SEAN O' FAOLAIN

by

MAURICE HARMON

CONSTABLE · LONDON

First published in Great Britain 1994
by Constable and Company Limited
3 The Lanchesters, 162 Fulham Palace Road
London W6 9ER
Copyright © 1994 by Maurice Harmon
ISBN 0 09 470140 7

The right of Maurice Harmon to be
identified as the author of this work has been
asserted by him in accordance with the
Copyright, Designs and Patents Act 1988

Set in Monophoto Fournier 12pt by
Servis Filmsetting Ltd, Manchester
Printed in Great Britain by
St Edmundsbury Press Ltd
Bury St Edmunds, Suffolk

A CIP catalogue record for this book
is available from the British Library

87,050

£16·95

SEAN O'FAOLAIN

For Diarmaid

Contents

	Acknowledgements	11
1	Cork	15
2	Education	28
3	Revolution	42
4	Civil War	55
5	Corkery's Glugger	63
6	Harvard	70
7	London	85
8	Killough House	100
9	Knockaderry	119
10	*The Bell*	127
11	The *Bell* Years	152
12	Italy and Newman's Way	165
13	Ireland	175
14	Princeton	191
15	A Wasted Life?	203
16	Acceptance	215
17	A Writer in Residence	230
18	The Wonderful Seventies	244
19	Rosmeen Park	265
	Notes	283
	Bibliography	307
	Index	315

Illustrations

between pages 160 and 161

Sean's parents with the three boys
Sean, aged twelve, with his mother
Presentation Brothers College, Cork
Revd Brother E.I. Connolly, LL.D
Eileen, Sean's wife
Eamon de Valera, December 1919 (*Hulton Deutsch*)
Frank O'Connor
Elizabeth Bowen (*Jonathan Cape*)
Edward Garnett (*Richard Garnett*)
Sean and Eileen with Julia
Sean with Julia and Stephen
Sean with his cat
Alene Erlanger in the mid-1950s
Sean and Eileen on holiday
The portrait by Sean O'Sullivan, 1963
Carol Smith
Elfreda Powell
In Rome in 1974 (*Godfrey Graham*)
1972, at home (*Godfrey Graham*)
1990 (*Mary Moloney*)

Acknowledgements

MY first and greatest debt is to Sean O'Faolain who gave me permission to quote from his published and unpublished work and answered many questions. I am grateful to Eileen for many helpful comments, to their daughter, Julia O'Faolain Martines for her help and also their son, Stephen.

There were many others. I have tried to associate some with particular chapters, by the use of footnotes, where their help was particularly relevant, although in some cases the information they provided covered much wider areas, or applied to different times. All the following have helped through letters, telephone calls, or interviews: Bryan MacMahon, James Plunkett, Eilis Dillon, Mary Lavin, Harriet Sheehy, Dermot Foley, Patrick Lynch, Nuala Mulcahy, Cormac Lankford, Tom Brosnan, Honor Tracy, Sean Ó Coileain, Margaret Phelan, Ita Daly, David Marcus, Sean Ó Tuama, Seamus MacGowan, Mary Hogan, Mairead Murphy, Sophia Mallin, Valerie Cooper, Sean Dunne, May O'Donovan, Joan O'Donovan, Evelyn Garbary, John Vernon, Maureen Charlton, Nuala Ni Dhomhnaill, J. Anthony Gaughan, Father Michael O'Carroll, Rüdiger Imhof, Frank Dorgan, Bill Twomey, Brother Terence, Brother Reen, Robert Greacen, Cyril Cusack, Daniel C. Donovan, Nancy McCarthy, Denis and Robin Mathews, Leon Ó Broin, Tim Pat Coogan, Seamus O Domhnaill, T. J. McElligott, Patricia Boylan, Gregory Allen, Elisabeth Schnack, Gerald Goldberg, Aloys Fleischmann, Isabel Healy, Kitty Madden, Declan MacSwiney, Brother Matthew Feheny, Madge Sheehan, Shevaun Lynam, Lis Pihl, P. A. O'Connor, Frank Johnston, Bridie Markham, Neddy Kennedy, Peter Brennan, Dan Frawley, Cathal MacDomhnaill, Dennis O'Driscoll, Catherine Brand, Virginia Teehan, George Hetherington,

Elfreda Powell, Finbar Dowdall, Tim Cadogan, Brian Murphy, Seamus Hilferty, Cornelius Buttimer, Hector Legge, Marjorie Linklater, Michael Parnell, A. A. Hampton, T. P. O'Neill, Brian P. Kennedy, Micheàl Ó hAodha, Aodh Ó Tuama, Nial McCarthy, Godfrey Graham, Fr. Mark Tierney, Brendan MacGiolla Choille, Ruth Moller, Tony Caldwell, P. J. Brophy, Rita Quinn, Helen Fahy, Eithne Jones, Michael O'Beirne, Leslie Rice, Finnbarr O'Brien, Muriel Spark, Carol Smith, Cristoir and Ray Ó Cinneide, Enda Delaney, Stephen O'Sullivan, Hugh Powers, Brian Lynch, Joseph McHugh, Maire McCarthy, Lily Twomey, Cornelius Cleary, Michael Sweeney, Patrick Henchy, Sean Ó Luing, J. F. Powers, George Garrelts, Liz and Julian Moynahan, Linda Howe, William Daniels, John V. Kelleher, Michael Erlanger, Alene Bricken, Sally Bierer, Ann Saddlemyer, Don Torchiana, Moody Prior, Jean Hagstrum, Francis Molloy, Robie Macauley, Jane and John Jacobi, Edward T. Cone, Jean McAndrew, Edmund Keeley, Hans Aarloff, Carol Szymanski, Earle E. Coleman, Joseph Frank, Paul Horgan, J. H. Wilson, John Anderson, Walton A. Litz, Peter Davison, William S. Rukeyser, Tina Hunt Mahony, Barbara Brown, James Robinson, Francis Molloy and Munira Mutran.

I owe a particular debt of gratitude to Lori N. Curtis at the McFarlin Library, the University of Tulsa; Michael Durkan, Librarian at Swarthmore College; and Shawn Holliday, my research assistant at Marshall University. It would be impossible to name all the people who helped me, but I wish to thank them.

The staff of the following institutions have been particularly helpful: the National Libraries of Ireland, Scotland and Wales; the Libraries of University College Dublin, Trinity College Dublin, University College Cork; the Military Archives in Dublin; the Royal Irish Academy, the Cork Museum, the Cork Public Library, the Cork Archives Institute; Department of Manuscripts, the British Museum Library; the Libraries of the universities of Reading, Bristol, Leeds, Durham; the BBC Archives at Caversham; the Morrow Library, Marshall University; The Graduate Records Office, Harvard University; Houghton Library, Harvard University; Bancroft Library, University of California at Berkeley; the Harry Ransom Humanities Research Centre at the University of Texas; the Mugar Library, Boston University; the Burns Library, Boston College; the McFarlin Library, University of Tulsa; the Butler Library, Columbia University; the Berg Collection, New York Public Library; the Special

Collections Department, Deering Library, Northwestern University; the
Beinecke Rare Book and Manuscript Library, Yale University; the
Manuscript Division, the Library of Congress; the Special Collections,
Southern Illinois University at Carbondale; the Radio Telefís Eireann
Sound Archives; the British Council, University College Dublin Archives
Department; the Irish Academy of Letters, the Irish PEN, and the Irish
Association of Civil Liberty.

References to published works are given within the text, abbreviated as follows:

Bird Alone	BA
Collected Stories	CS
Come Back to Erin	CBE
Constance Markievicz	CM
De Valera	Dev
The Great O'Neill	GON
I Remember! I Remember!	Rem
An Irish Journey	IJ
The Irish	IR
King of the Beggars	KB
Midsummer Night Madness	MNM
A Nest of Simple Folk	NSF
Newman's Way	NW
A Purse of Coppers	PC
South to Sicily	SS
A Summer in Italy	SI
Teresa	T
The Vanishing Hero	VH
Vive Moi!	VM

[1]

Cork

AT the time of Sean O'Faolain's birth on 22 February 1900, his family lived over Nicholas O'Connor's public house on the corner of Halfmoon Street in Cork. On one side they looked across the River Lee at the city's most famous landmark, Shandon Tower with its fish-topped steeple. On the other side they looked at the back of the Opera House whose dressing rooms, scene docks and stage door were directly across from the door of no. 16 Halfmoon Street where the Whelans lived. It was much later that Sean adopted the Irish version of this name. Halfmoon Street was quiet. While close to the busy Coal Quay and Clothes Market, it was relatively undisturbed by commerce. There was the pub at the corner, an old cooperage next door with sheds and a cobbled yard, a series of stables that housed horses belonging to the *Cork Examiner*, a forge, a small factory for making Kandy Sauce and an electrician's shop at the far end. Paul Street, behind no. 5, to which the Whelans would move within a few years, was a laneway of craftsmen's booths. There was a cork-cutter, a joiner, a woodcarver, a tinsmith, a basket-weaver, a plumber, a picture-framer, a statue-maker, an iron-worker, a painter, a cooper and a baker.

Cork was an Atlantic port. Great liners plying from Europe to America called downriver at Queenstown, later known as Cobh. It was a thriving market town which drew people from the countryside every week by train, horse and cart, or bicycle, the women in shawls and often carrying baskets of produce for the shops. Cork was not so much a city as a big country town with a folk atmosphere. Many people had moved there from the countryside, as O'Faolain's parents had done in the 1890s. They retained memories, customs and sayings from the countryside. Sean's mother would say of a cold day that 'it would skin the Danes', or of a rich man that he 'spent more money than would beggar Damer'. On Twelfth Night, as the youngest person in the house, Sean was sent outside to knock on the door with a freshly baked loaf to ward off hunger in the year ahead.

Cork was busy and colourful. It had a prosperous business class whose lives Sean did not notice until as a young man he saw their yachts at Crosshaven and realized that there were men in Cork who travelled abroad regularly, to London and Paris, kept their wives in style, and dined in city hotels. He was more aware of other aspects of the city. Unemployed men stood about the streets, people scrabbled in the Clothes Market to make a living, children often went barefoot. Bad housing was common in the low-lying flat of the city where the Whelans lived, and elsewhere in the laneways. Houses were overcrowded and in the slum areas where there was no sewage system they were dirty, poorly ventilated and had an inadequate supply of water. Half of the city's houses had no water closets. Sanitary conditions were bad and there was a high incidence of smallpox, enteric fever and tuberculosis.

The poor formed a teeming background throughout Sean's growing years. He found other aspects of life more exciting. Local militia and colourful ex-Munster Fusiliers strode the streets. He went to Glanmire railway station to see the old Parliamentarians – John Redmond, Tim Healy, Gussy Roche, Maurice Healy, William O'Brien – welcomed by bands and cheering crowds. Mobs howled, faction fights broke out, women shrieked and waved their coloured cashmere shawls before the landaus, and tar-barrels flung sparks into the air. He went to the station to see bands welcoming theatre groups, such as the Moody Manners Opera Company or Benson's Shakespearean Company. He enjoyed the annual processions, such as the one on St. Patrick's Day, in which the Master Masons, the Farriers, the Bankers, the Confectioners and the Brewery Workers marched behind their banners. The Lord Mayor wore his Wellington hat, fur cape and chain of office, and was accompanied by his aldermen, councillors and the city sword bearer. The National Foresters strode along in green jackets, snow-white plumes, white buskins and tasselled boots. School children sang hymns. Confraternities of men and women from the churches also marched and the Royal Irish Constabulary brought up the rear in black helmets and black uniforms. There was, too, the pomp and ceremony that attended the opening of the assizes, when Sean's policeman father was assigned to guard the judge at the courthouse. The judge always arrived in a horse-drawn carriage, accompanied by detachments of mounted police and military. His father, and the other policemen, wore full-dress uniform for these occasions, with spiked helmets with silver chin straps, gloves and patent leather belts. Sean could slip into the court to observe the trial, judgement and sentencing of the mere Irish whose cause he was as yet too young to understand.

Although Sean's memories included such colourful occasions, his writings about Cork are often marked by disenchantment. It was, he says, no place for sensitive people. 'To succeed there you have to have the skin of a rhinoceros, the dissimulation of a crocodile, the agility of a hare, the speed of a hawk' (IJ, 71). Nevertheless there were contented hours in which he viewed Cork from the top of Patrick's Hill, or from Orrery Hill, or from the top of Blarney Street, or when he watched the river winding and expanding to the southeast. Strolling about the city in later years he was enchanted by its physical beauty, and realized that he had formed a completely incorrect view of the place as a child. His perception of his native city then resulted from the kind of pressure put upon him by parents and teachers.

He was the youngest son of Denis and Bridget Whelan, who had two other children – Patrick, born in 1892, and Augustine, born in 1895. His father, born and raised in Killone, Co. Laois, had met Bridget Murphy when he was stationed in the town of Rathkeale, Co. Limerick. They were married on 10 February 1891 in Limerick's Catholic cathedral and moved soon afterwards to Cork. Denis was a tall, finely built man. Each of his sons would inherit his upright carriage. He was, in Sean's estimation, a humble, pious man, uncomplicated in his sense of duty, without ambition for himself but very ambitious for his sons. Conscious of his lowly position in a line of officials stretching downward from the King of England, he liked to trace 'the line of precedence'. He saw himself as part of that line, with sergeants, inspectors and various grades of official above him. A similar perception of his unworthiness pervaded his religious life. He went to Mass every morning and took his sons to meetings of the men's confraternity on Monday evenings. At night they heard his voice raised in supplication: 'O please, dear kind Jesus, look after my poor little children, Patrick, and Augustine, and John. Watch over my poor wife Bid. Guide them and guard them. Help me to work for them as long as I live . . .' (VM, 31). It was an attitude that Sean eventually despised. In his autobiography, *Vive Moi!*, Denis is an exemplary cardboard figure. He has praiseworthy qualities, but lacks humanity, diversity, complexity. The chapter devoted to him is entitled 'The Old Grenadier', which sums up the son's way of seeing him as a character out of *Baroness Orczy*, belonging to war, with a gentlemanly code of behaviour. One accepts O'Faolain's conclusion that he admired his father, but never loved him. He 'never knew him'. The little that he did know was that he gambled on horses, was interested in land auctions, dreamed of returning one day to his own county. He made use of this in his first novel. He did recreate his father's dream of returning to the rural background in one warmly evocative story, 'The Sugawn Chair'.

He illustrates his father's willingness to do whatever was expected of him in his account of his rôle during the siege of Watergrasshill. Sean was only four years old when this event took place but the sight of his father wounded and bandaged left a lasting impression on him. One afternoon, he tells us, he ran in from school and found his father lying on the sofa in the kitchen, his head bandaged, his right hand wrapped in layers of cotton wool and more bandages. His mother explained that Denis had been sent to Watergrasshill to help in the eviction of a tenant farmer. The man had barricaded himself in and the police had had to put him out. In the melée Denis was struck with a stone, and when someone thrust a heated iron bar through a hole in the window he had grasped it. It had seared his hand to the bone. Sean writes that it was 'his silence that wounded me and the bewilderment in his eyes. Could it have been that he was shocked by the passionate clash with his own kind of small-farmer folk in that early morning tussle on those windy uplands?' (VM, 31.)

The account is colourful but inaccurate. *Vive Moi!* is not strictly factual. The Siege of Watergrasshill took place in October 1904, before Sean went to school. He treats the incident as a clash between Denis Whelan and his own kind of small-farmer people, and evokes traditional accounts of cruel evictions. But this particular eviction took place on a hundred acre farm held by a relatively well-off farmer. The house was a sturdy two-storey building, with stone sheds about a sizeable cobbled yard, not a little Irish cottage. It was also stoutly defended. When the eviction order was served, twenty-three local men occupied and fortified the house. Such a large crowd gathered outside that the sub-sheriff, bailiff and police escort had to send for reinforcements from Cork, Fermoy and Middleton. Denis Whelan was part of the group sent out from Cork. The confrontation was fierce. The crowd jostled the police and jeered at them as they tried to force their way into the house. The police, who used scaling ladders and a battering-ram, faced a variety of missiles: iron bowls, pointed wooden poles, liquid tar poured down on them and the heated iron bar pushed through the door. In the subsequent trial, the injuries to Constable Whelan were specifically mentioned. He was apparently the only policeman to be injured.[1]

O'Faolain's relationship with his mother was closer and more complex. When he was a child she was tall, slim and very beautiful. He loved her very much. By the time he was in his late teens he ceased to love her, and as a young man he pitied her. He was her pet. He had her to himself in the hours after his brothers had gone to school. When he was a schoolboy they went walking together arm in arm like lovers. He accompanied her on frequent visits to the church. She was deeply pious, but it was not a happy piety. Her religious melancholy withered everything it touched and did not inspire him. Known to the lodgers as 'Ma Whelan', she lived anxiously from week to week and was usually in debt – she even had to borrow to pay for basic necessities. She was parsimonious to a fault. The Whelans were not all that poor. Denis's one pound a week salary was more than many families had and it was regular. Together with the money brought in from lodgers it enabled the Whelans to send their boys to a fee-paying school, but the habit of scrimping and saving was ingrained. Bridget's parsimony led to small deprivations and disappointments. When Sean wanted to become an altar boy, despite her piety and despite his enthusiasm, she refused to buy the soutane and surplice required. She once sent him to school in an outlandish coat made from one of his father's old uniforms. It hung out about him like a bell. She ignored the humiliation it caused him. Sean would use the coat to symbolise everything he later came to hate and despise in their shabby-genteel life. Bridget was also fiercely ambitious for her sons. She constantly urged them to 'rise in the world', a phrase he came to detest, and wore herself out working and saving to advance their progress. She made their lives truly miserable at times. The poor, Sean argued, can enjoy life, can go into debt for their pleasures, but the parsimonious shackle emotions and put restraints on their pleasures. In *Vive Moi!* he is painfully honest in his attempt to be fair to his parents. Clearly there was much about them that he disliked and there were some things that he hated, but he knew that he owed them a lot. They did their best for him, gave him a good education, wanted him to rise in the world, instilled their own brand of Catholic morality into him, although in the process they stunted his emotional life.

If Halfmoon Street was quiet, it was the kind of place, with its craftsmen, Opera House, horses, river and quays, in which three lively boys might have had a happy-go-lucky childhood, with lots of friends and casual acquaintances. In fact, they did not. Their parents constantly admonished them to keep to themselves, to be careful how they behaved because they could never know who might be watching them. His father would warn him: 'what would Jimmy Simcox [alderman and breadmaker] say if he saw you now with your tie crooked?' He addressed his father as 'Sir'. His mother often embarrassed him when they were out together by urging him to 'talk up nicely to the nice gentleman'. She called him 'pig' whenever his manners needed correction. She beat him with a rattan carpet-beater when he was disobedient or impudent. The boys went and returned from school together; they went on afternoon walks together. Throughout his childhood Sean did not have a single friend and the habit persisted in secondary school.[2]

As a constable Denis Whelan was expected to keep aloof from the general public. A sergeant's wife pointed out that it was inappropriate for him to live over a pub. She suggested better districts towards the university. Bridget and Sean visited her there in a fine house backing onto the university grounds and looking down upon tennis courts, playing fields, the river and a public park. They duly moved to no. 4 Mardyke Place, a cramped four-roomed house, 'two up and two down', in an alleyway running from the fashionable Western Road to the tree-lined Dyke Walk. They remained there for two years. They spent one year at no. 9 Adelaide Street, a two-storey, redbrick house with an attic, in a street nearer to the city centre. In the following year they moved back to Halfmoon Street, this time to no. 5, on the corner with Academy Street. This would be Sean's home until he went to America in September 1926. Here Denis and Bridget were able to make a reality of their ambitions for their children. Here they had room for lodgers, and being close to the Opera House they knew that there would be no shortage of custom.[3] When he was old enough Sean was sometimes sent to the railway station to meet the artists, displaying a printed card that advertized the attractions of no. 5 as a boarding house. It was a large three-storey house, above Charley McCarthy's plumber's shop. Later, Denis Mathews had a cobbler's factory there, employing as many as forty cobblers. Overhead there were two floors, and above them four attic rooms with ceilings that sloped to the floor, which had only one skylight window each. The boys slept in one bed in one garret, the parents had one each, the servant girl had the fourth. The large space outside the attics was used as a drying area for washing. The lodgers had the rooms on the two floors underneath, with fireplaces, proper windows, linoleum on the stairs on the second storey, carpet on the stairs on the first.

In each garret Bridget made an altar of disused orange boxes, draped in starched lace, with coloured statues of the holy family, Saint Francis and Saint Anthony set about an immense Christ in blue and red garments. All the statues were surrounded by little pious pictures in gilt-wire frames. Every night she came into Sean's room, made him cross his arms on his chest and recite the prayer: 'O God! I must die. I do not know when . . . or where . . . or how. But, if I die in mortal sin, I am damned for all Eternity'. She roused the boys every morning for Mass, sent them out to devotions in the evenings, saw that they attended weekly confraternity meetings in the church, and constantly implored aid and consolation from the saints. In Lent, when she roused them at half-past six for seven o'clock Mass, they heard her voice, in Sean's imaginative recreation, raised in exhortation: 'Up! Up! I come, said the Lord, like a thief in the night seeking whom I may *devour* . . . Woe to the weak and lukewarm of heart . . . Come to me all ye who labour and are burthened and I will refresh ye . . .' (VM, 49). On their afternoon walks during Lent, often compelled by Pat, they would call into a church to make the Stations of the Cross. 'Pat and his bloody discipline', according to Gus, 'was the real Cross; a proper pimp'.[4] Up to the age of seventeen Sean spent a great many hours in churches, with the result that he was filled with the sensations of smells, noises and incense. But in his inner self he felt silence and a remoteness from the world. He felt solemn and sad and, above all, that everything about him was unreal and otherworldly.

The hopeless tragedy of his mother's life began as an emotional burden and became a moral problem. 'I loved her so much that I could not bear to see her miserable, so I resolved to help her by becoming her private accountant'. He explained that she could keep track of expenditure and earnings simply by keeping a record of what she took in and what she paid out. Her trouble was that she never had anything left over from one week to the next. She was, she explained, just like her mother. 'Many and many's the time I saw her when she'd sell a cow or a pig at the fair of Rathkeale, and had the money in the heel of her fist, putting on her bonnet and tackling the pony and cart to drive up to Knockaderry. She'd pay a bit here and stop a gap there. So much against this. So much against that. When she had it she gave it. It's all I do from week to week. Rob Peter. Pay Paul' (VM, 78). Gus Whelan was sceptical about the accuracy of this report. Sean's portraits of both his father and his mother were fictionalized to give an impressionistic truth.

He questioned her acceptance of the will of God, by which any hardship, any misfortune, could be endured as part of God's scheme. Why, he asked himself, did God allow such suffering? Did life have to include so much pain? He went through most of his boyhood without questioning Heaven. 'The Will of God prevailed for a long time with me . . . What broke it apart in the end was pity and anger: the first for my mother, whom I loved so dearly that I could not bear the sight of her unhappiness; and the second, far later, for my people, in a bitter rage that they should be obliged to endure so much' (VM, 46).

Not everything in the Whelan home was dull. Family picnics to Blarney Castle, outings to the seaside at Youghal, visits to the races in Cork Park, an annual visit to Poole's Miorama and summer holidays in the country helped to relieve the monotony. Since they could not have friends, the boys invented a private world for entertainment. They made a puppet theatre from a kitchen stool draped with a towel, paper sets from old magazines, actors out of corks propelled by pins, wrote and performed plays, and gave one another names. Pat was The Emperor of Tuba, Sean The Pidgeon, Gus The Elephant. They produced a newspaper called *Capo* or *Da Capo*. They indulged in fantasies about shows they would see at the Opera House and anticipated the delights of their summer holidays. Sean, who was born imaginative, passionate, nervous and sensitive, often went alone to the attic to perform his favourite rôles – Bonaparte, Robin Hood, Bonnie Prince Charlie, or the Irish Parliamentarians.

He also enjoyed reading fairy tales, comics, such as the *Magnet*, the *Gem*, or the adventures of Sexton Blake. With the help of the Carnegie free library, he developed an interest in fiction: he read De Vere Stacpoole's *The Blue Lagoon*, Arthur Murphy's *The Grecian Daughter*, but in particular novels about war and chivalry – by Henty, Ballantyne, Dumas, Dickens, Scott.

The brothers responded in different ways to the family's emphasis on religion. Called to the priesthood in 1911, Pat went to All Hallows College in Dublin, where he was ordained on 5 May 1918, and went to Australia. Gus deliberately failed Irish in Matriculation so that he would not have to remain at home and attend university. Instead, he sat for the British Civil Service Examination, became a clerk in December 1914, and was posted to Limerick, where he met Ellen Dooley whom he married in Dublin in 1921. After 1922 he made his career in England. Sean, younger than Pat by seven years, and younger than Gus by five, was more susceptible to his mother's influence. Neither a conformist like Pat nor an outright rebel like Gus, he was for much of his life ambivalent about both Pat's commitment to Catholicism and Gus's rejection.

The religious influence sank deep. 'I used to get great joy as a boy from the Morning Offering which offered up every simple task and made it meaningful'.[5] Sean attributed the formation of his histrionic imagination to the Church. His imagination was engaged when his mother led him, as she often did, to pray at the tall crucifixion in the parish church. The Virgin's foot, she told him, had performed many miracles of healing. He liked to pray before a painting of Purgatory, fascinated by the arrested figure of a young girl, almost redeemed. Religion was an opiate. It was also a kind of fiction. The Stations of the Cross told a story, as did every stained glass window. He liked the Holy Week drama of Tenebrae, the stripping of the altars, the washing of the feet, the blessing of the Paschal candle. Stories fell from the pulpit where Fr. Dick O'Sullivan, Director of the Men's Confraternity, gave readings from Dickens instead of sermons.

None of this prepared him for life. Religion was sentimentalized. It created no bridge to the real world of poor tubercular children pushed around the city in soap-boxes on wheels, and Magdalenes flitting about the quays at night in dirty shawls. It induced a fear of the flesh. Because of this fear he thought, at the age of thirteen, that he had committed the sin of blasphemy. Reading how the Jews nailed criminals to a cross to die slowly from loss of blood, he imagined Christ naked on the Cross. That image, he thought, was not only immodest, it was blasphemous. Afraid of what the priest might say, he stopped going to confession. But he received Communion every Sunday as usual so that his parents would not notice and thereby he began to commit even more sins. Fortunately, when he did go to confession, the priest quietly reassured him that he had not committed blasphemy.

Nobody talked frankly about sexuality. Nobody explained his involuntary sexual emissions. He was startled and bewildered when his penis developed a 'night-life' of its own and for years endured 'a horrible sensation of guilt'. When, years later, he read of a father who explained wet dreams to his son in a sensible manner, he asked why he could not have had a liberating father like that. At the age of twenty Sean did not know the facts of life. He resented this betrayal. 'Whenever I think of the turbulence and agony of nubile youth, the terror of a boy at his first discovery of his manhood, of a young girl at her first experience of womanhood, I can only rage at our pious elders who so sweetly, so virtuously, so loftily and benevolently sent us naked to the wolf of life.' (VM, 16.)

The other formative influence was the theatre. Cork had two: Dan Lowry's Palace in King Street and the Opera House in Emmet Place. The Palace was a lovely, ornamental theatre with domed boxes, a richly gilded proscenium arch with the city's coat of arms in the centre, and a tiered balcony with an ornamental rim. It was a lively place, much frequented by Cork's poor and by British soldiers. Sean used to fight his way up the long white-washed stairs to the gods and even then often had to climb into one of the small windows to get a view of the stage far below. He saw the shows of the period – *Floradora*, *The Country Girl*, *The Merry Widow*, *The Girl in the Taxi* – and heard its popular songs: 'If Your Lips Could Only Speak', 'By the Side of the Zuyder Zee', and 'By the Light of the Silvery Moon'. But he preferred the Opera House to which he and his brothers got in free, courtesy of the doorman. He saw Frank Benson, Alexander Marsh, Charles Doran, Fred Terry, Maud Allan, Mrs Pat Campbell, José Collins, John McCormack, Esmé Percy in works by Shakespeare, Ibsen, Shaw, Sheridan, Goldsmith. He saw grand opera with the Moody Manners and the O'Meara companies, lots of Gilbert and Sullivan and many Irish plays.

The Opera House also captivated his imagination. In summer time when the great door that led to the backstage was open he could see actors and actresses in brilliant costumes and make-up. Scenery was carried through the double door by men he knew, such as Tommy Mulvany, Jim Dooley, Lazy Casey, and Georgie Campbell. The Cork Butter Exchange Band became the Napoleonic army in *A Royal Divorce*. Lazy Casey and Tommy Mulvany played in *The Scarlet Pimpernel*. And since visiting artists also lodged in his home, the intermingling of the real and the unreal became even more confusing. He chatted with the Vagabond King, Simon Legree helped with his arithmetic, Long John Silver helped with his Latin translations, the ghost of Hamlet's father smiled at him, Mrs. Wiggs of *Mrs. Wiggs of the Cabbage Patch* fainted onto the kitchen floor when his father told her that King Edward VII had died. They came into his life with all their dazzle and allure from the plays of the period – *The Light That Failed*, *The Little Vagabond*, *Bella Donna*, *The Sorrows of Satan*, *The Sign of the Cross*, *East Lynne*, *A Bachelor's Romance*, *The Bells*, *Alone in London*, *Sweet Lavender*, and many, many more. But he was forbidden to go to *A Royal Divorce* and Marie Corelli's *The Sorrows of Satan* which his mother regarded as sinful. He ran errands for the artists, brought a jug of porter to Claudius, a bowl of soup to Ophelia. They belonged to a world entirely different from what he knew, suggested tastes and a style of living very different from his. 'When our lodgers leave our house at night for the theatre I wander wonderingly through their rooms, their fires banked cosily for their return at half-past eleven, a late supper laid out for them on white napkins spread over the soft Paisley table-covering of ink-stained chenille. I gaze in awe at their exotic belongings – the travelling clock in red leather, the whiskey bottle with the patent lock, photographs of themselves and their friends in silver frames, all signed, their especially ordered bits of outlandish food on the sideboard, Gorgonzola, Smyrna figs, piccalilli, Palmyra grapes, Peak Frean's rusks, Whitbread's ale, Yorkshire relish, cold veal pie, their foreign papers and magazines, the *Stage*, the *Performer*, the *Red Magazine*, the *Strand*. I touch a lady's snow-white furry slippers, I lift and let fall a diaphanous nightgown . . . Once or twice in *London Life* I stared, transfixed by shame, fear, and delighted wonder, at my first picture of lusciously naked women'. (VM, 9–10.)

The two worlds of the church and the theatre seemed to fuse. From his attic room he could hear both the throb of the organ in Saints Peter and Paul's, and through the open skylight of the Opera House, the tenor taking the high 'C' in *Pagliacci*. Once, at a children's mass when the others sang 'Lord of Hosts we praise Thy Name', he sang 'Please don't flirt with me—e—e' and one night he walked down the aisle of the pit in the Opera House and genuflected to the advertisement curtain. There were times when he hardly knew where he was, as when one Sunday evening the entire chorus of the Carl Rosa Opera Company went into the organ loft in the church and sang the *Tantum Ergo*, as though it were the Venusberg music from *Tannhäuser*. No wonder he regarded the church itself as a theatre. All about him in the pews were familiar figures – Canty the tinsmith, Looney the cork-cutter, Bagsy Flynn the basket-weaver, the one-eyed man who boiled sweets, Nicky O'Connor the publican, Lombardi the ice-cream man, the two Sullivans who were coopers, his neighbours and the poor from the lanes. Ned Cooney, stage-door keeper at the Opera House, was also the church sacristan.

But, if the romantic world of Edwardian theatre bore little resemblance to the life he knew, the impact of Lennox Robinson's play *Patriots*, which he saw on 5 January 1914, was startling. All his accounts of the experience emphasize amazement and shock. Sometimes he combines it with seeing G. B. Shaw's *John Bull's Other Island*. In a letter to Robinson he seized upon Robinson's account of *his* moment of truth when he saw W. B. Yeats's *Countess Cathleen*. 'When you tell', he wrote, 'how *Cathleen* crystallized things for you in the Opera House I remembered again how your *Patriots* did precisely the same for me, in the same theatre, and by the same players'.[6] Robinson's play shocked him upright with delight in the real. When the curtain rose he beheld with astonishment the parlour of a house in an Irish country town and people who resembled his own relations. All its antimacassarish details were tenderly, delightfully, recognizably familiar: a geranium pot in the window, a chenille cloth covering the table, pictures of Robert Emmet and Pius X on the walls, old lace curtains, old padded furniture. The play brought back memories of relations who had been involved in the Fenian movement. He had read about the Fenians, had heard his father condemn them. Here on stage a Fenian, who had been jailed, returned to the little town still filled with ideals of freedom, intent on rousing the young men to rebel once more against English rule. 'The fantastic thought burst on me that in Rathkeale, even in Cork that night, there might be other real, living, exhaling-inhaling, dusty, scruffy, angry old men with these same noble, gallant, hopeless ideas. I will not say that I was changed, when I left the theatre and walked out into the wet streets of Cork. But I know that I was dazed.' (VM, 86.)

In 1912, when he saw a melodrama by George Sims, called *The Lights o' London* he wrote a short story with the same title, beginning 'Big Ben struck out the hour of midnight! The notes rang out over the lights o' London from Whitechapel to the East India Dock Road'. In 1913 he published two stories in the *Irish Outlook*. In the first he wrote, unconvincingly, about a Frenchman in the Hotel de Fulières in Paris. In the second Jack McBride, an

Irish emigrant in London, takes the Saxon shilling, rises to the rank of corporal, but deserts when his mother dies. Nevertheless, he 'loves his country as every Briton should'. He pretends to be a traitor as he leads the enemy against the British, blowing his bugle in warning. When asked when he began writing, Sean replied, 'It seems to me I was always writing'.

But he saw life through other people's eyes. He used to persuade himself that he had already written novels about eighteenth and nineteenth century France. When he was fourteen he loved to tell school companions about the works of a wonderful novelist called Jean François (he was christened John Francis). When he had finished telling them the story of the latest work by this writer and they asked where they might get it, he would reply 'It can be got nowhere. I am Jean François. I am just finishing my great novel'.[7] It would be years before he discovered his own world, but Robinson's play gave him a premonition of the untilled field that he would one day begin to work.

[2]

Education

JOHN F. WHELAN entered the Lancasterian School on 6 March, 1905. He was just five years old, 'a delicate, scrawny little lad', with red-rimmed eyes, who was very talkative and always very interested in whatever was going on. With its high wall and enclosed yard running all around the building, the school looked like a prison. It had three rooms; a single room for infants where Sean began, first and second grades; a double room for third and fourth grades; and a large room for fifth and sixth grades, where Pat and Gus were. The school was heated by a rectangular Quebec stove whose flue ascended through the high, glass roof. The playground was a gravelled yard, where the boys played football with a homemade paper or rag ball, which they also threw, in what they called the roof game, onto the roof (they would jostle to catch it as it fell back, if it did not stick in the gutters).

It was a tough school. The boys came from a variety of backgrounds. The 1905 register records Sean's entrance and lists the professions of the fathers: cattledriver (2), carman (2), smith (2), jarvey (2), fireman (2), carpenter (1), labourer (1), quarryman (1), maltster (1), painter (2), policeman (5). Many boys went barefoot; some were so poor that they came without lunch; many had to drop out to help parents by working; others worked part-time as messengers or newsboys; and there was a high mortality rate among the poor. No wonder Gus objected to Sean's description of the Whelans' poverty. By comparison with many other boys they were 'toffs'.[1]

Discipline was harsh. Boys were punished with a strap or leather. Physical culture took the form of marching and drilling in the yard. By O'Faolain's time the practice of 'histing' – that is, hoisting a boy on another boy's back so that his bottom could be slapped – seems to have ceased, but there was a 'black hole' into which the unruly could be flung amid the coal dust and the rats. Slapping was an everyday occurrence, but Sean recalls only two incidents of outright brutality. Brother Sebastian Rogers, a big man with a bull-like throat and voice, and a strong arm with which he wielded a leather strap an inch and a half thick, had an interest in boxing. Known as 'Battling Billy', he liked to put two boys fighting after school, bare-fisted and bared to the waist. The prize was a few pieces of bread. Once Sean saw two boys refuse to fight. He witnessed one other type of cruelty when the headmaster, 'Sloppy Dan', brought two senior boys into the science room to be punished for mitching. What he saw sent him shivering in horror to hide in the smelly toilet:

> Corrigan was a great burly fellow, so developed beyond his years that he looked about twenty, so strong that he could have knocked down Sloppy Dan with a blow. Feeney was slight, fair-haired, and back-bowed, but also more of a grown youth than a boy. Sloppy Dan himself was smallish but burly, with a round porcine face, always brick-red, big round glasses, a rounded, powerful back. His devouring pedagogic obsession was English grammar. He would wander from class to class to teach it, invariably carrying in his fist a punishment strap cut from a black leather harness trace, about one foot six long, two inches wide and a half-inch thick, and when, as he constantly did, he became excited over his parsings and analyses he had the odd habit of swishing his strap behind his back like a tail and roaring at the top of his voice like a bull. If we failed to give the right answer he would make us hold out our hands and give us one-two of the hardest he could draw. It was not the pain I minded so much as the sight of his round, empurpled face leaning over me with bulging eyes and bellowing mouth around which there would sometimes gather a pale-gray scum of frothy spittle.
>
> This was how he looked now through the eyelet hole, holding Feeney by the left arm and lashing with his leather strap at his naked thighs and bottom. Even through the closed door I could hear Feeney screaming, probably not so much from the pain as from fright and shame . . . The bigger fellow, Corrigan, stood by impassively watching the degradation of his friend. (VM, 37–8)

In later life Sean was critical of the school's educational shortcomings, occasional cruelty, Dickensian squalor, and lack of facilities for work and play. But he stressed its warmth and ability to make learning a pleasure. What made the school a happy place for him was its teachers, whose boyish innocence and camaraderie he cherished. Many were young men who came from the small farms and little towns of four southern counties – Cork, Kerry, Limerick and Clare. Not much more than boys themselves, with little experience of the world, they often mispronounced words in the manner of speakers of Hiberno-English, said Newfoundland, Hanover, coincidence, tay for tea, they do be for they are, and contrary for contrary. Brother Josephus explained that combustion was due to phlogiston, Brother Philip that circumcision was a small circle cut on the forehead of Jewish children. The boys were told that there were twelve minerals and were given their names without any further explanation. More subtly, Brother Magnus offered sixpence to anyone who would extract salt from seawater, and when one or two did, offered a silver watch to any boy who would extract sugar from a turnip. If most of the monks were simple men, the headmaster, Brother Declan, was in a different category. He joined the order when he was forty, had been trained at St. Patrick's Training College in Dublin and been principal of a school in Co. Cork. By the time O'Faolain arrived at the Lancs, Brother Declan was already old, grey-haired and reserved in manner, but given to outbursts of rage.

Sean got a good basic education. He became a good reader, with a particular liking for reading poetry aloud. He wrote essays regularly. In mathematics he progressed as far as stocks and shares, and he learnt the rudiments of physics and chemistry. Religious education followed the diocesan programme which was based on Butler's *Catechism* and the *Explanatory Catechism* that went beyond Butler to the prophecies and the Psalms. Languages were not part of the curriculum. The Brothers managed to create 'a lovely, happy, fairy world'. What he gained there, in addition to a good grounding in the three R's, was a happiness he would never know again. 'Life there was a succession of dream-days . . . they were the only days of my life that were really lived',[2] he wrote, but a sense of a harsher reality occasionally intruded. Once when Sean was on his way back to school after lunch, he joined two boys who were playing near a rubbish dump and became so absorbed in their game that he forgot the time. After about an hour his brother arrived, asking 'Why didn't you come back to school after lunch?' and added in the Cork accent that they all had at this time 'Ahadeee! Johnny Whalen, you were on the lang! You were on the lang!' He was, Sean recalled, overcome with 'cold horror' at the realization of what he had done. For the first time in his life, at the age of six, he became vividly aware of wrong, of Other People who expected him to be responsible. He became aware, after a fashion, of his own identity. Society was pointing its finger at him; he trembled in terror. 'I had disgraced myself. I had disgraced my family. . . . I had come out of the Garden of Eden'. When he went to secondary school, learning became a means to an end; he lost his sense of wonder.

Even as a small boy Jacky Whelan talked excitedly about holidays in Rathkeale. In ways which are almost inexplicable, being atavistic and subjective, Rathkeale was of enormous importance to him. It was where his mother and father came from, where all his aunts had lived before they scattered abroad, except for the three sisters who stayed and were reunited on the annual holidays. It was his first free country of the imagination, the first to seize upon his feelings with values, memories and a way of life attractively different from the restrictive life of Cork. In later years, when he would try to identify what he most valued about Ireland, he would plump for Rathkeale, even if he always found it difficult to explain why it was that it was for him the centre of Ireland. Two thirds of his first novel, *A Nest of Simple Folk* (1934) is devoted to Rathkeale and it appears in *Come Back to Erin* (1940), where his middle-aged rebel, Frankie Hannafey, goes back to Nan Cosgrave's cottage to confirm the source of his tenacious nationalism. 'All Ireland for me,' Sean wrote, 'is in and about Rathkeale; a dead, lousy, flea-bitten, snoring pig of a town that I cannot think of without going as soft as a woman' (IJ, 150). In middle age, memories of Rathkeale, of the 'almost sensual pleasure of turf-smoke', of leaning over the half-door at the end of the muddy street, gave him a 'beatific joy'.[3]

Once a leading town in west Co. Limerick, Rathkeale retained some of its former grace in architecturally attractive town houses adorned with Ionic and Doric doorways and delicate fanlights. In the nineteenth century it got its impressive courthouse, a police barracks, a national school, the convent of the Sisters of Mercy, a dispensary, a post office and an animal pound. But the town also deteriorated, particularly in the decades after the Famine. More than fifty-eight per cent of the population left in the years between the

Famine and the end of the century. Poverty was endemic. But the Catholic Church, inspired by a conservative, ultra-montane ideology, increased in strength. St. Mary's Church, built in 1880, has a magnificent spire that dominates the surrounding flat countryside. At this time the Catholic Church, which was heavily institutionalized, took a firm hold on the people through guilds and societies. Denis and Bridget were products of this institutionalized church and were deeply affected by its sentimental religiosity. For them, and for their generation of Catholics, religious life was based on the catechism which emphasized the Church's authority, and recommended regular reception of the sacraments, attendance at Mass on Sunday, and a regular round of prayers and devotions. Devotion to the Sacred Heart and the Blessed Virgin flourished.[4]

Sean's Aunt Nan lived in a long, whitewashed, thatched cottage on that muddy street, Roche's Road, just off Main Street. It had small, lace-curtained windows with white wooden bars to protect them from cattle coming and going to the fairs. To the left of the door was the cool kitchen whose high ceiling was the underside of the thatch. It had a large, open, turf-burning fireplace. Here Nan prepared and served the food on a sturdy wooden table. A large dresser with the usual array of delft had, in addition, rows of polished, empty Colman's mustard tins for Sean to play with. To the right was the parlour with starched lace curtains, family portraits, a coloured oleograph of Daniel O'Connell in his liberator's cloak, one of Leo XIII, a clock with weights, a canopy bed, a commode, a harness hanging on the wall, and in the centre there was a dining table with a family photograph album on it. Here the outside world hardly existed. Time seemed to have stopped. When war broke out Aunt Nan and Uncle Tom asked their fourteen-year-old nephew who and what were the Germans.

Behind the house was a yard with stables for Tom's horse and donkey, a piggery, a shed for the hens and a rain-barrel. From here Sean could enter the orchard, which had a high perimeter wall. There he could play, or read, undisturbed. The cottage had a half-door over which Nan liked to lean; she was remembered later as a white-haired old woman in a black dress and shawl, who would sell apples to the children and send them to the shop for 'a seedy cake'. Tom, a stooped figure with a red wen on the back of his neck, ran a hackney service and delivered bags of mail to the railway station. The childless couple welcomed their nephews and the woman who had left Rathkeale to live in the city after she had married constable Denis Whelan.

[32]

The barracks were just a short distance from the Cosgrave cottage, and from the shop where Bridget had worked underneath its famous statue of the chinaman.

There were days when Uncle Tom would take Sean out to the commons to work in the small fields on the shore of Lough Doohyle. The commons and the lake lie in a small saucer-like depression tucked away behind the low hill on which Rathkeale is built. The only sign of habitation is the spire of St. Mary's church, raised against the backdrop of the distant Kerry mountains. To a small boy it meant everything and nothing; he could wander about, lie in the grass and watch the clouds drift slowly over the low hills to the Shannon, chew a blade of grass, examine insects in the long reeds, be fancy free. He drew upon these inexplicably magical moments in *I Remember! I Remember!*. In Rathkeale ambition ceased to exist, competitive striving had no place, and nobody cared who might see him as he walked along. There he could be himself for a whole month of freedom. There is no evidence that he ever did any work. He was a city boy, expected only to be a gentleman, to succeed in ways in which middle-class urban children succeed. Working on the land was not one of them. He put this indolence to good use in his portrait of Leo Donnell, the spoiled son, in *A Nest of Simple Folk*. On Sundays Uncle Tom would drive them to visit grandmother Murphy's farm at Loughill, near Knockaderry, a small thatched cottage on a thirty-nine and a half acre farm. Sean enjoyed playing with his Hough cousins: 'We tumbled in the tall haybarn . . . We were put up on the mighty back of the working horse for rides. We chased the geese in the haggard. Once I stayed for a couple of nights'. (VM, 63.)

None of O'Faolain's accounts of his holidays includes memories of play with local children or of getting to know his contemporaries (even those written after his return as a man). The habit of being solitary persisted. Local people never got to know him. They would see him sitting outside his aunt's cottage, or going along the bog road to the commons, often with a book in his hand. It is quite possible that his mother discouraged him from mixing with local children. Bridie Markham, eight years his junior, used to see him sitting in a sugawn chair outside Cosgraves. She noticed how well-dressed he was, with his felt hat and half-belted coat, but although they often passed each other on Roche's Road he never acknowledged her. The only person he always went to see was Mrs. Houlihan, an old woman who lived across the street.

Those who had known him as a boy looked forward to his visits as a man. They knew he was 'clever', but apart from Bridie's father, few of them were readers. There was some local resentment about his comments on Rathkeale in *An Irish Journey*. John Hough liked to acknowledge the relationship, but resented his account of the farm in *A Nest of Simple Folk*. As the Hough family now say, 'They had land when others didn't'.

He lost touch with his Rathkeale cousins, but they continued to admire him. The younger generation resented his snobbery. Those who lived near him in Dublin ignored him, as he ignored them. When a cousin returned from New York and went to visit him, she got a cool reception. When another was introduced to him in Limerick, she felt his reserve. He did not even go to John's funeral, although he sent a letter. That was not enough.

In Rathkeale he had his first intimations of family history, and made his first discoveries of an identity that predated the move to Cork. There he sensed, faintly at first but later with a sudden access of faith, that he belonged to something larger and more liberating than the frugality of Cork. There his father's trust in Empire was challenged by a piety that grew out of the flat fields, the arable land, and the endless skies over the River Deel. It was holy ground. When he built a home for himself and his young family on the side of Killiney Hill outside Dublin, he called it 'Knockaderry'.

On alternate summers the boys went to Co. Kildare, to stay with his father's sister, Kate, and her husband, Owen Boyhan. They had three children: Tom, May, and Lena. Lena liked Sean less than his brothers, because he was always pushing himself forward. Sean liked his Uncle Owen, a simple unaffected man, but found Aunt Kate less easy to be with because of her pretensions to gentility. The impressions that stayed with him were of her being an overdressed old peasant woman pretending to be a grand lady, or her being a sick inelegant old woman suffering from migraines.

Kildare was different from Rathkeale. When he was very small the Boyhans lived in the gatelodge in Celbridge, close to Castletown House. His memories of holidays there included seeing a fox streaking across the demesne pursued by huntsmen, but his memories of Newbridge and the Curragh were clearer. They included bugle calls, military bands, gunfire from the rifle range, the jingle of harness, the rumble of gun-carriages, hooves thudding on the curragh, the smell of fodder, hay, leather and the

Cockney voices of British Tommies. His cousin, Tom Boyhan, a dashing young man several years his senior, took him on shooting trips across the bogland, to swim in the canal, to watch horses exercising. If Rathkeale was rural, timeless, steeped in history, Kildare was cosmopolitan, opening outwards and upward. The British Empire reached right into the camps. The romance of war touched him here just as surely as it did in the books he read and the plays he saw. There was, too, the romance of racing. Romance also presented itself through the talk of his female cousins about regiments, the affairs of officers and soldiers, and their gossip about trainers, owners and jockeys. Kildare educated him in ways quite different from the lessons absorbed in west Limerick.

Tom Boyhan took him to Dublin, a thrilling, eye-opening experience of bustling streets, fine shops, great buildings, gentlemen's clubs, visits to Tom's tailor and gunsmith, his first meal in a restaurant. Within a year Tom was married, had his commission, and went off to France where he was killed at Arras within a month of his arrival. By 1917 when Sean returned to Kildare, the Boyhans had moved close to the camp at the Curragh, Aunt Kate was dead and the girls were working. He spent his days idling about the plain or playing handball alone. Later on, his one indelible memory from this summer was of meeting a woman on whom he looked for the first time 'as a man looks at a woman'. She seemed the most beautiful creature he had ever seen, large-breasted, large-armed, hair as fair as corn, eyes sapphire blue, skin breathing like pale pink sweet peas, her white-toothed laughter a blast of sun (VM, 71). It seemed to him she was probably hidden in everything he had written. He captured that obscure sexual awakening in the lyrical-romantic story, 'Love's Young Dream'.

Presentation Brothers College, which Sean entered in September 1912, was much different in appearance from the dilapidated Lancs. Opened in January 1888, a Science Hall and a Junior School were added in 1901. The two buildings formed an impressive, grey façade along the Western Road and behind them was a spacious yard, a handball court and playing fields along the Dyke. The brothers wore soutanes, the lay teachers had bowler hats, and the boys school caps and celluloid collars. Sean, wearing a homespun tweed suit and brown leather boots, was enrolled in Class VI in the Junior School. The school applied itself seriously to preparing boys for particular careers. They could gain access to all grades of the Civil Service, to the banks, and to British military colleges, such as Sandhurst and Wellington, and to university. Seven subjects were taught: English, Irish, Latin, French, mathematics, history and chemistry. Religious education was also provided. Discipline was strict, corporal punishment a daily occurrence, and rote learning the preferred method of instruction. Brother Loyola ('Lolly') O'Sullivan, who was in charge of the Junior School, was a martinet, who used a strap and a cane freely and insisted, in a slight lisp, on cleanliness – 'a nice vite collar, me sonny'.

Parents expected results and Pres. accordingly was a cramming factory where no cultural interests were encouraged. Teachers knew what was expected of them. They instilled those expectations into their pupils who in turn knew that their parents – and most certainly this was the case with O'Faolain's – expected their sons to work hard, to endure whatever punishment they might receive, for the sufficient reason that success in examinations meant entry into a more secure way of life. If punishment was a spur inside the school, parental hopes were an even sharper goad outside. Sean lived in terror of tests and examinations. Denis and Bridget Whelan constantly reminded their sons of the 'great and unremitting hardships' they had to endure in order to educate them. There was no escape from their loving blackmail and there were times when Sean hated them. They were relieved when the headmaster reduced fees for Sean and through the years put some money his way for tutoring weaker pupils. During his last two years he was a pupil-teacher. He did well, was an honours student in all grades and a prize-winner in the middle and senior grades, but he felt helplessly coerced and was chronically unhappy. To illustrate his feelings of being coerced he later narrated the occasion in 1914 when the whole class, on being refused permission to go to the races in Cork Park, an annual event to which they were normally allowed to go, went anyway. Three boys, including Sean, returned to the school, explaining to the others that what they most feared was not punishment, but the hurt and shock to their parents. Next day, Brother Evangelis, also remembered for what he invariably said before a punishment, spoken as though it were Latin, 'by me to you for it', punished all the others, some twelve to fifteen, while the three non-rebels sat by in shame. The bitterness of the experience stuck in O'Faolain's mind. He wrote about it in *A Nest of Simple Folk*, associating it with his loss of innocence, and again in 'Up the Bare Stairs', a bleak account of the effects of parental coercion. It was a story, he said, about a man ceasing to love his parents, and it marked a decisive moment in Sean's relationship with his. From that day he developed 'an absolute craving for independence', although he never succeeded in feeling he was 'a wholly autonomous and self-responsible individual'. He always felt himself as existing in relation to somebody else or something else. From that day he had a terror of kindness, benevolence and gratitude. 'I have always felt, and often rebelled against, such bonds as human affection, loyalties and ties of the heart, pity for others, sympathy, the passions, which tie us to others by love or hate or envy or lust, human respect, ambition . . . All these things are the bonds that keep us in our place'.

The love he felt for his mother was also irrevocably shaken by another incident that happened about this time. One evening as they walked along arm in arm, he saw some school friends and ran over to talk to them. When he returned, Bridget was 'boiling with rage'. She violently rejected his hand, refused to talk to him, turned for home and when they got inside seized the rattan beater from behind the kitchen door. She lashed him across his calves up the three flights of stairs into the attic room, made him strip naked and flogged him all over until she was exhausted and he 'was reduced to the abject and final subjection of unheeded sobs of shame'. For it was, he felt, the shame that mattered both to her and to him. 'In my first year as a marriageable youth, *nubilis*, my masculine pride had been assaulted unforgiveably' (VM, 75). His anger festered. From then on he began to strip her as she had stripped him by silently noting imperfections and crudities in her nature that he had previously not noticed. The truth forced itself upon him that the woman he had once loved was a boor and not civilized. He deliberately recalled other incidents of her insensitivity: on some of their affectionate walks she would embarrass him by bending low in front of him under the pretext of buttoning his clothes, would spread her legs and urinate standing up. At home, instead of walking the six steps to the toilet, she would take a cup from the dresser and urinate into it, emptying it several times into the sink. As a boy he had wondered if he was becoming too romantic and refined as a result of going to the theatre, and if it was because of reading that he felt ashamed at her behaviour. Now he recognized her crudity.

Sean's suppression of his unhappiness at Pres. was a way to survive in the face of the coercion that he felt at home and at school. As a technique he would see it reflected in the lifestyle of an oppressed people and their leaders. If there was some obstinacy in his make-up, derived from the years at Pres., there was also the habit of masking his private feelings, of temporizing, of being secretive, and of escaping from the pattern of his life by weaving patterns of his own in fiction. That ability to live a double life, which he found useful later, originated in and was first successful at Pres. Gus may have had this in mind when he commented 'I think you were an unreasonable brat anyway: you wouldn't stay in the nest and quietly cheated'.[5]

In the end teachers made the difference. Christopher Flynn, his French teacher, could evoke the reality of Paris and France. 'Doggy' Sheehan, his English teacher, a shy, civilized man with a falsetto voice and a stammer, whom the boys badgered, gave him the run of his library. Doggy taught English poetry, drama and prose, English history, European history, and World Geography to his unruly, mischievous classes. He recognized and encouraged Sean's interest in literature and Flynn stimulated his interest in French.

Two teachers, Brother E. I. Connolly and Pádraig Ó Dómhnaill, influenced Sean profoundly. Connolly was a native of Cork. Largely self-educated and widely read, particularly in English Literature, he was reputed to be a fine classicist. Under his enlightened administration Pres. became one of the most prestigious secondary schools in the south of Ireland and was virtually a constituent college of the Royal University, preparing students for matriculation and all the arts degrees. He urged boys towards brilliant achievement and, when necessary, rebuked them. He told them they were 'consummate puppies' who deserved to be flogged, but he did not believe in corporal punishment. For him a gesture, a look, a tug of the ear, a mocking 'you young rascal' were sufficient. He recognized Sean's interests, encouraged him to borrow reference books, and when Sean took down notices from the notice board and replaced them with two pages of a school magazine that he had written and called *The Bugle*, 'The Man' merely asked that in future he should be allowed to see the 'magazine' before it was pinned up. Sean admired him, liked his affectionate, chiding ways and was permanently grateful for his having wide horizons. He was the first real influence in O'Faolain's life outside the home, and he was what Denis Whelan wanted his sons to be: a gentleman. He represented the conservative, conformist, loyalist, snobby side of Pres. Through him pupils received outlines of a world beyond Cork. Even his classes in religion evoked far foreign fields where the French generals, Pétain and Foch, were staunch Catholics, and where past pupils never lost the faith. He emphasized the brilliant careers of former pupils. 'You can become a Canadian Mountie. Or go into the Merchant Navy. Or there's the Indian Police . . . the whole British Civil Service is wide open to you. Look around you at all those photographs in the hall. Given to me, every one of them, by old boys from every corner of the world'. No wonder Gus Whelan opted for the Civil Service and Patrick sailed for the missionary fields of Australia. Brother Connolly also evoked the wonder of the classics. In Sean's final years he prepared a small class for matriculation and revealed that 'happy marriage of feeling and intelligence which is the very heart of the classical way of life' (VM, 95).

If The Man stood for one side of Pres., Pádraig Ó Dómhnaill stood for another. For all its conservatism and West Britonism Pres. was not immune to the changes taking place in Irish life as nationalistic feelings and aspirations became stronger. O'Faolain's years at Pres. (1912–1918) came at a crucial time. While the full force of the changes did not affect him until he entered University College, Cork, the seeds of those changes were planted in him at Pres. and nurtured by his Irish teacher, Ó Dómhnaill. Older boys, like Frank Gallagher and Pádraic Ó Caoimh, who later became active in the fight for freedom, were more receptive to nationalistic influences in those years. Boys began to walk homeward by Sheares Street, to see young Irishmen training as officers in the Irish Volunteers. 'There was a sort of rebel music in the air around the place they used for training; there were unspoken, undefined memories of the past, and a vague feeling of excitement about the future'. The Easter Rising of 1916 was ahead.[6] Pres. Brothers were not immune to the infectious music. One of them gave Ó Caoimh a copy of the writings of Arthur Griffith and some poems and stories by Brian O'Higgins. They talked together about hurling and football. The significance of these incidents is that they undermined the Intermediate Education System under which Pres. functioned. That system was designed to weaken the Irish sense of cultural identity, but the policy boomeranged, since the realization that Irish culture and racial identity were threatened with extinction motivated young men and women to explore their own history and culture. Resentment at deprivation encouraged young men and women to subvert a system of education designed to erase Irish identity.

Pádraig Ó Dómhnaill was born in the partially Irish-speaking district of Liscarney, Co. Kerry. He read Celtic Studies at University College Cork. Denied a university appointment because of his involvement with the Irish Volunteers, he got a teaching position at Pres. A quiet, handsome man, a good teacher and a natural scholar, he was committed to Irish culture. By virtue of his background, training and interests – he played football, loved céilidh dancing, and was active in the Gaelic League – he embodied the changes that were taking place in Irish life. His influence on Sean proved to be revolutionary. He 'let fall, in odd words and phrases, hints about a far-off free country called the West where the people talked only in Irish, wove and spun in it, fished and ploughed, drank and laughed in it, where . . . there was a wonderland where the star of Eden never died' (VM, 127). He evoked an entirely different way of life that outshone what Sean had found in Rathkeale. It was romantic and utterly seductive for an adolescent who had as yet no clear sense of the direction his life would take. One day O'Faolain, still known as Jacky Whelan, heard that Ó Dómhnaill had been seen at the head of a band of men wearing the dark green uniform of an Irish Volunteer. Because of his admiration for his teacher, he was unable to scoff, as he had earlier on seeing a similar band of ill-clad, poorly equipped men parading in Emmet Place.

It was the Easter Rising of April 1916 that broke O'Faolain's loyalist links. As the rebels in Dublin held out against superior odds, as he heard of British Lancers being fired upon in front of the General Post Office in the city where he had walked with Tom Boyhan, and when he read of their dignified surrender, his defences gave way. 'That day', he records, 'I stole away up to my attic . . . and I wept for them' (VM, 102). The *Cork Examiner* carried graphic descriptions of the destruction of Dublin and protested strongly at the execution of the leaders. Sean had not thought much about nationalism, but with the Rising feelings rose up in him of which he was previously unaware. His response was primarily and powerfully emotional. Now in the summer of 1916 when he went to Rathkeale he cycled about the countryside in search of historical remains, the ruined castle of the Desmonds, the friary of the Earls of Kildare, the home of Aubrey De Vere.

One day, sitting beside Ó Dómhnaill, he noticed that he was wearing a gold ring in his lapel. That meant, Ó Dómhnaill explained, that he would speak Irish to anyone who wished to be spoken to in that language. Sean decided that he, too, wanted to have a *fáinne*. Ó Dómhnaill prepared him for the oral test and lent him books in Irish. One of these, a collection of poems by Tomás O Súilleabháin, O'Faolain kept for years. 'I cherished it solely for its frontispiece – a smudgy photograph showing a rocky promontory on the Atlantic, a ruined chapel, a rocky graveyard, a few fields . . . they became my new symbols . . . I was creating a new legend, a new myth' (VM, 103).

[3]

Revolution

THE summer of 1918 was the beginning of a period of remarkable growth and change for Sean O'Faolain. In July he attended Irish classes at Pres. and met Eileen Gould, whom he would marry ten years later. In August he cycled westward for the first time to that Irish-speaking country that Pádraig Ó Dómhnaill had so vividly evoked. In October he entered university and began to enjoy the unexpected freedoms of student life. Within months he was caught up in the excitement of being an Irish Volunteer. He was young, he was freer than he had ever been, and he was in love – with Eileen, with Irish language and culture, with Ireland itself.

In his last year at Pres. he had become tall, spindly and more nationalistic. It was he, with two or three others, who went to The Man and asked that the school be allowed to form a hurling team. From playing this traditional Irish game to attending an Irish summer school was a short step. On the very first day a dark-haired girl sat directly in front of him. Seeing her ponytail sweeping back and forth across the inkwell on his desk, he dipped its tip into the ink and politely handed it forward to her. She turned and laughed gaily at him. 'She had deep brown eyes, red, glowing cheeks, and white teeth, one of which was gold-capped, an attractive little mole to the left of her upper lip, and a cloud of hair that I chose to think of as the colour of thunder.' (VM, 106.)

Eileen Gould lived at no. 4 Walls Terrace in Sunday's Well, a row of four houses with small front gardens, each of which leads onto a little path that runs to the hilly, winding road that leads from Sunday's Well Road to the Women's Jail, Convent Road and Strawberry Hill. Because their mother had died, the five Gould children were raised by her sister, Aunt Kate. The father, Jo Gould, was a bearded, well-dressed, good-looking, travelled man, who was reputed to be very clever.

From him Sean received a new sense of Cork. Denis Whelan saw the city as alien, felt respectful of its leaders, and was nostalgic for his familiar rural origins. Gould was proud of his Cork connections. Denis was loyal to the British Crown. Gould had been an ardent nationalist, a Fenian, and a supporter of Parnell whose fall he deeply regretted. Denis lacked self-pride and was humble in serving his superiors, but Gould was naturally independent, self-reliant and indifferent to British power. Sean commemorates his spirit in the larger-than-life portrait of the fiery, old-fashioned, anticlerical Fenian, Phil Crone, in *Bird Alone*.

As a family the Goulds were different from the Whelans. They were outgoing, uninhibited and indifferent to middle-class values. Eileen was free in a way that he had never been. She was vital, wilful, romantic, liked Byron, Shelley, and the bawdy Irish poets of the eighteenth century. She approved of the Russian Revolution, hated snobbery, despised convention in dress, loved the country. She took him on walks along the slopes of the river valley and shared her knowledge of the countryside with him. She knew more about sex than he did: she was bemused by the sight of condoms floating down the river.

Discovering that she spent her summers with Irish-speaking families in the West, he determined to join her. Cycling out from the city past the fields where they liked to walk, he began to feel the magic of the West. It was a matter of atmosphere evoked by the rocky landscape, the furzy fields, an old bridge, a weathered farmhouse, the old Norman castle at Carrigadrohid. In two hours he was on the little hill on the edge of Inchageelah, which marked, for him, his arrival in the free country. At that point Pádraig Ó Dómhnaill's Irish-speaking country began. What he had imagined from the cover-illustration of Tomás Rua Ó Súilleabháin's collection of poems was here a reality, an iconography he would treasure for years. He cycled through the village, past the lake, past little white cottages with thatched roofs, through the unforgettable aroma of turf smoke, through the village of Ballingeary to Tuirin Dubh, the townland where he was to stay with the O'Tuamas.

Tuirin Dubh is a small valley about a mile and a half from Ballingeary. On one side it backs onto the River Lee, which at this stage, just a few miles from its source in Gougane Barra, is but a small river. On the Ballingeary side it is bordered by a small tributary stream. On the other side, facing O Tuama's, is a rocky, tree-lined cliff. On the other, where the road turns sharply towards Gougane Barra, are a number of large rocks. This self-enclosed valley with three or four families was a haven for almost everyone from Cork who wanted to absorb and be renewed by contact with Irish language and culture. Sean, Eileen, Nancy McCarthy, and Michael O'Donovan, later to be known as the writer Frank O'Connor, stayed here. So did Father Tim Traynor, Terence MacSwiney, Daniel Corkery, De Valera, Erskine Childers and many others.

In appearance the O'Tuama residence was unpretentious. It had a plain, cemented front, a long garden leading out to the road, and a stone loft and byres to one side. Across the road was a barn with a galvanized iron roof and more byres. As Sean arrived Eileen emerged and introduced him to 'Nan Nan', the woman of the house, Bean Ui Tuama, whose welcome in Irish was as warm as the welcome he had received in the past from his Aunt Nan. He felt at home.

There were about twenty to thirty students who had travelled from various parts of Ireland, and one, Scottie McKenzie, from Scotland. There were clerks, students, carpenters, craftsmen, an electrical engineer, and two men who had been in the Rising in Dublin. The women slept in rooms in the house. The men slept in the Lochta Fada, a dry stone loft which had been turned into a dormitory. The entrance was up a flight of stone steps on the outside. Inside were three divisions: students slept in iron beds at the near end, the farm workmen in the middle, and servant girls at the far end. Should the loft become too crowded, men would sometimes take refuge in the barn across the road, which was also entered by means of stone steps on the outside and a door in the gable away from the road. They spoke only Irish, often helping one another with words, phrases, pronunciations and forms of grammar.

Their zeal to speak their native language bound them together. They were light-hearted and happy. All adopted, and many retained, the Irish version of their names. Jacky Whelan became Seán Ó Faoláin. In the mornings they went to classes at the Irish college in Ballingeary. In the afternoons they were free to swim in the lake, climb the mountains, explore the surrounding countryside. In the evenings they took part in céilidh dancing by the roadside or in the college, sometimes went on boating parties, or sat in Bean Ui Tuama's kitchen talking, or listening to songs or fiddle-playing. 'Nobody who has not had this sensation of suddenly "belonging" somewhere — of finding the lap of the lost mother — can understand what a release the discovery of the Gaelic world meant to modern Ireland' (IJ, 144). Not for many years did Sean get free of 'this heavenly bond of an ancient, lyrical, permanent, continuous, immemorial self, symbolized by the lonely mountains, the virginal lakes, the traditional language, the simple, certain, uncomplex modes of life, that world of the lost childhood of my race where I, too, became for a while eternally young' (IJ, 144).

Of all the places in West Cork, Gougane Barra was Sean's favourite. There, beyond its small lake, was the source of the River Lee, at the head of a dark valley, known in Irish as the Red Coom, in English as Valley Desmond. A tiny island near the edge of the lake was a hermitage with a ruined chapel and a small square cloister of cells where, according to tradition, monks had slept in the time of the early Celtic church. St. Finbarr, Cork's patron saint, had lived on this island. Sean and Eileen 'loved this valley, lake, ruined chapel and rude cloister because of their enclosure, their memories, and their silence' (VM, 112). For the landscape of his first collection of stories, *Midsummer Night Madness*, Sean drew upon his memories of Gougane Barra, of the valley and the mountains. His short story, 'The Man Who Invented Sin', captures the happiness and unselfconscious freedom of those who gathered in Tuirin Dubh. 'The Silence of the Valley' commemorates the beauty of Gougane Barra on the occasion of the death of its storyteller, the bearer of tradition.

Almost every summer from 1918 to 1926 Sean and Eileen went to the Gaeltacht. In 1920 during their long vacation from university they went to the island of Cape Clear to stay in 'Luí na Gréine', with Bean Ui Shúilleabháin. In 'Luí na Gréine', perched on the hill above the tiny harbour, there is a magnificent view of the islands off the Cork coastline. As they cycled westward they noticed strange looking forces, half-soldiers, half-policemen, along the roads. The year in which the Black and Tans arrived became known as the Year of the Terror. When they returned to their studies in the autumn they were aware of the increase in violence and tension.

* * *

University College Cork is situated on a wooded campus that slopes over grassy lawns from the hill on which its Tudor-style buildings cluster to the South Channel of the River Lee. Early in October 1918 Sean signed the College Roll and registered as a student in the Faculty of Arts. He had sat for a scholarship examination earlier in the summer and had been awarded an Entrance Exhibition, valued at £10. 'When I went up to UCC, it was a new world. When I was a boy it was a wonderful world and I thought of it as one that was made for me'.[1] He let his hair grow long, wore a black hat, Irish tweeds and a long overcoat that hung loosely from his lanky frame. Like any full-blooded, intelligent and inquisitive young man, discovering the delights of being free of parental and teacher control, he took advantage of his freedom. He spent hours lounging in the students' club or outside on the grassy banks, 'arguing, dreaming, hoping, mocking, conspiring, flirting and, so, learning from my fellow students' (VM, 124). He went to College 'hops', or dances, which were usually held in restaurants or in hotels in the city. Everyone knew that he and Eileen were 'doing a line'. Some wondered at this. While she was warm, outgoing and greatly liked, he was thought to have a chip on his shoulder, because his father was a policeman. Beside her high colouring and classical profile he seemed unattractive. But they had much in common – a liking for books, a high level of intelligence, a love of Irish language and culture and an involvement in the Republican movement.

He joined several societies. In 1919 he was a committee member of the Irish Society (An Chuallacht Gaedhlach). In 1920–21 he was a Council member of the Students' Representative Council, a committee member of the Students' Club and Auditor of the Philosophical Society. This year both he and Eileen were on the committee of An Chuallacht Gaedhlach. He was particularly active in his final year. On 23 February 1920 he became Secretary of the Literary and Debating Society, another name for the Philosophical Society, in addition to being the Auditor. In 1922 he was awarded the society's medal for oratory.

Student life, he discovered, was undemanding. He read English, Irish, Latin and French in his first year, did enough to gain a pass, then opted for English Language and Literature as his major subject, with Irish and Latin as subsidiary subjects. Although only Pass Irish was required he did the Honours course, attending lectures in both Old and Modern Irish. College life suited him and he read widely – Arnold's poetry and prose, Browning,

Shelley, Joyce's *A Portrait of the Artist as a Young Man*, Chekhov, Turgenev, Dostoyevsky, Tolstoy, Maupassant, Balzac and Hardy whose novels he read 'constantly'.

He loved English poetry, 'adored' Meredith's 'Love in the Valley', and was attracted to Hawthorne for his more passionate world. It was as the Irish revolution gained momentum that the revolutionary writers – Shelley, Stendhal, Dostoyevsky, Yeats – became relevant. He, and other students, liked to quote 'I met murder on the way/ He had a face like Castlereagh'. Yeats's political poems were popular. Everyone knew 'September 1913'. Sean's favourite, 'Easter 1916', captured his own progression from indifference to involvement. But his Book of Revelation was Kuno Meyer's 'simple, concrete, intimate' translations from Old Irish. They helped to 'blend him with his own people'.[2]

In the summer of 1921 Sean passed Irish and Latin and in September sat for his finals. He was awarded Second Class Honours, sharing first place with another student, and won the Peel Memorial Prize which was given to the most distinguished student of the year on the results of the final examination, taking into consideration also the student's participation in the public life of the College. It included the 'Old Corkonians' gold medal and £5 to be spent on books of his choice. Sean chose volumes of Chekhov. Next year he was awarded the Micheál Óg Ó Longáin Prize for his play 'An Dán'.

He returned to UCC twice, first in 1924 to do an MA in Irish, then in 1925 to do an MA in English and to obtain a Higher Diploma in Education. His dissertation in Irish was not much more than a long essay. Written with clarity and conviction, and applying the idea that a writer's growth depends on the combination of technical skill and personal experience, it focussed on two of Dáibhí O'Bruadair's poems, written ten years apart. O'Faolain placed his argument in broad literary and cultural contexts, with examples drawn from Goethe, Spenser, Shakespeare, Wordsworth and Tennyson. Two sections of the thesis were published in *Earna* (1925), a magazine sponsored by the Irish Department. His short story, 'Prendergast', appeared there in 1924.

The tendency to range widely was checked in his first thesis by his concentration on two specific poems. But his MA thesis in English, 130 pages in length, entitled 'The 'Prentice Years of English Poets: A Study of the Craft of Old English Verse by J. F. Whelan', is given over so much to

[47]

generalization that it lacks coherence. It is a passionate, whimsical and unfettered piece in which lyrical energy and impressionistic pronouncements take the place of scholarship. Unimpressed, Stockley gave it a mere pass mark.

The Professor of English, W. F. P. Stockley (1859–1963), was a gregarious, colourful man. With his tattered gown, long beard and absent-minded manner, he seemed a caricature of a professor, but he was a man of wide intellectual interests. His surviving textbooks suggest that he was disorganized in the way O'Faolain describes, but that portrait of him as a comical teacher, enthusiastic but incoherent, is malicious and unfair. He often got carried away by his enthusiasm, reading passages aloud and asking excitedly, 'Did you feel that? Did you savour it? Did you get the rhythm?' Some students found him stimulating, knowledgeable and a brilliant teacher. Sean thought him stimulating, but confusing and obtuse.

Stockley insisted that students wear gowns at lectures, frequently asked questions in class, put pressure on them to work and required an essay on an assigned topic each term. He warned them against plagiarism, hated generalizations, and was known to be a hard marker. He was a man of principle and sophistication. All agree on the value of his 'at homes'. He would greet his guests at the door in striped trousers and swallow-tail coat. Through these occasions Sean gained an insight to civilized behaviour and the niceties of social life, virtues he had seen previously only on the stage of the Opera House. The Stockleys often had musical evenings at which people were expected to perform. Germaine, or her friend, Tilly Fleischmann, would play the piano. They had play readings, favouring Sheridan's *School for Scandal* or *The Rivals*, Shakespeare's history plays, *Henry IV* in particular, or Goldsmith's *She Stoops to Conquer*. Germaine, a good reader and a clever mimic, spoke with a strong German accent and was outstanding as Mrs. Malaprop. Stockley also read well.

Sean's judgment on UCC is stern. If he was critical of Stockley's disorganized lectures, and lack of formal training – 'only a smattering of Old English and Middle English and . . . never even mentioned Old High German' (VM, 216) – he was even more critical of the professional deficiencies of his Professor of Old Irish, Tadhg Ó Donnchadha, who wrote under the pen-name of Torna, and knew no Sanskrit, no philology and very little Old Irish. His brother Eamonn taught Modern Irish. Both had been trained as teachers in the national schools. 'When I left that college I did not know what a bibliography was, how to compile a clear course of reading, how to attack any subject, ignorant of the difference between a conflation and a collation, a primary source and a secondary source, objective analysis and subjective feelings, how to compose a resumé, how properly to organise a theme' (VM, 128). There was, he also felt, in a characteristic snooty manner, a drawback to being a university student in a city that did not have museums, art galleries, periodicals, a publishing house or two, a sister university, a symphony orchestra – that is, a cultivated tradition emanating from wealthy drawing rooms, old houses, old families (VM, 162). But in fact UCC gave him time to discover himself, to read, to make friends, to develop, and to recover to some degree from the consequences of his lonely, puritanical upbringing. His election to positions of responsibility on student committees suggests that, despite his aloofness and affectation, his peers recognized his talent for organization. He had a reputation for being brilliant; he was pushy, strong-minded, aggressively argumentative, self-confident and always had to be superior.

But he was not without anxieties. Bothered by the 'frets' of adolescence, he was still deeply troubled by his mother's distress. Why, he asked himself, was his mother being driven to drink? She was, for him, Ivan Karamazov's one innocent child whom God allowed to be assaulted. He took these worries to Fr. Aubrey Gwynn who was conducting the College Retreat, and explained that he was unable to go to confession, because he found it difficult to accept a God who allowed so much suffering. In some irritation, Father Gwynn demanded why he should be expected to solve the insoluble problem of the existence of evil. Contrite in the face of that response, Sean backed off, unappeased. Next day he sought another priest, confessed his sins, was absolved, and concealed his doubts. But he heard 'the sucking noise' of Arnold's ebbing tide and knew that he was 'not only a fool but a stranded damned fool' (VM, 82).

There were two sides to him: on the one hand the lively student, the voracious reader, the intellectual, the competent administrator; on the other the self that questioned and doubted. As a boy he had experienced the conflict between God's omniscience and the demands of sexuality. The suffering of his pious, self-sacrificing mother made him question the goodness of God. Now at university his faith was so low, despite years of compliance, that unless he did something about it he felt he 'would soon be

[49]

left marooned on a sandbank in a sea of faithlessness' (VM, 80). Later he would understand the aridity of his childhood religious training. For now his faith was endangered. Becoming a rebel allowed him to forget this problem, but it also led to its exacerbation when the Catholic Church condemned and excommunicated Republicans.

Revolution – the Anglo–Irish War (1919–21), the Truce (1921–22), and the Civil War (1922–23) – formed the background to Sean's years at university. If his head was filled with wonder as he entered college, reality began to intrude the day a fellow-student with a gun slapped him on the back and said 'What about it?' 'Next thing I knew I was in the IRA'. More accurately he was in the Volunteers. His parents were horrified. His mother wrung her hands, his father prayed fervently against it and feared the loss of his pension. It was a tense time in the home as their youngest son went beyond their control, flew in the face of the British Empire, associated with 'blackguards', came into conflict with the Church, and as hostilities intensified came into personal danger. Sean tried to hide his revolutionary involvement by slipping over the back wall into Paul's Lane, but men in trench-coats would come knocking at the door with messages for him to attend a Section meeting. Those visits caused rows. Denis prayed for the protection of the British Empire and condemned his son's new associates. Sean answered back furiously. Bridget stood between them in tears. British military forces came searching for him and once his father found a revolver under Sean's pillow.

Sean never became prominent in the IRA, not so much because of his youth, as he used to maintain – Tom Barry and Ernie O'Malley were only two years older – but because of his inexperience and background. As an RIC 'get' he was regarded with suspicion and distrust. Like thousands of others he did the ordinary jobs: gathered information, guarded sleeping guerillas, carried dispatches, dug trenches across roads, felled trees, did police work, marched in the streets in defiance of military orders. But he revelled in his freedom. 'Never will I forget the first day I stood in a field, in a deep glen, somewhere to the southwest of the city, with a score of other raw recruits, being given my first drill by some older student, while along the two hills overlooking the glen other Volunteers stood on the lookout for police and military. Before we were dismissed our captain, Ray Kennedy

. . . spoke to us about what we were, and were there for, about the coming fight, about secrecy and loyalty. It was an autumn day of sun and shower, and just as he began to speak to us a faint, gentle sprinkling rain began to fall on us, and then the sun floated out again and sparkled on every leaf and blade of grass as if some invisible presence had passed over us with a lighted taper, binding us together not only in loyalty and in friendship but in something dearer still that I am not ashamed to call love. In that moment life became one with the emotion of Ireland.' (VM, 135.)

Involvement had its risks, particularly in the period from Spring 1920 to July 1921, when the violence intensified. Every separatist organisation, Sinn Fein, the IRA, the Gaelic League, was proscribed, every nationalist paper was banned, every prominent Republican was a wanted man. Faced with an invisible guerilla army that struck suddenly and then vanished, the British forces resorted to unofficial counter-terror. Reprisal begot reprisal. The IRA raided for arms, attacked police barracks, intimidated the RIC, burnt the homes of the Anglo-Irish Ascendancy, kidnapped and executed informers and hostages. The British retaliated in kind, sent in more forces, including the Auxiliaries in July.

Sean was aware of the increasing violence. In January 1920 he read that Thurles had been shot up by police and military. On St. Patrick's Day, Stockley was attacked by two Black and Tans. On 19 March Cork's Lord Mayor, Tomas MacCurtain, Commandant of No. 1 Cork Brigade in which Sean was enrolled, was murdered in his home. On Easter Sunday the IRA burnt out a hundred Inland Revenue offices and a large number of deserted RIC barracks. Six Volunteers were then mutilated near Cork. In July two were severely beaten and tortured; one died. That month Sean and Eileen cycled to Cape Clear. In August Terence MacSwiney was arrested. Refusing to recognise his courtmartial, he went on hunger-strike, was deported and died in Brixton Prison in October.

Cork honoured its dead Lord Mayor. Sean stood proudly in the guard of honour at City Hall, where MacSwiney lay in his Volunteer uniform, his face dark and shrunken in the candlelight. It was a moment of strong feelings: lament for his commander, resentment and rage at the manner of his death. After a solemn requiem Mass in the Cathedral, he marched with the UCC Republican branch to St. Finbarr's Cemetery. Along the way the band played the 'Dead March' from *Saul*, and every window was 'black with people and every face dark with anger or moist with tears'. UCC students lined the Western Road. MacSwiney's *Principles of Freedom* was one of Sean's revered nationalistic texts, together with Padraic Pearse's political writings, Thomas J. Clarke's *Glimpses of an Irish Felon's Prison-Life*, Tone's *Autobiography* and Mitchell's *Jail Journal*.

The winter of 1920–21 brought some of the most violent deeds of the Anglo–Irish war. In Dublin nineteen British undercover agents were assassinated. In Kilmichael Tom Barry's West Cork flying column killed eighteen Auxiliaries with the loss of three Volunteers. In February seven IRA men were executed in Cork. Outside the barracks Mary MacCurtain erected an altar, and while many women prayed, including the mothers of the condemned men, they heard the successive volleys of the firing squad. The young men, it was reported, went to their deaths in pairs at fifteen minute intervals, 'like schoolboys'. Because Mrs Lindsay of Coachford, Co. Cork, an elderly Unionist, had given the information that led to their capture, she was kidnapped by the No. 1 Cork Brigade and shot. Next day, in Cork city, six unarmed British soldiers were also shot. Sean was not involved in the notorious kidnapping but he wrote a memorable account of what happened in 'The Small Lady'.

The pattern of terror and counter-terror continued. In December the Auxiliaries set fire to Cork. Sean watched the fire from his attic room and in the morning he and Michael O'Donovan walked disconsolately amid the ruins. Their free Carnegie Library was no more. That day Bishop Cohalan condemned all violence, excommunicated the IRA and earned their resentment.

The last year of the revolutionary struggle coincided with Sean's final year at university. It was particularly intense: 'the aim of the British was not only to break the nerve of the fighters but to break a whole people . . . They closed life in on us tighter and tighter every month through a varied, incessant and inventive terrorism, constant and often pointless raids and arrests, humiliating and brutal beatings-up in city streets, casual murders on country roads . . . early curfews that locked us up in our houses and reduced the city to a desert hours before the sun set, after which the Tans, who operated outside every known law and war-convention, roved the dark streets in search of victims or loot.' (VM, 140–41.)

Once Sean was stopped by the Black and Tans. They searched and questioned him, threatened to shoot him, to throw him in the river, to flatten his balls, to take him as a hostage and made little of his protests that he was the son of a loyal member of the RIC. A young lieutenant took a volume of Shelley's poetry from Sean's pocket and wrote 'fine stuff' in the margin beside 'The Mask of Anarchy' and the 'Ode to Liberty'. They made him sing 'God Save the King', then sent him running to their jeers and a hail of bullets meant to frighten, not to kill. In a different mood they might have shot him, or have tied him inside the Lancia to be shot should they be ambushed.

In June, as Sean sat for examination in his subsidiary subjects, prospects for peace began to be more promising and the weather turned warm and sunny. But the centre of Cork was in ruins and the nights were still racked by rifle and machine-gun fire. In July 1921 came the Truce. The Troubles were over and a Treaty was signed in London on 6 December 1921. Sean prepared for his BA examination, but spent much of the time drinking, dancing and parading. He had had a good revolution:

I used to recite to myself, 'Bliss is it in *this* dawn to be alive but to be young is very Heaven.' I was at the University now – as an university fourth-rate but for me it was perfect, for it was a library, a workshop, a club and conspiracy. We drilled on Sundays in hidden fields outside the city, we route-marched, we learned to use guns, we studied Gaelic and went out into the mountains to drink it as from the pure undiluted Pierian spring, we combed the world's literature for revolution, talked in the manner of Dostoievskian intellectuals, despised the bourgeoisie, longed for nothing better than to be hanged by the neck for Ireland and to be buried under the tricolour. As those years hotted-up life took a quicker and quicker pace. I knew sensations I had never known, such as terror and rage and love, for in those days I came to love Stuttering Looney and Bagsy Flynn with a love more intense than I have ever experienced after or ever will. For about five years I lived on top of a Mont Blanc of elation.

In the autumn Sean took a job as a travelling salesman with the Educational Company of Ireland. He trimmed his hair, grew a neat moustache, and in order to make himself look older than twenty-one, abandoned the baggy tweeds and the ankle-length overcoat of the revolutionary in favour of a business suit. He bought his first motorcycle, owned a chequebook and set off to sell school books throughout the south and west of Ireland. He got to know every school, convent, monastery, bookshop and country hotel in Munster. He met the other commercial travellers. He experienced the slow trains and the cold hotels, the dull food, the depressing towns. But for a young man who had not travelled much in his own country it was an education. He read Gogol's *Dead Souls* with delight and formed the ambition of writing its Irish counterpart. But once more revolution intervened. De Valera and his supporters rejected the Treaty because it failed to offer full independence and by 28 June 1922 the Civil War had begun. Forces under Michael Collins were determined to defend the Free State of twenty-six counties established under the Treaty.

[4]
Civil War

SEAN'S decision to oppose the Treaty had little to do with the issues that politicians had wrestled with during the Treaty debates. Nor did it have much to do with viable political or social alternatives. At the age of twenty-two he was still idealistic, high-minded and able to be disappointed that the pro-Treaty side, motivated he felt by materialism, had settled for less than total freedom. He complained bitterly that the Free State forces had even used British artillery to shell Republicans in the Four Courts, and had relied on the British for ammunition and weapons in their encircling drive in the south. The fact that Daniel Corkery was fervently anti-Treaty weighed heavily with him. For both of them, De Valera represented principle over opportunism, pride above shame. Initially Corkery, like De Valera, tried to reconcile the two sides, but in April 1922 he denounced the Treaty in *Poblacht na hEireann*. His *Rebel Songs* (1922) expressed a confidence that the Republican cause was right. Sean gave up his job, offered his services to the IRA and was assigned to the bomb factory in Gilabbey, where he joined Ray Kennedy and other UCC men in the meticulous, dangerous and unglamorous task of making bombs. For the next two months he sat every day at the work benches among the jars of acid, the heating ovens, the boxes of powder, making incendiaries out of cardboard and cotton wool, filling bomb cases, constructing fuses, removing bullets from cartridges, refilling the charge grain by grain, inserting the wads carefully, shellacking the caps, drying them over warm metal plates, while outside lorries of armed men set off for the front. The tedium of the work can be seen in his story 'The Bombshop'.

While he worked in the bombshop he also helped Frank O'Connor, Sean Hendrick and Daniel Corkery as a censor on the *Cork Examiner*, then under Republican control. He wrote a marching song to the air of 'John Brown's Body'. He also wrote 'Khaki and Green' for *An Poblacht (Southern Edition)* which Erskine Childers thought summed up the political situation. Referring to the murder of T. Kenafick by Free State forces, Sean argued that the Free State were using the same methods that the British army had used during the Anglo-Irish War. He listed other examples: a man killed and his body flung into the hole made by the mine, children killed, prisoners beaten and killed. It was blunt and effective, the kind of propaganda that Childers himself and Frank Gallagher, another past-pupil of Pres., had formerly directed against the British in *The Irish Bulletin*.

But propaganda could not halt the Free State advance. Defeated in Dublin, the Republicans tried to form a defensive line from Limerick to Waterford, but that did not hold and the IRA in Cork began to unravel. On 10 August the city fell. Scottie McKenzie died defending the city against the advancing Free State Forces. Sean, Ray Kennedy and the others were ordered to move the bomb factory to Macroom, where they set it up once again. They were followed by the retreating Republicans. Frank O'Connor and Sean Hendrick sang Sean's song, 'In Clareside and in Kerryside we've buried fighting men', as they fled westward. The retreat became a rout. Incapable of forming another defensive line, the Republicans had to scatter. Some, including O'Connor and Hendrick who borrowed ten shillings from Sean to do so, made their way back into the city. The experienced fighters formed themselves into flying columns. The bombshop was moved to Ballyvourney, a few miles from Gougane Barra. Once again, the Republicans were denounced by the Catholic Church which issued an order of general excommunication, and called them 'riff-raff, scum, looters, and murderers'. They never forgot and have never forgiven the Church for this. The bombmakers worked in Ballyvourney until November 1922, but in increasing uncertainty as Free State troops closed in, captured Macroom Castle and moved on Ballingeary, where Sean's friend Christy Lucey was shot as he tried to escape from Tuirin Dubh.

Bored with their work and wanting to be more active, the bombmakers asked to be given a chance to fight when Macroom was attacked, but were refused. They were included when Dave Robinson planned an attack on a Free State blockhouse in Inchageelah. But when the regular fighters deliberately turned up too late to participate Robinson abandoned the attack in disgust. Sean's chance to see some real action had passed. On 7 December he was appointed Director of Publicity for the First Southern Division.[1] The Republicans had commandeered a printing press and set it up in a farmhouse in Guirtin Fliuch, a townland about three miles from Ballingeary. It was a large, old-fashioned model, with a fly-wheel and drawers full of lead, so high that a hole had to be cut in the ceiling to allow it to stand upright. Guirtin Fliuch is approached by a long, narrow, winding sideroad that runs deep into the valley. The valley itself is bordered by mountain on three sides and by a stream on the other. Lucey's second farm, where they had the press, is off the sideroad on a narrow track that winds along the foot of the mountain. A two-storey stone building, it is invisible from the sideroad and even when one approaches closer it is screened by trees.

As a boy, Dan Kelleher was sent down to the house with jugs of tea and slices of homemade bread. Peter Lucey dropped by occasionally. O'Faolain, he said, 'was the dictator' – he wrote the news sheet. Bob Langford, a printer and an experienced Republican activist, set the type and ran off a thousand copies; a city boy named Connolly acted as look-out. At night Sean and Langford would go to the O'Tuamas for a meal, sit by the fire in the kitchen, with Sean repeatedly flicking back a lock of hair from his forehead. Sometimes they stayed for the night. He got on well with Langford, but resented his going every day into Ballingeary to read the *Cork Examiner*. That resentment finally erupted into a bitter row. Later Sean was ashamed of his failure to understand that Langford, a family man, was anxious to hear the news from Cork. He himself had become abstract and inhuman in his dedication to Republicanism.

According to Peter Lucey 'the Civil War ended in this valley'. When the Free State forces approached, the Republicans fled west towards Kerry. Sean and Langford shut the door of the farmhouse, dumped the lead in a ditch and took to the hills. For a brief period they and a few others tried to evade capture, taking part in one engagement firing downhill at a line of green uniformed figures advancing towards the village of Ballymakeera. It was Sean's only experience of direct engagement, apart from an attack later on a Free State lorry in Cork, and finding the whine of bullets over his head not to his liking, he was filled with even greater admiration for the men in the flying columns.

The attack on the lorry became the subject of a poem and a story by Frank O'Connor:

> Whelan wears yellow gloves
> I see them hanging dead from his left hand
> In his right he carries
> A dark revolver.[2]

O'Connor and Hendrick wore the conventional trench-coat of the IRA fighter, with hats cocked to one side. Sean, like the Eric Nolan of O'Connor's story, 'Laughter', disguised himself as a gentleman by wearing yellow gloves, carrying a walking stick and smoking a pipe. 'He came in, tall, bony, and cynical, a little too carefully dressed for the poor student he was, a little too nonchalant for a revolutionary. There was a calculated but attractive insolence about his way of entering a house and greeting the occupants. He laid his walking stick on the table, and covered the handle with his hat'.[3]

Sean had one or two more brushes with the enemy as he wandered through the countryside, hungry and dispirited, sleeping in barns and outhouses, eating whatever he could get from the people, usually tea and bread. Not long before Christmas, suffering from itch, lice and crabs he sought refuge in a priest's house. The priest gave him a hot bath, a change of clothing, a clean bed, and a solid breakfast. He had no difficulty in persuading his guest to go home and fitted him out as a cleric to make the journey less dangerous. When Sean entered no. 5 Halfmoon Street, his parents welcomed the prodigal. Bridget kissed him again and again. Denis held his arms fondly and without reproach. He spent Christmas with them, happy to be back in his blue and cream room, with his fire and his books. After dark he would slip out to meet Eileen.

When Christmas was over he cycled to West Cork but was ordered back to the city to run publicity from there. He hid in his room. Only his three couriers, Eileen, Molly Fitzgerald and Mary Lucey knew where he was. They carried the newssheets into the city for distribution. Innocently Eileen had hired a room in a brothel – 'The Abode of Love'. There, the papers were wrapped in bundles and distributed once a week to wherever the headquarters of the First Southern Division happened to be. But in February 1923 Eileen was arrested and jailed. In March, Molly Fitzgerald was also captured. Sean wrote to her in prison, but carried on, by now so keyed up that he had no feeling for Eileen, Molly, the anxieties of his parents, or Mary Lucey's remorse at being the cause of Molly's capture. 'I was', he recalled in *Vive Moi!*, reflecting on his fanaticism, 'Ireland, the guardian of her faith, the one solitary man who could keep the Republican symbol alive, keep the last lamp glowing before the last ikon even if everybody else denied or forgot the gospel that had inspired us all from 1916 onwards. I firmly believed in the dogma of the minority's resistance to the majority, that the People have no Right to do Wrong. Like all idealists, I was fast becoming heartless, humourless, and pitiless' (VM, 165). He was in this a faithful follower of Eamon De Valera. As Corkery said to him, 'All idealists are callous'.

When Eileen was released from prison he was shocked by the change prison had made in her. While his heart had hardened, hers had been softened, not so much by imprisonment as by her father's suffering. She condemned the Republicans as abstract fanatics, and inhuman. Only their love for each other kept them together. It was a difficult time in their relationship, since he was also romantically involved with Mary Lucey.

But then he began to feel the strain of being confined. With the coming of Spring he slept away from home, with Horace Porter in Monkstown, with Stockley. He even stayed in homes that he knew to be supportive of the Treaty. In April he took refuge in an old country house in the hills south of the city and began to regain a sense of his own relative unimportance. There, on 24 May 1923, he read De Valera's proclamation to dump arms and observe a cease-fire. He walked openly back to the city only to be ordered at once to Dublin to become Assistant Director of Publicity for Sinn Fein, the Republican party. Mary MacSwiney, Director since September when Robert Brennan got sick, thought O'Faolain would never be a good editor of *Sinn Fein*, and doubted his ability as a leader writer.[4] When she was jailed in November 1923, he was made Director of Publicity under Patrick Ruttledge, Acting President.

At first he was elated to get away from Cork, and to be close to the centre of events. That mood gave way to despair when he realized how very short of leaders the Republicans must be when they had to appoint one so young and inexperienced to such a responsible position. He was editor of the blatantly propagandistic *Sinn Fein* (known outside Ireland as *Eire*) and worked with Mary MacSwiney on *An Phoblacht*. The real organizer was Mrs Erskine ('Molly') Childers who, grief-stricken by the execution of her husband and an invalid, ran *An Phoblacht* from her home in Bushy Park, Terenure. Fanatically opposed to the Treaty, a dominating, powerful woman, she drove O'Faolain to incessant work and goaded him to greater and greater effort. 'She was to me', he recalled, 'and to many others who worked closely with her more than human and less than human. She gave the overall impression on many occasions of a Madonna with a bomb'. When her home was raided she swept all her papers into a hiding place under the carpet beside her bed and Sean escaped through the French windows. Once again he was caught up in a frantic, idealistic defence of the Republic. 'I began to pour passionate cables all over the world protesting against the destruction of the Living Republic by a junta of traitors. I appealed by cable to the President of the United States, to the head of every Government in Europe, to the editors of newspapers in all parts of the state, to the Vatican, to high ecclesiastical personages everywhere'. He drew up messages to the Irish People to be printed as display advertisements in Irish newspapers (VM, 168–9). Although now he admitted to himself that there never had been an Irish Republic, he continued to write passionately in its defence.

The emotional cost was great. He was constantly exposed to stories of the sufferings and deaths of Republicans, including the agony of a hunger-striker who was force-fed. They were, he judged 'all idealists, self-crazed by abstractions' (VM, 170). He stayed in Dublin until the end of January 1924, met Eileen who was on her way back to a teaching position in Ballinasloe, then returned to Cork, to private life, 'a more than disillusioned and embittered young man' (VM, 172–3). There was little hope of getting a job. He returned to UCC, to the 'sheltered cloister' where he had once been happy. There he could try to recover from his trauma. But he could never recapture the magic that Cork had once had for him. For years he would wander its streets, looking for his 'lost dream', like the disillusioned self in *Bird Alone*, 'rewalking old walks, revisiting old haunts'.

There was much to be bitter about. The Republicans had been soundly beaten. For them, the war was 'a terrifying and horrible experience'.[5] 'It *was* a mistake but inevitable. We were bloody fools. Dev. was a wobbler that time. He had high ideals but no sense of reality and swung us with him – young men. The older men would never admit it was a mistake or be ashamed of it – quite the contrary'.[6]

Establishing military courts, the Government set out to break the Republicans, whom they now classified as 'criminals'. Unauthorized possession of a revolver was punishable by death and so Erskine Childers was executed. O'Faolain had seen Childers in Macroom and thought him a doomed man. That death left a bitter taste in his mouth. In just over six months the Government executed eighty-one Republicans, thirty-four in January 1923 alone when Sean was still in Dublin. Each death, he recalled later, was a bruise on his soul.

When the Civil War ended thousands of Republican prisoners were in jail, where they remained for months. They went on a hunger strike which failed and on their release were met by a largely hostile people, many of whom agreed with the bishops' pastorals that they had 'wrecked Ireland from end to end and had caused more damage . . . in three months than could be laid to the charge of British rule in so many decades'.[7]

It would be many years and many books and articles before Sean would be able to place himself and the events that had moulded him into some kind of rational perspective. His involvement with revolution had been instinctive. He had trusted the leaders. He had been led by the nose. In Dublin he discovered, in bitter disillusion, that if what they all knew about politics were written down it would not cover the back of a threepenny stamp. In that year, he said, he woke up.[8]

From any perspective the revolutionary years had affected him more deeply and more lastingly than any other period in his life. In the interplay of life and death, there were splendid scenes and painful scenes, such as the morning 'a chap with whom I had been to school and thought a crude, rude, barbarous lout was taken out after a drumhead courtmartial and shot – it took a long time to think that out'. Was it a good thing or a bad thing, he asked himself, to have had five heavenly years of youth and then to lose them in the Civil War when

> Stuttering Looney put a bullet in Bagsy Flynn
> And Holy Mother the Church rushed in
> With a terrible tale of the shoals of sin
> That must follow the dream, now the dream was over,
> Tear friend from friend and boy from lover,
> And nothing allowed but fear and greed,
> The stonecrop's grey and fluttering weed
> And the cress that chokes the throat of the stream
> That once was red with fire and the dream.

[61]

He was confused and bitter, but he did not lose his belief in Republicanism. At the unveiling of a memorial cross to two dead comrades on the eighth anniversary of the Easter Rising, he spoke in austerely idealistic terms: the cause, he said, glorifies the man who upholds it; no minority is too small as the unbeatable minority of the dead; the memory of what former patriots endured 'must infuse into every man who passes this spot a feeling of self-contempt and shame, if he cannot say that he, too, is doing his part to perpetuate their sacrifices and bring their work to its proper conclusion'.[9]

Five months later he launched a sweeping attack, in *Sinn Fein*, against a series of articles by Frank Gallagher on the 'Volunteer Spirit' and against Terence MacSwiney's *Principles of Freedom*, which was being serialized reverently with Irish and English versions side by side. The reiteration of principles, he declared, was unnecessary, the reiteration of propaganda offensive. The people needed facts. They needed Reason and Intellect. One could read *Sinn Fein* for a long time and not realise that Republicanism was an intellectual movement. What, he asked, does *Sinn Fein* think about the language movement? What does Frank Gallagher think about it? Or Mary MacArdle? Or any official Republican apologist?

Later he raised the issue above the bitter legacy of the Civil War to a more constructive and inclusive level. He would, he said, like to hear from someone who believed as he did that the people are fit to climb to any height if only they are led to it: 'a height or plane where we shall not sneer at everything the Free State population may attempt irrespective of good intentions: a plane where we shall not be afraid to say that Collins and Griffith were men of noble qualities; a plane where we shall encourage actively a Gaelic tradition as well as a Republican one, and achieve a tradition of Republican culture instead of a tradition of Republican sentimentality.'[10]

[5]

Corkery's Glugger

THE Anglo-Irish War was part-time and episodic. Sean could be a student by day, an IRA rebel in the evenings or on Sundays, and be available at times for routine activities. The Civil War occupied his attention more completely but throughout the period, from 1918 to 1926, he had time for other things. He formed friendships at university and in the Gaelic League. He went to evenings at the Stockleys', visited Daniel Corkery's home, where he met writers, painters, and musicians, joined the Twenty Club and became a familiar figure in the city's literary, cultural and Irish language circles.

He went to events sponsored by the Gaelic League in various centres, including the North City branch where Terence MacSwiney and Eamon Ó Donnchadha were enrolled. He joined the O'Growney branch whose meetings and céilidh dances took place in An Dun, Queen Street (now Matthew Street), became its Secretary and edited *An Grianan*, a twelve page literary annual produced for wearers of the *fáinne*. In it he published two of his own stories, 'An Teach' and 'An Malairt', and got contributions from Torna, Corkery, Alfred O' Rahilly, Frank O'Connor, and others.

As a supporter of the Gaelic League, he identified with the idea that Irish must become again the predominantly written and spoken language of the country and that the people would thereby preserve and develop their own identity in a way they could not if English remained their main language. In this he was allied with Corkery who remained steadfast to the Gaelic League philosophy, as it had been defined by revered figures like Douglas Hyde, Eoin MacNeill and Padraig Pearse.[1] Soon, however, he was to break with Corkery and this was painful. Both men were strong-willed and egotistical.

Corkery never forgave Sean for choosing to write in English rather than Irish. Sean felt that Corkery, like De Valera, had led him into his own brand of emotional nationalism. But in 'The Patriot', he gave a sympathetic portrait of Corkery, the middle-aged bachelor trapped, as he had been himself, by inhuman Republican passion.

An Dun was also where a small group put on plays by Daniel Corkery, T. C. Murray, Terence MacSwiney, and others. The plays, such as Corkery's 'King and Hermit' and 'Israel's Revenge', were typical, O'Faolain wrote later, of the Irish Literary Revival: they were forcefully conceived, tragic, even melodramatic, and romantic.[2] Nevertheless, on 4 April 1919 Sean played the part of Sean Falvey in an Irish language version of Corkery's 'Clan Falvey', performed by the St. Finbarr branch of the Gaelic League and produced by Corkery.

It was in An Grianan also, in a room above a stable across the street from An Dun, that on one night in 1918 Sean first met Michael O'Donovan. O'Donovan was then fifteen years of age, 'slightly hooped, all specs, and eyes and brow, the eyes myopic, the teeth ingratiating, the brow magnificent . . . He wore knickerbockers, long, woollen, hand-knitted stockings . . . and black boots'.[3] He was a lonely boy from an even poorer background than Sean with no-one to talk with about what interested him most, Turgenev, Goethe, and Old and Modern Irish poetry. He and Sean had many interests in common: the IRA, the Gaelic League, books, and the possibility of becoming writers. They became inseparable. Both were idealistic Republicans, but the deaths of MacCurtain and MacSwiney, the burning of Cork, and the executions brought the reality of blood and death close. O'Donovan looked up to O'Faolain, who had the advantage of being three years older, was brilliant, disciplined and a university student. O'Donovan tended to be emotional and argumentative and the differences between them made their friendship stimulating and amicably antagonistic. Corkery encouraged their rivalry.

It was Corkery's encouragement that led Sean to attend meetings of the Twenty Club, which took place close to his home in a laneway behind the Church of St. Augustine, almost directly opposite Sheila Wallace's little stationery shop where he bought those seditious nationalist newspapers that helped to shape him. When it was founded in 1915 the Club was non-political. Limited to twenty full members and forty associates, its aims were to publish each year, in addition to broadsheets and miscellanies, a work of aesthetic, economic or patriotic interest by a Cork writer. But it failed to generate a creative or intellectual renewal. Apart from Corkery, it lacked people of real ability and vision.[4] Real writers, like Lennox Robinson and T. C. Murray, tended to leave for Dublin or London. In the early twenties the Club published a Republican periodical called *An Long*, which ran for three issues before being suppressed by the Free State. Begun by Corkery, O'Connor, Sean Hendrick and O'Faolain its first issue in May 1922 carried Sean's review of Lennox Robinson's play, 'The Round Table', and of a new novel in Irish.

Corkery's influence on Sean was direct, through the Gaelic League, dramatic productions in An Dun and meetings of the Twenty Club. He also arranged for him to attend classes at the school of art and encouraged his literary ambitions. More importantly he was a published writer, a novelist, a short story writer, a dramatist, a painter, a nationalist, a Gaelic Leaguer, a political activist who spoke on platforms with Republican and other leaders. He behaved like an artist, maintained an aloofness that befitted the artist, just as Yeats did in Dublin. He was quite unlike anyone that Sean knew, the one person in the city, before his meeting with Frank O'Connor, with whom he could talk about books and writing.

His literary influence was more a matter of example than of direct guidance, although Sean and Frank O'Connor took their early writings to him. 'Let's see,' he might say, 'how Shakespeare would have done it'. That may have been impractical, but it set standards. Corkery taught O'Faolain to aim at greatness and he felt 'intense admiration and gratitude at being permitted to consort as an equal with a great man'.[5] He showed Corkery his own list of reading, which included the Russian novelists whom Corkery extolled as models. Sean already knew what he liked: *The Brothers Karamazov*, *The Torrents of Spring*, *The Kreutzer Sonata*, *The Death of Ivan Ilyich*. In later years he realized how frequently he and O'Connor had pestered Corkery, two lonely, penniless young men, forced to wander about the city, often in the rain, and inevitably turning up Gardiner's Hill to Corkery's home where they were always welcomed.

He was also an example of someone who was able to create an imaginative life by surrounding himself with books, music, paintings, and periodicals. Over his mantelpiece he had his own large water-colour of a man with a scythe standing on Fair Hill and looking across the river valley. For years he lived in the belief that Cork could be a sustaining place, maintaining that the small city could be a world in itself as Concord had been for Thoreau. The Twenty Club was based on this idea. He involved himself in drama, gave lectures, encouraged young talent, made his home a cultural centre. He played classical records for Sean and other visitors: Beethoven symphonies, Mozart's 'Violin Concerto in A', Schubert's 'Unfinished Symphony', Strauss's 'Till Eulenspiegel', Delius whom he particularly liked and some Bach. When he went out sketching or painting, he took Sean, or Frank O'Connor, with him. They carried his easel and called him 'Master'. He was their mentor who actually bought books, *The Studio*, and *Times Literary Supplement*. Corkery in turn regarded O'Faolain as a born literary man. He allowed him to look through his copy of *Ulysses* which he kept in a locked drawer. He was, O'Faolain said, in his final comment on him, 'a most kindly, hospitable and sympathetic man'. Sean became his best friend.

But Sean could see that Corkery was trapped. With a nearly blind mother and a devoted sister depending on him, he had few opportunities to live a normal life, to marry, to devote himself to writing, and he could not get away. He told Sean about his fear of being provincial, something they all feared. Sean understood the older man's defensiveness, seeing it as a compensation for his personal frustration. Irishness and nationalism gave him a significant set of references. But, while Corkery was becoming entrenched in his beliefs, Sean was learning to be objective and critical. By developing a doctrine of regionalism Corkery, he saw, 'tied the knots of provincialism about him, instead of kicking the ropes from his feet'.[6] By contrast, O'Faolain and O'Connor grew out of provincialism. 'The disillusion of the post-revolutionary period helped us to spit on it all'[7] and to outgrow their dependence on Corkery.

Unfortunately Corkery's defensiveness made him more narrow. When Sean first met him he was enthusiastic about Russian literature, thinking that Ireland and Russia had much in common, that Irish novelists could emulate the Russian novelists. But after the Civil War he opposed the idea, said Irish writers should not learn from foreign models, turned against the writers of the Anglo-Irish Revival, and had no time for O'Faolain or O'Connor once they began to write in English.

The publication of Corkery's *Threshold of Quiet* (1917) was an 'event' for O'Faolain. He welcomed a novel that dealt with popular life and admired it enormously. Corkery, he saw, faced the frustration of life in

Cork and admitted it. Sean was elated by Corkery's *Hounds of Banba* (1920). Its self-sacrificing, dedicated and disciplined heroes were ennobled by action. But when O'Faolain became less starry-eyed, he saw that they were not at all like the IRA he knew. His own stories in *Midsummer Night Madness* consciously reflect a more realistic picture. When this collection was attacked in *An Phoblacht*, he acknowledged that it had been written in a spirit of disillusioned revolt against the glorification of the gunmen, but he argued it was books like *Hounds of Banba* that were 'the really vicious and immoral books', because they gave a false picture of the fight and thrust young men into a 'blind and thoughtless struggle'.[8] He had been one of those thoughtless young men and he was bitter at being deceived by Corkery. The age difference between them was also a factor. How, he asked, could a white-templed man with a lame leg 'dare be romantic when young men are in hot blood and know that the w.t. man with the l.l. goes to confession, sniggering at having to do it'?[9]

When Corkery's nationalistic ideals infected his creative writings O'Faolain could not admire them. In addition, as he began to think out his position on nationalism, on Republicanism, on the revival of the Irish language and on the future directions of Irish literature, he found himself questioning Corkery's beliefs. In particular he questioned the view of the Irish past that Corkery expressed in his influential study of eighteenth century Irish poetry in Munster, *The Hidden Ireland* (1925) which Corkery gave to O'Faolain on Christmas Eve 1924. Calling it the bible of the Revivalists, O'Faolain objected strongly to Corkery's identification of modern Ireland with a 'cowed Ireland, a land of poverty, bad education, or none, and defeat'. He pointed instead to the classical, scholarly Ireland he had discovered through Kuno Meyer. He objected to the Revivalists' advocacy of an uneducated peasant culture at a time when Ireland was already part of the European tradition and would contribute, both in Irish and English, to world literature.[10] He criticized the emphasis on eighteenth century Irish texts at the university on the grounds that Irish should be read for its intellectual content.[11]

Objecting to Corkery's narrow, influential and representative definition of an acceptable Irish tradition, he insisted, as he had in *Sinn Fein*, that no one man was the custodian of the national tradition. The work of others should be recognized: that of Horace Plunkett and AE in the rural cooperative movement, the 'gunmanning' of Michael Collins and Rory

O'Connor, the visions of W. B. Yeats, the work on the hydroelectric scheme on the Shannon, the work of the Gaelic League, the publication of a weekly paper in Cork, and the quiet efforts of craftsmen of all sorts throughout the country. He had, he declared, faith in his own generation to make a better tradition for Ireland than was made in Corkery's generation. Corkery's view of tradition had come out of a memory of long defeat and was a narrow tradition fearful always for its own safety. Theirs came out of an Ireland of fight and conquest and was a wide tradition that opened its arms to the ideas of every country in the world.[12]

These articles reveal an O'Faolain that his contemporaries remember: serious-minded, intelligent, argumentative, aggressive, prepared to speak out for what he believed. They carry a tone of proud assertiveness. He had seen enough self-abasement in his home, had fought to free his people from oppression, had identified with Sinn Fein's call for self-reliance. Now, as he began to articulate his belief in himself, in his generation, and in the possibilities for the future of his country, he did so with pride, rejecting Corkery's identification of modern Ireland with a defeated Ireland. He became Corkery's glugger, a term given to O'Faolain and O'Connor by Denis Breen, meaning that Corkery's protégés did not hatch out as expected. Knowing he had been swayed too easily by feeling Sean sought to balance feeling with judgement. He found guidance in Walter Pater's ideal of noble living in *Marius the Epicurean*, in John Donne's intellectual refinement, in Joyce's combination of romantic style and cold realism. In taking on the Gaelic Revivalists and Corkery, in criticizing educational changes, O'Faolain opposed the most influential people of the time and attacked what many revered. His attack on Republicanism in *Sinn Fein* also made him enemies. He constantly stressed the primacy of intelligence, was strongly European-minded and was vehemently opposed to narrow definitions of Irishness. He detected the first signs of that acquisitive middle-class which, in combination with an uncultivated Church, threatened the Republic he had tried to create.

In the summer of 1924 Sean, Eileen, Molly Fitzgerald and Frank O'Connor were together in Cork. Fresh from her job in Ballinasloe, Eileen was the only one who had money and Sean borrowed heavily from her. In September he got a position as Head Class Teacher in the Christian Brothers School in Ennis. Initially he was content. He had a salary of £150 per annum, which he supplemented with private tuition, and paid back what he owed Eileen. He could afford to subscribe to the *TLS*, the *Irish Statesman*, the *Spectator*, and the *Labour Monthly*. But Ennis was a smaller and duller Cork. It had no cinema, no theatre, no library, no bookshop. As the months passed he felt trapped and when the teacher with whom he shared lodging at Mrs McEvoy's on Francis Street, running his hand through a thatch of prematurely grey hair, said 'Would you believe, Sean, I'm twenty years a teacher', Sean decided that he could and that he must get out.

At Christmas he and Eileen decided to resign from their jobs. In September Sean went back to UCC thinking that an MA in English and a Higher Diploma in Education might equip him for a better job. Frank O'Connor got a job as a librarian in Sligo, then in Wicklow. Eileen got a teaching position in Naas, within easy reach of Dublin, and Molly Fitzgerald left. Alone in Cork, Sean did not even have Corkery's company. Now when he visited, Corkery did not invite him in. In his loneliness he began to write. At Christmas he went to Dublin and met AE and Lennox Robinson. Then in February 1926 he published a short story called 'Lilliput' in the *Irish Statesman* and began to feel that he might be a writer.

[6]

Harvard

W H E N AE and Lennox Robinson agreed to recommend him, Sean applied for a Commonwealth Fund Fellowship in January 1926. Under the terms of the Fellowship he could spend two years at an approved American university, receive about $3000 a year and spend three months travelling within the United States at the end of the first year. He was called for interview in April. The Award Committee included Sir Walter Buchanan-Riddell, Principal of Hertford College, Oxford, as Chairman; Sir T. Percy Nunn, Professor of Education at the University of London; W. B. Reed, Professor of English, Yale University and Director of Education to the Commonwealth Fund; and Viscount Chelmsford, sometime Viceroy of India and Honorary Fellow of Magdalen College, Oxford. According to Sean his selection was a matter of luck: 'About twelve or thirteen went for interview. They had just come to the twelfth when someone said "What about giving the Irish a chance?" '

He heard that he had been awarded the Fellowship with mixed feelings. The opportunities provided – escape from Cork's provincialism, intellectual challenge, variety, an expansion of personal life at all levels – threatened what he clung to: the subjective, inner world of the writer and the haven of the familiar. Not only was he writing challenging articles about what he knew and valued, but he was exploring his own nature in short stories, trying, as he told Edward Garnett 'to get away into the recesses of myself free from the desire to be as others'.[1] By accepting the Fellowship, he took on, but was neither quite ready for nor, as he discovered, fully committed to, the life of the professional academic and scholar. At this time he thought he would have to make a choice between being an academic and being a writer.

In July he was presented to the Prince of Wales, Patron of the Commonwealth Fund. It was a splendid occasion, and a considerable alteration in stature for the defeated Republican propagandist. The Prince, who was shy and ill at ease, talked with each Fellow for about five to ten minutes, asked each the same questions: 'Where do you live? Where were you at school? Where are you going in America?' and invariably concluded with the injunction: 'Remember you will be an ambassador for your university and your country'.[2]

Meeting the future King Edward VIII at the Palace of St. James was one kind of achievement. Meeting the other Fellows made Sean realize some of his own limitations. They had their eyes firmly fixed on opportunities in England once they had concluded their years in America, whereas he had few prospects; while he had spent summers in West Cork, they had travelled widely in Europe and further afield. He had never even been to the Continent.

When he returned to Cork he decided to rectify that. In August Frank O'Connor, Eileen and Sean went to Belgium, pausing on the way to visit Oxford. They stayed for a week at Damme, a village about four miles from Bruges. O'Connor bought a large-brimmed black 'poet's hat' and sat immobile for hours in an outdoor café. Sean and Eileen cycled to Zeeland and to neighbouring beaches, then took the train to Paris, to wander 'hand in hand around the quays, the island, the old city'. They saw their first play at the Comédie Française, visited the Louvre and the Conciergerie, Sean's favourite, since he had read every novel he could find about the Revolution. They went to the Grand Guignol, where Eileen became so terrified that, fearing she would not sleep that night, she asked Sean to sleep with her. Sean's account of these days in Paris stresses their innocence. He was 'ardent and romantic,' Eileen 'with her high colouring, brown eyes and black hair, was like a rose with the sultry yet brilliant effect of a dark-red rhododendron' (VM, 203). Years later Frank O'Connor confirmed the truth of Sean's portrait.

In the summer of 1926 Sean also met Liam O'Flaherty: 'the most handsome man I had ever seen'. He was the embodiment of muscular strength and well-being, bursting with energy.[3] O'Flaherty told him how helpful Jonathan Cape's reader, Edward Garnett, had been to him as a writer, and suggested that Sean should send him samples of his work. On 15 August before leaving for Belgium, Sean sent Garnett 'The Bomb Shop' and 'Under the Roof'. He also put in a good word for Frank O'Connor, 'a friend of mine who writes very finely . . . We are both dry for criticism'. Garnett's reply, together with an invitation to visit, arrived in Cork after Sean had left for Belgium.

It was in the summer of 1926 also that Sean and Eileen first met Alene Erlanger, who was a frequent visitor to Ireland because of her interest in drama and horses. Vivacious, open-eyed, friendly, and welcoming, she invited Sean to visit her in America.

Bridget and Denis were proud of his success: degrees, a Fellowship, acquaintance with well-known people, and being presented at Court. They lavished affection on him. Now, too, he was capable of an affection for them that he had not felt since childhood. His mother delighted in packing his new cabin trunk. Under the terms of the Fellowship he received an equipment allowance of two hundred dollars and his fare was paid both ways. He bought a book of etiquette and equipped himself with a tennis shirt that fastened between the legs, dress shirts, expanding cufflinks, patent leather pumps, silk underpants, cravats, visiting cards.

Then he went forth. He spent the night of 13 September 1926 at 'Springfield' with his College friend, Joe Healy. Next day Joe accompanied Sean on the tender out to the liner anchored in the bay under a full moon. The S.S. München had arrived from Bremen on the morning of 14 September. As the tender moved out in the moonlight, bonfires blazed along the coast, with one just for Sean in the back garden of 'Springfield'. The band played 'Come Back to Erin'. But his mood was far from sentimental. When Joe said, 'I hope, Sean, you won't be too homesick in the States?' he answered, bitterly, 'For Ireland . . . I don't care if I never see the bloody place again'. All his 'latent disillusion with Ireland, with life in general' welled up in him, on hearing the music, at seeing two girls weeping softly beside him 'in a sudden, bitter satisfaction at yet another instance of human stupidity' (VM, 204).

If the portrait of Eileen in *Vive Moi!* is of the 'good girl', the portrait of the woman on the boat, whom he calls Anna Maria Kauffman, is her opposite: the experienced, sexually-liberated woman, 'blonde, blue-eyed, strongly built, handsome'. In between the two portraits is the awkward, inexperienced, young man, embarking uncertainly on adventure. Anna Maria, Swiss-born, educated in a wealthy east coast American college, married to a German exporter, was interested in modern poetry and

American politics. From her, Sean first heard of T. S. Eliot. Their flirtation was slightly impeded by the presence of Alfred O'Rahilly, UCC's Registrar, who was also going to Harvard, accompanied by his wife and daughter. Nevertheless Sean enjoyed this ship-board romance with an older woman, the secrecy imposed by the Registrar's presence only adding to the excitement. In the course of the voyage O'Rahilly gave Sean the impression that if he distinguished himself at Harvard, there could well be a job for him in Cork as successor to W. F. P. Stockley.

When he arrived on 22 September, Sean was taken aback by the noise, heat, and dirt of New York. He visited Alene Erlanger and for the second time on this journey came into contact with an experienced, older woman, who received him with kindness, took him, and her mother, to see *The Pirates of Penzance*, and eagerly begged him to visit again. Then he took the train for Harvard.

At Cambridge he found lodging at 48 Irving Street. He bought an alarm clock, a teapot, one cup, saucer, plate, spoon, knife and fork, tea-towels and paper napkins from the five-and-ten.[4] Usually he had lunch and dinner in one of the noisy, crowded student cafeterias.

He went to see Professor F. N. Robinson, his academic adviser, who worked out the year's programme for him: 'Celtic 1. Old Irish' given by F. N. Robinson; 'Celtic 20. Investigation of Special Topics in Celtic Philology' under F. N. Robinson; 'Comparative Literature 20e. Irish and Welsh' given by F. N. Robinson; 'English 4. Middle English. English Language and Literature from 1150-1450', given by F. N. Robinson and J. S. P. Tatlock; 'Romance Philology 3. Old French. Phonology and Inflections', given by J. M. D. Ford. For his special topic in Celtic 20 he proposed 'The Possible Influences of Old Irish Verse on Anglo-Saxon Metrics'. The second year brought more of the same: 'Celtic 3. Old and Middle Welsh', under F. N. Robinson. Celtic 20 and Comparative Literature 20 continued; 'English 20c. A course of Special Study' under John Livingstone Lowes; and 'English 86. Studies in Shelley' under Professor André Koszul.

It was a formidable programme. But Sean settled into the austere life of the graduate student, rising at 7.00 a.m., working until 9.00 a.m. in his room, then walking across to his carrel in Widener Library, or else to a morning lecture or seminar, after which he would return to Widener and work there until dinner time. Widener was well stocked and its system of open access favoured the serious student. After dinner he went to a student cafeteria, with Frank Chambers, who also lived at number 48, with Ernie Simmons, or in the following year with F. W. Bateson. He and Freddy saw a lot of each other and often went together to a cabman's cafe, because the food was cheap, if unvaried.

The classes were gruelling, particularly Old Irish with Robinson in which there were only two students, Sean and Ernie Simmons. He was somewhat put off by Robinson's lukewarm approval of his special topic. Since he had studied Old English with Stockley, had done his MA thesis on Anglo-Saxon verse, had done Old Irish with Torna, and felt an affinity with Old Irish poetry he thought himself well-equipped to investigate his special topic. Robinson patiently listened to O'Faolain's enthusiastic account of his proposal. 'Well,' he said, drily, 'it might be worth while. To spend two or three years on it. Just to see. If there is anything in it.' (VM, 215.)

Although he entered enthusiastically into his new rôle, for which he grew a small beard, Sean was not entirely happy in it. The proposal he had presented to the Commonwealth Fund had been ambitious to the point of absurdity: 1) the study of early and modern English in its relation to coeval Celtic literature which may have influenced or been influenced by it; 2) an examination of Celtic influences on Anglo-Saxon literature with regard to a) the genius of both, b) the forms of both, c) the simultaneous growth of both in lyric poetry, folk-epic, court literature, religion, towards the definition of the genius of Anglo-Saxon literature as seen before and after Romance and Renaissance influence and a comparison with Celtic (chiefly Irish) literature which was so much less affected from the outside; 3) to present a work on these lines for a D. Litt. degree. What he had not realized was that Harvard's graduate system did not lend itself to such literary interests. At that time it was not possible to do a Ph.D. in English Literature, only in philology and for this one had first to cover the entire field: Old English, Old French, Old High German, Gothic, Icelandic, Middle English.

In his first letter to Edward Garnett, in November 1926, Sean complained about the 'unbelievable amount of drudgery-work here at linguistics'. But, he added, he suffered this 'gladly', since there was much to be gained from such 'methodical work', but he had had no time for his own writing, apart from translating one poem from Irish. Part of the trouble was that he was not well prepared. Robinson was 'amazed' to find that Sean had got as far as an MA, 'without doing any really scientific work in grammar'. As a result Sean struggled. He worked ten hours each day, and his appearance indicated that the work was a considerable strain. He had grown to his full height of five feet eleven inches, but weighed only one hundred and forty pounds. He found the Ph.D. work 'heavy, dry and uninteresting'. While Robinson was pleased with the work Sean did for him, he appreciated his difficulties. He agreed that Sean should drop Old French and do some research either in Irish literature or in drama with John Livingstone Lowes. He was 'inclined to agree' that Sean should not continue towards a Ph.D.[5]

Sean was both happy and unhappy. He thought of staying in America but he was lonely and homesick. He missed Eileen and wrote to her frequently. As the first winter set in Cambridge became dark and snowy. He dreamt of home, saw himself as a small boy beside the Lee, heard the bells of Shandon in his sleep. He had a picture in his mind of every street and alley in Cork, particularly those he had walked in with Sean Hendrick. He varied his activities, played tennis and squash, and went to the theatre, the symphony and the opera. As the first term ended he discovered he was quickly forgetting what he had studied and began to fear he was not cut out to be a scholar. When he asked O'Flaherty's advice, he got a blunt reply: if he kept at his studies, he would ruin himself as a writer; Garnett thought he 'had genius', and was 'deeply impressed' by his writing; he should chuck Harvard and encounter the raw material of life. 'Murder that fellow O'Rahilly,' O'Flaherty said, 'then write a good short story about the murder . . . Don't write home . . . Be a scoundrel'.[6]

Harvard's emphasis was 'fanatically rationalist, emotionally arid, and fundamentally anti-aesthetic' (VM, 211). John Livingstone Lowes' *The Road to Xanadu* was the ideal, but Sean resented the envy and rivalry of some of Lowes' colleagues in their comments on the book before it was published. Sean admired Lowes whose 'Tradition and Revolt' underlies his later response to Irish society and was reinforced by his reading of Arnold's *Literature and Science*. Had Harvard's Germanically-based methods been as intolerable as he suggests in *Vive Moi!* he would not have stayed on for a third year and voluntarily sat in on courses by Babbitt, Kittredge, Lowes, and others. Harry Levin's judgement on the philological syndicate in *Irving Babbitt and the Teaching of Literature* (1960), a copy of which he sent to Sean, when he was writing *Vive Moi!*, helped to confirm Sean's later view that the method was arid. It is significant that he switched to Lowes for his second Special Topic on the philosophy of W. B Yeats. Robinson, equally sceptical about this proposal, was not alone in thinking Sean was pretentious. Babbitt's *New Humanism* attracted Sean. Its emphasis on poise, a sense of proportion, the imitation of great models, decorum and the Inner Check appealed to him.

His loneliness was alleviated by the kindness of Albert and Edith Kennedy who ran the South End House, a settlement house at Union Park. They welcomed him, invited him to their summer cottage in Duxbury, and introduced him to their friends, with the result that the doors of several wealthy Boston families were open to him, and to Eileen, when she arrived later.

In March he met Anna Maria Kauffman in the foyer of Symphony Hall. She and her husband invited him to spend a weekend at their summer house on the Cape. There, not far from the Miles Standish monument, in delight and excitement as they looked across the bay at the lights of Plymouth, Sean put his arms about Anna and kissed her. Her response shook him to the 'marrow'. 'Not here! Not now!' (VM, 222.) He met her soon again for tea at the Parker House. About two weeks later he sent an especially made engagement ring to Eileen. At Christmas he and Anna exchanged gifts. In the New Year they met more frequently, went together to concerts at Jordan Hall, once to an art show, and once to a performance of Joyce's *Exiles*. In February, when her husband was conveniently absent in New York, they dined together, returned to her house, went immediately to her bedroom, and undressed. But when he looked for the first time at the body of a naked woman, he felt no desire. The image of Eileen interposed itself. Anna Maria threw him out.

At Easter he took a train south, travelling through Washington and Charlottesville, to the western side of the Alleghenies, to the small village of Hindman, Kentucky, where, as planned by Albert Kennedy, he stayed in a settlement house for three weeks. It was a good place in which to ponder the difficulties of his situation: his disaffection with scholarship, his literary yearning, the temptation of Anna Maria, his loneliness for Eileen. He rode through the hills and valleys, went to a Revivalist meeting, gave a talk on Ireland in the local school, had to defend his virginity from an assault by a female companion, and made up his mind.

He wrote a long letter to Eileen asking her to join him. If she did not, he would leave and go home. This thoughtlessly self-centred request put the burden of choice for his future on her shoulders. In effect he asked her to abandon her job and travel three thousand miles to join him in a strange country. Her reply was positive: she would come out. Would he, she asked, see if there was any chance of her getting a teaching position in Boston? Impractical, as usual, he had not thought about this side of things. All he could do was consult the Kennedys whose solution was that both he and Eileen should live and work at South End House. Waiting for him also on his return was a chilly note from Anna Maria which he did not answer.

His behaviour at one level is easily understood. He was not ready for an affair. Immature and inexperienced, he enjoyed the sensations, but was frightened. While he loved Eileen, he was attracted by the older woman and encouraged her. But there is something else: a coldness, an ability to make use of someone, to take a half-risk, to be self-protective even when apparently adventurous, and in the process to deceive. There was, too, a readiness to rely on Eileen's level-headedness when it suited him.

He spent the summer of 1927 idling along the shore in Duxbury, walking in the woods, sailing in the bay, waiting for Eileen. He met her at the boat, drove her straight to the South End House, realizing, too late, what a shock the skid-row side of American life could be. That afternoon, making amends, he took her shopping, and that weekend they went to Duxbury. When the second academic year began he and Eileen lived at South End House and did voluntary, part-time social work, taking neighbourhood children to poetry readings, rehearsing a play, or driving newly arrived immigrants into the countryside. They had an enjoyable social round: skating on the Charles, skiing in New Hampshire, going back to someone's house after a concert. It was a change from the rigours of Cambridge and Sean felt less cloistered and more content. As he drove to Harvard each day in his shabby clattering car he was happier and more cheerful than he had been the previous year. But his room at South End House had a little too much of the get-together spirit and in January 1928 he and Eileen moved to Cambridge, to Appian Way.

But the year was difficult in other ways. At the settlement house they were close to a couple going through the process of getting a divorce. The rift between the Kennedys involved them: Edith confided in Sean who responded with sympathy and may even have flirted with her; Albert was attracted to Eileen. But there was an even more serious difficulty. On that first trip to Duxbury Eileen realized two things: Sean had been changed 'completely' by his year in America and his image of her was unreal. He had been living with an ideal in mind. She was like a girl he used to know when he used to live in Ireland. In his distress at this discovery, on that first visit to Duxbury, he went alone to the beach one night and wept. Next day he told her he had made a mistake in asking her to join him; he saw she would never fit in; he begged her to go home. But Eileen had little choice. She had no job in Ireland and no money. All she could do was wait patiently in the hope that the love they had shared in Ireland would be revived. Meantime, discovering that her Irish qualifications did not make her eligible to teach in America, she took a secretarial course and pondered on what had happened. Sean, she realized, had expanded his horizons, had read and thought a lot, had distanced himself from Ireland, and had been absorbed by a different culture. She had been excluded from all that.

In his second year at Harvard things improved. He had less philology. He enjoyed Babbitt's lectures on antiromanticism and changed his Special Topic. It says much for his intelligence and his doggedness that he got As or A minuses in all his courses and was awarded an MA in Modern Languages in June 1928. He was also awarded a Harvard University Fellowship under which he still had full use of Widener, could go to what lectures and seminars he wished, and avail himself of the guidance of any professor he chose to consult. He was one of seven recipients of this Fellowship which was 'given on the grounds of high scholarship and promise' on the recommendation of the Faculty of Arts and Sciences.[7] This third year turned out to be the one he enjoyed best. He got a job teaching an extension course in Anglo-Irish literature in Boston College; he had more time for his own writings; and he had Eileen.

He wanted to continue his graduate studies, even if he did chafe against the philological system. As early as December 1927 he applied to the Commonwealth Fellowship for an extension of his tenure of the Fellowship for another year, arguing that he needed a third year in order to complete the programme of studies which he had proposed when applying for the Fellowship and to complete his anthology of Old Irish lyrics before undertaking 'the routine of professorial work'.[8] One month later he wrote another letter to say that Robinson had informed him that when he completed his present work he would be awarded an MA with an A grade. Furthermore, Robinson also thought that the anthology, with comprehensive notes, glossary and appendix, would be published. But he needed 'a modest subvention' to give him time to complete it and he would like to employ a full-time assistant, if the Fellowship could provide the necessary funds. He backed up his request with a summary of the work he had already done and the work he would complete by June 1929.

The earnestness with which Sean submitted his proposal and the fact that Robinson continued to support him suggests that he intended to pursue an academic career in conjunction with his literary career. At this stage, early 1928, he had only slight proof that he might be able to become a writer and no proof that he might be able to support himself from writing, but he had evidence that his professors approved of him.

The letters of recommendation that he gathered for his file in the Harvard Appointment Office provide a judgement of his stature and achievements at this stage. F. N. Robinson said 'Mr. Whelan is an excellent scholar, of an unusual range of attainments, and an experienced and skillful writer'. J. L. Lowes expressed 'a very high opinion of him as a man . . . He is really a man of letters, widely read, cultivated, interested in many things, with the ability to do also thoroughly scholarly work'. Lennox Robinson found him 'charming, modest, sympathetic'; he had written one very interesting play and several excellent short stories; he had a liberal breadth of view refreshing in a young man. 'I thought him, two years ago, one of the most promising young Irish writers and I see no reason to modify that opinion now' he said. President Merriman of University College Cork called him 'one of the most brilliant students who passed through the College'. George Russell believed him to be 'a young man of very great literary ability with a good intellect . . . He has intensity and independence of mind.' W. C. Lyon, from the Educational Company of Ireland, reported that although Sean had not much experience of business, he did his work in a competent manner, and Brother Hoctor praised his abilities as a teacher. He was characteristically thorough in getting these recommendations into his placement file.

The day before he did his German language examination on 3 June 1928, almost ten years after they had met at Pres., Sean and Eileen were married in the Cathedral of the Holy Cross, close to South End House. The celebrant was Father Harry O'Connor. The fee was $10. Father O'Connor remembered them, because of what Sean said: that he intended to win a place for himself as an Irish writer. 'He aspired to greatness and was certain he would attain it'.[9]

[79]

After the ceremony he and Eileen, with Ernie Simmons, the only one in on their secret, had breakfast in Shraft's restaurant on Harvard Square. Within a few days they set off on a honeymoon across America. Sean's Fellowship, in which $750 was set aside for three months of travel, was not meant to cover a honeymoon, but there was not much anyone could do about it. Although he had intended to postpone his marriage, he made himself ineligible for further funding from the Fellowship when he did marry. They were away for eight weeks. They drove south, camping the first night on a hillside in Virginia, then on to Tennessee, to the Mississippi, crossing the river by ferry about two hundred and fifty miles below Memphis, on to the mesas, climbed up the Rio Grande from Albuquerque to Sante Fe, and spent two weeks on a hilltop outside Taos with the Rio Grande at their feet and the Rockies ahead. On the way they had from time to time discussed the question, could they live in America? In the darkness above the Rio Grande they made up their minds. 'We belonged to an old, small, intimate and much-trodden country, where every field, every path, every ruin had its memories, where every last corner had its story' (VM, 243). They had travelled through a vast land, but it held no historical vibrations for them. In the end their choice came from little, familiar things that drew them back to Ireland, instinctively, subliminally, in ways that no amount of analysis or rationalization could hope to explain.

It was inevitable that Sean should have felt a conflict between the demands of scholarship and the lure of creative writing. Already his promise as a writer had been confirmed by others, by AE who published 'Lilliput' and told him 'I think that you have a great talent',[10] by Torna who had published 'Prendergast', the first story in which O'Faolain's literary personality may be detected, and by Garnett. As early as February 1927, he began to work on 'Fugue', which he based on that short period in the winter of 1923 when he had been hunted by the Free State forces. In it he drew upon accounts of Willie Twomey and Christy Lucey escaping from Tuirin Dubh. He worked at it until early summer, changing a simpler story called 'Three Women', first written in Irish, into a more literary one. He also began to jot down images, characters and scenes that would eventually make their way into his first novel. From a distance he could recreate what he found most alive in his imagination – the life he had known around Rathkeale and in Cork – and thereby learn about himself. In March he had the satisfaction of seeing 'The Bomb Shop' in *The Dial*. Later it was chosen for the *Best Short Stories of 1927*.

After their honeymoon Sean and Eileen went back to live at 'The Cottage', 10 Appian Way, in Cambridge, Massachusetts, a tiny partly-furnished, clapboard house, just off Brattle Street, which they rented from Mrs. Theodore Noon. At that time Appian Way was little more than a paved lane with three or four white frame houses looking across at Radcliffe College. No. 10 had an ell to which had been added a dependency so fragile-looking, so amateurishly constructed that it looked like an oversized playhouse for children or an undersized home for servants. This was 'The Cottage'. It had a tiny porch, with steps, some trees in the yard, and from the outside looked quaint, but inside it was dark, cramped, and draughty. An old-fashioned boiler in the basement supplied inadequate heat. The floors tilted, the walls leaned. It had a tiny kitchen, a living room with two arched windows, and a bathroom on the ground floor. Upstairs there was a long, porch-like corridor on one side, with windows, and off it two small bedrooms, and a third towards the front which was subdivided.[11] Years later a literary map of Cambridge listed no. 10 as the home of Sean O'Faolain and John Berryman. John Kelleher, emerging from a Yeats seminar, announced humorously to Helen Vendler and Maurice Harmon that 'that house has associations with Irish literature!'

But it was home for Eileen and Sean. Various friends loaned them furniture. They lived frugally, sharing a package of cigarettes, going to the movies perhaps once a week, never dining out, avoiding alcohol. Sean, in fact, avoided alcohol while he was in America. Through careful husbanding they saved enough money to pay their fares back to Ireland and still have £200. From 'The Cottage', on 4 February 1928, Sean asked Pinter to be his agent. One month later he registered with the Harvard University Appointment Office as John Francis Whelan, the name he had used at Harvard, giving his permanent address as 5 Emmet's Place, Cork. On 28 May, writing again to his agent he gave a change of address to 5 Halfmoon Street. What that implies is that he intended to return to Ireland, perhaps after the wedding. What it also reveals is that Sean's impressive account of looking down at the Rio Grande and up at the Rockies is 'poetic license', contrasting the grandeur with the Lilliputian attractions of Cork, the Rockies with Patrick's Hill, the Rio Grande with the Lee. On the other hand by registering with the Appointment Office he kept his options open: a job might turn up in

America. He tried in vain for a professorship in Iowa at the end of 1928. He was pleased with his job at Boston College and Eileen got a position in the Shady Hill progressive school. He had his Fellowship. They could survive for another year. In that year also he applied in vain for a Guggenheim Fellowship, hoping to get time to devote himself to his writing.

In the Autumn of 1927 Lincoln Kirstein founded the *Hound and Horn* and chose Richard Blackmuir as editor. Through contact with these young men Sean's literary life quickened. He used to drop in occasionally to the journal's offices at 1430 Massachusetts Avenue. Kirstein or Blackmuir would call in to the little house on Appian Way. In the company of those who owned, ran and edited the magazine Sean was in a world that suited him.

In turn the young men valued his intellectual gifts, the easy hospitality of his home, his ability to correct and update their understanding of Ireland, which they saw very much in the aura of the early Yeats and *Ulysses*. But here was someone who had helped to shape a revolution, who had first hand experience of what became of Kathleen Ni Houlihan and held strong views about literature, language and culture. Furthermore, he was a published writer, a friend of AE and O'Flaherty, and corresponded with Garnett and Eliot who, as Blackmuir notes on 7 January 1929, spoke 'highly' of Sean again in *The Criterion*. Sean's essay, 'Style and the Limitations of Speech', was thoughtful, well-planned and knowledgeable. T. S. Eliot approved of it and had, he said, read O'Faolain's article on 'Censorship in America' in the *Irish Statesman* 'with great interest'.

He kept up his Irish contacts, read the *Irish Statesman* every month, learned with disgust of the assassination of Kevin O'Higgins in 1927. In August 1928 he got word of his father's death. Denis Whelan died on 23 August in Shanakiel Hospital, aged sixty-seven. Augustine bought the plot and when he returned to Ireland Sean erected a white marble headstone, recording his father's name, date of death, and age. In September 'Fugue' appeared in *Hound and Horn*. Sean sent a copy to Garnett. 'Some day,' he said, 'I hope to prove to others that your original criticism was well founded.'[12] 'Am I a writer?' he asked and got the welcome reply, 'You are a writer' (VM, 247). Garnett asked Sean to send him everything he wrote and to call on him should he ever be in London. It was a heart-stirring moment, confirmation of an identity he had been searching for. This year he also published a number of articles in reputable periodicals, one in the *Virginia Quarterly Review* and one in *The Criterion*.

In February 1929 he gave Garnett a full account of his stewardship: he had not written three good pages since he left Ireland and this made him doubt that he was 'a God-sent writer'. He was caught 'between the wish to be like Turgenev, Pater, Moore, the early Joyce and Mozart and the need to make a living in order to write'. He also had to consider 'the wife'. He was afraid that he was 'born to be a nice, bothered, troubled person rather than a Protean outpower of beauty', but he did feel confident; he was between first promise and fulfilment. If he wrote 'but one perfect lyric or novel or book of stories I shall meet the great doom — which frightens and horrifies me very much — with equanimity, if not happily'. Reading George Moore on his 'dead life' and *The Untilled Field* filled him with 'agony', with a wish for colour and balm, and a fear of 'Ireland's harsh, *skinny*, uninspiring ethic'. Although they would sail to Ireland in June, he really hoped to get a job teaching in London. He wanted to cut Ireland off as thoroughly as he could before returning to take up the Chair of English in Cork. 'I want to return a disinterested stranger'.

Meanwhile he continued teaching at Boston College downtown in the old Jesuit high school in James's Street. The course helped him to sort out his views on Anglo-Irish Literature. He prepared an edition of the *Lyrics and Satires from Tom Moore* and while he had the run of Widener, collected, and made his own translations of early Irish poetry which he subsequently published as *The Silver Branch*, the anthology he had described in January 1927. He gathered material for a life of the early Yeats and prepared a bibliography of Yeats's writings.

In April he wrote again to Edward Garnett. 'It is getting late now and I feel my mind is changing. I am trying to hang on to my idealism — such as it is — in the face of many experiences that deride it, and even attack it. My religious beliefs have gone by the board long since, though that was merely under the stress of a more implacable idealism still: now I am in the backwash of that event and I am rather terrified by all I see around me ... Unless I find some unity in myself to recompense me for what I have lost — I am lost'. He had read Spengler's *Decline of the West*, but found the mood very much of its time; his sense of a lost generation was one which included Eliot, the Sitwells, and Joyce. Each one, he declared, 'must henceforth be his own universe and hope for nothing from his contemporaries, for nothing from the social world about him, from religions, or morals or society'.

In June he and Eileen cleared out their little house, packed their possessions into four suitcases, sold the Model T for $25.00, embarked on the ninth, and were in Cobh seven days later. Again the band played 'Come Back to Erin', but this time he did not object.

[7]

London

WHEN Sean and Eileen moved to England they had $850 and no job, but they were lucky. Sean got a position as Senior Lecturer in English Language and Literature at St. Mary's Training College, Strawberry Hill, Twickenham, a position he held from September 1929 to June 1933. Eileen got a job teaching Commercial Subjects at a convent school in Gumley House, at Isleworth, where she taught from September 1929 to December 1930. They were fortunate, too, in finding attractive accommodation in Richmond. Their apartment at 51 Queen's Road had five rooms, one with French windows opening onto the garden at the back. They lived there until June 1930 when they moved to no. 19 Cambrian Road, off Queen's, just a short distance away. This was a two-storey, red-brick house in a short cul-de-sac leading to a side entrance to Richmond Park. Charles Stewart Parnell used to visit Katherine O'Shea in a house closer to Cambrian Gate.

Richmond was ideal. Sean and Eileen could go for walks in the Park, stroll to the top of Richmond Hill and from there enjoy its fair and famous prospect, walk along the towpath from Richmond Bridge, and enjoy the old hostelries – 'The Three Pigeons' or 'The White Shore'. The Park, a nature reserve with two large herd of red and dappled deer, many thousands of trees, thousands of birds, and all the common woodland animals, was lovely at any time but particularly when the Autumn colouring touched the bracken and the wild flowers, as it did when Sean and Eileen moved into Queen's Road that September. When they moved, on 1 December 1931, to Merton House, 73 Cambridge Road, a quiet road off Teddington High, not far from the Lock, they exchanged one set of riverside walks for another.

Whether at Richmond or Teddington Sean was only a short distance from Strawberry Hill.

In 1925 St. Mary's was moved to Strawberry Hill, where it acquired over thirty acres of wooded country on the historic site of Horace Walpole's castle. There the pseudo-Gothic architecture of the old buildings was combined with new college buildings, the 200-year-old lawn with modern playing fields. Sean admired the elegant rooms in the castle and, as a future biographer of Daniel O'Connell, the Liberator's large mahogany dining-room table which the College acquired for the centenary of Catholic Emancipation.

St. Mary's was a residential Catholic Training College for men run by Vincentian fathers, all of whom were Irish. The principal, Father Vincent McCarthy, from Sunday's Well, was in his final year. His successor, Dr. James Doyle, from Killorglin, Co. Kerry, held three doctorates and was a man of considerable style. The vice-principal, Father Joseph ('Bunt') Leonard, had many literary and artistic connections. He was, O'Faolain wrote, 'a most genial, good-humoured, and cultivated man'.[1] Another interesting teacher was Father William Hastings, who lectured in History, and was regarded by colleagues as a genius. A man of strong, conservative views, he took exception to Sean's habit of questioning opinion. The most interesting of the lay teachers from Sean's point of view was P. J. Dowling, who had written a thesis on the hedge schools of Ireland.

Sean's teaching duties amounted to ten hours a week. He lectured to about sixty students in 'scum English', preparing them for the Teacher's Certificate Examination; to students in Intermediate Arts; and to one class studying for the BA degree certified by the University of London. Ten hours a week left him considerable free time but teaching, preparing classes and reading student essays left less time than he would have liked for his own writing.

He was regarded as a good teacher. Father McCarthy was pleased with the success of the students in examinations. Most comments on his teaching are favourable. Students knew he had three MA's. Later they discovered that he was a writer. Frank Naughton to whom he lectured on Donne, Crashaw and Herbert says he was 'most pleasant and agreeable in manner', and that his lectures were scholarly.[2] A. J. Dopré remembers his appearance – 'neatly dressed and looking over us through his glasses, Sean would survey us with friendly but observing eyes and deliver his lectures clearly and forcefully without allowing any diversion'.[3] Michael Fitzpatrick thought he was aloof, since he left the school every day after lunch, but was 'a great teacher' who made them work and regularly gave them essays to write. John McHugh, whom Sean taught for three years, had a poor opinion of his teaching: he seemed bored, poorly prepared and aloof. Students used to say his lectures must have been prepared by his wife. Although Sean grumbled in his second year when salaries at St. Mary's had to be reduced by 10%, these were among the happiest years of his life. But his happiness came not so much from teaching as from writing. In these years, too, his first child was born and his first book was published and promptly banned in Ireland. He failed to be appointed at University College Cork, but he completed his first novel and became more professional about his writing.

During these four years he served a literary apprenticeship to Edward Garnett who was the best friend that Sean and Eileen had in London. He often invited them to dine with him in an Anglo-Russian restaurant on Harrington, to lunch in Soho at the Commercio and gave them tickets to concerts or to performances of his own plays. Sometimes he visited them in Richmond. Through Garnett, Sean met other aspiring writers – H. E. Bates, Malachi Whitaker, H. A. Manhood. He also met T. S. Eliot and Herbert Read and renewed his friendship with Eric Linklater and Freddie Bateson. According to Linklater Sean was foremost of the young men whom Garnett was advising at this time.[4]

Garnett, an unselfish and enthusiastic reader, critic, and guide, had infallible judgement and grasp of the potentialities of a talent. Already a legend, when O'Faolain met him, a friend of Conrad, Lawrence, and Galsworthy, he was now encouraging a new generation including O'Faolain who had, H. E. Bates noted, 'arrived permeated down to the roots by an admiration for Joyce and had promptly been sent packing, like O'Flaherty, to write of the fat, wet Irish pastures of his childhood'.[5]

The first work that Sean showed Garnett in London was a play on Charles Stewart Parnell called 'The Red Petticoat'. It was 'all talk' (Autumn 1929). Garnett wanted greater historical accuracy, but Sean argued that his Parnell was 'half-real, half-imaginary'. For months he and Garnett argued, until Sean admitted that his Parnell was too abstract and his approach 'too intellectual'. He explained his position: since he had been betrayed by 'leaders' and 'heroes' in his youth, he had no time for them now. He submitted the play to the Abbey Theatre, but it was turned down.[6]

This reluctance to romanticize patriots characterizes almost all the stories he wrote at this time and included in *Midsummer Night Madness*. He refused to glamorize what he felt had been overglamorized. Sending 'The Death of Stevey Long' to Garnett and apologizing for its 'vulgar melodramatic strain', he said he disliked the patriots so much he wanted 'to have a slap at the cruel devils' (11 July 1931). Stevey Long is cruel and irresponsible: guilty of betrayal, murder, lechery and arson.

Sean worked hard at the stories. He had he knew a tendency to 'bite off too much' (November 1929), to go for 'the big canvas, slow symphonic movement', but he tried to make the stories less subjective than they had been in 1918 or 1926. He revised constantly, watching 'every word, every line; every adjective'. He rewrote sentences over and over and read them out to himself and to Eileen.[7] The surviving manuscripts are heavily revised. Garnett wrote a Foreword for *Midsummer Night Madness* in which he identified O'Faolain's dominant gifts; he noted the delicate rendering of atmosphere, the feeling for landscape, the artistic quality of the writing. Here, he said, was 'the Irish sensitiveness to place and emotional mood, in a style free and flowing, punctuated by passages of that brutal frankness which is the conscience of the younger generation' (MNM, 13–16).

Sean was delighted. 'Such encouragement is almost enough to live on for the rest of my life' (27 July 1931). But Garnett's Foreword was also hard-hitting. Ireland, Garnett wrote, was the most backward nation in Europe, the most indifferent to art and literature, the least aware of critical standards. It was time, he declared, that the Irish people realized that a nation taking so little interest in its own writers and leaving them dependent on English attention and English alms is culturally contemptible. The reviewer in the *Bookman* called it a 'tactless diatribe against the Irish people'.[8] John Chamberlain, while saying in the *New York Times* that it was the best book of Irish stories since *Dubliners*, found Garnett's introduction 'suffused with a brilliantly caustic bitterness towards the Irish'.[9] Sean was caught between delight in Garnett's praise and anxiety about the possible consequences of a particularly anticlerical statement in the Foreword. He consulted Father Leonard who left him in no doubt as to what could happen. In view of Garnett's anticlericalism, he was careful to describe Father Leonard as 'a very broad-minded priest, an Irishman, a friend of the Desmond

McCarthys and the Harold Nicholsons and the Bernard Shaws'. Then he told Garnett what Leonard had said: a) I shall certainly be attacked because of that reference to the priests; b) I shall have to defend that reference, for I have agreed to its publication in a book over my name; c) I shall have a hard time doing so without getting assassinated; d) The reference would put his Principal – *might put* – in an invidious position; e) 'it would certainly mean I'd never get a public (or private) job in Ireland if the clergy knew anything about my trying for it. I don't want their rotten jobs but it might follow that I couldn't live in Ireland at all'. He felt the reference could be toned down without any loss of principle and suggested that the same charges could be made generically. Garnett agreed. At Sean's request he also pointed out, in response to Daniel Corkery's criticism of them in *Synge and Anglo–Irish Literature*, that writers like O'Faolain were expatriates because they could not get tolerance or understanding criticism at home. Sean reacted angrily to Corkery's dismissal of expatriate writers and his accusation that they exploited their country for money.

The relationship with Garnett was the most important in Sean's entire literary life. 'I cannot tell you how much it has helped knowing of your interest in me. Where nobody else is interested it is, in fact, priceless knowledge to me'. (April–May 1931.) Six months later he wrote, 'You don't know what it means to be able to say – I hope E. G. will like this, to have an audience before one's mind which is discriminating, ready to praise and blame with justice' (27 October 1931). From the beginning Sean trusted and respected him. He usually addressed him in letters as 'Mr. Garnett'. He tried 'Dear Edward', but found it inappropriate. He reverted to 'Dear Mr. Garnett', remarking that if he called him anything, he'd like to call him something like grandpère – 'something to indicate the difference in our ages and at the same time the affection I know I shall always have for you' (20 June 1931). Eventually he relaxed into a less formal, and occasionally jocular, mode. Despite the abundant evidence of Garnett's generosity – many letters, visits, exchanges of gifts, repeated encourage-ment and helpful criticism, Sean remained inhibited. But he became more open and intimate with Garnett than he ever did with any other man.

The relationship had its strains. Sean defended his work whenever he felt Garnett was unfairly critical. When Garnett told him that his view of

Parnell was that of a peasant, Sean bristled. 'I and peasant in the one sentence! My God, am I a peasant? Do I look like a peasant, think or talk like one? Should I drown myself to think so? I beg of you to understand that my father and mother tore the soil with their hands but I have torn myself out of their blighted, blinded, uncivilized, intolerant, shutminded tradition at no small cost to my nature and my immortal soul . . . Have I not warned you I am an Anglo-Irishman now?' (1929.) With the change in ancestry went a change in accent, although his reactions could still be extreme. Once, when Garnett commented on his 'negative nature', his response was rude and violent: 'It pains me that you should be such a fool . . . If that's all the help you can give a man on his way through this bitch of a world you should be content to shut up. Do you think you have helped any? If not what was the purpose of such an intrusion? You surely have heard that young men take themselves seriously — and most seriously when their egos are out of order? You will allow me tell you to go to hell? Consider it said'. If Garnett came *out* to him (26 September 1931) he went out to Garnett and not only about literary matters. Again and again his letters express gratitude and appreciation of the older man's many kindnesses to himself and Eileen. He shared his hopes, fears, ambitions, satisfactions with Garnett, and his disappointments.

He and Eileen longed for Ireland. In March 1931 he told Bliss Reed that he wanted to return to Ireland without delay. 'I have a good veneer on top of my Celtic temperament so that few who meet me realize that there is all the cunning and unscrupulousness and temper, the treachery of the Celt — or attributed to us — under the superficial disguise of a London cut of clothes, spats, kid gloves and attaché case. But the Celt is there'.[10] A job in Cork was the ideal solution.

Ever since Alfred O'Rahilly had mentioned that he might succeed Professor Stockley in the Chair of English Language and Literature at University College Cork, the idea had stuck in Sean's mind. He knew Daniel Corkery was also interested and had written a 'venemous' letter about him to AE.[11] In November 1929, knowing that Stockley had retired, he began to prepare his application. He thought of doing a Ph.D. at the University of London. He got letters of recommendation from Sir Walter Buchanan-Riddell, W. B. Reed, and John Livingstone Lowes. He had, he told Reed, 'a wonderful good chance of getting it'.[12] But all this was premature. The position was not filled promptly and these letters had to be updated in the Spring of 1931 when the vacancy was finally advertised. Since there was only one professor in the Department, Sean was puzzled by the delay. He wrote to O'Rahilly and got an ambiguous and unsatisfactory reply:

I am replying promptly – if I defer I may never answer! The Governing Body is considering the English Chair on 21st March. That will be the first bit of news. They may decide to advertise it or they may postpone it. I will let you know immediately. Mrs. O is still in bed, not a bit better. No servant for the past few days – her father died. Kids have measles. I need make no comment. Professor from St. Louis stayed with me two days recently to discuss matters. I may go out temporarily next year – permanently if I get salary and security. Any man under 35 ought to leave this country. No influence, no peace, no elbow-room. Kindest regards to Mrs. O'F. Let my promptness excuse my brevity. Consider yourself very lucky. Best wishes.

A (VM, 261–62)

The professorship was advertised. It had a salary of £600 per annum with a yearly increment of £40 to a maximum of £800 and it was pensionable. One hundred copies of applications and testimonials had to be submitted by 27 April 1931. The process was not simple. Three separate bodies were involved: the Academic Council, the Governing Body of the College, and the Senate of the National University of Ireland which made the appointment. The Governing Body was composed of widely different people: four Bishops, the Lord Mayors of Cork, Limerick, and Waterford, and County Council members from Cork, Kerry, Limerick and Waterford, made up of business men, farmers, doctors, and others. The Governing Body at the time of Sean's application had co-opted The Man and D. J. Leahy who had been associated with the Twenty Club.

Taking advantage of his Spring vacation Sean travelled to Cork and spent a month seeking interviews with as many members of these various bodies as he could. The whole operation, with the travel and printing costs, came to about £50.[13] It was a disheartening experience. While he encountered people who might be expected to consider the merits of his candidature in a rational and unprejudiced manner, many were either too busy, or too uninformed to pay much attention to him. In *Vive Moi!* there is a hilarious account of his interview on a windy day with a farmer who was saving hay. The farmer shouted 'A professorship of English? Can you talk Irish?' He even faced Bishop Cohalan who was courteous, but gave nothing away. A publican informed Sean that any fool could teach English and that it was a waste of money to pay people for such 'bloody nonsense'. He went to see Stockley and was furious when he refused to support him. He left that house in a rage.[14] When he heard that Father Gwynn, in whom he had confided, also opposed him, he felt betrayed. The strain told: when he presented himself for interview, he collapsed in the stone corridor outside the Registrar's office.

Sean had impressive testimonials: from President P. J. Merriman; Dr. Alfred O'Rahilly; Sir Walter Buchanan-Riddell, F. N. Robinson, John Livingstone Lowes, Sir Percy Nunn, E. B. Reed, Robin Flower and Revd V. McCarthy, Principal, St. Mary's Training College. President Merriman confined himself to an outline of O'Faolain's academic career at UCC and at Harvard. O'Rahilly wrote that he was acquainted with him while he was a student at UCC and also for a year at Harvard. 'I have,' he said, 'a very high opinion of his ability, of his literary attainments and critical faculty.' He pointed out that Sean studied philology at Harvard, 'for which few facilities exist here.' He was, O'Rahilly concluded, 'eminently fitted for a Chair of English'.[15]

The three people associated with the Commonwealth Fund were more complimentary. Buchanan-Riddell pointed out that his success in obtaining a Commonwealth Fellowship out of one hundred and seventy eight candidates was in itself 'evidence of distinguished intellectual gifts'. Percy Nunn wrote a gracious letter, saying that he 'was so much struck with Mr. Whelan's qualities of mind and personality' that he made it his special duty to maintain an association with him and to follow his achievement after he had received the Fellowship. 'Everything I have seen and heard of Mr. Whelan has strengthened the extremely favourable impression he produced on me the first time we met. I do not know a young man whom I would recommend with more confidence for an academic post in English'. Reed visited Sean several times at Harvard and spoke with F. N. Robinson about his work. Robinson 'had a very good opinion of him and considered him a mature scholar who needed but little guidance'. From the Fund's point of view his scholarship 'was eminently satisfactory'. Reed's recommendation was striking: 'I can recommend Mr. O'Faolain without any reservation for this post because he has a somewhat rare combination of qualities: he is not only a scholar but he is an excellent critic and a creative writer. So many scholars are out of contact with creative work, but Mr. O'Faolain is a writer and thinker, and for that reason I consider him a very desirable man. I feel certain that he has a real gift for writing, and that he will make a name for himself. As for his scholarship, it is sound; one need say nothing more'. He went on to praise O'Faolain as 'an interesting and attractive man who has the gift of getting on well with people'. He thought he would make 'an admirable teacher, partly because of his human interests and his keen sense of humour', but chiefly because he had 'a deep love of literature and an enthusiasm for it which must affect his pupils'. From a man in Reed's position this was a most impressive judgement.

Both Harvard professors were supportive. Robinson said he had had the opportunity to know a good deal about O'Faolain's 'training and equipment' and was glad to testify to his fitness for the professorship. 'By natural endowment he is a good writer and an intelligent and sympathetic critic of literature'. In his graduate training at Harvard he covered a considerable portion of the philological programme required of candidates for the Ph.D. His studies in Anglo-Saxon, Middle English and Old French, as well as in Early Irish and Welsh, gave him a good equipment for teaching or for research in the comparative philology of the Middle Ages. During the latter part of his residence he had continued his investigations in Irish, and availed himself of opportunities for instruction and research in English literature of the modern period. 'He combines', Robinson concluded, 'an exceptionally broad range of scholarship with literary ability and with personal qualities which ought to make him a successful teacher'.

The letter from Livingstone Lowes was short, but equally positive. 'I have not the slightest hesitation in recommending him strongly for such a position . . . He is a man of mature critical judgment, widely and learnedly read, and he is over and above all this, a writer. I can think of few men who seem to me to be better fitted, both personally and through scholarly attainments, than Mr. Whelan.'

Corkery had testimonials from W. F. P. Stockley, the Revd T. Corcoran and Stephen Gwynn. Stockley praised his qualifications in comparative criticism: he had, he said, 'read and assimilated much of German and French literature'. Corcoran praised his 'scholarly depth of thought and precision of expression', Gwynn his 'luminous and beautiful English style' and the 'high courtesy and chivalry of temper' in all his work. None of this counted as a recommendation for scholarship.

Clearly in the area of testimonials Sean's support was more impressive than Corkery's. But in the area of publications he was at a disadvantage. Much of what he listed, such as the Yeats bibliography and proposed biography, the bibliography for F. W. Bateson, was unpublished work apart from the slim collection of Moore's poetry, the fourteen page article in *Folk-Lore*, and the two essays in *Earna*. *The Silver Branch* was almost completed, but was not published until 1938. Instead of listing his periodical publications, he named the periodicals. This meant that there was no real evidence of the kind of articles he had written for such journals as *The Criterion* or the *Virginia Quarterly Review*. He also omitted the Irish journals, and ignored his short stories. He wanted to be seen as a scholar, rather than a creative writer.

Corkery, on the other hand, included both creative and scholarly work in his list of published works: *A Munster Twilight* (1916), a collection of short stories; *The Threshold of Quiet* (1917), a novel; *La Pléiade*, literary criticism (1919); *The Labour Leader* (1920), a play; *The Yellow Bittern and other plays* (1920); *The Hounds of Banba* (1920), short stories; *The Hidden Ireland*, literary criticism (1925); *The Stormy Hills* (1929), short stories; *Synge and Anglo-Irish Literature* ('On the point of publication by the Cork University Press'). On the next page of his application Corkery had two lists, one of 'Lectures and Addresses Delivered During the Past Twenty Years', the other of 'Literary Articles', all of them in non-scholarly Irish periodicals and newspapers. As evidence from a middle-aged applicant for a professorship they were not impressive.

But there were other considerations that weighed against O'Faolain. Corkery was respected in Cork where he had been a cultural force for many years. He was prominent in Gaelic League and nationalist circles. *The Munster Twilight*, *The Threshold of Quiet*, and *The Hidden Ireland* were widely known, influential works. The announcement that Cork University Press was about to publish *Synge and Anglo-Irish Literature* was a tactical strike against O'Faolain that would not have gone unnoticed within the College. Even the basic fact that Corkery was not academically qualified did not work against him. His method of setting out his achievements, lectures, publications and experience as a teacher of adults tended to blur his deficiencies. When the Governing Body met on June 19 1931, Sean got three votes in the first round, two in the second. The rest went to Corkery.

Sean was impatient to know the outcome. He wrote to the UCC Secretary on 3 May asking when the Governing Body would meet. He wrote again asking the same question on 26 May. He knew by the end of the month that the decision had gone against him. It was a bitter blow to his pride. He had very good testimonials, three MA degrees, experience of two universities, training by some of the leading scholars of his day, had held two Fellowships, but had been passed over for someone who was untrained, unqualified and inexperienced. Corkery had qualified as a primary school teacher in 1907 and had spent his career as a primary teacher and in teacher training. He had no primary degree, and apart from a vacation course in England, had no formal academic training.

Sean had not realized that Corkery was being coached for the job, through being allowed to do an MA thesis, not an honorary degree, as he mistakenly thought; that his thesis was about to be published; that he was backed by Stockley at a time when the outgoing professor had a strong voice in the selection of a successor; that he was backed by O'Rahilly, and favoured by Republican, nationalist and Gaelic League elements for whom *The Hidden Ireland* was a sacred text. O'Faolain needed someone within the college to highlight his qualifications. It is clear from the voting pattern that no one spoke up for him, certainly not O'Rahilly whose influence, had he chosen to use it in O'Faolain's favour, could have been decisive. In fact, O'Rahilly fought 'tooth and nail' to get Corkery elected and admitted that he had 'blocked' O'Faolain, even though he had voted for him.[16]

Sean had been betrayed. 'I am', he wrote to Garnett, 'so unhappy this week that if I write to you I may work it off. I had built some hopes . . . on returning to Ireland via the post I have been seeking in Cork. I should not like Cork but it would be Ireland anyway'. He believed that O'Rahilly had encouraged him so that it would appear that Corkery had triumphed over someone substantial.

Work was a cure for disappointment. He wrote 'The Death of Stevey Long', mapped out *A Nest of Simple Folk* and in August he and Eileen returned to Cork. They revelled in the beauty of the countryside. It was 'beautiful and as it rains every night it is washed fresh and new each day'. They walked out their old country roads each day. 'Yesterday we walked out to Blarney. Every step was a joy. Every smell!' (14 August 1931). They walked to Gougane Barra, going in a circle via Skibbereen, Castletownsend, Glandore, Drimoleague, Bantry, to stay in Cronin's hotel. 'The lovely country all about us is so satisfying that I can neither read nor write. Thank God I feel that I am living again . . . We swear we are returning next year!' (25 August 1931.)

When they got to England he pressed ahead with *A Nest of Simple Folk*. Asking Garnett to send him a copy of Turgenev's *Torrents of Spring*, he said he wanted to mould himself on Turgenev. He was trying to 'pour everything' into the book, thereby making it 'an enormous salad, so that it would be a criticism of Irish social life, religion, politics as well as a personal account'. This was the novel he had begun in America. Now it flowed. By 2 October it was half-written, despite being slowed down by 'bloody lectures and bloody pupils and bloody Spenser and Chaucer'.[17] There were, he knew, good things in the novel even though Garnett thought it too long. Essentially it was an account of Sean's ancestors as they struggled for survival on a farm in Knockaderry, made their way into Rathkeale and then to Cork. It stressed the hardships of their lives on the one hand and on the other the explosive attraction of Republicanism. Leo Donnell, an irresponsible, weak character becomes involved with Fenianism, is jailed twice, and becomes a symbol of nationalistic rebellion in the final section for young Denis Hussey in Cork. Through him and through stories of racial injustices, garnered here and there, Denis is drawn into sympathy with the rebels of 1916. 'From some hidden well of memory all the stored hate of centuries jetted into his mind . . . they fountained in him like the blood that surges to the head and blinds the eyes with rage' (NSF, 147).

Garnett wanted stronger scenes in the final section, but Sean could not write them: city life, he claimed, was 'anaemic', but he admitted that the writing was too Joycean and too personal. It was odd, he reflected, that what he had experienced was anaemic and what he had only recreated was 'strong' (May 1933). He was very happy with this work: 'such a real, simple, *truthful* book. I don't think you realise how much so it is. It is very precious to me. I feel like saying damn strong scenes. This is my Villette, my Nichee de Gentilshommes, my Mill on the Floss . . . I finished with wild scenes in *Midsummer Night Madness*. I wanted calm and dust and the pollen of the bogflowers on my boots . . . This is a bloody great book. Hurrah! I read it again all over and I loved it. It's *true*. It's simple. It's Ireland. It's my old boot. Christus! What more can one ask?' The letter has 'Hurrahs' written all round the page (May 1933). He found the typing 'exhausting'; he was at it ten hours a day, but he was elated: the novel, he told Cape, was far too good to get 'wide recognition' and much better than Garnett realized. 'I am very pleased with it'.[18]

Meanwhile the publication of *Midsummer Night Madness* early in 1932 brought the kind of acclaim that helped Sean's reputation. It had a literary rather than a commercial success but that meant that every important literary editor in London knew his name. The British reviews were good. Gerald Gould, Rebecca West, Compton Mackenzie, A. E. Coppard, Eric Linklater, H. E. Bates, Cunninghame Graham, 'all either wrote or reviewed in highly complimentary terms'.[19] Sean was particularly pleased by Linklater's comment that it was 'a wild and lovely book', because so far as appearance and outward nature were concerned, he was far from being 'dishevelled'; he cherished that tribute to his 'antithetical self'.[20]

He sent a copy to AE and got a warmly appreciative reply. 'I have,' AE assured him, 'read your tales with great admiration for the continual beauty of the writing and the power of invention, quite in accordance with so much of Irish character, ironical and wild and passionate.' AE went on to say how pleasant it would be to have him back in Ireland. 'Your generation must create its own ideals as the generation to which I belonged . . . One man alone can do little, but with a couple of comrades it is comparatively easy. Frank O'Connor is full of vitality and out of your discussion with him and others you may do for your generation what Yeats and others did for my generation'.[21]

Frank O'Connor wrote an enthusiastic letter. 'Lilliput' was not a patch nor a stick on the best Sean could do, he said. The descriptive writing was often superb in one or two scenes. He professed, 'I take off my cap and walk on tiptoe'. He saved the highest praise for 'The Small Lady': 'the monastery scene is magnificent . . . better than anything Corkery, O'Donnell, O'Flaherty, or I could do. Nothing else in the book is as good'.[22] Sean was less pleased with O'Connor's review in *The Dublin Magazine* which praised O'Faolain's respect for his craft and his descriptive power, but faulted his description of states of mind. By way of illustration he referred to 'The Small Lady'. This had the best writing in the book, but O'Faolain's handling of fundamental issues displayed a lack of sensitivity, O'Connor wrote. O'Connor wrote explaining his criticism, but O'Faolain was not placated.[23]

[97]

Ironically the story that O'Connor singled out was the one that caused most offence in Ireland. The seduction of the young rebel by the Anglo-Irish lady in the Trappist monastery shocked contemporary taste. Francis O'Reilly, Executive Secretary, Catholic Truth Society of Ireland, complained about the book to the Minister for Justice on 14 March 1932. He enclosed a copy and referred to specific offensive pages, which he had marked, over twenty in all.[24] The Censorship Board banned the book as 'being in general tendency indecent'. The banning shocked O'Faolain.[25] He felt infuriated and humiliated and regretted his mother's distress. He received anonymous letters. Eileen maintained that the experience made him introverted. The IRA, angered by his account of the abduction of Mrs. Lindsay and his generally unflattering portrayal of rebels, ordered him to appear before a court-martial. He ignored the order, but avoided Cork for some time.[26] The Cork IRA never forgave him.

Before they could return to Ireland Sean wanted to achieve some degree of financial security, now that he had failed to get the university appointment. The birth of his daughter, Julia, in June 1932, after a protracted labour of forty-eight hours, made that even more advisable. He cultivated his connections with London editors; reviewed regularly for the *Spectator*, and the *New Statesman and Nation*; gave talks for the BBC; contributed articles, mainly about literature and politics, to a variety of periodicals, to the *Nation* and *Commonweal* in America, to the *Bookman*, *The Criterion*, the *Listener*, *New Statesman and Nation* and the *Spectator* in England and wrote a column for the *Sunday Chronicle*.

He tried to get *Hound and Horn* to publish 'The Small Lady' which he initially called 'Fugue No. 2' and when they were slow in doing so succeeded in getting payment of $100 on the grounds that the delay had cost him $150. 'I begin to think', he told Lincoln Kirstein, 'I have the makings of a shrewd businessman in me'.[27] He conducted a prolonged and detailed correspondence with Robert Gibbings at Golden Cockerel Press about the terms for the publication of a limited edition of 'The Small Lady'. He pressed his agent, Pinter, for prompt and accurate payments.

He tried to secure some ongoing income from his publishers. Viking Press offered £200 advance on *Midsummer Night Madness*, but Cape were slower. Had Cape matched Viking's offer, he might have 'thrown down the glove and bolted for Ireland – secondary teaching and all'. But it was, he felt, better to wait to see what the effect of the short stories might be. If they made 'a stink' in Ireland, he wouldn't get even a secondary school job. He and Eileen knew what it meant to be poor and therefore feared poverty so much as to be 'over-prudent perhaps'. Had they £400 from the two publishers, a book of stories out and half a novel written, it would be 'a fair gamble to chuck his good semi-university post and sail for Ireland' (27 July 1931).

He pressed Cape to finance him for a couple of years, arguing that *Midsummer Night Madness* had earned all but £20 of the £150 paid on a/c of royalties and that the French translation would bring in a further £20–25. *A Nest of Simple Folk* must, he thought, be worth at least £125–150 to Cape, probably far more. He saw it as a potential Book Society choice and book of the year (7 April 1933). Finally, Cape confirmed that they would pay £12 per month over a period of two years, the amount to be set against royalties on *Midsummer Night Madness* and any future work they might publish. He would give them the manuscript of two novels, one already delivered, and one volume of short stories.[28]

Sean was ready to go. He wrote 'a long and loving letter' to Michael O'Donovan saying he would be home in July.[29] He was tired of cities. He completed the bibliography for F. N. Bateson and finished *The Silver Branch*. He received an appreciative letter from AE for a long essay he had written on his work for *Inishfail*.[30] Cuala Press rejected 'A Born Genius', but *Midsummer Night Madness* was recommended for the Femina Vie Heureuse Prize and he was elected to the Irish Academy of Letters.

[8]

Killough House

IN July 1933 Sean and Eileen realized their dream of returning to Ireland. They rented Killough House in Co. Wicklow within sight of the mountains. Sean set about exploring the political and social developments that had taken place during their absence. That exploration took many forms – articles in British, Irish and American periodicals, three biographies, a novel, a collection of stories and a play. Together these form a developing view of Irish life and in particular of the place of the artist and intellectual. In these years he became the spokesperson for his generation.[1] Often depressed and weary, he worked hard through the Irish Academy of Letters and PEN to alleviate the lot of the artist. Most importantly, in his study of the life of Daniel O'Connell he found a hero he could admire and emulate.

Killough House was about fifteen miles from Dublin. It had four rooms upstairs, four downstairs, hot and cold running water, a w.c. inside and outside, but neither electricity nor gas. It had an orchard, a kitchen-garden and a vinery. Sean set one room aside upstairs for his study, painted the floor, made his own desk and got a photograph of Edward Garnett to whom he continued to pour out his gratitude: 'it is all due to you, Edward! You got me working at the stories, you boosted them, you wrote me a smashing preface – you put me before the public. That one success gave me my chance. And you made Cape back me! I am your slave for life. We are both eternally grateful for it all' (1933).

At first the garden was a source of food and they enjoyed working in it. 'There's great fun so far. Taking bags of apples into Dublin to the Markets at 7 a.m. is fun. Watering plants by moonlight is fun.' Life was 'very idyllic and pagan' as they washed in the river behind the bushes in the early morning' (1933). 'It is all just as we wished it to be. Isn't that great? We are as happy as Eden. If I can only hold out it's all grand' (1933).

But Killough was not Edenic. Eileen was bored there and both were depressed at the thought of winter coming. By December, with the car off the road, they felt their isolation. There was only one bus each day to Bray and only one coming back. The butcher and the baker let them down; the maid was difficult and impossible to replace, and Julia was 'too full of beans'. Sean found her 'fat and jolly and fetching', but Eileen, he noted, slaved with 'that bitch Anna Julia' and was dotty about her: 'Bad Thing!'

They gave up gardening when the mountain winds flattened their beans and peas. They planted sturdier vegetables 'all over the place', put rock plants in one part of the flower-garden and hardy annuals everywhere else, but the orchard did not do well and the vines were only fair. Sean missed London. He got away to a PEN conference in Edinburgh where he and Eric Linklater, whose ability to make money impressed him, were blind drunk for a week.[2]

Sean had much to do. They had saved £400 from London, even after buying a Morris Cowley saloon for £75. Now they found it too expensive to run. He had contracts for £150. The *Sunday Chronicle* paid him £4.00 per week; he reviewed for the *New Statesman and Nation*, *The Tablet*, *The Spectator*. Viking gave him an advance of £550 and Cape's £12 per month would continue through 1934 and 1935. But living costs were higher than expected. They worked out that they needed roughly £400 a year: holidays (£50), clothes (£30), incidentals (£50), car (£40), housekeeping (£80), insurance (£45), relative (£22), rent (£68). Total £385. Keeping a careful record of what he wrote, the number of words, and the money earned, Sean tried to average about five hundred words a day, after revision. If he did, and if he made enough money, he could spend time writing fiction. He followed this system for years.

Killough was isolated, but Michael Farrell, a small, humorous man who loved talk and argument lived next door. He was writing a long semi-autobiographical novel which he discussed frequently with his new neighbour. Frank O'Connor was a frequent visitor. Having Sean around 'created the old interest and affection and sense of friendly rivalry'. He found him as 'charming' as ever, but Eileen was 'a bit hard, a bit lacking in kindness'; she was, he judged, a bad mixer and needed to be liked. He noted that she preached birth control,[3] although she and Sean had refrained from full sexual intercourse until the summer of 1929, when it happened accidentally. 'Oh', Sean said, apologetically, 'I seem to have done something this time'. As always O'Connor and Sean complemented each other, Frank bursting with ideas and intuitions, Sean steadier and less combustible but greatly stimulated by the other's enthusiasms. Other friends occasionally travelled out from Dublin. Desmond and Mabel Fitzgerald lived nearby. Desmond had known Eliot, Pound and the Imagists, had fought in the General Post Office Rising in 1916 and been Minister for External Affairs in the first Free State Government. Mabel had been George Bernard Shaw's secretary. Through them the O'Faolains met writers, artists and politicians. They also went to Sarah Purser's afternoon teas at Mespil House in Dublin. The regulars at these gatherings included W. B. Yeats, Lennox Robinson, Denis Gwynn, Robert Lynd and several others.

About a month after they moved to Killough, Sean wrote to Francis Hackett, who lived at Kiladreenan House a few miles away with his Danish wife, Signe Toksvig. She invited the O'Faolains to tea and recorded her impressions in a diary. 'I liked them, he was gentle, not argumentative, not self-centred, and as he stayed he got more animated'[4] but, she observed, he could be 'quite schoolmastery and oracular' (23 August 1933). He was, she decided, 'very introvert'. Eileen told her he was self-conscious and 'all angles' when he tried to talk to 'the people' (22 September 1933). Christo Gore-Grimes also recalled Sean's 'natural shyness and sensitivity which he attempted to conceal by adopting a cynical and slightly aggressive attitude. This he softened with an impish sense of humour'.[5] Francis Hackett found him supercilious, sarcastic and cantankerous. Jan Bateson found him 'flamboyant'. Sean admitted that he loved 'being contrary and irrational' in his judgements, 'like a woman'.[6]

Signe's favourable impression of Sean wavered when she went to Killough and found him unshaven, even though he knew she was coming, and Eileen not very tidy. She thought them reserved and guarded. 'Why', she asked herself, 'is there coldness at their core?' (31 October 1933). Garnett told her that he admired O'Faolain as the 'best of the young Irish writers' (20 November 1933). Less than two weeks later, Sean had thawed out, stopped being 'clever' and drove her home. Their friendship developed. He went to see her on his own and seemed more natural. They talked about religion. When she played Sibelius's Third, he 'was greatly moved'. He called it amoral music. It was, he said, like her, 'un-human'; she had 'cold blue eyes'. She remained suspicious. Irish temperament she judged to be 'very largely verbal'. She was not the last woman to believe that Sean's flirting confined itself to words. She was convinced that he had not 'liberated himself yet'.[7] He was liberated enough, however, to be attracted by this blonde, blue-eyed, fastidious and self-confident woman. 'Be kindness to her,' he told Garnett. 'I liked her and would love her if she let me' (3 November 1933). She did not.

Francis and Sean played golf together, read each other's work, met for lunch occasionally in Dublin, discussed the need for a literary journal, and worked together to get an Irish PEN Centre started. For Signe Sean was sometimes attractive, sometimes unpleasant. When he returned from Scotland she found him 'clean, easy and very nearly charming'.[8] Now the O'Faolains looked 'ten times better, freer, healthier. . . . His hands are scarred with garden work. She had on a pretty dress. I really liked them: they are peeping out of their shells'. Eileen told her how they had saved and scrimped and denied themselves in order to get back to Ireland – to heaven – and their disappointment.[9] Another time Sean was bent on contradiction and condemnation. 'Utterly positive and rude'. He returned a book and two magazines 'in a filthy state. Brr! Lord!' (26 March 1934). He made a good impression on her friend, Alfhild Huebsch, but Ottoline Morrell thought he was 'not well bred' and Signe decided she 'would never trust him.' (16 April 1934.)

By Spring Sean was depressed, sick of Irish politics and bored. There were no ideas, only foolish prejudices and much Holy Roman fervour. They were, he complained, 'not only insulated from world ideas but isolated and icebound'.[10] Sean's weariness and depression came in part from overwork, in part from the lack of variety. They lived frugally – 'no drink, no buying books, not much clothes, little furniture' – and he missed 'sparkling talk or highbrow conversation'.[11] Apart from the Hacketts he met 'practically nobody keen and alive and European'. But his depression also came from his analysis of Irish society. As a result of the revolution the whole social position was 'upside down'. Ireland, he argued, was 'hedged, and walled and fettered'; it was deprived of intellectual life by a junta of Gaelic Revivalists and Catholic Actionists.[12] Such people, he said, had not the courage to be what they all were – 'the descendants, English-speaking,

[103]

in European dress, affected by European thought, part of the European economy, of the rags and tatters which rose with O'Connell to win under Mick Collins — in a word, the modern Anglo-Ireland'.[13]

He deeply resented Corkery's 'priggish' and 'ill-mannered' rejection of expatriate writers. Corkery's exclusivist literary judgements ran counter to his own appeal for the acceptance of all Irish writers. He was disturbed by the political motivation of Corkery's argument. Behind its devaluation of Anglo-Irish literature, he saw fear of the possible emergence of an Anglo-Irish nation. Corkery's idea that the Irish Celt, suppressed by the British, and the Anglo-Irish, was about to re-emerge was taken up by De Valera who pointed backwards to days of glory, condemned an England that had crushed the native language and tradition, and promised the resurgence of Irish culture and civilization. The trouble with this enthusiastic dream, O'Faolain argued, was that it fed the heart on fantasies and obscured historical actualities. One of those actualities, he frequently insisted, was that virtually every feature of modern Irish life came, not from the Celtic past, but from Catholic Emancipation and the Land Purchase Act, both of which took place in the nineteenth century.[14]

Eamon De Valera was central to Sean's struggle to understand the new Ireland. He interviewed him in December 1933, almost ten years since he had last seen him, on a wet day in the mountains of North Cork. Then he was an outcast, leader of a lost cause. Now he sat in the office in Government Buildings where Arthur Griffith had worked as first President of the Irish Free State and had a large built-in plaque of Michael Collins facing him. Sean had mixed feelings about him: 'Sometimes he's a hound of hell to me. Sometimes I see him lyrically. All the high pressure I was capable of I put into my little biography of him, which is not really an honest book'.[15] That book embarrassed him for years. Hackett was shocked by its florid passages and its dishonesty. Sean called it 'arrant nonsense', 'shamelessly pro-Dev and pro-Irish propaganda' written at a time when those who had followed De Valera saw their hero coming into power at last and their dreams and ideals, they hoped, about to be realized.[16] Its final chapter sums up De Valera as an idealist and absolute nationalist who not only believes in the Sinn Fein policy of self-reliance and separatism but adds to that the idea of separatism in language and culture, and stands for a Christian state within an individual culture based on the old Gaelic state. The final chapter refrains from stating what Sean actually thought of De Valera.

[104]

He disagreed fundamentally with De Valera, rejected his pietistic simplicity, and saw him as an intellectual obscurantist who had no sympathy with the women's movement and censored advertisements and photographs in the *Irish Press*; Sean rejected a philosophy that left out 'everything that was magnificent and proud and luxurious and lovely'.[17] He disagreed totally with De Valera's view that modern Ireland began in the year five hundred and was great and glorious. He was weary of De Valera's metaphysical debate about policies, objected strongly to his isolationism, and saw that his economic programme of protective tariffs for native producers favoured the middle-class. That which he had first detected before he went to America became a reality under De Valera's protectionist and isolationist policies. All the other ills followed: censorship, conservatism, the indolent glorification of things Irish and the sentimental, low church Catholicism. De Valera's ideas were, in O'Faolain's judgement, out of line with the 'great, infectious, germinating ideas of democracy' which originated among men of learning and culture – Cirey, Montmorency, d'Alembert, Diderot. The original Irish advocates of Republicanism – Tone, O'Connell, the Young Irelanders – were humanists and steeped in European thought. O'Faolain identified himself as a Democrat and a Republican in the European sense.

Within two weeks of moving to Killough House, Sean attended a meeting of the Irish Academy of Letters. The Academy had been established to represent Irish writers in the fight for artistic freedom from censorship. In that fight it had to rely, but without much success, on its moral authority, but it was able to highlight literary achievement through the Harmsworth, Casement and O'Growney Awards. Its annual dinners, at which these awards were presented, brought members together, as did the Annual General Meetings. Although not elected to Council until 1937, Sean was active in the Academy's affairs. He was usually on the Committee of Selection for the O'Growney Award for work in the Irish language, was sometimes one of the Trustees and eventually became both Honorary Secretary and Honorary Treasurer. Sometimes he was master of ceremonies and sat at the head table as he did on 5 December 1934, when the Harmsworth Award was presented to Lord Dunsany. In May 1937, at a gathering in the Peacock Theatre attended by ambassadors, writers, painters, and scholars, he presented the Gregory Foundation Medal to Douglas Hyde.

His work in the Academy was often hampered by Yeats's domineering presence, but he had more freedom at PEN which he helped to re-establish in Ireland. As Secretary he did much of the work. Largely through his efforts there were about forty members at the first AGM and this increased to seventy-five by the time of the second AGM in November 1935. He tried to make PEN more heterogeneous than the Academy and was attacked by Denis Devlin and Peadar O'Donnell for lack of standards for admission. He was also attacked by Francis Hackett who felt that his commitment to internationalism was qualified by Catholic and nationalistic reservations. 'You have', Hackett said, 'a kind of opportunism that I do not understand. You actually oppose Wells, and favour Chesterton, and are in, and yet out of, the Catholic Church . . . You must make of PEN what Yeats failed to make of his Academy, a stockade against the barbarians, a place in which the literary are strengthened to maintain themselves in the condition of freedom that alone makes for authentic, and internationally viable, work!' Offended by these 'highly personal' remarks, Sean explained that he opposed Wells because he did not think he was a suitable speaker for the occasion. Hackett suspected that it was Sean's Catholicism that made him oppose Wells. 'I want to know', he said, 'what your real convictions are about Catholic Ireland being the essential Ireland'.[18] He could not understand Sean's ambivalence. 'You are a Catholic, and I am not . . . I do not believe in an Ireland that rejects birth control and divorce on principle. You do. I don't want an Ireland that looks on sex as sinful and on women as an occasion of sin. You do . . . but as you are honest enough to say you are a Catholic, it makes my cooperation absurd'.[19] But for Sean it was not that simple. His ambivalence about his Catholicism was endemic.

A Nest of Simple Folk appeared in September, 1933. Sean was still delighted with it. 'Eager' to get his book into 'the out of the way places', he advised Cape on distribution, declaring that since he had once been a book salesman, he knew how this should be done. But sales were disappointing: Cork, six copies, Limerick, five, Galway, three, Dublin, about twelve. At least he had a better response in America. His publisher cabled: PRESS WELCOMES SIMPLE FOLK WITH ENTHUSIASTIC PRAISE. SENDING CUTTINGS. CONGRATULATIONS.

The novel received wide coverage – in the *New York Herald Tribune*, the *Sun*, the *New York Times*, *Time*, *Chicago Daily News*. *The New York Times* placed him in the front rank of contemporary novelists. Many reviews mentioned his literary promise. Photographs showed a serious looking author with a moustache and short beard.

A Nest of Simple Folk left many unanswered questions, but none so pressing as the causes for the explosion of 1916 that swept Denis Hussey, and Sean O'Faolain, into violent rebellion. *Constance Markievicz* tried to explain why this daughter of the privileged Ascendancy threw in her lot with the nationalists and identified, after the Rising, with the needs of Dublin's poor.[20] In it Sean idealized Dublin society in the years preceding 1916 when, he wrote, 'everything was in full swing – the theatre, the new literature, the new Gaelic movement, Sinn Fein, Labour . . .' (CM, 74). Political, social, and literary life were intense and writers drew upon a complex social scene, before revolution flattened society into something less exciting. It was, he declared enviously, a good time to be a writer and a good time to be Republican. Far from being hare-brained idealists, the I.R.B., he argued, were practical revolutionaries who manipulated the idealists and deliberately primed the pump of revolution. That made sense of his own irrational response, and of hers. Like him, Constance only began to wake up to the complexity of the Irish problems, or the complexity of the Irish mind, when the disillusionment of Civil War made her think harder.

By the time Sean had finished the book he was feeling the strain. It took six months to complete. He was paid £150 and he was weary by the end. Reckoning that he had written 175,000 words since September 1, he knew that he must get away – from Julia, from everything. Eileen was run down, Julia seriously ill. They went to Glengariff and revisited Bantry, Baurlinn, Lochnambreachdearg, and enjoyed themselves. They took Frank O'Connor with them because he was feeling depressed when Nancy McCarthy married someone else. He never forgot this kindness. But Eileen was sick again when they came back to Killough, this time with a throat infection.

More than anything else Sean wanted to write a novel that would examine moral issues. *Bird Alone* developed from a long short story, one of a number that reflected Cork's suffocating middle class, but it drew upon an earlier period. Instead of trying to describe the kind of breakdown and disillusion of his own experience, Sean hit upon the idea of using the Parnellite period.

The high point of Parnell's career would correspond to the high point of the revolutionary struggle, while the trauma of Parnell's fall and the bitter divisions it caused would correspond with the demoralization brought about by the Civil War. At the same time he could draw upon his experience of falling in love, his conversations with Eileen's father, his memories of the Old Parliamentarians returning to Glanmire station, and his memory of De Valera being brought around the city in defeat. He put a lot of his own experience, his youthful dreams and later disillusionment and his present sense of frustration into this novel. While Corney Crone, the young hero, is not a mirror image of his creator, his condition at the end of the novel, the consequence of his proud refusal to be part of a society he rejected and his sense of having been betrayed by an older nationalist, is close to Sean's own at the time of writing.

Bird Alone was Sean's attempt to write a Catholic novel which would not shirk the gustier emotions, would avoid the methods of both the naturalistic and the psychological novel by highlighting character and incident in order to illustrate the society in which the young lovers, Corney Crone and Elsie Sherlock, lived. Dealing with the issue of sexuality in a puritanical society, it exposes the human costs. When Elsie becomes pregnant, she is terrified of the shame she will bring to her Catholic family. Like Stephen Dedalus, Corney breaks the links that bind him to home, church and society and exploits Elsie Sherlock for his own sexual and intellectual satisfaction. But faced with her attempted suicide and imminent death he has no answer to her need to confess their sin. This part of the novel, Sean explained, depends for its failure or success on whether or not the reader gathers from the first half the 'Scarlet Letter-ish rigidity of the community code'. What he wanted to show was that Corney was made into a *rara avis*. When he rejected the world that ought to have shaped him, and which he ought to have accepted, he became free, but it was a barren freedom: he had killed life, he belonged nowhere, he had taken individualism to its logical and tragic conclusion. Sean had wanted to carry the story forward to the point where Corney would again find a place in society 'with a proper sense of independence', but as yet had not found out how any individual could find a niche in the Scarlet Letter code. He had wanted to express 'the spiritual tragedy of a lost soul – two of them. I wanted you all to remember that Hell does exist, that Elsie's in it and as for Corney, why this is hell nor is he out of it. Beyond my powers! As yet!'[21]

The banning of *Bird Alone* hurt. The book, he knew, was neither anti-Catholic nor anticlerical, but anti-Irish Catholic and anti-Irish cleric. He wrote to the Minister of Justice asking him to withdraw the ban. Frank O'Connor protested in the *Irish Times*. Several academics signed a petition requesting that the Minister lift the ban, but it remained in place. Once again Sean was branded.

Sean also explored the state of barren isolation in *A Purse of Coppers* (1937). Just as Corney Crone could not be fitted back into society, characters in these stories cannot go beyond the dead end in which they are shown to exist: the girl ostracized because she has offended the Scarlet Letter-ish code of her community ('Kitty the Wren'); the girl trapped by sectarian opposition to her love for a Catholic ('There's a Birdie in the Cage'); a man seeking escape in fantasy from the provinciality of his surroundings ('The Old Master'); and artists denied fulfilment in the same society ('A Born Genius'). Hanafan cries out in 'Admiring the Scenery' that every man lives out his own imagination of himself and every imagination must have a background. But for these characters there is no sustaining background. Loneliness is a metaphor for a society in which the individual is denied the God-given right to personal fulfilment. The condition is defined in the prologue story, 'A Broken World', where the priest-narrator, remembering the vision of wholeness that had once moved him to action, enunciates the view that where there is no moral unity there is no life. 'Life', he argues, 'is a moral unity with a common thought. The *compositum* of one's being, emerging from the Divine Essence, which is harmony itself, cannot, unless it abdicates its own intelligence and lives in chaos, that is to say, in sin, be in disunity with itself. Since society, however, is an entity composed of many members, life becomes a moral unity with a common thought' (PC, 12).

'A Broken World' concludes in a romantic wish for some image that would rouse the people, some messianic figure that would lead them out of apathy. It came from the emotional, 'soft' side of O'Faolain's temperament. The alternative, Sean felt, was to accept Irish life as he found it. He thought of Chekhov who said Russia was a lousy country where the writers love frowsy women and laundresses and eat woodlice and sleep in the gutter and have nothing to write about. Nevertheless, Chekhov made golden glory out of the woodlice and 'be Jasus why can't I out of the dungheap and the donkey' (1 February 1936).

But it was not easy. He knew only too well how difficult it was for the estranged writer, who felt surrounded by a hostile environment, was faced with a diminished social reality after the revolution and felt out of sympathy with large areas of that society, to keep his imagination free and unembittered. Knowing the risks of impotent anger, Sean carried Stendhal's warning in his pocket: 'For all our anger the Government will be much the same in twenty years as it is today . . . There will always be something to drive us mad in politics, and one of the saddest ways to spend one's life, I feel, is in a state of impotent rage'.[22] He needed magnificence. He needed the kind of novel in which an exaltation of mood would transcend the merely familiar and in which character would achieve timelessness. The Catholic novelist, he thought, writing out of a body of beliefs and a community of faith might provide a solution. 'For I know no other art but this: the art of a man who writes out of his naked nucleus of self, his original, primal core of being, with and about those associations of thought, habits, opinion, desire that common life or traditional life wraps about each one of us.'[23]

Sean's decision to accept the dungheap and the donkey was strengthened through thinking about the character of Daniel O'Connell. The concentrated power of this portrait lay for Sean in its being a manifesto akin to Yeats's early essays. It holds the mirror of O'Connell up to modern Ireland and highlights the attitudes and achievements that are directly relevant – such as O'Connell's Europeanism by which the intellectual ideas he absorbed in France and England broadened his thinking, the Benthamite utilitarianism that enabled him to abandon Gaelic Ireland in the interests of progress, and his exemplary freedom from sectarianism. Sean also emphasizes here his rôle as a liberal Catholic layman mediating between Church and State and ensuring that neither should be allowed to dominate the other. O'Faolain's O'Connell is a rationalist and 'the greatest of all Irish realists', but he is also deeply moved by the needs of his people. The biography demonstrates Sean's long-held conviction that modern Ireland must be dated from O'Connell's time, not from the collapsed Gaelic world of the seventeenth and eighteenth century. The appeal to the sanction of the Gaelic past, made by Corkery and other nationalists, O'Faolain again argues, was merely Republicanism faking a tradition independent of O'Connell's acceptance of the mingled strain of Anglo-Ireland. He is ultimately, what the concluding passage in 'A Broken World' expressed a desire for, a redeemer taking the broken world of eighteenth century Ireland

and moving it forward to a new and fruitful synthesis. When modern Ireland looks for its origins it finds, not Celtic heroes, but the dispossessed people whom O'Connell taught to appreciate the power and possibilities of popular agitation. 'The native instinct was wild and uncultivated, haphazard, fumbling, largely negative, denying clearly, but not affirming clearly – as it is, to a lesser degree, even today. It could not affirm because it had no concrete way of affirming its genius, as free nations affirm their genius, in educational institutions, political institutions, great buildings, social behaviour, art, literature, and so forth. It had only one way of affirming what it instinctively regarded, and that was by political manoeuvres' (KB, 213). O'Connell had lived at a time of social breakdown comparable to the social disruption and diminishment that had taken place in Ireland through the revolutionary period. That lesson was particularly relevant to O'Faolain's shrewd assessment of De Valera as successful rebel but failed social reformer.

At times the biography rises to a crescendo of semi-mystical praise for a creative reformer who was linked instinctively with his people: 'In body and soul, origin and life, in his ways and in his words, he was the epitome of all their pride, passion, surge, and hope – their very essence' (KB, 138). The characterization is a psychological *tour de force*, but Sean's hero-worship clouds his judgement when he regrets O'Connell's decision to call off the monster meeting at Clontarf. Had he led or sanctioned a rebellion, he argues, and gambled on the possible reaction to a mass killing, O'Connell would have satisfied the natural human desire for the magnificent ending, would have become part of the tradition of romantic, patriotic Ireland. That claim contradicts the cold pragmatism that O'Faolain praises elsewhere in the book and calls for the kind of blind irrationality that he condemned in *Constance Markievicz*. It is in keeping with the rhetorical excess in 'A Broken World' and indicates as well how deeply moved Sean was by his involvement with O'Connell's character.

O'Connell was a challenge: a mirror image in which Sean saw aspects of his own nature, the outline of what he admired, and the elements of a character he viewed with disgust. 'All we can ever hope to create', he confesses 'is an image of ourselves' (KB, 214). But O'Connell was more than a mirror image. He was many of the things that O'Faolain instinctively disliked and that his upbringing had taught him to condemn. The O'Connell that Sean discovered challenged him in a fundamental and revolutionary manner. While he confirmed many of his beliefs about how a leader could bring about a creative social renewal and illustrated principles of thought and behaviour that Sean valued, as a man he challenged him to change his attitudes. His mind he saw as shrewd, hard, ambiguous and self-protective. He was dogged, tortuous, resourceful and secretive, but he was also crude, cunning, coarse, dishonest, brutal and untrustworthy. He was no gentleman. 'I wrote pages blasting him for a crook, until I saw that I was writing like a Protestant and a bloody idiot, so I went all over those pages changing the hard words to admiring words'.[24] O'Connell's wavering, ambiguous personality seemed to resemble his own day-to-day uncertainties as he tried to cope with the new Ireland and to accommodate his own moral dilemmas. When he characterizes O'Connell's brand of Catholicism as wavering, barely stopping short of complete revolt from orthodoxy, he includes most of the Fenians whose anticlericalism he had once shared. The issue touched him closely. O'Connell acted, O'Faolain says, as do most Irishmen: 'piously Catholic in practice, indeed, vociferously Catholic, while retaining at bottom a strong reservation of independence, some smothered scepticism, the widest tolerance of other religions, and great elasticity in action' (KB, 77). Men, as he knew from his own experience and from his reading, could live for years in the most equivocal condition of mind about the most vital subjects; this could include a gnawing unease about religion (KB, 80). There was in the human heart, he noted, a terrifying power to resist an inevitable conclusion and the power to deceive itself into thinking it has made a decision when in fact it has again escaped into a simulacrum (KB, 81). O'Connell perpetuated, in O'Faolain's view, that type of Irish nature 'where truth is always in hiding and where the very soul ends in being in hiding from itself' (KB, 254). 'Minotaur and Sphinx', he notes, 'lie in ambush in his countenance, where, as in that of most men, there is the differentiation of his double nature in the play of his looks; always the right eye held the secret calculation; always the left had been a challenge and a doubt. One corner of the lip is likewise turned upward in a half-smile; the other is gripped downward with a horrible suggestion of latent ruthlessness and brutality' (KB, 253). With O'Connell's coarse, extrovert, complex nature, he was faced with someone he would normally not have accepted. He could explain some of it in terms of the sphinx-like mind, he could show historical origins for this, could explain that the elastic conscience was part of a mode of survival for an oppressed people. But, in the end, he praises O'Connell the pragmatist and realist who accepted what he found, and thereby turned Ireland's hardships and infirmities into advantages, and knew that if he could but once define, he could thereby create. 'He imagined a future and the road appeared' (KB, 320). For Sean that was the essential fact. Once accepted it directed all his intellectual and imaginative life.

Sean's acceptance of the whole man marks an important stage in his development as a writer. After *A Purse of Coppers*, he moved on from depicting man caught in a cul-de-sac to depicting complex, contradictory figures. 'The Lonely Woman', submitted to the BBC in October 1938, as 'Mrs. Moore Makes a Friend', portrays a woman, in essence Bridget Whelan, who is 'a damn nuisance' — stubborn, pious, self-pitying, vain, falsely humble, contradictory, and suspicious. But she is emphatically herself, and O'Faolain accepts her. His fiction became more receptive and tolerant. He was able to write with satirical amusement about the contradictions of the Irish character in 'Childybawn' and 'Unholy Living and Half Dying', and with profounder insight in 'Lovers of the Lake'. He moved from the moral straightjacket of a strict ethical view of human nature, the damned souls in *Purse of Coppers*, to a more tolerant, more understanding response. He liked the Christian humanism of Father Gerald Vann's *On Being Human*, but the major source of the change came through the example of O'Connell.

Early in 1937 Sean told Elizabeth Bowen that he looked forward eagerly to meeting her. He had been reading her *Friends and Relations*, finding 'so much trembling loveliness' in her books that they disturbed him. 'Lonely folk shouldn't read lovely books.' Meeting her gave him the impetus to go back to his novel, which he had had to put aside in order to get on with his life of Daniel O'Connell, and to prepare *Purse of Coppers* for publication. He told her how 'addled' he sometimes became between all the writing he had to do – a biography, stories, articles, reviews, and his novel 'tormenting him' when he was not working on it. He told her he admired her writing, her control, her sense of drama in small things, that he 'adored the underdefined atmosphere in *Another September*', which she sent him. 'I could smell the hay, the wet, the mountain-line'. It was, he said, 'entirely Irish'. He sent her a copy of *A Nest of Simple Folk*.

[113]

When he got home from London, he invited her to Killough. She invited Eileen and him to Bowen's Court instead. Sean replied that his wife would hardly be able to accept, but that he would love to see Kildorrery which must be wonderful these days; would the weekend of 8 May be convenient? As those visits were repeated Eileen used to complain that 'la Bowen' never invited her, but Sean was a welcome guest at Bowen's Court. He found her fascinating. She was a fellow-writer, a successful novelist and short story writer, she had travelled abroad, been educated abroad, was intimate with writers, intellectuals, politicians and diplomats in Oxford and London. She was naturally warm, gregarious and loved to entertain. They got on well together. Excited at the thought of his arrival, Elizabeth would say to her housekeeper, Molly O'Brien, 'Who do you think is coming?'

They enjoyed their walks along the paths and through the great woods of the estate. They would walk down to the crossroads at Farraday to watch the open-air dances, would sometimes rest in Elizabeth Cleary's huckster's shop at the corner, would drive to Kinsale to buy lobster and crab, and when Elizabeth went into the garden to cut flowers, he would accompany her and then return to the house to watch her arranging them. They talked and talked. Once they drove to see the ruin of Convamore, former home of the Listowels, which the IRA had burnt. Elizabeth was also sexually liberated and they quickly became lovers. That first summer they went to the Salzburg festival with Isaiah Berlin, Stuart Hampshire and Sally Grauer, and were joined by Cyril Connolly and his wife.

They spoke to each other across a religious, social, cultural, and racial divide, but they spoke as writers who knew that literature could, even should, transcend such divisions. It was one of his particular interests and he soon began to urge her to write a novel that would break down these divisions. He recalled the discomfort he had felt the previous summer when he stayed at Alta Villa, a Big House near Foynes, County Limerick. He and the Griffiths sat on the steps looking at a far line of hills from which his people had come: 'As we sat on the steps a man came *sidling* with his hat in his hand, an old man with drooping moustaches. He might have been my father. The butler came out to fend him off from the lady of the house. The butler was possibly the old man's second-cousin, and he might have been mine. I felt something turn over in my bowels to see the two men talk to one another in that way, and to have to keep silent, and not to say, Hello Tom, or Jerry, or whatever his name was. It seemed the wall was just as high as ever. It made me feel like a spy inside it.'[25]

In his relationship with Elizabeth he was not free of this ambivalence. He was not entirely at ease among her friends whose accents and attitudes tended to offend his Irish sensibilities.

From the beginning Sean wanted her to become a member of the Academy. She was elected in 1937. He tried to have her *House in Paris* considered for the Harmsworth Award but was overruled by Yeats. The following year she was elected to the Council which meant that they met at monthly meetings over the next two years, whenever she was able to attend. She wrote to Virginia Woolf. 'A friend of mine from Ireland . . . wants to meet you so very much . . . he is a very nice young man'. On the morning of their meeting, in February 1938, Virginia Woolf had received a ring-casket from Lady Ottoline Morrell's estate. O'Faolain described the scene: 'The foreheads of the two women almost touched as they bent over the little casket to inhale the undying scent of its little, pale-green cleft. The two profiles, Virginia's exquisitely beautiful, Elizabeth's not beautiful but handsome and stately, were . . . like two young faces on an obsolete coin. Within months their world was under fire. Within half a dozen years it was dotted by ruins . . .'[26]

The war disrupted the relationship. Academy records show Elizabeth's presence at Council meetings in June, September, October and November of 1939. In the summer of 1940 she rented a flat in Dublin, went back to London for September, but was in Ireland again in November. She went to Bowen's Court in December and returned to London in February. She seems to have attended only the July meeting in 1940, and the January, June, and October meetings of 1941. By 1942 Elizabeth was attracted to Charles Ritchie and her visits to Ireland became less frequent. She felt it a duty to be in London where she was an air-raid warden, and saw Sean less frequently. In his diary he noted her sadness. Her 'nice young man', only one year younger than herself, also became very busy as the editor of a monthly magazine.

Sean was enthusiastic about the 'noble work' that might be done through the Academy. He could see the Academy getting at the young and persistently coming before the public in a courageous, intelligent, and politic way. 'I want a Congress of Irish Writers here next Summer . . . I want . . . a kind of Irish Literary Society, that will come before the provinces publicly, in debate or lectures'. He urged Hackett to become a member.

Knowing that Yeats had blocked his nomination initially, Hackett was not enthusiastic. O'Faolain urged him to 'sink his personal feelings'. He, too, had 'always' found himself cold-shouldered by Yeats and 'felt a certain umbrage at it'. Others had shared that fate, but had not allowed it to deflect them from unselfish service. 'What a fine job of work we could do with you on Council! You, O'Connor, Higgins, O'Malley, Miss Bowen, I, O'Neill, Lennox'. He was, he added, 'in a more earnest frame of mind than I have ever been in'. He wanted to make the Academy into a 'real live institution, exercising its rightful influence on the country'.[27]

He felt that the time was 'identical in every way to the time after Parnell'. The young were as Yeats found them then, bits of wax. They needed to be moulded. 'We have a magnificent opportunity to save the fine things that we all believe in'. But the Hacketts had decided to leave Ireland. Sean was shocked. The news left him feeling 'very lonely and solitary down here in the hills . . . By Jesus if we don't get something out of this ffing Ireland – so challenging, so torturing, we're no men'.[28]

He looked forward to Frank O'Connor's play, *The Invincibles*. 'It's going to raise a little dust', he told Patrick McCartan, because the memory of the murder of two British officials was still fresh and O'Connor treated the assassins as men whom Ireland let down. The producer, Hugh Hunt, was 'comically timid about the funny old men in greening hats who have been wandering into the Abbey since the bills went up – antique Fenians like desiccated bats come out of their winter sleep . . . Hunt imagines them with rusty knives in their bottom drawers . . . Ancient relatives . . . keep cropping up'.[29] On opening night there was an air of apprehension as O'Faolain, Hunt, O'Connor, Evelyn Bowen, Dermot Foley and Richard Hayes gathered in the foyer. The arrival of Maud Gonne McBride added to the tension, but the play went off without incident, apart from a woman fainting in the stalls.

While Eileen and Nancy McCarthy were on holidays in Paris he also worked at a play, 'a piece of gay, Chekhovian light-heartedness', which he called *She Had to Do Something*.[30] Based on incidents that took place during the visit in May 1931 of the Anna Pavlova Company to the Cork Opera House when priests spoke against the show with the result that people stayed away, it dealt with the conflict between Art and Puritanism. Sean was uneasy when Aloys Fleischmann turned up at one of the rehearsals. He knew Aloys would recognize some of the characters, since the play portrayed Germaine Stockley and Fleischmann's father, who was a recluse but not pathetic as he was portrayed, and showed Dean Sexton and his son unfavourably.

There were difficulties over the casting. The Abbey Company favoured Shelah Richards for the female lead, but O'Connor urged O'Faolain to put Evelyn Bowen, Robert Speaight's wife, in the part, arguing that she was just like Germaine Stockley. Evelyn wrote to O'Faolain saying she would like the part. He said that he was leaving the casting to the producer, but would make his views known.[31] Casting her for the lead was both a tactical and artistic mistake. It antagonized the company and risked the success of the play. Casting Fred Johnston, a large man, as the ballet dancer compounded the error. Realizing she was not being welcomed Sean sent her flowers and invited her to lunch in the Hibernian Hotel. Knowing that Sean had little money, Evelyn accepted, but chose carefully from the menu to minimize the expense: no wine, no soup, a medium priced entrée, no dessert, coffee. Sean was furious. When the waiter turned to him, he ordered 'sardines on toast'. She was deeply offended by this put-down.[32] She would have been even more offended had she known that Sean could afford to buy land and build a fine house in Killiney.

The first night, 27 December, went off badly. There was applause, but also hisses and boos. Adopting a Yeatsian stance, Sean made a combative speech in which he compared the audience to the puritans in the play. He reminded them of what AE had said: if the Abbey ceased to be controversial, it would cease to live. He was glad, he said, echoing what Yeats said about rocking the cradle of genius, to have rebaptized the little pagan and help rescue it from the applause of the foolish. But the Yeatsian mantle was a poor fit. It was one thing for Yeats to have defended Sean O'Casey's *The Plough and the Stars*, quite another for O'Faolain to try to defend a much weaker play in the same manner. He was appalled by the way his play was changed in performance. By the third night gags had been introduced and by the end of two weeks he hardly recognized what he saw on stage as the play he had watched in rehearsal. His 'light, frothy piece' had become 'the regular, low-brow, Abbey, heavy-handed, farcical, cut-and-slash, guffawing kind of thing'.

Before the play went into rehearsal the O'Faolains moved from Killough House to Killiney. The move brought them closer to the city and to schools. Julia was now five years old and Eileen was pregnant. They paid £100 for an acre of land and built a two-storey house with four bedrooms, one large living room, a small study, bathroom, kitchen, all fully wired, for £1100. The house looked towards Dublin across a pleasant, wooded landscape. Within its clusters of trees were 'big and little houses . . . a clock-tower in the foreground, a gazebo pricking an inky rim of trees . . . the obelisk at Stillorgan glinting like a little spire. From the delicate blue smoke reclining over the Liffey there uprises cupolas, domes, chimneys, spires, gasometers, masts and funnels'. It was, O'Faolain concluded, 'all urbane, and civilized, and soothing'.[33] The house's only claim to fame was that as a small boy James Joyce had ridden his tricycle wildly downhill through the public park and bashed his head against the wall.

As the time approached for Eileen to have her baby Sean felt 'a bit shot-up' and could not work. In that period of waiting he accompanied her to early mass on the Feast of the Ascension, but reacted badly to the behaviour of the congregation. 'The awful craw-thump! How it all surged back on me. What can you do with a people like that? It did neither of us any good. But Dublin from the hills at morning. Cold and fresh and vernal!'[34] Stephen was born on 5 July 1938. Sean sent telegrams to Nancy McCarthy and Frank O'Connor. O'Connor, who already had a male child, replied: 'All the appropriate sympathy'. Sean wrote ecstatically to Eric Linklater. 'He is tiny and he is full of life, and desire, and will – he is activity, he is urge, he is man – a man-child, a doer, a wanter, a plucker of fruit, a breaker of old bottles, he is Adam and Manfred and Nelson and De Valera and Bill Sykes – he is male. He has balls! I – feminine male – call him Steve that he may complete me and be a stevedore; not a bloody romantic author like me – and I am delighted with him . . . God love you, God love you, God love you. I love you. I love everybody just now. (Except nurses)'.[35]

[9]

Knockaderry

As Sean finished the De Valera biography in May 1939, he felt depressed. He stopped going to the Abbey, gave up writing letters to the papers, feeling that his social conscience, 'thank God,' was dying. He was conscious of leading a double life, holding 'high ideals' in private and a 'casual indifference' in public. In the six years since his return he had grown bitter about Dublin, 'an empty provincial town, and would go back to London, if Eileen could bear it' (March 1939).[1] Fifteen years before it had been an exciting place, when it meant a visit to AE, to Yeats, and the Abbey Theatre. Now AE and Yeats were dead and the Abbey was a shadow of itself. Only Frank O'Connor spoke his language, 'the language of the artist, with whom I can create a mood in which life around us takes on stature, and the moment trembles with a feeling that something is about to happen, as if revelation were immanent — the feeling we always got with AE or Yeats' (IJ, 298). It was a mean city: 'no sooner does any man attempt, or achieve, here, anything fine than the rats begin to emerge from the sewers, bringing with them a skunk-like stench of envy and hatred, worse than the drip of a broken drain' (IJ, 299).

He missed O'Connor who had moved to Wexford with Evelyn Bowen. Although he wrote to him frequently, that was not satisfactory, since O'Connor did not like to write letters, whereas Sean did. He and Eileen could not afford to visit the O'Connors as frequently as they would have liked and O'Connor only came to Dublin occasionally. When he did, he stayed with them. Sean begged him to come back. 'When will you come out of that hell-hole and give me a chance to squabble with you again? . . . Kiss Evvie for me — one of them wet smacky wans you learnt in Bantry. Come

and see me sometime for Christ's sake or I'll begin thinking I'm Ahaseurus
. . .' 'Write to me you ungracious son of a bitch'. 'I do wish to the High
Heavens you would have some hoss-sense and live in Dublin. I'd fight you,
and hate you, and you'd get fed up with me, but it would be all *alive*'. He
passed on bits and pieces of news about himself, his work, the family,
mutual friends, the Abbey, books, and ideas. He was flirtatious about
Evelyn, the Welsh witch, whom he had failed to lure. 'I'd have given her
chocolate and thick cream, held her hand in a movie, listened to her
assiduously . . . Scorned and outcast, I hug myself with hateful malice . . .
May ye ate one another. (Lave her go out now and feed her chickens! Does
she powder their backsides?)' The letter rattles on about Michael Farrell,
Freddy May, Bob Collis. 'Come — I have schemes and schemes. And don't
be an ass about your novel'.

In May he became embroiled in a row between O'Connor and the Abbey
Board. The Board had given a dinner for Richard Hayes and had not invited
O'Connor. O'Faolain felt guilty, since it was he who had told O'Connor
about the dinner. O'Connor sent in 'a violent letter of resignation' (May
1939). At a party at Lord Longford's, Sean refused to shake hands with
Hayes. Eileen told Sean he must confront him. He told Hayes he 'was
pained and shocked at his treatment of my friend — I had a secret sadistic
hope I could make him cry' and wanted to punch 'his red nose'. Hayes got
emotional, declared O'Connor had changed towards him, blamed
O'Connor, took refuge in his wife, 'a cheap minx of forty two with pig's
eyes, flirtatiously arch'. O'Faolain felt angry with himself for having
spoken to Hayes at all, but then Eileen declared that Hayes 'was a bloody
ould hypocrite and that he made her sick'. The incident did not spoil 'an
otherwise excellent night'. Sean cast a satirical, gossipy eye over the
company. Good copy, he judged, had 'the art to be satirically contemptuous
. . . One could make it seem very comical in a provincial way' (May 1939).
He urged O'Connor not to be bitter (May 1939). Knowing that Frank was
not in good health and that he and Evelyn had many worries, he felt like a
'friendship-wrecker' and blamed himself intensely for talking about 'that
blasted dinner.'

O'Connor had asked him to go on the Abbey Board, but he did not wish
to be involved with people whom he did not respect and urged O'Connor to
make a clean break.[2] 'Let it go at that. You love the theatre and you will miss
it, and you hate seeing it (in the Abbey) fall into the gutter'. O'Connor, he

advised, had better things to do. 'Remember that I said, and I am not a fool in these things, that if you do six more books of short stories like the last two, you will be with the immortals — the Tchekov of Ireland. But it is necessary that you do about six. Books float one another. They comment on and enlarge each other. A man's corpus of work is his achievement, not one book or two'. Nobody, he told him, had written stories like his for years, and years.

Sean was restless and irritable. Knockaderry was too small, Eileen was sick, Stevie threatened with a cold, Julia was 'walloping about the place'. He felt claustrophobic and wanted to build a hut in the garden (1939). He worked at *Come Back to Erin*, put up a trellis in the garden, read *At Swim Two Birds*, and got his 'Garden Study' in August for £100. That summer, sometimes accompanied by Paul Henry, he went on several trips in order to gather material for a book on Ireland. He went to Kildare, then south through Kilkenny, down the rivers to Waterford, into Cork, out to West Cork and Kerry, northwards to Rathkeale, Limerick, Clare, Galway, and further north to Mayo and Sligo. He crossed through Northern Ireland to Belfast and from there completed his circuit down to Dublin. He kept a log, wrote up his experiences in the autumn and winter, completed the book in December 1939 but felt that it was 'scrappy' and 'unfinished' (December, 1939). *An Irish Journey* combines impressionistic descriptions, memories, bits of history, and topographical notations in an easy, relaxed style. Towns and people are viewed with the eye of a novelist; O'Faolain selects, heightens, invents, alters. When he got to Bowen's Court he found the Irish army camped on the great open field. He and Elizabeth sat on the steps and heard the soldiers singing in their tents. It was like a scene from *Another September*. More from memory than with the aid of the faint lamp-light from the hall he read 'the lovely stanzas' about change from Spenser's fable of Titan.

In Limerick he heard a story about Bishop Michael Browne of Galway. 'Great feck about new Bishop Browne of Galway, bully, arrogant, heard Father Mac was going to pics with femme, rang up pics. Is Father Mac there? Who's that? The Bishop. Yerrah gwan out of that. I'm coming down. Does. Sends in for Father Mac. Father Mac, the bishop is outside. Yerrah gwan out of that. Honest to god. Some joker. Out comes Mac grinning. Get into my car you pup. Drives him to new parish in Letterfrack or like, and orders him first to a week in Melleray.' According to Stan Stewart, the

Limerick chemist, the Bishop was 'closing all the Davis escape chambers in town'. He urged Sean to 'stick a knife in the hoor'. But not all the Galway pubs were closed: Stan and Vin Barry took Sean to three of them and he got home 'soused at three a.m.'

He went to London at the end of July but 'was hauled back' to his mother's bedside in the North Infirmary in Cork. The experience upset him. He did not do a 'stroke of work' for a week afterwards. He went to see her four times in August (29 August 1939). She had become a pathetic, shrunken, stubborn creature who clung to her familiar home in Halfmoon Street even though it was much too big for her. Once, in exasperation, Sean threw her down the stairs and broke her leg.

At the end of August Eileen and Sean went to the first night of Daniel Corkery's *Fohnam the Sculptor* at the Abbey. Sean 'never sweated so much for shame and rage'. The play, he told O'Connor, was 'beyond *all* human words. Corkery with a rainbow on his arse and feathers in his ears standing on his toes and blowin' himself up like a bullfrog'. O'Connor must see it. 'See our youth. See the mind (sic) of the man who ruined us.' He mocked the play's language – Holman Hunt, Rossetti, wishywashy Tennyson. 'This is our suck, our pap, our mush' (29 August 1939).

On 1 September 1939 Germany attacked Poland. Sean read about the outbreak of war as he sat on a wall below Croagh Patrick. On the second De Valera summoned an emergency session of the Dail to declare that Ireland would be neutral. On the third Britain and France entered the war. The war made the O'Faolains uneasy. They decided to move away 'permanently', wherever they could get a house, but preferably near Kilkenny, but there was no house available there and Eileen did not want to live in a town. She was 'dreaming of Bantry Bay, rowing a boat, or sailing' (November 1939). Eight estate agents put Knockaderry on their books but nobody was interested. By November they were resigned to staying.

The war affected his overseas markets. His earnings decreased. As the English market shrank, he turned more and more to Irish radio. Since his first appearance before the microphone in Dublin in 1935 he had done occasional book reviews and talks. Now he reviewed regularly, took part in discussions, gave the Book Talk almost every month, usually at five guineas a time; the remuneration never matched what he got from the BBC. Records in Radio Eireann show that he made £45 in 1940. The station's internal comments on his performances were favourable. His talk on Hardy: clear delivery; trenchant style; literary abilities evident. His book talk: interesting; first rate. One on new short stories: A1; very good – another: excellent. Frank O'Connor disagreed. He found the talk on Hardy 'very bad, pedantic, over-accentuated, confused, using twenty words and twenty ideas where one should do'.[3] Sean still sent out stories and articles, but it was difficult to sell material now. He put pressure on Pinter, sent him 'Cadenza for Christmas' for *Harper's Bazaar*. Pinter sent it to the BBC who turned it down. He asked him as well to insist on Penguin paying for *De Valera* immediately: he was 'stoney'. Five days later he wrote again: he was very hard up. He went to London in March to do a talk for the BBC, but did not enjoy himself: the food was bad and his sleep was disturbed by air-raids. On the twenty-fifth he sent Pinter the manuscript of 'Teresa' and enclosed two new stories. He thought of doing a life of Oliver Cromwell. Pinter advised against that, but suggested an autobiography instead. Meanwhile unsold material began to pile up. The BBC held on to his story 'The Machinery of Life', Pinter had 'The Warder', *Lilliput* turned down 'Wrong Number'. The BBC returned his talk 'The Secret of Walter Pater'. In all there were nine articles that Pinter was unable to sell. The agent was still slow forwarding cheques. In June O'Faolain told him he was on his 'beam ends'. In October he again asked for money. In November he asked him to send what was owed from *London Opinion*, *John O' London* and Penguin. He thought of going to teach in America to make a living, to escape from the war and to be able to continue his writing – he did not want to be silenced. Paris had fallen. His English friends told him London would soon be under threat. He himself thought that Ireland might be invaded. In Dublin there was a lot of scare talk: the Americans would take the ports, there would be an Allied fleet in the Irish sea, and dogfights over Killiney. Eileen was so frightened that she ran down to Dunlaoghaire and bought two tins of corned beef and half a stone of flour.

When the Bishop of Galway took legal action because of the story about him in *An Irish Journey*, Sean was desperate. He felt 'buggered up' with the libel action which he could not hope to fight given his lack of money. His Irish publisher had no intention of fighting a Bishop. Sean and Eileen went to Kilkenny for three days and had 'rest, quiet, great food'. But when they got home he was on the phone all night trying, unsuccessfully, to stop the publisher from inserting 'their lousy disowning ad' in the paper.[4] He lay awake another night trying to see what he could do 'to save a bit of amour propre and common decency from that small town bully and these small-town publishers'. 'I do not like arrogant people. I like decent firm pride not jack-in-the-office' (1940). Browne and Nolan withdrew the book and told Macmillan to sell it in Ireland themselves. O'Faolain thought the incident killed the hope of getting Irish books published in Ireland. It was a defeat; he 'got over the humiliation', and lived to fight another day. 'Round to Them. Next time. Round to us.' (9 August 1940.)

O'Connor proposed that he, Denis Johnston, Sean O'Faolain, and others should form a National Theatre Society. They would collect plays and offer them to the Gate or the Abbey, keeping control of the plays in their own hands. In view of O'Connor's explosive exit from the Abbey, Sean urged him to consider if it was worthwhile becoming involved again. He discussed O'Connor's idea with Lord Longford and Denis Johnston and voiced his concern about finances. Why, he asked, would dramatists bother with them unless the scheme seemed financially attractive? Johnston suggested a guaranteed season: they would form a Society, get ten shillings from two hundred people for four tickets, and guarantee the dramatists £50. Sean questioned O'Connor's idea of a writers' group, because it cut off the stage from the writer. 'If you have ideas about the theatre you must have a theatre to have them in . . . Let's copy Yeats if we do anything. That makes for reality — writing for time, and place, and men . . . I took up what I'd written of a play last night and it was all in a vacuum. What audience? What players? What producer? If I write a play I must have the stimulus of a theatre and an audience'. Concerned about standards, he made it clear that he was 'a confirmed intellectual and literary snob and that his idea of a good theatre was a theatre that produced good plays well — better still, great plays greatly'. Despite much discussion the scheme never got going. Instead the Dublin Drama League was revived.

But he was really too busy to become involved and was determined not to be secretary of the proposed society. Between meetings of the AE Memorial Committee, on which he represented the Academy of Letters, and launching the Friends of the Academy, which took weeks and weeks of work, he had little time or energy to consider O'Connor's plan. It was, he said, the same old story of man-power. Three people did all the work. In the Academy, as both Secretary and Treasurer, he was trying hard to revitalize it. In August 1939 he proposed setting up a Financial Sub-Committee, in September he became a member of this committee, in October he proposed

[124]

that members should consider finding homes for the children of writers affected by the war. In January 1940, he wrote to members, enclosing the minutes of the meeting of the advisory Financial Committee which had been set up to consider the Academy's difficult financial position. The Committee had three further meetings and worked out the details of the proposed Society of Friends. Sean felt stretched. He told O'Connor he would see these through and then the Academy could go to hell: he had to attend to his own work. He attended meetings throughout the years of the war, then his name disappears from the records, although he did not formally resign until January 1969.

He welcomed Frank O'Connor's 'masterly' novel, *Dutch Interior*, and was delighted when it got a sensitive and appreciative review in the *Irish Times*. The novel recreated his own memories of Cork's oppressive, stultifying atmosphere, he felt. He found its dull hatred 'unbearable'. Were it not for the fact that 'you are a man of genius and a poet, and that it is shot through with the lurid light of the pity of a damned soul for damned souls, (terribly moving), and that it has all the lyricism of nature in pain . . . I could not have borne to read it. I adored – perhaps because my poor starved heart shrieked for some release – the sexuality of Eileen . . .'. He told O'Connor that he had sympathized too much with his characters and they 'clawed' him 'into their hell'. He should have kept 'more cold and distant'. 'You felt involved in their misery – hence the lack of humour (I did the same with that silly book *Bird Alone*) . . . It's a hellish, lovely, lousy, filthy, bloody, pitiful, terrifying novel'.

Meanwhile, *Come Back to Erin* was not going well. He kept on with it through the summer and autumn, but in the end, despite some impressive writing in the first two parts, he knew it was not good. He wanted to examine the predicament of an old style Republican, Frankie Hannafey, who tries to continue with his cause as late as 1936, and is forced to realize that there is nothing he can do. When he goes to America, he revels in books, music, theatre, sexual feelings, all the things he has missed because of his dedication to the nationalist cause. Everything draws him farther and farther from the cause that he has served. The idea that he may be fitted back into Irish society is absurd. And O'Faolain knew it. He called the novel 'unmitigated . . . *bilge* . . . all melodrama and romantic escapism . . . I feel a washout . . .' (November 1939).

Sean put much of his own frustration and alienation into the character of

Frankie Hannafey. Frankie's conclusion that Ireland is on top of him like a load of hay is an extreme expression of Sean's own situation. Frankie is a man who has been so involved with politics that his nature has been starved of imaginative and sensuous nourishment – like Sean when he sailed for America in 1926, when he revelled in the opportunities to enjoy theatre and books, and was tempted by the woman on the boat. Frankie's love-affair with his step-brother's wife, whose beauty and sophistication he cannot resist, is based on Sean's own involvement with a wealthy American woman. Indeed Frankie's awkward handling of the relationship reflects his own lack of subtlety in handling his relationship with Anna Maria Kauffman. But the problem he still found beyond his powers, since he still found it beyond his reach in real life, was how to reintroduce the rebel to the society he had rejected, when that society was still the same and there was no sign of it changing. All of Sean's frustrated characters in *Purse of Coppers* and Corney in *Bird Alone* externalize his own predicament. What one can say about Sean in the summer of 1940, seven years after his return, is that he clearly understood Irish society, had examined and explained it over and over, had demonstrated the problems faced by the writers, could find satisfying imaginative surrogate leaders in the past but remained disillusioned with and unattracted by De Valera and his policies. While he wanted to write a novel that would encompass his love-hate relationship with his own country, he found himself thwarted by his concept of the novel as a reflection of a multi-layered, complex society, since that idea does not fit the Irish situation of a one-class, lower middle-class, Catholic, non-intellectual society. For O'Faolain to identify with a great creative leader and reformer like O'Connell was to court disappointment. He could not emulate his political achievements and the attempt to be equally creative by writing was a daunting task. He could examine, he could define and try to show a way forward through these examinations of past leaders and these analyses of the contemporary situation. He could thereby hope to create a new sense of political, social and cultural life and create the condition in which change might happen. It is not surprising that when he was asked to edit a monthly magazine, he seized the opportunity and threw himself into an even more direct and powerful engagement with Irish life. He had in any case been thinking about the need for such a magazine since his return.[5] Behind *The Bell* lay *The Fortnightly Review*, *Hound and Horn*'s successful mix and behind *Hound and Horn* lay their model, *The Criterion*.

[10]

The Bell

EARLY in August 1940 O'Faolain began to work consistently on *The Bell*, but he had been preparing for weeks, interviewing Frank O'Connor's mother in Cork,[1] obtaining short stories and an article on AE from O'Connor, encouraging Elizabeth Bowen to do something on the Big House, asking Michael Farrell for something 'objective' on the theatre. He cast about for an appropriate name. Some members of the Editorial Board favoured *This Ireland*, but he hated the self-conscious use of the word 'Ireland'. He asked Norah McGuinness to design a cover with a small, very green harp on the right hand corner. Then any title would be Irish. He wanted *You*, or *Now*. Eileen suggested *All of us*. In the end he chose a title with an indirect allusion to a Russian magazine and prepared his first editorial.[2]

The Bell, he announced, had in the usual sense of the word no policy. It would in time grow into character and meaning. Avoiding old symbolic, nationalistic words, they had chosen for title a 'spare and hard and simple' word that had a minimum of associations. The symbolic words – Banba, Roisin Dubh, Kathleen Ni Houlihan – belonged to a time 'when we growled in defeat and dreamed of the future'. That future had arrived, and with its arrival, killed them. 'All our symbols have to be created afresh, and the only way to create a living symbol is to take a naked thing and clothe it with new life, new association, new meaning, with all the vigour of the life we live in the Here and Now'. Their only job was to encourage Life to speak. He put his faith in a raw, inarticulate Ireland in which there were men and women itching to speak, to express intimate corners of the land, familiar details that mean Ireland to the individual. He opted for Life over Abstraction and opened the pages of his journal to the ordinary, the familiar, and the everyday. Their only 'policy' was to stir themselves 'to a vivid awareness of what we are doing, what we are becoming, what we are'. *The Bell* was quite clear, he said, about certain practical things – the Language, Partition, Education – and would deal with them from time to time, but it stood for Life before any abstraction or generalization. 'We prefer, likewise, the positive to the negative, the creative to the destructive . . . We are absolutely inclusive'. He ended with the declaration that *The Bell* belonged to the reader – 'Gentile or Jew, Protestant or Catholic, priest or layman, Big House or Small House' (October, 1940).

Peadar O'Donnell got financial backing from Joseph McGrath, a former Republican and Government Minister, who founded the Irish Hospitals Sweepstakes and became wealthy. Eamon Martin, the brains behind the Sweepstakes, was McGrath's appointee on the Editorial Board all of whose members – O'Donnell, Maurice Walsh, Roisin Walsh, Frank O'Connor and O'Faolain – had Republican backgrounds. O'Faolain did most of the practical work. He dealt with contributors, read and edited their submissions, answered the correspondence, handled the details of printing, illustration, lay-out and publicity. *The Bell* never looked elegant. It was, according to one contemporary comment, the only magazine in the world printed on lavatory paper with ink made from soot.

It was printed at Cahills where O'Faolain was already employed by the owner, J. J. O'Leary. As a young man J. J. had worked with Barry Fitzgerald in the Irish Land Commission. They left on the same day. Fitzgerald went into acting. J. J. went to Fleet Street, became a printer's devil, became acquainted with Lord Northcliffe, came back to Ireland and bought Cahills which had the only large scale letterpress in Dublin. He printed *The Bell* in between many profitable and complex jobs of a very different and more difficult nature, ranging from the printing of Bibles for Africa, the printing of bus time-tables, the late-night printing of each day's Dail debates, the ruthless abridgement of famous novels in paperback, the printing of end-of-term scholastic examination papers, and of each month's *English Digest*, which he imitated with his own *Irish Digest* (VM, 321). At the same time he was interested in the arts, kept a box in the Gaiety theatre, was a close friend of the Abbey actress, Ria Mooney, a friend of Sean O'Casey and kept up his friendship with Barry Fitzgerald. A short man with sharp features and a keen yachtsman, who occasionally took Fitzgerald and O'Faolain sailing, he may be detected in a number of O'Faolain's later

stories, including 'The Inside Outside Complex' and the novel *And Again?*
Hearing that O'Leary wanted someone to help run his publications,
O'Faolain had gone to see him at his large factory on the corner of Parkgate
Street. Seeing a door marked 'Mr. O'Leary' he was about to knock when a
man came out. 'Are you Mr. O'Leary?' 'No', the man said, 'I'm his brother'.
The brother, William, ran the company. J. J. made O'Faolain editor-in-
chief of all his publications and editor of the *English Digest* and paid him
£1000 a year. O'Faolain used his office at Cahills as *The Bell*'s headquarters
but did his work for J. J. in a room behind the Bank of Ireland in College
Green.

Material poured in to 43 Parkgate Street: poetry, short stories, essays,
plays, biographical material. To Sean's great delight the first issue sold out
in Dublin on the first day. Not since the publication of *The Nation* in 1842
had a magazine been so eagerly received. 'This magazine is going to be
famous. So watch for it'.[3] Looking through it he realized that O'Connor had
written about half of it. 'And the best half at that! If you and I dropped out of
this country, I ask you, what would be left?'[4] He wanted O'Connor to act as
Poetry Editor and to find him two good poems every month. He told him
he would pay him a guinea per thousand words on acceptance and not less
than five guineas 'which isn't bad these days'. He soon discovered that
O'Connor could not be relied upon to deal with poems quickly, return
manuscripts or answer letters. Pestered by poets looking for their
manuscripts, Sean begged him, repeatedly, to return specific poems and
devised a number of schemes to try to make the arrangement better, but
nothing worked satisfactorily and eventually he had to give the job to
Geoffrey Taylor.

O'Connor's failure to cooperate disappointed O'Faolain. He wanted him
to be part of the scheme just as he had wanted Hackett to join him in the
good work that the Academy might do. But he underestimated O'Connor's
capacity for envy. In this and in other areas O'Connor acted as the spoiled
child who wanted things to go his way and sulked when someone else was
the centre of attention.[5] His criticism of Sean's earnings and his suspicion of
other members of the Board and of their attitudes to him worried and
infuriated Sean. 'Your letter', he responded, 'is the last bloody word. I knew
you could do things like this well, but by Christ this beats the band . . . It's
bad enough to have to face the post every morning with a set mouth – and
sigh with relief like a boy let off a whipping if it contains no venom from

[129]

some stranger. But from a "friend" '. He asked O'Donnell to allow him to act as Secretary of the Company so that he could call a meeting. Since O'Connor accused him of wasting time and money, he wanted to have the details clarified. He circulated to the Board members a summary of expenses based on the first issue:

Editor's salary per month	£20
Contributors	£25
Managerial	£20
Printing	£48
	£113

Ads. income	£63
Sales? 2000?	£40
	£103

That meant a monthly loss of £10. It was better than they had expected and meant they could carry on for quite a while.

He objected to O'Connor's using phrases like 'making a mug of me', 'a phrase deliberately intended to deceive me', 'blinding me', 'take sides with O'D', 'my suspicions'. Not merely was this offensive but, he pointed out, it created an unsavoury atmosphere which made it difficult for them all to work together. He defended O'Donnell's skill in getting advertisements; his rôle was 'essential' (1940). He liked working with O'Donnell, finding him 'enlivening and on the ground'. He himself was, he told O'Connor, a willing part of a practical scheme. 'It is there – a scheme, some money, good will, talent, an opportunity. The result is quite a good little magazine . . . I try hard to get the thing down to a basis which warrants my time financially. It eludes me. People will not turn in stuff. I waste days. I have wasted weeks – months. I have done virtually no work since the end of August'. If O'Connor took The Belfry that would be 'practical, solid work' and there was nobody else to do it.[6] He felt O'Connor was being 'doctrinaire and idealistic' in objecting to the association with J. J. O'Leary. 'You preach the new democracy. A fellow who began life as a messenger-boy makes good. He sees people like you and me around. He wants to do well. He gives the £50. . . . The main point is that an Irish business-man becomes a patron of letters (for mixed motives, of course.) It is not the Yeats atmosphere – there

[130]

is no grand manner hanging around. It is just Jacky O'Leary . . . replacing Edward Martyn. Do I like such a metamorphosis? Do you? Do you like this Ireland we helped to bring into existence? Do we accept the universe or not? It strikes me that it is all very well for you to sit among the woods and streams, and get emotional about "Farewell to Patrick Sarsfield", and all very well for me to write, *King of the Beggars*, but when the beggars say, "Well, here we are, boys," – what do we do about it? I must be purblind, crass, dishonest, self-deceived, if you are right and I am wrong when I pretend that "a piece of cheap publicity was a generous action" – for I *do*'. Where they differed, O'Faolain concluded, was in the handling. He, O'Donnell and a few others did what they could in the circumstances in which they found themselves: 'the whole diary of every day's decisions of give or take, refuse or accept, with nothing to guide us but the wish to produce as good as can be produced under *actual*, and far from *ideal* conditions'. It was in that spirit that he urged O'Connor to take on The Belfry. 'I feel downcast. The hell with it all. *When shall I do a spot of my own work??????????*' (1940.)

By December he had a clear idea of what being an editor meant and he described it for the Editorial Board. In most cases, he pointed out, it was not sufficient to invite contributions in general terms. The editor had to state what he wanted clearly and fully. For example, say he wanted an article on The Country Bookshop. This would be the procedure:

1.   He turns over and over various possibilities to get the matter of country reading into the magazine and decides on the bookshop.
2.   He selects a possible writer. He selects Bryan MacMahon of Listowel, because he runs a bookshop. He writes at length to him.
3.   He reminds him.
4.   The article arrives. It is three parts MacMahon's great thoughts, and one part bookshop. He reads it, cuts it, marks it. He writes to MacMahon again, explaining how good the good bits are and what he has left out.
5.   He will probably have to remind him again, and when the article arrives
6.   will probably have to do some more cutting.

This was, he said, the general rule with every article. In the case of professional writers it was 'heavenly' not to have to do this. Yet, in the case of Lennox Robinson's play in January, it meant two interviews. Edward Fahy meant much more. M. J. MacManus's article had to be retyped completely, Michael Farrell involved interviews. Jack Yeats always meant several letters. A good piece like 'Twenty Five' or 'Poachers' would mean refusing up to four efforts with enough encouragement to keep him trying. Norah McGuinness's article 'Make Your Windows Gay', took, literally, two days at the end to get it in – phone calls, wires, visits, letters – apart from arrangements with Brown Thomas, block-makers, etc. Five times, in vain, he had approached another writer for an article. This was in addition to the ordinary routine.

He realized that it would take time to 'educate' the public up to the kind of periodical which was 'totally new' in Ireland. The public was still puzzled as to what they were getting at and most writers 'aren't worth a God Damn for this sort of work' and would not, he thought, support them. 'We must keep our policy tight and hard and unyielding for a year at least – cost what it may'.

From the beginning O'Faolain knew what he wanted. In his hands the magazine was restrained, constructive, rational, and documentary. He advised would-be contributors in the second issue to notice that every contribution came from actual experience. Michael Farrell went to Birr and saw the local theatre, Francis MacManus described life in the Teachers' Training College which he had attended, Frank O'Connor wrote of AE whom he knew, 'Orphans' and 'I Live in a Slum' documented real life. First they must see clearly, have the facts and understand the picture. This had never been done before. 'When Ireland reveals herself truthfully, and fearlessly, she will be in possession of a solid base on which to build a superstructure of thought, but not until then'. There would be no abstraction until then.

In this second issue he had a good mix of stories, poems, and articles; there were established writers like Peadar O'Donnell, Arland Ussher, Frank O'Connor, and O'Faolain; stories by M. J. MacManus, Niall Sheridan, Michael Murphy, Michael Burke and Lynn Doyle; poems by Patrick Kavanagh and John MacDonagh; an article by Norah McGuinness on the art of window display; one by E. M. Wells on the Dance Board; the second part of Edward Fahy's article on prisons; Farrell's coverage of plays for the country theatre; book reviews; and a new feature called 'Mise Eire' made up of short quotations from newspapers sent in by readers, with a prize for the best quotation each month. That mix was representative. He drew in writers – John Hewitt, W. R. Rodgers, Cecil Day Lewis, Donagh MacDonagh, Elizabeth Bowen, Denis Johnston, Maura Laverty, Anna Sheehy, Jack Yeats, Elizabeth Curran, Robert Greacen, Joseph O'Neill, Margaret Barrington, H. L. Morrow, Hubert Butler, Margaret Corrigan, Josephine MacNeill, Michael MacLiammoir; poets, novelists, short story writers, dramatists, theatre people, and artists from different parts of the country.

There were some innovations and changes over the years. The magazine had regular articles on current theatre, art exhibitions, concerts, painters, poets. There were several series: one called 'Personal Anthologies' in which contributors discussed their favourite poems; one on the 'Old School Tie' in which past pupils described their schools; another on 'What it Means to be a Presbyterian, or Unitarian, or Methodist, or Jew'; a series on careers; a 'One World' series that he wrote himself, addressing the issues likely to emerge in various countries after the war; one on people's incomes that described how people lived on incomes ranging from £800 a year down to £100. 'The Fourth Estate' was a series on newspapers. 'Meet the Bellman' had portraits of Ernest Blythe, Denis Guiney, Richard Hayes, Elizabeth Bowen, Christine Longford, Maurice Walsh, Jimmy O'Dea and Margaret Burke Sheridan. Occasionally there were extracts from work in progress. In every contribution the essential ingredient was realism and actual experience, the more gritty and specific the better. Never in an Irish journal had so much time and effort gone into the preparation for an article, the search for facts, for verifiable evidence. In many cases O'Faolain himself did the spadework, researched the subject, thought out its parameters, sought out a suitable contributor and guided him.

The range of material covered in the factual, informative, investigative articles was impressive. From the beginning, as in the case of Professor Fahy's two articles on prisons, he tried to get well-informed articles on particular topics. He sought the most appropriate contributors, such as Joseph O'Neill, an experienced music teacher and adjudicator, whom he took on as Music Critic. He organized a series of articles on censorship, beginning with C. B. Murphy's 'Sex, Censorship, and the Church'. In November 1941 Henry Bellew set out the legal position in 'Censorship, Law and Conscience'. In January 1942 Murphy responded with 'Principles and Practice'. When Monk Gibbon wrote in defence of censorship, that article was met by two articles, one by T. C. Kingsmill Moore, the other by James Hogan. Gillman Moorhead wrote on 'Hospitals, Finances, and the State'; P. R. O'Sullivan on 'Anti-Clericalism'; Maura Laverty on 'Maids versus Mistresses'; Hanna Sheehy Skeffington discussed 'Women in Politics'; Eileen Webster discussed the teaching of history in schools. In 'Two Dublin Slums' Sheila May exposed conditions of poverty, overcrowding and hunger. Some articles were anonymous; they included such subjects as 'The Decline of English' by a secondary teacher; 'The Life of a Country Doctor'; 'Gaelic – with the Lid Off' by a national teacher; 'A Day in the Life of a Dublin Mechanic' by 'Night Shift'; 'Speaking as an Orangeman' by 'One of Them';' 'I Wanted to be a Nurse' by 'Probationer'; 'Publishing in Ireland' by a master printer; 'Defectives in the Dock' by 'Medicus'; 'Insanity in Ireland' by 'A Psychiatrist'; articles on jockeys, yacht racing, libraries, crime, fly fishing, reforming the legal system, dog racing, women in public life; and 'I Did Penal Servitude', an exposé of the Irish prison system.

For a while O'Faolain ran a section called 'New Writing'. Each month he published a short story with a critical comment. He would say, 'Keep apart from your characters'; 'Preserve some sense of irony'; 'The story is told with modest simplicity and no trimmings. It begins and ends naturally, it has point'; 'I like cold writing'; 'Every detail is observed'. He was pleased with Michael MacGrian's 'Myself and Some Ducks'; 'What delights me,' he said, 'is the delicacy of its feelings and its pictures . . . the whole quivering response to Nature . . . the gropings after some bond between the life of the ducklings, the beauty of the nights, the love of the girl, and the growth of the boy to some fashion of selfhood . . .' He liked a story sent in by Mary Lavin, but wanted her to work at it – 'worry it as dog with bone'. Val Mulkerns felt he had the right to comment, because of his experience. His rejection slips often had handwritten notes – 'I liked this a little better. I'm hoping for more'. 'Not this. Send more soon. Be less subjective'. When she became the Assistant to Peadar O'Donnell who succeeded O'Faolain as editor, she had the salutary experience of noting that even a letter to the editor from O'Faolain had been much revised: he practised what he preached. He preached hard work: 'You must not', he told Maura Laverty, 'turn back from the strait and narrow of artistic slavery, but perfect and perfect and perfect everything you write'.[7]

For Bryan MacMahon in Listowel, Co. Kerry, the appearance of *The Bell* was momentous. He sent a poem to The Belfry; it was published in November 1940. He sent his article on his bookshop (March 1941) and was reprimanded by O'Faolain: 'You have been incontinent'. O'Faolain wanted 'facts' not 'fancies'. He rewrote it and got the first of the magic postcards. 'Bookshop now fine. Will publish next month. SO'F.' He sent in a short story, 'The Breadmaker' and got another welcome, laconic postcard. Sometimes O'Faolain would sub-edit a story, sometimes change an ending, sometimes fire off cryptic advice: 'Lag your pipes'. 'Keep your balance'. Once on a visit to Dublin MacMahon met with O'Connor and O'Faolain and asked how a short story was written. O'Faolain spoke about the harmonization of disparates, the mating of opposites, advice MacMahon never forgot.[8]

The young James Plunkett sent in a story. 'Apart from anything else,' O'Faolain told him, 'it is a mile too long'. But he liked its 'high spirits' and asked to see something shorter and more recent. Plunkett promptly sent two stories: 'Fiddler' and 'As It Was in the Beginning'. O'Faolain commented in the margins. 'Fiddler: Better. I don't feel it quite comes off. Sorry. A bit sentimental'. 'As it Was: style not developed, e.g. "Prolonged struggle for existence" is cliché and means you are not identified with character. Do you feel in such language? No! Talk: yes, but not feel. Say "There was no more furniture: he was too poor".' It was steadying, precise advice, good for young writers.[9]

His correspondence with Dermot Foley about his story 'The Verger' shows a mixture of kindliness and irritation. He advised him to cut it back, to avoid 'literary phrases', not to allow his own pleasures to interfere with character. Dermot was an old friend, a man of great enthusiasms and zeal, who could be irascible. 'My Dearly Beloved Dermot', O'Faolain began, 'you have robbed more of my time than any six young men put together. I read and reread the Verger when I got it, I made careful suggestions, I suggested that it be cut. I went over it with a fine rake . . . you now send it back written all over again with some of my cuts . . . but you have still and again been wilful . . . Cross as a wet cat'. Foley reacted sharply. O'Faolain wrote soothingly: 'Angel . . . I've written angry letters like that, too, when I thought I was Shakespeare. Have pity, O Bard of Ennis. I also am Shakespeare . . . For four months I have devoted myself single-handedly to the creation of this magazine . . . There are umpteen other manuscripts . . . stop working your temperament off on me . . . he has to be compressed . . .

What is the nodal point or motif of the character? I see it quite plainly. I feel it should be stated more succinctly ... I like it and think it full of integrity. I want to print it. Now, angel, is not that all right?'[10] He got L. A. G. Strong and Elizabeth Bowen to read the story and they found it wanting.

Lochlinn MacGlynn's story 'The Dam' intrigued and teased him as much as if it were one of his own. He read it over and over, but felt it needed to be rewritten. Cutting or patching would not be enough. He sensed that MacGlynn had enough of the genuine writer in him to enjoy conquering the technical difficulties. His suggestions reveal the hand of the master. He marked the ms. carefully. The character, Bella, should be mentioned in the second sentence, but something should be added about this being known to everyone 'except to me'. His brackets meant *cut*. Flowers at the end of paragraph two were not observed enough. – 'Get something unusual, even the celandine.' The last sentence on page two, second paragraph, was not subtle enough. 'Play up the gushing life of Spring. Pull out the vox humana stop, work the tremolo, go all out, don't be afraid to be luscious and sensuous there – good pointer to Charlie's inner swell of emotion. Get a sharp black and white contrast to the chill and the fire'. On page seven, he advised, 'get a sense of thick night, smells, bourgeoning life. Some gesture is necessary here – a lift of his head to the first star (Venus?), a passionate movement.' Make him roar at the boy to go, hunt him home, do something outrageous and unusual like flinging a stone after him, he suggested. 'The boy goes, bewildered, frightened a little, and then looking back up the banks, in the dim starlight, sees some unusual pose, facing the wrong way, and hears the roar of the water. Runs back. Sees what he has done. Keep last three lines of page eight and let him follow, see Charlie go in, close the door, and sit by the fire. "Outside the water was hissing as it poured away, the long stored water, feeding the drouth of the spring flowers on the bank, etc. I stole home. I can still smell the sweetness of the night, and hear the roar of the wasted water running through the dark".' You can do it, he urged, and make a lovely story of it. He would like to use it in his October issue (1942), deadline 1 September. It is not hard to imagine the excitement of the young writer when he got this long letter at once so responsive and so practical. He rewrote and sent it back in. 'Blast it', O'Faolain responded, 'not right yet'. 'But this time careful cutting should get it right. At first it was too reticent, but exciting because of that suggestibility. Now it is too overt, and the excitement of the "hint" quality is lost'. He would cut out some of the statements and leave only what was necessary for an alert reader to understand, he said. The story appeared in November. O'Faolain sent a cheque apologizing that it was so meagre. He should have explained to him that it was because this was a story 'reaching to the top class' that he did not print it right off, as they did with far inferior work which could not be improved since such work did 'not ambition high'. It was only because 'The Dam' was in the tradition of the great stories that he had tried to get it 'absolutely as good as can be'. He enjoyed seeing a man trying to get the last ounce out of his idea and hoped MacGlynn would forgive his 'efforts' and 'interference'. He ended with 'send us more'. He continued to encourage MacGlynn, published three of his stories, and hated, he told him, to turn down anything by him.[11] His practical kindness may be seen in a letter he wrote to MacGlynn in October 1943, telling him that there was work available at Cahills on the Irish and English *Digests*. It should be worth a minimum of £350.[12] He agreed to read part of a novel for MacGlynn who wanted him to tell him 'the naked truth'.

O'Faolain had an infectious enthusiasm for what he liked. He told Edward Sheehy that he had a 'lovely subject', a perfect ending, but a fumbled beginning. 'It can all emerge as a lovely, delicate, ironical, tender story'. If Sheehy brought out the poetic tenderness and poetic irony, he'd love to print it. It was just the kind of story, he said, that 'we Irish' could write better than anyone living. It revealed the Irish genius at its best: 'cynicism become irony, irony become sympathy, sympathy become humour, humour become philosophical, and so, a synthesis of our essentially civilized attitude to the human comedy. Without the sympathy and humour and poetry we should go the way of Manchester, and be just "realists"'.[13] He had a good sense of what worked in a story. Although he admired O'Connor's 'Uprooted', he knew that the ending in which the priest speaks about a girl he had known in Bundoran was 'too explicit'. O'Faolain queried this. Would he speak in this personal way to a brother? 'Brothers', O'Faolain said, 'are so separated from one another'. O'Connor made the incident more subtle.

O'Faolain wanted writers to write about what they knew. By now he had a better understanding of the art of the short story. His own writing had developed from the relaxed style and the more crowded canvas of stories in *Midsummer Night Madness* to the more compressed, suggestive and concentrated stories in *Purse of Coppers*. He gave three talks on Radio

Eireann in May 1942 on the 'Art and Craft of the Short Story'. They were rated 'excellent' inside the station and at least one aspiring writer listened avidly. 'I remember it', Eilis Dillon recalled, 'the way an outcast member of the Foreign Legion would remember his first drink after he had crossed the desert on foot. I had been waiting for it all my life, or at least all my conscious life, and here it was, unmistakeably'. He began with a quotation from Flaubert that expressed one of his fundamental beliefs: the secret of masterpieces lies in the concordance between the subject and the temperament of the writer, and he went on to stress the importance of personal experience, and spoke of practical things and illustrated them from particular stories.[14] Later he published a series of articles in *The Bell* (January to July, 1944) all of them filled with practical advice and all of the advice based on and illustrated from specific literary sources. Later still he incorporated these articles and stories in *The Short Story* (1948).

'Those who examine nothing and question nothing', O'Faolain wrote in his first extended editorial, 'end up knowing nothing and creating nothing'. Political nationalism had, he believed, for too long absolved the country of the need for constructive thought. He frequently pointed out that the generation that had planned and carried out the revolution failed to think ahead to the kind of society and economy they would wish to create.[15] Sinn Fein's policy, which once had an attractive ideal of self-reliance and self-confidence, had been replaced by one of self-protection and isolationism.

He called attention to the results of introversion and exclusiveness on Irish writing and recalled that forty years previously a magazine like *The Bell* could have relied on contributions and readers from all over Ireland. 'When we look back at that great period of forty years ago we see what the ideal might be and what has been lost — an extraordinary catholicity of interest, a fine intellectual curiosity, a bond with the civilization of the wide world, a sympathy and understanding with all human sorrows and tragedies which give a universal quality to the best work of the time'.

He worked to introduce new thinking, to promote ideas by frequent repetition, to make readers aware of the actual conditions of Irish life. He asked questions, avoided controversy, preferred patient and constructive thinking. As a matter of policy and strategy he explained present developments in the light of history or by comparison with developments elsewhere. Before commenting on the state of the Gaelic League he outlined its initial aims and showed how and when politics had affected its development. Before attacking the middle-class he explained how it had evolved. Before condemning censorship he explained why it existed in such an extreme form in Ireland. He gave a roll-call of banned Irish writers: Frank O'Connor, Liam O'Flaherty, Kate O'Brien, Austin Clarke, Francis Stuart, F. R. Higgins, W. B. Yeats, George Moore, Sean O'Casey and others.

Ireland's censorship, he explained, arose because standards and tastes had not been developed. Kate O'Brien's *Land of Spices*, praised by Catholic journals abroad, was banned in Ireland on the basis of a one sentence reference to homosexuality. Louis D'Alton's *The Money Doesn't Matter* was banned for caricaturing a public figure in a tasteless manner. When the Censorship Board banned Halliday Sutherland's *The Laws of Life*, he had proof of what he had been saying for years: the censors abused the law. In this case they had not realized that the book had received the imprimatur of the diocese of Westminster. He got a copy of the imprimatur. The Minister for Justice refused to admit that the Board had made a mistake, and asserted 'that whether or not a book was legally banned, he would over-ride or ignore the Act of Parliament and ban it on other (unspecified) grounds.' O'Faolain pointed to this admission as evidence that books were improperly proscribed. The banning of Eric Cross's *The Tailor and Ansty* was particularly objectionable. The book was a collection of stories, sayings, and opinions gathered by Cross from Tim Buckley at Gougane Barra. At a time when the official Gaels promoted the revival of Irish language and culture it was contradictory and outrageous for them to ban the words of someone who had a direct link with that culture. In October O'Faolain prepared a resolution for the Irish Academy of Letters, protesting to the Minister. He and Frank O'Connor wrote to the *Irish Times*. In the Senate Sir John Keane put down a motion asking that the Censorship Board be reconstituted and pointed to the unfair banning of *The Land of Spices*, *The Laws of Life*, and *The Tailor and Ansty*. The Board's Chairman, Professor Magennis, would have none of this. He called the Tailor a sex maniac, said his wife was a moron, and accused Keane of taking his arguments from letters by O'Connor and O'Faolain in the *Irish Times*. Keane's motion was defeated. 'How the hell', O'Faolain asked himself, 'can anyone work in a country where the mob creates such an atmosphere of bigoted ignorance?'[16]

* * *

Perhaps O'Faolain's most famous editorial was 'The Stuffed Shirts'. He began by mentioning some 'extraordinary' incidents: the Gaelic Athletic Association had proposed that the Minister for Defence should be removed from office because some members of the Army played games like golf, or soccer, which were not 'national games'; a member of the Dublin Corporation had proposed that the Press should be prevented from reporting details of unpleasant crimes and this in Holy Ireland where such things did not happen; the censors had banned the last two volumes of Proust even though only a tiny fraction of the population was likely to read them; a bookseller in Limerick complained that the Readers' Union of London had refused to send him any more books because he had refused to distribute their last choice, a book by H. G. Wells, to their members. 'There were other blokes dodging about in the shrubbery quacking at us through their fingers, but that is enough'. His generation, he declared, had lost all sense of its origins. The very history being taught was a complete fairy-tale. 'The main notion of it is that we have since the dawn of our history been united here in our efforts to eject all foreign ways, people, manners, customs – which is, of course, arrant nonsense: on this fancy there has been piled up a gospel of the sanctity of the West and the evil of the East, the generative power and utter purity of all native custom and tradition, as handed down by an army of, mainly legendary, saints and heroes; a thirst for not only what little remains of this custom and tradition but for the revival of what of it is actually dead or obsolescent; a drive towards authoritarianism to enforce these ideas and a censorship of cold-blooded economic pressure . . . to down everybody who opposes them. This farrago is called Nationalism'.

How different all this was from what they had dreamed of as young men. 'We had looked forward to seeing all classes united, all religions equal, all ideas welcome. We visioned fresh and eager life sloughing its old skin. Those things I poked fun at in the beginning of this article are not young and eager. They are very old, and very silly, and very cowardly.' He did not believe they were characteristic of Irish people.

He deplored the country's inward-looking, defensive posture. Ireland's future, he argued, lay in a European Federation. World history led him to observe that all the greatest cultures had been the creation not of separate racial units but of blended hordes of peoples of various ethnic origin. There was, he concluded, no such thing as an independent nation. 'It took a war to teach me that obvious fact' (VM, 318). He described the kind of Republican he could admire and in the process defined himself: 'the sort of Republican who . . . wishes his country to take her part in this terrible evolution of European civilization which is and always may be a recurring series of periods of achievements and defeats, of full living and hard enduring, of rebuilding and new starts, of Peace in which men create splendidly, and interruptions of every kind which they struggle to control . . .'

Towards the end of 1944 he began to feel that there was a weight of inertia on the country, 'some large psychological frustration', whose removal would be essential for the release of the people's energy.[17] The climax to O'Faolain's reaction to the whole post-revolutionary period came in his condemnation of all that had come into existence under De Valera. It arose out of a controversy in *The Bell* with M. J. MacManus who had published a biography of De Valera. Sean gave it an unfavourable review to which MacManus replied in the form of an open letter to the editor. He began by contrasting the high hopes with which the magazine started out, praised many of its contributions, but noted the 'catastrophic decline' in the editorials. They no longer rang 'a joyous, stimulating appeal; the sound that comes from the belfry is a death-knell'. The magazine had become defeatist, the editorials were bad-tempered, crabbed, peevish and nagging. Then he proceeded to draw attention to the contradictions between what O'Faolain had written in his 1933 biography and the Penguin biography of 1939, between a biography written for the home market and one written for a foreign audience. The facts, MacManus said, were unchanged yet O'Faolain had once used them for adulation and then for condemnation. He went on to give evidence of De Valera's achievements as evidence to disprove Sean's charge of 'masterly inactivity', and ended by urging him to have faith in himself, his magazine and his country. He should not, he urged him, supply fodder for Ireland's enemies; he should criticize all he wanted to, but do so on the basis of fact, not on personal prejudices and dislikes.

Sean's response to this attack began quietly. He recognized, he said, that in a small, intimate country those engaged in public controversy often pretended to be highly incensed. So, while M. J. addressed him as 'dear Sean', he nevertheless charged him with despicable behaviour, e.g. writing for foreign consumption, showing up his own Government, writing an acid, hostile biography, and so on. Then, with 'superb impertinence', his friend implored him to have faith in himself. Obviously, O'Faolain pointed out, if 'dear Sean' were that kind of person, M. J. had been keeping very low company for years. Just as obviously Sean was not expected to take the attack seriously, since if he did, the result would be a punch in the kisser or a libel action. He dismissed the charge of inconsistency by saying that the 1933 biography was pro-De Valera propaganda and that a man must have the right to change his mind. As for De Valera's achievements, he readily granted them but referred to continued emigration as in itself a judgement on the worth of those achievements. De Valera's policies, he said, were determined not by Republicanism but by the concept that the function of the State is to provide conditions in which men of property may prosper and that the growing prosperity of the new, 'hard-faced' industrialists would keep the working classes grateful and happy. The emergence of a middle-class, he went on, happened after revolutions, when one class replaces another, and the Irish middle-class come from decent stock; middle-class Ireland could be much worse than it is. MacManus should recognize, however, that the quality of life had never been so low since the death of Parnell; he should stop propagandizing for a party against a profession (the writer) and stop trying to shield this exhausted generation of politicians against the indignation of the people and the honest anger of the writers. At this point O'Faolain's editorial rises to a vehement condemnation of the state of Ireland under De Valera:

The truth is that the people have fallen into the hands of flatterers and cunning men who trifle with their intelligence and would chloroform their old dreams and hopes, so that it is only the writers and artists of Ireland who can now hope to call them back to the days when these dreams blazed into a searing honesty — as when Connolly told the wrecked workers of this city that he found them with no other weapons but those of the lickspittle and toady and that his job and theirs was to make men of themselves. Surely these are honourable footsteps to follow? Surely it is not to let the country down but to try to raise it up, to reveal the drab poverty level of life which has sent our youth stampeding to the wartime cities of Britain and now threatens another exodus of their wives and children? Surely it is the duty of our writers to keep hammering at such facts as that our children today are as hopeless putty in the hands of morons who have imposed on our generation a parody of an education system beyond all ignorant, narrow and unrealistic, at which parents growl helplessly, at which the superiors of schools and convents can only wail and ring their hands, but in which the authors thereof obstinately and bearishly persist year after year against the protests of every class and creed? Surely it is not defeatist to protest to high Heaven against a censorship of bosthoons over letters and opinion in such a country? It is the natures of writers to have a passionate love of life and a profound desire that it should be lived in the greatest possible fullness and richness by all men: and when we see here such wonderful raw material, a nature so naturally warm and generous as the Irish nature, so adventurous, so eager, so gay, being chilled and frustrated by constant appeals to peasant fears, to peasant pietism, to the peasant sense of self-preservation, and all ending in a half-baked sort of civilisation which, taken all over, is of a tawdriness a hundred miles away from our days of vision – when we see all that we have no option but to take all these things in one angry armful and fling them at the one man who must accept them as his creation, his reflex, his responsibility. In a nutshell, we say that this is surely not the Ireland that Wolfe Tone would have liked to live in, or even Dan O'Connell, for all his peasant coarseness and cunning, or the aristocratic Parnell, or any man like that old eagle John O'Leary, or the warm-hearted Jim Connolly, or any man who really loved men and life, and we accuse it. (June 1945)

He was disillusioned. He had grown weary of attacking the bourgeoisie, the 'Little Irelanders, chauvinists, puritans, stuffed-shirts, pietists, Tartuffes, Anglophobes, Celtophiles, *et alii hujus generis*' (April 1946). There was also the fact that *The Bell* never achieved the intellectual range or level of *The Criterion*. It lacked sustained, in-depth discussion, partly because the academics, as Sean noted, refused to become involved. He was virtually on his own. His abrasive personality rubbed people up the wrong way. There was little he could do about that. He knew he was not good at working with people. He liked to be in control, was not always tactful in his comments on contributions, had a razor-sharp mind that pierced into the minds of others, was bossy and domineering, and was seen to be disagreeably arrogant. He received many abusive letters, was frequently attacked in Catholic newspapers and periodicals, and at a time when the country was conservative and pietistic he had a bad public image. Even M. J. MacManus's 'Open Letter' was not as naive as he pretended. MacManus urged Daniel Corkery to continue the attack. By adopting an amused response,

O'Faolain defused its mean spirit, but he was well aware of the treacherous nature of an attack from someone he knew. It was symptomatic of much of what he detested. Therefore he raised the issue to a general attack on De Valera's Ireland, on its mealy-mouthed, secretive mentality.

He objected strongly when O'Connor selected a non-Irish poet for The Belfry, since it went against the policy of encouraging Irish writers and contradicted the advice O'Connor himself had been giving. But soon he was faced with a more serious issue. In March 1941 Evelyn and Frank O'Connor went to see Louis D'Alton's play *The Money Doesn't Matter*. When they realized that Denis O'Dea was playing the part of Philip Manion as a caricature of Lennox Robinson, they walked out. O'Connor sent an indignant letter to the *Irish Times* to which the dramatist replied. For the Directors of the theatre, O'Connor said, to permit one of their members to be portrayed as a dipsomaniac and a thief was the foulest treachery. O'Connor followed up with a letter to *The Bell* which criticised the Abbey, *The Bell*, the general lack of literary standards and, by implication, O'Faolain himself. He accused *The Bell* of being a dog that did not bark. O'Faolain took up the challenge. Barking, he replied, was not their line. They set out to be 'a natural sort of sane, and quiet, and constructive paper such as any normal country would produce . . . a corner of sanity and intelligence and decency'. He liked that part of O'Connor's letter that protests against 'grossness and pointlessness and vulgarity', but was not impressed when he adopted Yeats's stance of 'noble indignation'. That, he thought, was 'sheer masquerade'. Living men, he reasoned, have often been caricatured. D'Alton was entitled to caricature Robinson, but not to do it stupidly, i.e. without taste. He wanted to tone down O'Connor's letter. He was worried about libel and concerned about Robinson's feelings. Therefore, O'Connor should not identify the stage character as a real person or as a member of the Abbey Board. O'Faolain underlined sentences which struck him as 'ludicrously excessive', the sort of 'rhetorical exaggeration' that spoilt the good impression O'Connor had made. 'If you write as a cultured, decent person, that is good; if you write as a wildly excitable person, people say "he's wildly excitable".' It was a great temptation to behave like a genius in public, he said, with the Yeats touch, the grand performance, but one had to carry it off always. It was not natural for O'Connor, or himself. He said:

Now the facts are that we are poor, without a tradition, without standards, beginning, ignorant, goodhearted, openhearted, timid, generous, emotional, eager, proud of country, and so on and so on. There is no use hurling oneself against the stonewall of the fact that we are not a Renaissance people, nor even a people who have fed on the Middle Ages. There *are* no Turkish slippers or pretty women. We must work with the material available. If I can get William O'Dwyer of Sunbeam Hosiery to give me £50 for *The Bell*, in advertising, by writing to him as a literary man, on behalf of literary men, and putting it up to him that it is *his* job to help letters, then I am doing good work. He is, of course, flattered, and I play on that. If I can get O'Leary of Cahills to give £50 to the Academy (in the teeth of the church) I don't care what little vanity or anything else comes into it. The breach is made. If I can get a Book Fair run by the Friends of the Academy with people like Aubrey Gwynn's sister, Duffys, Alice Curtayne, Farren all identified, I am delighted . . . I am making the Academy get recognised, and breaking down the grand arrogant Ivory wall which Yeats built up about it. I have to pay for that in humiliations of various sorts, and it is always a delicate and vital question, 'Am I going too far?' If I can get *The Bell* to take in every sort of person from Kerry to Donegal, and bind them about you and me and Peadar and Roisin do you not see that we are forming a nucleus? Take the long view – bit by bit we are accepted as the nucleus. Bit by bit we can spread ideas, create *real* standards, ones naturally growing out of Life and not out of literature and Yeats and all to that. It is going to take years and years. Explosions and rages get us nowhere. You sit down there on your backside and do the highfalutin' artist, while up here, painstakingly, I am doing a spot of real construction. That may not at all be how you see it. You may say I am undermining, giving away all along the line. *Ok.* I am merely telling you how I see it, and that's that. To me your irascibility is sheer nihilism. To me you are a magnificent anarchist. You drop out of the Abbey, you drop out of the Academy, you want to drop out of *The Bell*. You will probably drop out of Cuala. A grand time for a bit of excitement and let somebody else do the patient work. Can you imagine how your wildly explosive emotionalism strikes me, then? It just gives me a very large pain.

He urged him to keep on with The Belfry and as poetry editor; it was about the best piece of constructive work he could do.

O'Faolain put O'Connor's letter before the Editorial Board. Denis Johnston held firmly to the view that the Abbey was dead and not to be taken seriously as a theatre, but O'Faolain and O'Donnell held that it had to be taken seriously as an influence. All agreed that the caricature should not be brought out into the open since it was not the point at issue. *The Bell* would print O'Connor's letter, but without dragging in the issue of the caricature of Lennox Robinson. 'I asked for a Blitz on the Abbey', Sean told O'Connor and it was agreed, but they wanted to choose their ground. The plan was to mount an attack on the Abbey month by month. It would have to be done slowly and not have the appearance of a 'conspiracy'. They hoped, as a matter of public interest, to expose various 'scandals' connected with the theatre (1941).

He had O'Connor's letter checked by the solicitor, Herman Good, who advised that one passage was dangerous. He sent the relevant page to O'Connor, advised him as to the changes he was making on the proofs, told him they could not risk the Abbey Directors taking action. The Abbey would only have to serve a writ to get an injunction to prevent them from further comment, pending a case. 'It is far better for us to say what we can say, and keep on saying it, rather than be shut up at the outset' (1941). There was no question of the Editorial Board standing firm or risking financial loss (May 1941).

Louis D'Alton replied at length, but the reply would have exacerbated the row and O'Faolain tried to soften it. He redrafted D'Alton's letter and returned it. To his relief D'Alton reacted mildly and wrote a humorously dismissive reply to O'Connor's criticism. But the libel action was still possible, although O'Faolain thought the whole thing 'too intricate' to come to anything. He urged O'Connor not to write letters to the papers, to keep in touch with him, and to remember that they must act in concert (1941). He also suggested that O'Connor devise some alternative to The Belfry, if he thought it was not getting anywhere. 'You could try *the hostile witness* and criticise the whole bloody issue if you like?' He did not want to have to replace him as Poetry Editor. He would prefer to 'squabble' with him 'forever'. 'Please won't you let us go on squabbling? ... You are a lousy critic but you are as alive as a bucking bronco, and there must be someone to offset my academicism' (1941).

O'Connor's attack on *The Bell* drove O'Faolain into a bitter and furious response: 'I never see you *do* anything. Academy, Abbey, Bell, Drama

League, and I am sure in time Cuala – you will enjoy yourself blowholing at them all, and then chuck them. I suppose you think you are the Strong Man? To me you are in these matters of practical work, just one gigantic bubble of fart. That is your rôle – to stand up on the ditch and roar, and be the bullfrog blowing himself out, and saying all the time, "I am the Big Noise. All these other chaps are mean little whinging whining vaccillating conspiring Do Nothings". You co-operate with nobody, work with nobody, resign in a huff when you get tired, and go off feeling Pure and Noble.'

O'Faolain regretted this disgraceful outburst, admitting that not since 1923 when his irritation with Robert Langford burst had he behaved 'so outrageously . . . What maddens me is the toxic effect on my system. I alternately curse you, Evelyn, myself, and Ireland. So for Christ's sake let's keep away from one another until we, I, you, it heals' (SOF to FOC, 1941).

The libel case was scheduled for the New Year. O'Faolain briefed two senior counsels at a fee of £100 a day and suggested that O'Connor should pay off his part of the costs at the rate of a pound a week.[18] In the end J. J. O'Leary had to pay £250 in damages and *The Bell* £79. O'Faolain was sick of O'Connor. 'If Michael is down and out financially I am just miserable about it. But I am far more miserable, furious and miserable, at the way he is going sour and cockeyed . . . just now even I, and I've stood years and years of him, couldn't stand another hour'.[19]

The threat of libel was not the only worry. *The Bell* also had financial troubles. They raised the price to one shilling and sixpence in December 1941 and sales fell by a fourth. They had to pay for paper in advance and in September needed about £360. O'Donnell's business friends agreed to put up the £360 but wanted a businessman's control. The Board made over their shares to Eamon Martin on the understanding that the business men would not interfere with the editorial side. Even with this immediate financial problem solved, O'Faolain had to run the next three issues on 'buckshee articles' and he asked O'Connor had he 'any old stuff' (19 September 1942), but it was not easy to get material from O'Connor. O'Faolain asked repeatedly for an article, 'James Joyce: A Post-Mortem', which he could share with *Horizon*, and for the story 'Uprooted' which he wanted 'badly – both for its beauty and because it's buckshee!!' (12 October 1942.)

Although he was fully absorbed, O'Faolain felt isolated and depressed. 'Here it is cut off. Here it is the shut-eye of the year. Here nobody hears from anybody. Here England is a far away land. Here there's neither light nor life nor any hope but Joyce dead'. So, too, was his friend, F. R. Higgins, whose funeral he went to in Laracor, and the painter, Sir John Lavery. He had little inclination to write. 'You can't work when it seems as if nobody ever wants to see anything you do, and it all seems utterly unimportant'.[20]

Mentioning several examples of censorship and obstruction to O'Connor – the printer blocking his open letter to the Minister of Justice, the banning of a radio debate on education, the Minister inviting him into his office for a 'talk', the mixture of promise and threat in the Minister's remarks, his own hope of getting the incident in which five boys were flogged at school into *The Bell* – he made it clear that 'fighting' was hardly the word for what they were able to do; he could call it 'rear-guard action', or 'strategic withdrawals', or add a bit about 'near misses'. What they were doing required a 'long and patient process of attrition . . . the little drops that may or may not wear a dimple in the stone'. They had tried a frontal assault in the O'Dea case. He was not sure if that could be counted a success. 'We're still floating but barely just'.

Meanwhile O'Faolain had to do his work as editor. There were confusions in O'Connor's story 'The Mad Lomasneys', delays in getting 'The Grand Vizier', 'fey' bits in 'More Churches'. There was no subtitle for section 2 in that article and Evelyn, whom he had appointed as drama critic, was sometimes slow in getting her material in. He made two proposals to Sean McEntee, Minister for Local Government and Public Health: (i) that the Government should introduce an export subsidy scheme for periodicals, and (ii) that Government Departments should increase their advertising in *The Bell*. McEntee supported both, but the Departments found *The Bell* unsuitable for advertising and De Valera thought it would be unwise to promote the periodical abroad at that particular time.[21]

In June 1945 O'Faolain decided to give up being editor. The strain had become unbearable. He could not 'get free of dialectic . . . I grow totally pessimistic about Ireland and yet argue incessantly with myself about it'.[22] He stayed on as Book Editor for almost a year and brought about an immediate improvement in this section. He brought in new reviewers, both Irish and English. But he could not be associated with Peadar O'Donnell's 'concealed communism' at its peak, he thought, in his 'blatant support for the Jews without *one word* about the unfortunate Arabs'. O'Donnell had said that a Jew should be given a little farm in Donegal. But, O'Faolain asked, would 100,000 Jews be given farms in Ireland, with the intention of letting in thousands more? 'The shocking and brutal dishonesty of such a statement revolts me'.[23]

His farewell editorial does not tell the whole story. Editing *The Bell* was both stimulating and challenging. For the first time he was in charge. In all the other organizations with which he had been, and was, involved, he was frustrated by the apathy of members, or their timidity. Now his natural enthusiasm and energy could be channelled to good effect; he did not feel alienated. 'I was fully integrated because I was on the attack. I had accepted responsibility as a citizen and thought of myself as speaking for a great silent majority'.[24] He believed in an inclusive, non-sectarian democracy. He believed in the importance of ideas admitted from the outside. He believed that tradition must be examined and questioned. He respected individual independence of mind. He opposed censorship and clericalism. All his editorial attacks came from these basic beliefs. He set out to see clearly and to encourage others to see clearly, to get the facts and thereupon try to build for the future. In these demanding and stimulating years his true measure as a man appeared. Liberal, intellectual, Irish, Catholic, Nationalist, democratic, European, he was a man who spoke out with courage, conviction and concern. The note of lament for a lost idealism, and for a generation that had been short-changed gave his remarks a warm human dimension. He did not allow the pressures to warp his feelings. In the end he got tired, not embittered.

The Bell had only a small staff: Peadar O'Donnell, who was the General Manager, O'Faolain as editor, a woman secretary, Paddy Rooney, the accountant, an advertising manager, and the Assistant Editor Harry L. Craig, a student at Trinity College, who was well-known for the lack of order in his life and his sexual pursuits. He is portrayed mockingly in 'Charlie's Greek'. Craig attributed his success with women to his having a double duct in his penis. But he was a useful jack-of-all-trades who solicited material, helped with the proofs, wrote an editorial in the editor's absence and did the shopping when Eileen was in hospital.

At the end of the war, when *The Bell* had moved to no. 2 O'Connell Street, close to the Bridge and with a pleasant view over the Liffey, Honor Tracy joined the staff, but she worked first at Cahills where Sean gave her editorial responsibility for the French and Spanish editions of the *Irish*

Digest. J. J., however, could be an inconsiderate employer. He boasted about having Sean as a friend and often brought friends to Knockaderry, but Sean, and Eileen in particular, resented his phoning Sean at inconvenient times. Finally Sean resigned. The immediate cause was a row between them when J. J. rebuked a member of his staff. Sean informed J. J. of his fury and sought a guarantee that J. J. would not go over his head again. Unyielding letters went back and forth.

On the afternoon that he resigned Honor arrived back from a boozy lunch. Telling her of his relief, he said he felt so happy that he could kiss her. 'Why don't you?' she asked. When he did her eyes, to his astonishment, filled with tears and she blushed. That kiss and that blush transformed her in his eyes into a shining, warmhearted, responsive girl who liked him. He saw how 'handsome' she was and when she also wrote out a one sentence letter of resignation he kissed her again for her loyalty. She was, he realized, 'as vulnerable as a girl of fifteen'. In his elation he swept the eight photographs of J. J. off the office mantelpiece and together, laughing, they slammed their heels into the glass of the frames.

To some people's surprise they became lovers. One day in her small room in Nassau Street as he looked out at the grounds of Trinity College, he heard her ask, impatiently, 'Well? Are you going to make love to me?'. Her bared figure, he declared, would have delighted a Rubens, a Brueghel, a muscular Maillol, a fat-loving Titian. Afterwards, she said, 'If I had known you were as good as this I would have had the trousers off you long ago'. He was 'shocked at this coarse flattery' and pointed out that he could not know whether he was, or was not, 'good'. Her 'erotic expertise' continued to delight him.

Thirteen years younger than him, with flaming red hair, a pug nose and a curiously quilted face in which the eyes were barely visible, she was stocky and unattractive. But she was argumentative, outrageous, brilliant, witty, and intelligent. She cultivated an uproariously funny stage Irish manner and although nominally Catholic was outspokenly anti-clerical. O'Faolain became her mentor both in her writing and in the acerbic Irish Catholicism that characterized his thinking at this period. In her was externalized, in a liberated form, the tension O'Faolain himself felt between an atavistic Catholicism, based on early training, and a modernist antagonism based on his reading of Maritain, George Tyrell and Maisie Ward.[25] No self-respecting intellectual, he felt, could remain a Catholic in that Ireland.[26]

Honor's uninhibited clarity was valuable to a man still struggling to free himself from 'pietism, puritanism and patriotism', youthful idealism, romanticism, his later Platonism and Berkeleyism, and his inextricable bonds with Ireland (VM, 330). Her extrovert, rebellious personality and what he saw as an amoral nature attracted his more cautious temperament. She came into his life at a time when he was feeling particularly desolate, starved of affection, recurrently dispirited and unable to write. Known as 'hot pants Tracy', she swept aside scruples, and for years he was caught up in her emotional, exciting personality. He found her 'faithful, clear-cut, unselfconscious' and altogether and refreshingly different from the type of Irish woman to which he was accustomed. She was dangerous: 'a charming, unbeautiful, fatal woman'.

[11]

The *Bell* Years

THE thinking behind O'Faolain's management of *The Bell* permeated his biography of Hugh O'Neill, Earl of Tyrone (1550–1616), which he wrote between the summer of 1940 and February 1942. O'Neill's greatness, he argued, came from his realization that, by joining his struggle for independence from Tudor colonization with the Counter-Reformation movement in Europe, he could break through tribalism to create a confederacy. At the same time, while he understood the advantages of centralized power and of Renaissance manners and thinking, he was proud of his own culture. For him the patriarchal, pastoral Gaelic world, which the Tudors saw as antique and savage, was home. He was torn between an instinctive bond with what he loved and an intellectual awareness of what he must do to save it. O'Faolain defined him as a pragmatist who knew the weaknesses of his people, but gave them the chance to become part of something greater. By thinking creatively he made his people self-critical and objective about themselves and the world around them. He led them into contact with a Europe in which the principle of change and development was supreme. He was not, as often portrayed, a romantic patriot rising blindly and instinctively against Tudor aggression. That myth failed to include, because its originators did not accept, his repeated submissions to Elizabeth I. O'Faolain saw these as a strategy of survival, the calculated policy of a man who knew how to deal with a superior power. His dissimulations, mock obeisances, constant truces and frequent pardons were deliberate. Like O'Connell's, his mind was usefully whorled with reservations.

Patient, constructive, intelligent work, composed of success and failure, advance and strategic withdrawal, was exactly how O'Faolain viewed his own work at *The Bell*. He attacked when it suited him, bided his time, prepared the ground, gathered the evidence, enforced his policies on contributors, wore down the middle-class, officialdom and the Church, undermined and affected what they stood for in steady constructive criticism. When the risks seemed too great or endangered *The Bell*'s freedom, he quietened down and urged his colleagues to stay calm. His need to keep Frank O'Connor on a tight rein resembled O'Neill's need to restrain the impulsive Hugh O'Donnell. O'Faolain had to steady those who wanted an all-out offensive on the Government, the Church, the Language Policy, Education, Censorship, or whatever. For years *The Bell* avoided controversy and abstraction. The differences between O'Faolain's praise of O'Connell the semi-mystical leader, and his praise of O'Neill, the intellectual, measures O'Faolain's development in these years. He admired O'Neill's ability to assess and act on evidence. He identified with him. One of the great faults in the Irish character, in his view, was lack of analysis, indifference to self-awareness and a preference for unrestrained emotional response. Like O'Neill with his sense of a people locked into an outdated and unexamined system of loyalties, O'Faolain saw himself trying to work with a public who complacently accepted Irish life as they found it. Like O'Neill he wanted to inject speculative energy into that situation. Like O'Neill he believed that the past must be examined in order to move the country forward with new, fertile ideas. The tragedy of O'Neill's defeat at Kinsale, by the very forces he had sought to transcend, resembled Sean's feeling of defeat when he gave up the editorship. In O'Neill's predicament he saw the lineaments of his own situation and the shadow of his own eventual defeat. The pressure of that realization contributed to his breakdown in the summer of 1941.

O'Faolain, too, was torn between attraction and disaffection. Ireland was his fated field, but he was recurrently so alienated by certain aspects of it that he despaired of being able to write about it intelligently. The more he analyzed it, the less amenable it became to imaginative interpretation. The dichotomy emerged in almost everything he wrote: articles and editorials that condemned political or ideological shortcomings yet claimed that Ireland was not such a bad place; Frankie Hannafey's ambivalence in *Come Back to Erin*, and stories in *Teresa* (1947) that on the one hand pour out love for the Irish way of life and on the other reveal its drawbacks.

In some respects *Come Back to Erin* was an apologia. It explained Frankie Hannafey's behaviour after he had escaped from the straightjacket of his political idealism in the same way that O'Faolain explained T. E. Lawrence's love of books and music as 'his recompense for the starvation of that active life of the soldier. He had lived for years under the lash of his own idealism until he had become almost inhuman in trying to be superhuman, as pitiless to himself as to others, almost brutish'.[1] That explained Frankie's embrace of theatre, music, books and Bea Hannafey. It explained O'Faolain's behaviour both before and after he had disentangled himself from nationalism. In *Teresa*, stories like 'The Silence of the Valley', 'The Man Who Invented Sin' and 'Lady Lucifer' show a deep love for the Irish countryside. The doctor in 'Lady Lucifer' expresses love of country together with rejection of its narrowness. Human feelings, he avers, are composed of a shifting tension of opposites. He can admire the pride of the nurse who devotes her life to minding the madman she loves but hates the humility that makes such self-denial possible.

O'Faolain was relieved to escape from 'the prison of a biography'. He felt he could breathe again. He wanted to visit London, to write fiction; he suggested subjects for talks to the BBC and submitted work to Radio Eireann. He objected strongly when Radio Eireann began to pay contributors in pounds rather than guineas. In April 1941 he wrote to the *Irish Times* condemning the 'miserable fees' paid to Irish writers by newspapers and radio. The papers gave ten shillings for a thousand words, the radio two to three guineas for a thirty minute programme. The BBC paid ten to thirty guineas. PEN had twice approached RTE about their low fees. What writers needed, he said, was a trade union to fight for better treatment. He would try to form a union, if he got a sufficient response to this letter.[2] WAAMA (Writers Artists Actors Musicians Association) grew out of this invitation.[3] He told Roibeárd Ó Faracháin, Director of Talks, that he would not give his talk on *Knocknagow* unless they paid him what they owed. Ó Faracháin promptly cancelled the talk.[4] O'Faolain objected, but when Eileen had to withdraw her talk on 'I Went to Gettysburg', he quickly substituted one on 'American History in Fiction' and used the occasion to illustrate the amount of work and time involved in preparing a talk and the inadequacy of the remuneration: he worked at it at full belt from 3.00 p.m. on Monday until Wednesday at 12.30 p.m. He did this just to see how fast he could do it, turned over all his old American notes, consulted two books of reference, ran through a history of the American novel, and skimmed through six novels. Had the talk been prepared under humane conditions it would have taken four or five days. A fee of five guineas for such work, he argued, was shocking. He asked Ó Faracháin to pass his letter on to Dr. Thomas Kiernan, Director of Broadcasting, with a request on his behalf that it be passed on to the Minister for Finance. Were he, or any other scriptwriter, to work consistently at this slave-driven speed, he would break up in a fortnight.[5]

July and August 1941 were bad months. The threat of the libel action remained and he was trying to complete his biography of O'Neill. He had a nervous breakdown, could not read manuscripts, hated the telephone, resigned from four committees, and was 'ill' and 'idle'. He just 'couldn't keep up with the silly running and racing to which his nervous glands condemn him'.[6] The doctor told him he would be subnormal all winter. He took a glass of plain porter three times a day and each day walked for a mile and a half. He and Eileen cycled in Co. Wicklow for three days and decided to move away — to a five-room cottage in the country, preferably near Kilkenny.

He was 'exhausted' by *The Bell* which made him feel 'like a wet nurse to a family of about ten puling children every day'. He worked to keep boredom at bay. Even when he went to see Mac Liammoir in *Antony and Cleopatra*, he did so 'without enthusiasm'.[7] He was cheered by the publication of *The Great O'Neill*. While he knew it was not 'sparkling', it was 'pretty accurate'. He had based the historical record on J. K. Graham's thesis, 'An Historical Study of Hugh O'Neill', done at Queen's University and on his own research, but the psychological portrait was his own. Foley liked it, but O'Connor thought that the subject did not suit O'Faolain who attributed too much significance to O'Neill's ambiguities. Had he done it, he would have written it as comedy. O'Faolain was unimpressed with this view.

He was pleased by Frank O'Connor's article on 'The Future of Irish Literature'. 'When O'Faolain and I began to write,' O'Connor said, 'it was with some idea of replacing the subjective, idealistic, and romantic literature of Yeats, Lady Gregory and Synge by one modelled on the Russian novelists' but, O'Connor said, the comparison had been overworked. The Russian writer handled all levels of society; in Ireland 'the moment a writer raises his eyes from the slums and cabins, he finds nothing but a vicious and ignorant middle-class, and for aristocracy the remnants of an English garrison, alien in religion and education'. O'Connor described the progression in O'Faolain's work from the quiet lyricism of *A Nest of Simple Folk* to the horrified vision in *Bird Alone*. Of *She Had to Do Something*, he wrote that for the first time O'Faolain looked at his material through the eyes of an outsider and saw how preposterous it was. He praised the central section of *Come Back to Erin* in which the revolutionary falls in love with his step-brother's wife.[8] Almost for the first time, O'Faolain told O'Connor in response, he felt he was a real writer – 'the kind of feeling one wants to feel when fourteen'. He suggested that O'Connor do a series of articles for *The Bell*. 'You know the way AE and Corkery excited us with fine familiar generalisation. There are lots of young fellows who want this stimulation. You can do it'. He concluded his letter: 'Affectionately and with all my old admiration. When you write you come to life. We live on the points of our pens. How disgusting'.

When O'Connor was banned from Radio Eireann, O'Faolain used WAAMA to oppose it. Concerned for O'Connor's loss of income, he offered to lend him money, and arranged to pay him in advance for material to be given to *The Bell*. He also got a job for Evelyn at Radio Eireann. It was not clear why O'Connor had been banned. O'Faolain could think of three possible reasons: a broadcast that O'Connor did for the BBC in which he was critical of Irish neutrality, his article in *Horizon*, or his relationship with Evelyn Bowen, Robert Speaight's wife. He went to see P. J. Little, Minister for Posts and Telegraphs, got Frank Duff to act as go-between, talked with Roibeárd Ó Farachán and kept in touch with O'Connor. Little agreed that O'Connor could do radio work under a pseudonym, but O'Connor refused.[9] O'Faolain went to see the Minister's Secretary, 'a most cautious and careful and sympathetic bloke', and reported on the delicate stages of his meeting: he had intimated his suspicion that the so-called 'moral issue' was being raised but that on that they (he and WAAMA) would fight; he got assurances that this was not the main issue. Was it political? he asked, and was told it was. He asked if a man was not entitled to criticize Radio Eireann and gathered that he was. He asked whether it was external and gathered that it definitely was. He knew then that it was O'Connor's BBC broadcast that was the issue. He also got the impression that the Department felt that they (O'Connor, O'Faolain, and WAAMA) would find that hard to fight. O'Connor's divorce action complicated his efforts to negotiate him back into Radio Eireann. Feeling that the Minister's reservations were likely to have been strengthened by concern about the attitude of the Archbishop of Dublin, John Charles McQuaid, he asked Duff to find out what the Archbishop's views were. Duff advised O'Connor to send the Archbishop a memorandum on the facts of the case.[10] O'Connor wrote to the Archbishop but was put off by the way in which the matter was handled. 'Your A', he told O'Faolain, 'is a pretty fencer . . . It's all quite futile . . .'[11] O'Faolain disliked having to discuss O'Connor's private life. 'I feel rotten about this poking about in your affairs, and people talking about you, as it is the thing my extremely private soul loathes for myself'.

O'Faolain felt that the Left were being driven underground. 'Let's come out', he said, 'and eat the Right'. He arranged a dinner party at Knockaderry to which he invited Peadar O'Donnell, Frank O'Connor, Frank Duff, Head of the Legion of Mary, and Leon Ó Broin, editor of its journal, the *Maria Legionis*. O'Connor and O'Donnell complained that censorship was supported by the Catholic Church. O'Faolain expressed the view that the Legion of Mary was largely responsible for the atmosphere in which it was possible to suppress writers. But Frank Duff argued that the Legion also suffered at the hands of ecclesiastical authorities. Should they not get together to discuss the matter?[12] That was the result O'Faolain wanted. They decided to found the Common Ground Society with the intention of bringing the Left and Right together to discuss ideas without acrimony. The first meeting took place on 20 December 1942 in the Gresham Hotel. O'Faolain had promises from O'Donnell, Maurice Walsh, D. J. Giltinan, Sean O'Sullivan, to attend, and he hoped O'Connor would 'drop in'. These represented the Left. From the Right he expected Frank Duff, Leon Ó Broin, Roibeárd Ó Faracháin and Francis MacManus. 'I intend to attack the Church, and leave them to say it's allright or else admit it needs a Reformation' (19 December 1942). Early meetings were well attended but Frank Duff, as chairman, was too authoritarian. Mervyn Wall compared him to Savonarola and Peadar O'Donnell walked out because Duff would not allow people to speak freely. There was little common ground between the two sides and by August 1943 O'Faolain lost faith in the Society.

Even though he was supposed to take life easy, he could not avoid being busy. A diary entry for the period records a day's events: 'morning: *Bell* leader and letter to *Times* re censorship; 2 – Unicorn to meet Frank Duff and discuss the ban at Radio Eireann on Frank O'Connor; 3.30 to hospital to see Julie; 4. Meet O'Connor at Anne's Tea Shop; 4.45 to Bewleys to get

Bell ms from H. L. Morrow. He did not as usual turn up; 5.30 to WAAMA meeting at 17 Harcourt St; 7.30 to Jury's to WAAMA Writers Guild meeting; 9 drink with Michael Farrell whom I found very sensitive and discouraged about his novel'; 'Tired and headache at home 11 p.m.'. 'That is No way to write a novel!' Nor was it a way to write short stories. *Teresa* (1947), which represents about eight years of work, is a slim collection. Before Christmas 1942 there was sickness at home: Eileen had flu, Stephen was sick, Julia had a tubercular gland, he himself had diarrhoea. He wished he were going to London. 'A visit to London keeps one in good humour for about a month.'[13] Looking over the January 1943 issue he noted that he had written seven of the entries himself, thereby keeping expenses down to £15, the amount O'Donnell said was available for contributors.

On 2 January 1943 he took down his novel for the first time in several weeks. Eileen was still in bed; he was not sure if she was ill. He went shopping with Julia, but Stephen had a sick stomach and he was soothing him until 1.30 a.m. On the fourth he again worked at the novel and was pleased: 'Good at novel'. Next day he went to Cahills to discuss the cover for the next issue, met O'Donnell at five, went to a WAAMA executive meeting at five thirty. The following day he lunched at the United Services Club with J. J. O'Leary. Eileen was still sick; he thought she had flu. Later in the month he worked hard on proofs for *The Bell* and was so tired he could only go to a film. He took part in a radio debate on social life in Ireland. On 20 January he gave another talk to the Common Ground and wrote a thousand words of his novel, but *The Bell* could not be ignored. 'Day after day *The Bell* occupies my time and attention'. At least O'Donnell liked his editorial on 'Gaelic. The Truth'. He noted that the happiness of seeing Julia and Stephen in one chair and she telling him Jack and the Beanstalk 'is so keen that if it were prolonged one would not be able to bear it'.

The pattern continued: an occasional party at the Van Hoeks', or the Collises', meetings with O'Donnell, Duff or Ó Broin about the Common Ground, work on *The Bell* or the *English Digest*, meetings with contributors, lunch or dinner with Elizabeth Bowen, the 'Encore' series of review essays for the *Irish Times*, book reviews, work on his novel, frustration over the apathy at the Academy. Recurrently he was 'tired', or 'very tired'. On 14 February he was 'under the weather. Feel I don't want to write ever again: that if I had a private income of £750 per annum I'd idle life away.

Urges come to write but they are weak and die out. Is this just flu-depression or being 43 next week?' He also noted 'Remarkable ms. by Behan (from Mountjoy) on Terrorism'. 'I find myself monthly having to face the task of filling 96 pages with a most exiguous budget, and cheese-paring poor devils who would welcome a guinea extra'.[14] 'My life', he judged, 'is just a blank. I have been scratching *hard* for a living – that is all. Perhaps *The Bell* is a little use?' A week later he noted the blank days. 'Man's life dribbles away'. In April he woke each day to boredom which he killed with work. He had made £111 since February. 'All is drudgery! Utter and mind-doping drudgery!' In October he wrote 'Never have I been so suicidally depressed. The frustration of this island is now complete'.

His mood was often affected by work on his novel. When it went well he was contented, when it went against him he felt frustrated. But there were compensations – swimming and sunbathing with the family on Killiney beach, picnics with friends on Dalkey Island, holidays in Graiguenama-nagh, or Kilkenny, or Gougane Barra, weekends in Hunter's Hotel in Co. Wicklow.[15] In 1944 his birthday was 'a very happy day . . . much petting all day', gifts from Eileen, Julia and Stephen, a telegram from Elizabeth Bowen, and in the evening he and Eileen went to the Marine Hotel and met an 'amusing' crowd. In 1945 he got gifts, worked 'happily all day' on his novel and 'everyone was forbearing and gentle'.

He got a letter from John V. Kelleher asking him to comment on his 'artistic development'. He professed not to have 'the foggiest idea' what Kelleher was talking about; the phrase gave him 'stage-fright, lock-jaw and house-maid's knee'. What Kelleher wanted, he realized, was an autobiogra-phy and he felt too much that the human mind was a 'whorl' to be able to speak of it as though it were a 'plate'. Nevertheless he had a shot at identifying the most important influences: 'the Catholic Religion (God damn and blast it) and Ireland (Ditto); add England, i.e. the Empire'. They were, he said, half-English no matter what the Gaels said. As for literary influence he identified the Russians – 'a bit like the Irish' – and Flaubert, 'so solid'. The Troubles, too, he felt, must 'have edged people's minds' and made them wake up to the problems based on all this – 'the Humanistic problem, and the difficulty of working out a way of life . . . In the end one becomes a European . . . and is merely an Irishman by local pigmentation.' Ireland was 'a bit of a bore' because the Catholic Church had got on top on the lowest possible terms, and everything was tiresomely elementary. There was no intellectual life worth speaking of. Writers, therefore, tended to write sourly. 'The dilemma of a few intelligent people in a very unintelligent milieu is without precedent'. Intellectuals can't help being that way, he thought. 'One really wants to enjoy sensuously, humanely, and write of the triumph of form over chaos – anything which is passionate, which destroys, or which creates, or which seems to be striving towards something. The story of defeats or achievements of the soul'. He attached a list of his favourite books: *Torrents of Spring*, *Charterhouse of Parma*, *Return of the Native*, Chekhov's tales and letters (the essence of intelligence and form), anything speculative, but he had no time for poetry. He praised Pater's *Marius the Epicurean* and its 'unforgettable chapter on the New Cyrenaicism'.[16]

That July the O'Faolains went on holidays to Gougane Barra, and stayed in Cronin's Hotel. It was a relaxed place. Dinny Cronin would often leave the hotel to look after itself while he went off for a day's fishing or shooting.[17] The whole family had a lovely time. The weather was fine and when they went to Bantry they were 'baked'. Jack Hendrick came out from Cork and Fr. Tim Traynor was on holidays as usual. Known locally as 'The Saint', Traynor was a large, overweight, easy-going, emotional man whom O'Faolain and O'Connor liked immensely. He humanized the Church for them. The three men cycled through the Pass of Kemeneigh to swim in a pool in their pelts. The children also had a good time. Stephen, an attractive, curly-headed boy, with blue eyes and long eyelashes, developed a crush on Fr. Traynor, Julia went 'all romantic' and sat plaiting rushes in a boat all alone. In the evenings they visited Tim Buckley, 'The Tailor', and his wife, Ansty. Their little cottage on the side of the road leading into the valley was a gathering place for those who enjoyed The Tailor's almost non-stop commentary on neighbours, local incidents, past events and the world at large. He had an endless supply of stories. His conversations were natural, coarse, opinionated, and enriched by his memory of what people said, did and thought in the past. O'Faolain enjoyed the characters in the hotel bar: 'Drunks, dipsomaniacs, teachers, jackeens from Dublin, civil and uncivil servants, wild men from the hills, etc. come and go and make the nights resound'. So far there had only been one fight. 'The days disappear unnoticed. It is surely a last and magical corner'.[18]

He went to London in January 1944, was caught in two air-raids, but had an enjoyable visit. He had lunch or dinner with Elizabeth Bowen, Tom

Sean's parents with the three boys:
Sean, Pat and Gus (from left to right)

Sean, aged twelve, with his mother

Presentation Brothers College, Cork

Revd Brother E. I. Connolly, LL.I

Eileen, Sean's wife

Eamon De Valera, addressing a meeting, December 19

Frank O'Connor

Elizabeth Bowen

Edward Garnett

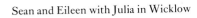
Sean and Eileen with Julia in Wicklow

Sean with Julia and Stephen in a
hired tinker's van, touring West Cork in 1946

Sean with his cat

Alene Erlanger in the mid-1950s

Sean and Eileen on holiday

The portrait by Sean O'Sullivan, 1963

Carol Smith

Elfreda Powell

In Rome in 1974, during the filming for his programme on the *Vatican*, in the RTE series 'Personal Account'

1972, at home

1990

Lindsay, Nicholas Mansergh, Violet Connolly, Rose Macaulay. But London was not as it used to be: there were 'no golden afternoons and golden wine, no luxury, little suavity, much courage and gutsiness and more friendliness, through all the dust and grime and grimness'. He enjoyed the pubs where all ranks of all armies drank weak beer and sang strong songs.[19]

In April he visited his mother in the North Infirmary. She was dying, but he could not face it. It was an emotional time for him, although his distress at his mother's decline was alleviated by meetings with Nancy McCarthy. He told her he did not want to be involved. Instead she was to phone him when his mother was near the end and he would go down. She phoned almost every day, because Bridget was very weak. She died on 13 May. He phoned Gus, notified Aunt Nan, and sent a telegram to Fr. Pat. Her remains were removed to SS. Peter and Paul's Church and buried on 15 May. Because of petrol rationing they used a horse-drawn hearse. Nancy and Sean, the only mourners, followed in a tattered carriage. He was very upset. The driver who wore a black hat above a very white face and red nose leaned into the carriage and inquired mournfully 'A walk or a trot, Sir?'

He brought his mother's old handbag to Dublin and examined it with revulsion; it revived his sense of her miserable, self-denying piety. Going through it was a 'painful business . . . with its pathetic snuff-tin, bits of holy bread . . . her specs and a brass ring . . . I burned the lot in haste and horror — a childish further effort to blot out. Now I have a feeling it is all going to come back to me like Mr. Asinine Wordsworth's "emotion recollected in tranquillity" (*my eye*)'. His mother's affairs were in disarray, but he was in no mood to sort them out. He felt 'all sore inside and physically weak'. He paid her doctor's bill, but she had other creditors, bookmakers and pawnbrokers. The only way to deal with them was to return to Cork. He went down in July. Meanwhile he thanked Nancy for her support. It helps 'enormously', he told her, 'that so many of those hours were happy with you'. But now he was 'fed up with humanity and feeling and emotion' and was going to use his 'nut for a few days' rest'.[20]

In July Sean and Eileen were invited to Cork by William Dwyer, Director of Sunbeam Wolsey, for the Kermesse week that he organized. The festival included a performance of *Midsummer Night's Dream* by the Cork Symphony Orchestra, conducted by Aloys Fleischmann, with massed choirs. In the course of the official dinner Alfred O'Rahilly came over to the table where the O'Faolains were seated and was fulsome.[21] But there was no reconciliation. O'Faolain had housed that grudge for many years. When O'Rahilly was President of University College Cork and wanted to confer an honorary degree on him, O'Faolain contemptuously dismissed the offer. Some years later when they happened to be on the same plane going to London, O'Rahilly invited O'Faolain to sit with him. O'Faolain replied that he had some reading to do and remained in his seat.

When they got back to Dublin they had a scare about Julia who was almost drowned in the baths at Dunlaoghaire. She returned home looking very pale and limp and had very bad headaches afterwards. In November Eileen had to enter the Portobello Nursing Home. She advised Nancy McCarthy to take an egg flip every day. Last year, she said, she had lived on liver injections and this year on raw eggs. Sean discouraged her from returning home early in December because the children had whooping cough, their friends were in and out of the house, and there was 'pandemonium'. She described her examination with some glee: strapped in a gynaecological chair with her legs aloft 'like a dead hen's'. 'They poke all sorts of evil looking hooked instruments into you. Honestly I thought some of them would come out through my mouth!' She was said to have 'a really beautiful peroneum . . . I am beginning to think I ought to have it photographed and used as a Christmas card for my friends! Do I shock you? Can you take it?' Despite the good report, she was weak, could get up for only thirty minutes each day, and had to remain in the Home for another ten days.[22] Sean coped as best he could, but he had a cold, was on a jury list, and his work piled up. He asked Nancy to send him perfume for Eileen for Christmas – Chanel or Coty. Eileen returned home on 14 December 'very groggy'. She had a restless first night: the children had their father up at two a.m. and at five a.m. with bad paroxysms of whooping.[23] On the day Eileen returned Sean began his short story 'Passion', which was based on his love for Honor Tracy. Eileen was slow to recover, found walking difficult, and was very ill on the nineteenth as though from food poisoning. Nevertheless she enjoyed Christmas. Sean was rushing about looking after things. Julia, who was wild and spirited, fell into a horse pond and came home dripping wet. She was put to bed with a hot water bottle, but when her friend, Marie Rush, arrived they opened the bottle and threw water at each other. Four blankets were soaked. On another occasion Julia nearly set the house on fire putting candles on her toy theatre.[24] Eileen returned to the nursing home for another examination at the end of January.

A publisher in Buenos Aires asked O'Faolain to edit a collection of Irish short stories. Writing to O'Connor requesting permission to use two of his stories, he loosely outlined the terms: about thirty pounds divided between twenty-three writers, which amounted to two guineas for each of O'Connor's stories. The balance after paying for typing, postage, cables would be his own editorial fee. *The Bell*, he said, was also thinking of producing a similar collection: *Irish Short Stories Today*. Would O'Connor allow them to reprint the same two stories for a further fee of four guineas? (September 1944.)

He got no reply. He wrote again, saying that everyone, except O'Connor, had agreed. He made changes in the proposed terms. They had paid O'Connor twelve guineas in November 1943 for 'the privilege' of reprinting three of his stories. They received one. That left eight guineas. 'Suppose we wash that out in return for the permissions I am now asking?' If the idea of a British anthology did not come off then O'Connor would only owe them one story. At the end of this letter he remarked: 'we are a little hurt to notice that you refused us a poem for *Irish Poems Today* (1944) and gave one to the *Irish Times* for their anthology, *Poems from Ireland*. Are we as awful as all that?' Their book, he said, had sold about 2000 copies and WAAMA made £50 (21 January 1945).

O'Connor accused O'Faolain of megalomania. He told Sean Hendrick that he had given up writing for *The Bell*, when O'Faolain started sending him letters written by the office boy, beginning Dear Michael and ending per and pro S. O'Faolain. 'Among the forms of hallucinations of grandeur I never before heard of a man that thought himself a limited company'.[25] He explained to O'Faolain that he gave a poem to the *Irish Times*, because its anthology was a serious attempt to present Irish poetry and not a stunt to catch customers or provide funds for a trades union. He offered O'Faolain two Hull lectures by way of wiping out his debt to *The Bell*. He would not go into the *Bell* short story anthology with O'Faolain acting as his agent.[26]

In reply O'Faolain urged O'Connor to distinguish between Irish surroundings that had hurt him and fellow writers who had not. 'The true facts are that there is not a person of any intelligence or discrimination in Ireland, or elsewhere . . . who does not admire you enormously . . . even those whom you have been grossly rude to, time and again, can surmount their disgust and still admire you as a writer. Do you remember the last time I had the pleasure of reviewing your stories – I think in *The Spectator*? I said that half a dozen more books like that and your position was as assured as Tchekov's, and I indicated, too, some flaws as they seemed to me. The day that paper arrived I drove into Dublin from Killough and found you in the Pembroke Library and you made a friendly swipe at me and we were satisfied that we were two normal people and two normal artists watching each other's work in emulation and admiration.'

When O'Connor refused a poem for their anthology and refused to allow review copies of his books to be sent to *The Bell*, 'then everything', O'Faolain told him, 'collapses into something really filthy and destructive and uncivilized. Personal dislikes and prejudices and all sorts of maggots ruin everything.' He was making things too hard when he refused a fellow-writer the right to make an anthology for South America, for he would not do it unless O'Connor was included. 'You will realise, please do try to realise that I would not waste half an hour writing to you like this for any other reason than your own true worth. I am not holding out an olive branch. I recognise that things get to a point and get stuck and we have both, at most, twenty years of life and either of us might snuff out like Fred Higgins any year, and I recognise, with sorrow, that things are nevertheless going to remain "stuck" now for ever'. He was not irked about the eight guineas. He was not trying to be his agent. He would very much like to see the Hull lectures.

But O'Connor would not be placated. His reply was uncompromising: 'The gall and bitterness is all yours . . . I don't want to have anything to do with you in the way of business . . . you're no longer capable of doing anything except with a multiplicity of motives . . . All the motives are honourable, but all together they're awful'. *The Bell*, O'Connor added, was 'the reflection of a mind swamped in a multiplicity of motives . . . like Corkery's stories . . . gives him the horrors. You and Dev how you both love the second-rate!' After that final thrust he invited O'Faolain to meet him for tea.[27] They continued to meet for lunch or a cup of tea, but O'Faolain's energy was poor and he felt gloomy. He had low blood pressure and about once a year would 'fall down a dark hole' and could face nothing. With Eileen and Stephen he went to Hunter's Hotel to rest.

[12]

Italy and *Newman's Way*

WHEN Graham Greene invited him to go to Italy in 1947 to write a travel book, Sean's first reaction was that he could not afford such a journey, but when Greene said Eyre and Spottiswoode would cover expenses with an advance of £500, he gladly accepted. It was the beginning of a new life, the first of many journeys. The articles and books he wrote on Italy opened a career for him as an international journalist writing for glossy American magazines that paid well. For the first time he did not have to worry as to where the next penny would come from. The cosmopolitan European writer replaced the embattled Irish intellectual. He wrote less about Irish conditions. Even his fiction became non-Irish in settings and characters, although he still wrestled with the problem of how to be an Irish writer. More than anything else Italy helped him to find a new perspective on human nature. He found there a different kind of Catholicism, a happier balance of opposites than the doctor had outlined in 'Lady Lucifer', and a much more lenient view of life than he himself had revealed in *Purse of Coppers* and *Bird Alone*.

The immediate result of Greene's offer was *A Summer in Italy* (1949), a mixture of romance and realism, in which O'Faolain, the traveller from the cold, puritanical north luxuriates in the sensuous delights of the warm, easygoing south. 'I do not understand', he wrote, adapting happily to the new life, 'how moralists divide the flesh from the spirit. To the Italians who live life to the full, brimming it over, throwing their whole bodies and souls into everything they do, life must be an indivisible oneness; whereas we, of this forbidding North, who measure and strain, tuck God away in the Church and Venus away in the bed, and miserably and foolishly drain each part of life on the richness of the other . . . For them sacred and mortal love are confederate, all rolled into one big, warm featherbed' (SI, 22–23).[1]

Italy had a profound effect on him. Whenever he crossed the Italian frontier, he shed hundreds of uncomfortable inhibitions and felt at home.[2] Year after year Italy opened his mind to the 'successful complexity' of a culture very different from Ireland's (VM, 336). He saw all those devout Catholics forgetting to go to mass, having passionate love-affairs, screaming at each other, but above all smiling. His return to Catholicism, which he called a conversion, was the outward mark of a profound internal change brought about by his contact with Italy. He had not been to confession since he had been excommunicated during the Civil War. Now in 1947 he entered a confessional in St. Peter's and, in his initial enthusiasm, which he later called 'a purely emotional sentimental illusion', said that he left a nation to join an empire (SI, 162). For the first time in his life he could be 'spontaneous and unrestrained about every element, attractive and unattractive' in the way of life he described. He 'felt emancipated as man and as artist' (VM, 334).

But he was not liberated from the moral dilemma caused by his affair with Honor Tracy. He could make his peace with the Catholic Church by embracing a less puritanical version of it, but the rules were essentially the same. Not even Rome condoned adultery. The euphoria he felt on leaving St. Peter's, in itself indicative of his need for belonging, inevitably came up against the force of his passion for Honor and the force of her more wilful, turbulent temperament. For a while she respected his submission to the moral law. She sent a telegram to her friend, Enriqueta Harris (later Frankfurt), saying 'Come to Venice'. When Enriqueta arrived she found Sean already there and realized that she was meant to give respectability to the situation. In *Summer in Italy* she is Rebecca, the young Jewish art historian, and the red-haired Honor is the man, Ginger. They went round together, visiting churches, eating in restaurants, swimming in Torcello. In the book Sean romanticised the whole experience. It seemed odd to Enriqueta that she should have been summoned to Venice.[3] But she was not so much a figleaf as a sword between the lovers. She found that Sean and Honor had been to confession at San Marco and now needed her to help them from relapsing into 'sin'. While she was there Honor slept in her room. Then Honor was called back to London, sent on assignment to Japan and the moral problem was resolved for the time being.

When he got back to Ireland, Sean worked at his Italian book through the Autumn of 1947 and the Spring of 1948. He found writing it a 'pleasure and a torment'. Nothing, he declared, would make a cosmopolitan of him. He struggled with 'the fascinating but exasperating problem' of where Saint Peter was buried and recognized that compulsion to get at the truth as part of his need as a rationalist. He could not abandon himself to sensual experience. After Rome there was Venice, but he feared the 'last terrible mile when the bloodtide is low and a breakdown is round the corner'; 'dear Honor Tracy' he added, was in Japan.[4]

Longmans asked him to write a life of Cardinal Newman and offered an advance of £1000, but he was not happy with the prospect of writing two books so far removed from what he really wanted to do. He got liver-injections for his 'annual low-blood pressure collapse into inertia', took Benzedrine, hammered away at his Italian book, corrected proofs of *The Short Story*, prepared talks for the BBC, did his book reviews, and dropped a big log on his toe. When the travel book was done, he went to London for a holiday and then to Oxford to begin reading for the book on Newman.

At the end of 1948 the BBC agreed that Sean should do a programme on the excavations at St. Peter's. Buoyed up by the success of 'Return to Cork' which he had done in September, he pressed them to think of a feature rather than a talk. He wanted to go to Rome with a camera crew and a microphone to interview archaeologists and historians in the crypt of St. Peter's or the crypt of Lucine. He attached a draft of the 'flow' of the treatment.[5] He was furious when the BBC told him by telegram that they had decided not to go ahead. He had already booked plane, train and bus tickets, made hotel reservations, paid deposits, made appointments. 'I'm involved up to the neck'. He rejected the excuse that there was an embargo on the subject. There can be no embargo, he said; there is nothing private, secret or copyright about the excavations and he gave them examples of articles already published about them. As to their objection that it would mean basing a programme on speculation, he said, of course it would involve speculation. 'I should not dream of making a definite statement about these *scavi*'.[6] He went to Rome as planned and afterwards went to Naples for which he developed a particular fascination.

In September he and Eileen travelled to Rome via Paris and Lausanne, then went on to Naples and Ravenna. They stayed on the island of Ischia, where they went swimming at the little beach of Carta Romana, and sunbathed beside the warm salt-water springs. After Ischia, Eileen went home and Sean wandered south until November to collect material for his second travel book, continuing his love-affair with Italy. In *South to Sicily* (1953), the fascination is less with sensuous delights, although these are always there, than with the nature of life, the attitude to religion, the racial mix, and the huge social problems.

Naples, he said, was where one passed from one Italy to another, from the more stable North to where no civil pattern had lasted long enough to create any stable tradition (SS, 47). He noted the distinction he found in the South between amorality and immorality, but gave up trying to understand it. 'Perhaps one of the reasons why I am a Catholic is because it is all beyond me and I have to have Somebody in whose hands I can leave it all with that sort of hope and trust that springs from despair. I do not know how it all works. I gave it up long ago.' Observing the emotional intensity of people crying for the blood of Januarius to liquefy, he was dazzled and bewildered, but found his imagination could not rise to that level of vulgar credulity. He responded more readily to the quiet, traditional celebration of Mass and the administration of sacraments in a nearby church. Both, he judged, were part of the folk world of the Neapolitans. 'The Beast is always scratching at their doors. In fear they pray to their saints or curse them. What Irishman 'familiar with the same dark anarchy of the soul, of all life, would not recognise the signs at once!' (SS, 45).

He was in Taranto in late October 1952. He gives a heightened account of storm, sudden darkness as the electricity went off, and lightning illuminating the great temples. 'I saw another temple. And another. They kept coming up and vanishing at every flash . . .' Heedless of the cool rain, he went out naked on to the balcony and 'gazed and gazed into the dusk for these erratic apparitions of Grecian gold. Was that honeyed line the temple of Juno? There was Zeus!' (SS, 144). On this night of fierce autumnal storm Honor Tracy joined him. They had hot reviving drinks in the bar, and a good meal in the dining room. When Honor went to take a bath and found the water cold, she flung open the French windows, stepped out naked on to the balcony, a red-haired, splendid pagan goddess upstretching her breasts to the black downpour, the thunder, the lightning. That night the storm, the place, the pagan myth made them one with the temples of Hercules, Concordia, Juno, Zeus.

After that night of passion it was, he says, some months before they met again, this time in Venice, near St. Mark's. It was the Feast of Portiuncula. He told Honor how his mother loved this feast, because of the vast number of indulgences she could earn by repeated visits to the church of SS. Peter and Paul. Honor was immediately enraptured. 'Let's do it, Nicky! What fun! The Ins and Outs! We must do it!' He pointed out that first one had to go to Confession and Communion. She insisted that if he loved her he must do it. He pointed out that he had already made and broken his peace with Rome solely because of her. Was he to make another treaty for her sake and then break it that night? She begged, with tears in her eyes, and he submitted. He 'confessed, recanted, fore-promised, expressed contrition, lied, was forgiven, emerged doubly apostate'. Like the woman in 'Lovers of the Lake', a story that recreates their situation, she emerged, tardily, radiantly: she had refused to give him up, argued, wept, got conditional absolution. 'I won', she said. They went to Mass and Communion. Honor was happy, but he was in despair, feeling they had betrayed the Church and themselves. In Paris he consulted a priest who made him face the truth: he loved Eileen, he could not make Honor happy, so what was the point of continuing the affair? (VM, 344–46).

Honor was very upset. She told Frank O'Connor that Sean had written to her saying 'Eileen won't let me see you anymore'. She thought that a spineless way of dealing with the problem.[7] Sean struggled for consistency of behaviour. When O'Connor left Evelyn and took up with Joan O'Donovan, he confessed to being a poor judge of 'such emotional intensities and convolutions'. He could understand a man having an affair with another woman, could understand that his marriage might be wrecked by it, but he could not understand him setting up all over again with yet another woman. 'I can only swear to God he's not so madly in love as all that!' In these matters, he decided, men have no will whatever. Therefore a man is always alternatively behaving like a cad or a gentleman. The only solution is to behave like a cad constantly. Alternating between the two can only bewilder himself and the women, neither of whom can decide what to make of him – 'if you are a cad to one woman, damn it, you are a cad!'[8] Was it consistency of behaviour or a desire for peace at home that made him give up the affair with Honor? She was still his 'dear Honor Tracy' whom he revered in late 1953, but within six months there was yet another woman. Honor meanwhile had a nervous breakdown and was in a nursing home in England.

In Calabria in November he was excited by the scheme by which the land was being given back to the people, and houses and villages being built for them. He wrote about it passionately in *The Bell*, and with more detachment in *Commonweal*, relating how he had gone down into the wilds of Calabria to see the Land Scheme in operation. He drove onto a bare plateau of rolling, leonine clay, without schools, without houses, without telephones, without roads, without enough water to drink, without a shrub or a tree, where 90% of the peasants did not own a square inch of soil, where they lived in remote, stinking villages. He admired the way the Americans poured in millions and millions of lire to reclaim the exhausted soil, to recreate and establish on it a peasant life. Tears had often blinded him to see old men, 'who might be my grandfather, or yours, getting at last the amazing gift of liberty for their children and their children's children'. It was, he said, as though Americans came to Ireland in the 1840s, took the English landlords off the backs of the people, poured dollars into the soil, made the landlords share the land, and saved Ireland from Famine and the miseries of revolution. He rejected the arguments, advanced by others in *The Bell*, that America was helping Sicily for reasons of self-interest.[9] He went to Calabria again in November 1952, and noted with satisfaction after driving through the countryside, that the Land Reform had taken root. 'Something has been started that can never be stopped' (SS, 223). But when he went back in 1964 he noted that the experiment had failed in Crotone although it had succeeded in Sybaris.

O'Faolain's writings about Italy consist of impressionistic descriptions that give the 'feel' of a place; reflections on the Italian mind; observations on the character of people from particular regions; references to novels he read; and accounts of particular encounters with local people. His assignments for *Holiday* took him back and forth across the entire country. He appears as the eager traveller, full of curiosity, reading the guide books, the novels – Carlo Levi's *Christ Stopped at Eboli*, Lampedusa's *The Leopard*, Guiseppe Borgesi's *The Woman of Syracuse*, Elio Vittorini's *Conversation in Sicily* – and the accounts of former travellers, Cardinal Newman, George Gissing, Norman Douglas. By the mid-fifties he was writing with authority and self-assurance. The articles reveal successively how deeply attached he had become to Italy and its people, particularly those in the South. One could not be in Calabria for three days, he wrote, without falling in love with it. His writing from this time has an attractive, persuasive, unhurried manner, as in his description of the sensuous pleasure of Taormina. He wrote of there being nothing to do all day 'but glut the senses on colour, and light, and wine, and shapely forms in art or nature', that 'Taormina is total picturesqueness: a village on a hilltop commanding one of the most glorious views in the world from lofty terraces, balconies and gardens drowned in bougainvillaea, pale-pink almond, saccharine-sweet syringa, jasmine, acacias, tuberoses, oleanders, barbarously scarlet tropical hibiscus, hedge-rows of wild geranium – a single street swung like a hammock between the Graeco-Roman theatre to the north and the undying plume of Etna to the south'.[10]

He responded to memories of the past. The sight of Mount Soracte from Rome was a reminder of reading Latin with The Man. A bald entry in a guide book – The *Torre de Milo* – enabled him to retrieve from college days Cicero's *Pro Milone*, in which the orator defended Milo from the charge of murder. That memory brought with it a host of other memories – Antony and Cleopatra, and Fulvia who stuck a hairpin through Cicero's tongue after he had been beheaded. Only scraps of memories, O'Faolain said, but enough to send him and us, if we felt so moved, to the history of the last century before Christ. Would we, Sean asked, travel in Greece or Egypt without doing our homework? We should not travel in the South of Italy without making ourselves aware of its richly layered history. In this cunning account of his own response, he refrains from giving an extensive or detailed background. Instead he uses one incident to point the moral and then proceeds to outline other attractions besides – 'memories of Magna Graecia, dying Rome, Gothic kings, Norman invaders, French and Spanish monarchies'. He says there is not a town that has not something to hold and please the eye: 'a carved Norman-Romanesque doorway, perhaps a Frederican castle, a Saracen watch-tower, a Byzantine apse, a remnant fresco, an Aragonese castle, a tesselated pavement, a School of Mantegna triptych or an after-Giotto altar-piece . . .'[11] But when the records of contemporaries or the intimate researches of historians are available, the effect, he declares, is 'more intense, more intimate, more moving'. Place, knowledge and imagination work best when all three are together – as they were in his response to Milo's tower. On this trip he was deeply moved by his discovery of a lonely pond where he beheld the round tops of some Grecian pillars and the foundations of a few brick walls. He turned that discovery to good account in his story, 'Something, Everything, Anything, Nothing'.

O'Faolain's experience of Italy was inseparable from his interest in John Henry Newman whose life he studied from April 1948 to June 1951. Newman, too, had experienced 'inexpressible delight' in the beauty of Sicily and its Greek temples. For him, too, Italy had been a transforming experience. Sean also experienced emotional confusion in these years as he responded to the impact of Italian culture, struggled to achieve consistency in his dealings with Honor and Eileen, ironically found himself taking the high moral ground in dealing with Stephen and with Frank O'Connor. He developed a complex tolerance of inconsistency, contradiction, belief and disbelief that enabled him to accept the Church's teachings while at the same time disregarding them, when it suited him. It was not an easy solution, since it went against his training. Fundamentally he preferred logical conclusions and hated obfuscation. Irish life might be murky, but he wanted his own life to be clear. He condemned De Valera for muddying the waters, he praised O'Neill for clarity of judgement and self-analysis, and he exhorted Stephen to be manly and forthright. Harvard taught him to respect rational proofs. O'Connell showed him that the human mind was a whorl. Newman showed him that reason is not to be trusted. There were contradictions in his own responses: he could fall in love three times a year and realize it was nonsensical to do so; he could be a Catholic, go to confession once a year, receive communion, and see it all 'as a vast metaphysical nonsense' but nonetheless the essential Truth. 'So here I am, a good mediaeval Catholic (pre-tridentine) and it's all balls of course'. There was, he knew, another type of Catholic, such as Bloy, Peguy, Bernanos – 'intense believers, men who thought you must live according to your faith, to the last word. To find their counterpart in Ireland, one must pick a Protestant'.[12] 'I may say I believe', he told Richard Ellmann, 'but I practise only in the most raggedy-arsed way, with a host of mental qualifications based mainly on the Modernist viewpoint'.[13] Not much had changed since he wrote the life of Daniel O'Connell.

He was profoundly interested then in the mental and emotional processes by which Newman made his way from his initial conversion to a narrow brand of Calvinistic Evangelicalism to leadership of the Oxford Movement and his final conversion to Catholicism. *Newman's Way* (1952) elucidated the ramifications of that process. O'Faolain examined his training and temperament, investigated family history, his home, the financial troubles, the differences in the make-up and interests of family members, and, in particular, the differences between the brothers.

But his interest, above all, was in Newman's explanations and judgements, his respect for reason, his eventual distrust of reason, and his final trust in the imagination to carry him to the doorstep of Heaven. Sean was not entirely sure why he studied Newman, but he was clear about the result: Newman destroyed his belief in reason and rationalism. 'All his life', O'Faolain says, 'he oscillates between the intellectual, expressible thing, which emerges from man as law or morality, and the irrational, inexpressible thing, which enters into man as faith or mysticism. He is perpetually torn between the exaltation which overleaps nature, and the intellectualism which would shape, control, reform and legalise it' (NW, 189). As a grown man, he argued, Newman would always blend a meticulous intellectual accuracy with a delicate perception of the subtleties of the mind, while omitting totally to record the simultaneous war of the emotions; he always transferred emotion into intellect so that his versions of experience, recorded later, are, in a sense, falsified by having passed through the refinery of his mind. That process resembled what happened in O'Faolain's own life. His fiction transforms experience, creates a new reality. Even his autobiographical writings select and reshape for the sake of poetic truth.

Ultimately what attracted O'Faolain was that Newman was primarily an artist. It was the artist in him, he argued, who finally admitted defeat in considering the mystery and the miracle of the Eucharist. Newman 'observed the great truth that any miracle is not against reason, but against imagination'. We can accept a miracle rationally, but we cannot imagine it. Since he was a boy, O'Faolain argued, Newman's intellect had been rising to where the Imagination on the very brink of heaven seemed alone fit to rule. There his reason told him that Imagination would not do and that the last flight was with Faith. He moved beyond the language of objective reason to the language of the mystic or the artist. One has to develop a new kind of mind to pass from Protestantism to Catholicism; this was the transition O'Faolain had had to make when writing about O'Connell. Protestantism with its emphasis on right behaviour is splendidly common-sensical. It stands in some entirely different intellectual world from Catholicism, which is magnificently non-sensical or super-sensical, and has a glorious emphasis on mystical communion. Sean's experience of Italy

[173]

confirmed this view. He would have argued at one time that all essential experience comes in boyhood, but no longer. 'The things I've learnt in the past sixteen years or so!' during which he had cast off 'boyhood romanticism'.[14]

He went to Paris on 29 July 1951 to work on his Italian book, but there were interruptions. The weather was bad, the flat was old and gloomy, and he could not get into a writing rhythm. Eileen and Steve arrived about August 12 and they had the worry of Stephen's spinal infection. When they left early in September Sean did some work, but then Julia arrived from Venice and that interfered with it. On his way home he visited Gus and Eileen in Epsom for a few days, did some work for the BBC, recast his book on Newman and arrived on about 14 October. By the end of the month he was 'on the last lap' of the book on Italy. He longed to get back to writing stories, could not even mention his novel, because 'the old demon of finance' dogged him once again.[15] Eileen continued to have stomach trouble and lived on a diet of white fish and white wine. Sean himself got a stomach upset in London. He had been doing his first televised story and felt the strain.[16]

He felt that his new novel, *Alien With a Passport*, was quite different from anything he had done before. He had 'a vague, vague feeling, a vague, vague, vague theme, and I poke about for characters and tiny incidents to convey these feelings. It has begun in Venice, and should move to Paris, and then to Dublin, and then to Paris and then to Dublin. I *know* the key idea roughly but I do not know any of the incidents and this is to feel a queer feeling of moving forward in the dark'.[17] At Christmas 1952 he had an attack of bronchitis and was suddenly 'very hard up'. He gave four talks on Radio Eireann, entitled 'Storm over Calabria', and two on the Newman family for the BBC. He enjoyed his birthday. Eileen made a 'lovely dinner', Julia gave him a cigar, and Elisabeth Schnack, his German translator, sent a blue tie. He was fifty-three.

[13]

Ireland

IN March 1946 Penguin Books invited Sean to write a book on the Irish. He agreed but said he would have to be paid much more than the £50 they paid him for his De Valera.[1] He set out his terms, but was glad of the chance to make some money, £50 down and £50 on publication, and felt the book would not require much work. He had a model in the *History of the French People* by Charles Seignobus which considered the contributions made by a variety of races – Gascon, Fleming, Norman, and others – to the formation of France. In the introduction O'Faolain defined his purpose: to write a creative history of the growth of the racial mind and to tell the story of the development of a national civilization. All the existing histories, he pointed out, with two exceptions, were nationalistic, patriotic, political, and sentimental. He quoted Collingwood with approval: 'History proper is the history of thought'. In a broad, lucid, revisionist sweep he analysed what successive peoples and particular events had brought to the creation of modern Ireland, and omitted the 'tiresome' material of histories – invasions, reigns, parliaments, dynastic risings and fallings.[2]

He wrote the book in six months. Even though he had to leave out many formative things – 'No word about Trades Unions or workers, or social life of the poor Irish in the towns and cities; no word about British law and Irish adaptations of it'[3] – the book was intellectually rigorous and compressed considerable reflection into its short form.

In June 1946 Sean began to organize the Russell Circle. He invited a selected group of people to have lunch together once or twice a month at the Bailey restaurant or the Dolphin Hotel. Among those contacted were T. W. Moody, H. O. White, Sean O'Sullivan, Jack Yeats, Elizabeth Curran,

Father Leonard, P. S. O'Hegarty and Frank O'Connor. It was a loose combination of historians, artists, an art historian, and writers, who would exchange ideas in a civilized manner.[4] He organized a similar but smaller group in the early Fifties; he founded The Cancan't Club, a discussion group that included Owen Sheehy-Skeffington, Patrick Lynch, and Christo Gore-Grimes. It was mainly a gathering of friends, who met occasionally for a meal in the Unicorn and discussed contemporary issues. In the summer of 1946 he enjoyed the company of the American scholars, Richard Ellmann and John V. Kelleher, intelligent, civilized young men who were deeply interested in Irish literature and history, and admired and understood what he was trying to do. As a result of his association with *The Bell* he was a prominent figure in Irish life and his standing abroad amongst writers and academics in England and America was strong. He stood out at a time when the Irish literary scene had been drastically diminished through the death or exile of many of the writers. Because of his stature as a liberal, he was invited in March 1948 to a meeting in the Royal Hibernian Hotel for the launch of the Irish Association of Civil Liberty. At that meeting he proposed that one of the objects of the Association should be to oppose the spread of totalitarianism, whether it took the form of Communism, Fascism, or any other form. Together with Owen Sheehy Skeffington, Christo Gore-Grimes and Michael Yeats he was elected to the Provisional Committee and in April 1949 was appointed to a sub-committee to draft a Constitution for the new body.

In the summer of 1946 he worked hard on *The Irish* and by August was ready for a holiday. Feeling the need for something at a leisurely pace, he hit upon the idea of travelling slowly through West Cork in a horse-drawn caravan. The whole family went to Cork by train and stayed at the Victoria Hotel. Stephen had a recurrence of fever, so Eileen remained with him at the hotel, while Sean, Julia and Nancy McCarthy ambled towards Gougane Barra. Julia, who was very close to her father, resented Nancy's presence and sulked. When they reached Inchageela, Nancy stayed in Creedon's hotel while the other two continued on. They parked the caravan in the yard of Cronin's hotel. There were a number of Dublin people staying, including Pat and Roger McHugh, Tim Traynor, and Honor Tracy. Sean and Honor went about together; they walked along the shores of the lake and spent hours out rowing. At night she slept in the caravan, since the hotel was full. Local people disapproved of Honor's wearing slacks, particularly when she went to Mass in the little oratory where Fr. Traynor said Mass. They were annoyed that several of them could be identified in the extracts from *The Tailor and Ansty* published in *The Bell*. They were unhappy also at the prominence given to the Tailor, since he was not the only story-teller in the area. The result was that one day when the men went grouse-shooting in the mountains and had the usual feast that evening, O'Faolain was not included. Eileen descended the stairs at the height of the party, like Lady Macbeth, to complain of the noise. Sean enjoyed Gougane and wrote enthusiastically, if superficially, about it in his column in the *Sunday Independent*.[5]

They went on. Jacky Buckley, the Tailor's son, led the horse down the hill, since Sean, being unaccustomed to horses, was nervous about the descent. There were 'heavenly views', Sean reported, on the road to Killarney; Hannah MacCarthy's pub was straight out of Synge; he enjoyed Guinness and bastable cake with butter; he recalled his days in Leaca Bawn; he described the Rock of Weeping where people gathered to watch friends and relations, supporters of the Great O'Neill, being executed; the Hollands still had the portable anvil used by their ancestor, a soldier in the Tudor army. It was too stormy to cross Mount Gabriel, so the O'Faolains made their way towards Ballydehob and Schull by way of Skibbereen and 'travelled slowly to happiness'. Often mistaken for tinkers, Sean was amused to discover that around Skibbereen he was thought to be the Duke of Windsor travelling incognito as a writer. Eileen was not amused. He described the holiday to his London agent. 'I took lots of photographs . . . I should expect $1000 for the script and pictures from *Holiday*.'[6]

When they got back to Dublin it was time to enrol Julia at the Sacred Heart School, The Hill, Monkstown, a small school with classes of about five or six pupils. She settled in well and her father, somewhat sceptical at first about clerical education, was pleased with her progress.[7] Stephen was enrolled at a Protestant kindergarten near his home; a local priest complained. He was transferred later to the Sacred Heart and from there to Willow Park, a preparatory school for Blackrock College.

When Sean sent the much-corrected manuscript of *The Irish* to Penguin on 2 November, he reminded his agent that his stories were not 'shiny magazine stories' and could be sold to magazines that pay less.[8] Unable to write potboilers, he put all he could into his book on the short story and even into his reviews for *The Listener*. Every writer, he declared, half-jokingly, should marry a wealthy, beautiful, kind woman who would let him walk on her. Because he spent so much time at his desk he was lonely. 'I am', he declared, 'a hopeless solitary'. He feared another breakdown.[9]

He had flu for three weeks in January 1947, was in low spirits and longed to be out of Ireland. The weather was 'damned disagreeable'. Eileen slaved 'trying to make wet turf burn, gathering twigs in Killiney Wood, drying sodden bits of timber, slacking the fire when it does burn so that our exiguous stock shall not burn too fast – and all the household, including myself and the maid, in bed with flu'. He read Dickens, played chess with the children, and worked at Meccano with Stephen. Kelleher sent two tons of coal, the first the O'Faolains had seen in years.[10]

Eileen was very sick in the Spring. It required three x-rays to diagnose that she had a duodenal ulcer. When Honor came to live at 'Camelot' a castellated round tower with an arch straddling Victoria Road, just a short distance from Knockaderry, her presence deeply disturbed Eileen who knew about the affair even though she told some people there was no truth in the rumours about it. Eileen's anxieties about her health persisted. When doctors diagnosed chronic appendicitis she decided to have it out. Sean complained about the endless illnesses in his family. His stomach began to give trouble. Marriage, he reflected, was 'an impossible institution'. One imagines a girl to be what one wants, but then one grows and changes, whereas she does not. She seems to change because her natural self emerges 'out of the haze of imagined personality with which one had endowed her'. The man, however, changes all the time. The woman becomes real. If a man would only be content with the reality, let her be what she is, let her go her own way, let her live as she wills and as a free human being is entitled to live – then all marriages would succeed. But people would not accept reality. It was 'Oh, a most difficult institution', hardest on the woman because she didn't change. The man changed; she remained what she always was, inevitably feeling that the man had no reason to complain. He concluded there was no solution 'except a great respect for one another, a great formality of behaviour, a perfect acquiescence in the autonomy of each other's nature . . . It's people wanting to force other people to be the same as themselves all along the line that makes all the trouble'.[11] With this especial pleading Sean struggled to rationalize his loosening of the marriage bonds.

He confessed to being a dutiful rather than a good husband and made up for his recurrent neglect by being supportive and attentive when he was home. More single-minded and loyal, Eileen, who was often lonely and withdrawn during his absences, concentrated on her writing and her gardening. Not that she was merely the traditional pious Irish Catholic; she too was sceptical, groaned about the puritanical church, grumbled about the Government, listened to the Anglican service on the radio and read the Saint James version of the Bible. She too had been romantic, idealistic and nationalistic; she too experienced the disillusion and let-down of the Civil War, had loved Ireland so much that she wanted to return but had to recognize how unlike the Ireland of her dreams this Ireland was. She shared much of Sean's disgruntlement, but she coped better. He ran after illusions and needed, or thought he needed, more than she, or Ireland, could give him.

Irish bonds chafed. In a bitter mood he summed up Irish commandments. First, Thou shalt not leave Ireland. Second, Thou shalt honour this thy father and thy mother, thy wife and child. Third, Thou shalt say no ill word of her, him or it. Fourthly, Thou shalt be perpetually miserable but always say utterly the opposite. Fifthly, Thou shalt dig by the sweat of thy brow for scraps of goodness, sweetness and light, and with thy hands like Jews in German privies, and when thou has found it thou shalt proclaim that the fields of Holy Ireland are paved with sunbeams. Sixthly, Thou shalt shut up when thou hast done this. Seventh, Thou shalt not covet anything, anybody, anywhere, no least pinch of them. 'What does it all mean? Why was I born in Cork in 1900 and not in Paris in the days of the Goncourts? I wish I could think up a theme for a play and spew it all out, all the love and all the hate . . .' He thought of moving into town. 'I grow more and more dotty from contemplating my navel up on this hilltop'. But he could thank God for one good thing: De Valera 'that elongated walking bottle' was in America. The new Coalition Government was 'a new era, a vast weight off our backs'.[12]

'It's the longing that makes life short, the endless bloody romantic ache; and no way to relieve it but to kiss the earth, or a woman, or write a story, or remember'. He pondered Henry James's description of Hawthorne's New England: the flower of art blooms only where the soil is deep, it takes a great deal of history to produce a little literature, it needs a complex social machinery to get a writer going. Irish writers, he wrote, understood what James meant by 'social dreariness', 'juvenility', a life that has begun to constitute itself from the foundations, begun to be simply, by the difficulty of the artist's 'enjoying' uncongenial circumstances, and by the lack of companionship. Just as James had commented on Hawthorne's provincial, simple surroundings by drawing an analogy with English life, so O'Faolain commented on Irish life by analogy with European and English life. 'Here is a country with few monuments and these most drearily paid for, few traditions that have projected themselves, no palaces here, no triumphal arches, hardly a statue outside Dublin, no provincial Pinacoteca, or Piazza Dante or ancient amphitheatre, or towering cathedral, no Siena or Rouen, no gay café life, no mellow Dorset towns, few, if any, really pretty villages, no clever cooking, no wine'.[13]

He could see no solution to a novel about Irish life except the 'surrender' of emigration. He would prefer to be able to show Irish characters conquering their daemon at home. He was stuck with the traditional, realist approach, although he appreciated that others had more flexibility. William Saroyan sent him his new play. 'Does he care about characters embedded in time and place? The scene is an egg: which contains (I take it) *all* life. Jesus! And people like me mucking about with Paddy Sullivan of Balyecks, in January, 1944, indeed in Batt's Lane, indeed in Number 4 Batt's lane, and indeed on January 4th 1944, 4 Batt's Lane at 4 p.m. exactly in the year x . . . Frank O'Connor keeps to 4 Batt's Lane and I don't. Loss of nerve? I wander off to the silence of valleys: damn it, a romantic must have some caparison'.[14]

But he was 'bored to exhaustion with the peasant mentality' which seemed to dominate all thinking in Ireland. They should see Ireland from a universal point of view, that is, with the eyes of the artist who is always spiritually homeless – 'The Man Without a Passport'.[15] It should be possible, he felt, to create one's own humanism inside the Catholic Church, by calmly ignoring it when inconvenient.[16] He had made a discovery. 'The real and best Irishman is the stage-Irishman: full of fibs, yarns, goodhumour, rascality, kindheartedness and blarney. Paddy Kavanagh is a caricature of this'.[17] When Eileen went to West Cork in the summer of 1948, he went to London and saw some plays and foreign films. Her account, combined with his reading Bryan MacMahon's *The Lion-Tamer*, raised the 'whole problem of Irish life and letters'. In West Cork, he commented, everybody was interested in this and that, but he judged it was all seed falling on barren ground because their intellects were shut in. MacMahon was a perfect example. 'The Irish thing, good, the Irish environment, terrible. How can a man become a writer in Listowel? It is not a case of Hardy in Dorchester. It is a case of MacMahon in ballybehind-beyond. Dorchester is in the English stream, i.e. in the continental stream. Hardy was a rebel. MacMahon is a conformist. Nuff said. The pianos are playing and then they go to the Confraternity'.[18] He thought Irish writers must 'denationalise'; as another generation had deDavisised they must deDevaleraise. They must emancipate themselves from Catholicism.[19]

In July the O'Faolains got some peace. Julia went again to Chambéry and they sent Stephen to Ring College in Ardmore, Co. Waterford to learn Irish. They hoped to go to Venice but Eileen's stomach was not right and they did not have much money. Sean had the offer of a lift by car to Venice but felt mean about going off and leaving her at home. He felt tied down. Honor was in Japan. Dublin was no place for someone who enjoyed 'a good old abstract intellectual discussion'. He was romantic. He wanted '*heroines*'. Eileen was suspicious of other women. When Margaret O'Neill visited Knockaderry, at Sean's invitation, Eileen 'devoured' him for not telling her that 'she was a charming young girl'. He was cursed, he thought, by being born emotional among a race mad with emotionalism. 'I naturally grow colder and colder . . . I am thus driven to being intellectual without any qualifications and wholly against my grain and in the worst country in the world for intellectuals. Nothing however is so infuriating, it is the last straw, as to be told, let us say by my wife, that I pretend to be cool and cold and balanced and I am really one of the most emotional people in the world; and to have to deny it passionately. Thank God I can write. There I can let my feelings go. Otherwise I have to be drunk or in love to be myself, and I can't get drunk because I have a bad tummy and who the hell is there in Ireland for any man to fall in love with? I awsk you?'[20]

The introspection of these letters arose in part from the autobiographical writing he did at this time. In September 1948 the BBC sent a sound crew to Cork to do recordings for his 'Return to Cork', which had grown out of six autobiographical talks he had given on Radio Eireann. It was a busy and emotional few days. Because the No. 2 Army Band refused to work on a Saturday, he and Aloys Fleischmann had to go about the city finding and equipping members of a defunct band, known as the Butthera, or the Cork Butter Exchange Band. The band played 'Brian Boru's March' and 'Skibbereen', the North Cathedral choir sang 'God of Mercy and Compassion' and Myles MacSweeney sang 'The Banks of My Own Lovely Lee' with passion. But at forty-eight Sean looked 'slight and frail'. After a night of heavy drinking in the backstage bar of the Opera House, he was still tipsy when they entered the North Cathedral and had to be discreetly supported by the parish priest. He was 'a wreck' when he returned to Dublin, but he had got an 'enormous kick' out of the experience and was bitten with the 'features bug'.[21] 'A thousand thanks', he wrote to Aloys Fleischmann, 'for a thousand kindnesses. The bells, the choir and the band came over most effectively'.[22] He went to London to do the recording and worked from 10 a.m. to 9.30 p.m., 'rehearsing and timing and cutting and improvising'. When 'Return to Cork' was broadcast he claimed not to have heard one word. 'It was a bit Passionate and *Personal*'.[23]

Apart from 'The Death of Nationalism' which he wrote with approval, O'Faolain wrote little now about Ireland, but he was drawn into public comment by the controversy over 'The Mother and Child Scheme'. His article in *The Bell*, 'The Dail and the Bishops', was a model of lucid analysis and comment. In April 1951 public discussion over the merits and demerits of the Scheme was suddenly overshadowed by disclosures of opposition to its proposals by the Catholic Church and the Cabinet. On 11 April Dr. Noel Browne, Minister for Health and the originator of the Scheme, resigned in protest and released the relevant correspondence between Mr. Costello, the leader of the Government, the hierarchy, and himself.

O'Faolain saw the controversy, the sudden death of the bill, Browne's dismissal, the assertive letters from the bishop, the compliance of the Government, and the secrecy with which the representatives of Church and State had acted as a telling reflection of the true nature of Irish democracy. The basic issue was the nature of the authority exercised by the Catholic Church. It was, he argued, not merely a question of the right of the Church to comment on Government action. In practice the Catholic Church commanded, since alone of all the churches, it exercised the weapon of the sacraments. 'The Dail proposes; Maynooth disposes'. The Catholic member of Parliament must obey. In view of this relationship, in which the Church has enormous power but very little social responsibility and the Parliament has all the responsibility but only limited power, he reiterated his belief that the relationship of Church and State must be one of constant tussle: the Church would properly, but always prudently, fight for power and the State would always try to restrain that power within due limits.

O'Faolain concentrated on the Church-State conflict, but there was also the power of the medical establishment, which strongly opposed the introduction of free community services. Alfred O'Rahilly opposed O'Faolain's position in the *Standard* and the Bishop of Galway defended the authority of the Church. That in turn led to O'Faolain's article 'The Bishop of Galway and *The Bell*'. He regretted the Church's suspicion of Catholic intellectuals. At the same time he disapproved of Catholic periodicals that emphasized their Catholicism which should, he argued, be inherent in their thinking.

Irish life went 'from folly to folly'. The latest foolishness took place at a meeting of the International Affairs Association on 31 October when Hubert Butler said that Cardinal Stepinac was a 'dupe'. The Papal Nuncio, whose presence had not been made known, 'rose up in wrath and strode out', the County Kilkenny Archaeological Society expelled Butler from his office as Secretary, the Dublin Vocational Committee then turned on Owen Sheehy-Skeffington for having been with Butler at the meeting of the Association. And, Sean told Theodora Fitzgibbon, 'if this sounds to you in England as the croakings of frogs and the squeakings of Aristophanic mice you have forgotten that these exasperations and irritations of Irish life follow on one another's heels week after week with the effect of a series of small boys continually ringing one's front door-bell and running away derisively'.[24]

Sean wanted the best for his children. He sent them to good fee-paying schools, kept a careful eye on their progress and expected results. Julia did well at the Sacred Heart, went to Chambéry in the summers, developed a proficiency in languages, acquired a sophisticated accent, and became poised and self-confident. Sean encouraged her interest in literature. She was, he told Sylvia Beach, 'pretty, eager, inquiring, and ambitious' in some ways, but 'quite a child'. She was suddenly gone 'boy-mad'. He wanted to find a French family for her to stay with one, 'not necessarily Catholic – but anyway (God between us and all harm!) not blatantly "free-thinking"'.[25] He was not pleased with Stephen's work. Eileen spoke of him as her 'problem child' and Sean worried about his lack of application. The difference between the two children was striking: the girl successful in her studies, fulfilling her parent's expectations; the boy not interested in academic work and disappointing them. That he was good with his hands and naturally gifted at electrical matters was not enough. Sean complained

about the expense of raising children, whose motto, he declared, was 'Bleed
'em white'. From this, he confided to Eric Linklater, 'you will gather that I
am in love with my daughter, which is true. And that my son is at the stage
of telling me, which is true'.[26]

In October 1949 Julia entered University College Dublin where she was
a successful student in foreign languages. Her friends noted how conscious
she was of parental pressure and approval. In November Sean began to
negotiate for Stephen to be admitted to Glenstal Abbey, Co. Limerick, an
expensive, all boys boarding school run by the Benedictines. He had to
explain that Stephen had fallen 'a bit' behind in his work due to recurrent
slight illnesses, but received special tutoring at home in the afternoons. He
was, his father assured Father Columba, a pleasant boy; very friendly and
sociable; impressionable; good-humoured. Sean was 'very anxious' that he
should mix with 'the right sort of boy, develop good manners and establish
his personality'.[27] Stephen had spent only one year and one term at Willow
Park. Not studious and inclined to be troublesome, he was remembered
more for one unruly incident than for any signs of promise. On a bus
'outing' he threw another boy's cap out the window. When the parents
complained, he denied that he had done it. At first Sean accepted his version
of the story, but then wrote to the school admitting that Stephen had lied.
He said he would have to send him to boarding school far from the city. It
was then that he began to negotiate with Glenstal. He and Eileen were also
'perturbed' that Stephen had to mix constantly with children in the village
of Killiney 'whose language and ways are more colourful than admirable'.
They wanted, above all, in Newman's phrase, that he should mix with men
of parts and breeding, of his own age.[28]

They kept a close eye on him. He was forbidden to play with children in
the village and had to ask permission to go there. His parents bought him
many toys and he had a superb electric train set which was installed for him
in Sean's former garden study, on a ledge running all about the sides. Alone
much of the time, he pestered the 'daily' to talk with him, invited her to the
shed to see the latest addition to his train, asked wistfully if 'Sean' was busy,
saying he would like to talk with him. Sean was often busy and insisted that
his morning schedule should not be interrupted. Stephen was closer to his
mother whom he resembled in appearance. He could be lively. Once, calling
the daily to an upstairs window, he squirted her with his water pistol.
Accustomed to the ways of boys, she was not greatly upset, but shouted 'I'll

break your neck when I get you', remembering too late that Sean was downstairs. He was very angry, compelled Stephen to apologize at once, and urged her to change her pullover for one of Eileen's. It was clear that Stephen needed companionship. When they heard that a place might be found for him at Glenstal, Sean increased the afternoon tutoring from one-and-a-half hours to four hours a day.

Stephen got bronchitis that Christmas. His father thought it was a chronic condition and hoped he would improve before he went to Glenstal. He handed over his 'dearest possession' in poor shape. Stephen, he explained, had been under the weather since November and should have 'a spot of early and late sleep'.[29] Eileen's remedy was an iron tonic in the form of milk after meals and a half-hour's rest after lunch. They hoped Glenstal could follow this remedy.

Within a year Stephen developed back trouble which was diagnosed as osteochondritis, a spinal infection. They took him to doctors in Dublin and London. One doctor prescribed a programme of bedrest for six months, then modified that to three, then, at Sean's urging, allowed Stephen to return to school but on condition that he wear a brace. This meant that he was not able to take part in games, but, as Eileen wrote to Fr. Columba, since Sean was in Paris, 'mental activity could go on'. By Christmas x-rays showed that his spine had made bone on the weak point. By Easter the spinal condition was cured, the brace came off and Stephen could be more active again, but he still had to avoid sports.

Glenstal only prepared boys for the final examination, but had a system of coloured, weekly cards and end of term reports with comments by the teachers. Since Stephen hardly ever sent his card home and wrote infrequently, Sean found it very difficult to assess his progress. At school discipline took the form of fines and detentions and these fell heavily on Stephen. Sometimes he was punished. Once he got a 'ten-stroke flogging'. He told his mother about this. When Eileen told Sean, he could only hide whatever concern he felt, remembering the floggings he had seen at the Lancs and at Pres., in the hope that Stephen would be compelled to work. He continued to urge him to succeed. At Easter he told him that if Stephen was satisfied with himself he would be satisfied with him and offered him five shillings for every gold card. Stephen got one and then there was silence. Sean wrote a 'stinker' of a letter, threatening to send him to a stern school and complained to Father Columba that Stephen had only written

[185]

home once since Easter (11 June 1951). The only reply Sean got to his stern letter, was 'a request for a Hornby train for his birthday!!!!' Sean hoped Stephen was making a novena they had promised to make with him. He finally insisted that he must have a letter and card every Tuesday morning. What they wanted, as they kept saying, was 'a decent, Irish, clean, gentleman who tells the truth and doesn't give pain to others'. But at Christmas comparing the various reports, Sean found it difficult to graph 'so uniform an indistinction'. They got Stephen a tutor for French (22 January 1952).

In the Spring Sean was more hopeful: Stephen seemed happy, his manners were improving. But these hopes faded: the reports were not good. Sean wondered if Stephen might be keeping bad company: he was beginning 'to get a bit rattled and worried' about him. He went to Glenstal to advise Father Columba that, in his opinion, one of Stephen's companions was unsuitable. Fr. Columba did not agree. Sean put greater pressure on Stephen, warned him that there would be no further concessions, such as a visit on Sports Day, or a birthday present, and sent back his last semi-illegible letter to be rewritten. But this 'Press Stephen' policy did not pay off. Stephen went back to school in September 1952 but by 17 October had sent only one card and had not written 'much'. Sean felt at a loss. He formed 'a depressing picture of him as the dunce of his class, ignoring and perhaps ignored'.

The Benedictines found Stephen difficult. He was disruptive and responded neither to encouragement nor discipline. They felt he 'had no moral guts'. Even his father commented 'Stephen is not a person'. Stephen could have been handled with greater understanding, but Father Columba was an old-fashioned disciplinarian, and Sean insisted on Stephen becoming the kind of person he wanted him to be. His behavioural problems gave cause for concern. When he stayed with the Childers in Wicklow, the Foleys in Ennis or the Lucys in Cork, he behaved badly.

Sean was embarrassed when Stephen got into trouble during the Easter holidays in 1953. The father of one of his school friends telephoned to say that he did not wish Stephen to associate with his son. The boys had stolen a box of cigarettes from the sideboard. Sean cross-examined Stephen at length, making it clear that he wanted to get at the truth, that there was no question of punishment, that his main interest was in helping the boy 'not to kid himself'. What concerned him most, he told Father Columba in a two page letter that he first read over to Eileen, was 'this conscience-confusion. If a man does a thing, right or wrong, I do feel very strongly that the one thing he must always be clear about is the actuality of what he has done. Otherwise there is no man there at all – just a horrid mess. We Irish are so prone to this horrid game of self-deception that I am always trying to get Stephen to be honest *firstly* with himself'. He decided that Stephen responded best to 'encouragement, kindness, man to man talk, putting it up to himself to master himself' (20 April 1953). Sean had never been close to his own father and found it difficult to cope with his own son. He was stern and rigid, and understood, but found it hard to tolerate, Stephen's reluctance to study. Smart boys could get away with that. 'Dull, slow, old clods like Stevie, poor boy, can at most hope to dodge'. But, in another mood, he was convinced that Stephen had 'buckets of brains'.

Memories of how he had been coerced into religious observance also affected his handling of Stephen. At the end of Stephen's first year in Glenstal the parents noticed that he was not going to communion, although he had been sent to confession several times. It troubled Sean that Stephen's 'religious sense seemed weak'. In a long talk with him he discovered he had not been to confession for about eight months. He tried 'to induce him to go to confession', but did 'not press him to come out on Sunday morning to communion'.

Stephen had a bout of flu and bronchitis at Christmas 1953. That put an end to their plans to have him tutored during the holidays, but they were pleased with his general 'manners and morals', and were surprised one night when he read some of his favourite poems to them. When Sean went to Princeton in February 1954, Eileen had to take over the supervision of Stephen's progress. The priests found her aloof and thought that her hypochondria communicated itself to her son.

Sean and Eileen were deeply shaken when told that he would not be kept on at Glenstal. Sean had a long 'interview' with him and wrote to Father Matthew expressing his fear of what being dismissed might do to the boy's 'precarious self-pride'. They hoped the school could give him one last chance. But the school had had enough. Sean was 'appalled' at the suggestion that he be sent to another college. 'He'd not only be at the bottom but the back of the class, hauled through in the most rough-and-ready-way . . . At his most impressionable age'. He begged to meet with Father Columba. 'You have thrown us into a state of sad dismay': all he had asked was that Stephen would be able to pass the one necessary examination for a career; he would be satisfied if he left Glenstal 'with the instincts of a Catholic, Irish gentleman'. They arranged for Stephen to have private lessons.

The previous year Julia graduated from University College Dublin. In celebration her parents took her on a picnic to Dalkey Island. She went to Rome for the following academic year. Eileen made preparations – sewing, mending, washing and buying for her. They thought of going with her, getting an apartment in Rome, but Julia wanted to be on her own.

Sunday evening 'At Homes' were a regular feature of life at Knockaderry. The people who went there varied from one Sunday to the next and over the years. There were summer visitors, scholars like Ellmann or Kelleher, English journalists or writers, like V. S. Pritchett, John Betjeman when he was at the British Embassy in Dublin, and a variety of Irish writers, artists, painters, actors, musicians, Republicans, editors, intellectuals. The list included Peadar O'Donnell, Frank O'Connor, Patrick Kavanagh, Brendan Behan, Maurice Twomey, Arthur Power, Con Curran, Eilis Dillon, Elizabeth Curran, various contributors to *The Bell*, James Plunkett, Honor Tracy, Norah McGuinness, Mervyn Wall, Brian Boydell, Frank Duff, Christo Gore-Grimes, Patrick Lynch, Owen Sheehy Skeffington, Nial Montgomery, Cyril Cusack, F. R. Higgins and many others. O'Faolain was urbane and sophisticated, a kindly father-figure to young writers, talking of European writers whom he had met, of places he had been, mentioning current events as he moved about, chatting with different people.

Impressions of Sean from the years of *The Bell* and afterwards describe him as professional, professorial, or like a Civil Servant. He exercised a certain authority in his person and had an air of superiority and detachment backed up by a sardonic humour. But he was guarded; did not reveal himself; could occasionally be snappish. In appearance, Honor Tracy recalled in *Mind You, I've Said Nothing!* (1953), he was like a respectable English burgher, tall and spare, rosy and blue-eyed, urbane and imperturbable. His presence soothed and restrained. But she knew he was quick to anger, wrote furious letters to the press, most of which he tore up. In professional dealings he was cold and abstract, never thawed out and expected things to be business-like. Unlike Frank O'Connor who had no respect for conventions, he wanted life to conform to convention. He took a high moral tone in commenting on O'Connor's love-affairs, giving the impression that he himself was above reproach in such matters.

He had a reputation for being abrasive and aloof, but that was unfair. He was always kind and courteous to Michael O'Beirne, advised Paul Henry on how to write an autobiography, gave David Marcus a story for the first issue of *Irish Writing* although he refused to be the editor, gave a story to John Ryan for *Envoy* and wrote a provocative reply to Conor Cruise O'Brien's interpretation of *The Irish*. When Frank O'Connor and Evelyn arrived at Dunlaoghaire with the body of O'Connor's mother and found no hearse waiting, he responded at once to Evelyn's phone call and made the necessary arrangements. There were numerous instances of personal kindness.

In the fifties the O'Faolains began to enjoy a better style of living. Sean began to look cosmopolitan, to wear European-style clothes. Knockaderry gave evidence of sophistication with artifacts collected abroad, paintings on the walls, books, newspapers and magazines everywhere. Sean's book-lined study, looking onto the garden through a bay window, had a small desk with a portable typewriter, a rack for his beloved pipes, a mobile of pale circles, and well-cushioned high chair. A gun propped in the corner was a reminder that he liked to go rough-shooting in the mountains, or sometimes in Corofin, Co. Clare. He liked to entertain friends and casual visitors in the garden. Even this was done with style. If the day were sunny he wore a panama, and held forth genially about himself and his work. To interview him was to receive a generous, thoughtful response in which nothing was revealed beyond what he chose to reveal. Eileen would appear with a silver tea service, bone china cups and plates, scones, brown bread or cake. She might, if the visitor were a mutual friend, join the group, but often she returned to the house or went back to her gardening which she loved. The garden was a tribute to her taste and skill. The house itself, hidden by trees and shrubs, and facing a wide sweeping lawn, showed her strong visual sense.

Sean gave the impression of being at ease, as indeed he increasingly was the more he detached himself from Irish issues. He worked, usually, from 9.00 a.m. to 1.00 p.m. The afternoons were free. He and Eileen might drive up to the mountains to collect turf mould for the roses. They might go for a walk on Killiney Hill, through the woods, to enjoy the fine views of the bay and the coastline. Sometimes they drove to Hunters or Glendalough for afternoon tea. In the evening he would read the *Irish Times*, the *Manchester*

Guardian, Figaro or some current fiction. They avoided television for years. He played the part of the successful literary man. His travels, the tastes and interests he acquired, and his new and satisfying sense of himself as a cosmopolitan figure, who kept one foot in Ireland, required, and in a sense, created a new image. He was no longer the embattled polemicist on the hill, the recipient of hate mail, the controversial letter writer. He was more relaxed, could afford to take it easy, to work hard on assignments abroad, buy time in which to write in his slow, methodical way, revising a ms., putting it away, taking it out again after weeks or months, revising, putting it aside, revising, sometimes as often as fifteen times, until he got it right. There were always several stories being worked over in this manner. The casual air masked the intensity with which he worked.

Eileen was not over-awed by his more public persona and greater literary reputation. She was outgoing and friendly, despite her hypochondria. She worked quietly at her own writings, voiced her opinions firmly and often disagreed with Sean. She sounded at times like the voice of his hidden conscience, reminding him of traditional moral values. To some she seemed bossy. Friends and dinner guests noticed she was faddy about food, worried about her digestion. People remarked the plainness of her bedroom with its single bed and crucifix. She was also very practical. Many writers used the same tax consultant whose fees kept increasing, but when she noticed an error in the statement sent out by Russell Murphy, she removed the portfolio and thereby saved them from the kind of loss suffered by other clients, when Murphy died and it was discovered that their money was unaccounted for. The fact that the O'Faolain estate was surprisingly wealthy was due more to her understanding of the stock market than to Sean's earnings, although these improved significantly.

[14]

Princeton

SEAN welcomed Richard Blackmuir's invitation to give one of the Christian Gauss Seminars in Criticism at Princeton. It was agreed that he should be in Princeton for three months beginning in February 1954, and would have a 'suite' in the Graduate College. The arrangement included three meals a day at the college, all for about $500 dollars for the term. His fee was $5000.[1]

Sean proposed to examine the work of James Joyce, Graham Greene, Evelyn Waugh, Jean Anouilh, and two others – Marcel, Sartre, Camus, Mauriac, Aymé, or Julien Green. He would search for the instinctive, unintellectual, perhaps moral, urges that marked off modern literature from the period before 1920.[2] During the Autumn of 1953 he began reading and thinking about these novelists and wrote for information or advice to Father Gervase Mathew, T. E. Hulme, Arturo Barea, Raymond Mortimer, Theodora Benson, Eric O'Gorman and Evelyn Waugh. He accepted Barea's opinion that Hemingway's portrayal of the relationship of the American with the Spanish girl in *For Whom the Bell Tolls* was unrealistic. Theodora Benson's letter about *Vile Bodies* he used, almost verbatim, when his lectures were published as *The Vanishing Hero*. He also made use of Raymond Mortimer's advice that Moore's *Principia Ethica* provided a rationalization for the aesthetic approach to life. Waugh, however, claimed never to have heard of the *Principia*.

By 1 December he had written five of his six talks. He sent the titles to Ellmann – Greene: *The Jansenist Fallacy*; Waugh: *The Sanity of Eccentricity*; Hemingway: *The Pelagian Vertigo*; Bowen: *The Pursuit of Sensibility*; Faulkner: *The Subjective Impasse*; Joyce or Virginia Woolf: *The*

Individualist Illusion. He would, he said, make cross-references to Mauriac, Julien Green, Bernanos, Aymé and a reference to Sartre. Ellmann advised him not to use two Catholic titles as this gave the wrong image. 'I don't find the Church in your pores'.³ Sean felt uneasy about what he had proposed. Since this would be his first experience of sustained university lecturing, he wondered if he was inviting trouble, if not disaster, by these cross-references. He felt ill-equipped for a 'full dress discussion' of modern French literature and, although he had included Joyce, he did not feel competent to discuss him either. He decided to keep Jansenism, because he had worked it out carefully, but to drop Pelagianism. He changed that title to 'Men Without Memory'. He told E.B.O. Borgerhoff, the Director of the Seminar, that he was looking forward to Princeton 'in fear and trembling' but 'with the fullest anticipation of a very interesting stay'.⁴ Borgerhoff still had the idea that he would include continental fiction and had organized attendance accordingly. Now he asked whether Sean intended to discuss European writers *passim* or at a particular point.⁵ Still uneasy about all that he seemed to have taken on, Sean revised his original plan by dropping the French writers and Joyce.

He sent Borgerhoff his list of novelists, a bibliography, the titles of the individual lectures, and said he would include some continental fiction. The bibliography consisted of the chief novels of the writers to be discussed and the following: Mauriac, *Le Noeud de Vipères*; Bernanos, *Sous le Soleil de Satan*; Julien Green, *Moira*; Alberto Moravia, *L'Amore Coniugale*; Marcel Aymé, *La Nausée* and *Les Chemins de la Liberté*; C. E. Magny, *L'Age du Roman Américain* and *Les Sandales d'Empedocle*; Virginia Woolf, *Diary*; Lord Keynes, *Two Memoirs* (*My Early Belief*); G. E. Moore, *Principia Ethica*.

He was angry with Frank O'Connor. First he had had to act as go-between when O'Connor and Evelyn Bowen were being divorced. Then he had to look after Joan O'Donovan when O'Connor went to America without her. Now when he wrote to Richard Ellmann saying that he thought this relationship was 'cracking', Ellmann replied that O'Connor had married Harriet Rich. Sean felt that at least O'Connor should have told him how serious the break with Joan had become. It was not a question of morality, he told Ellmann, but he felt that O'Connor should be avoided.⁶

But he could not be detached about him. O'Connor was 'like a brother with whom a fellow was once intimate, or a woman he once loved. He's part of Cork and Gilabbey and Spangle Hill and Corkery and youth and stars and the river and dreams and the ache of it all and the things he does and says are not observed by me with the same detachment I'd apply to anyone else in the world . . . It's like watching a younger brother becoming a drunk. The balls he talks is an agony to me: the more so because I have to defend him — why I don't know.' The fact that he gave up Evelyn for Joan and Joan for Harriet did not bother him so much, O'Faolain explained, as O'Connor's need to abuse and belittle one woman as he took up with the next: 'he seems to believe that to break with a friend or a lover you must first smear them, cod yourself, deceive everybody, cause the greatest amount of pain, dirt and general misery and indecency, all without, all with the utmost and most solemn or passionate self-righteousness . . . I think he is a bore and damn near a shit . . . I'm fed up with trying to be gentlemanly about him — and, I imagine, not succeeding ever . . . I feel very sad. Is it smallpox or O'Donovanitis?'[7]

In the middle of November 1953 Sean sent Kelleher 'Lovers of the Lake'. The ending, in which the lovers kiss and then go off to separate rooms, worried him. Nobody out of Ireland, he thought, would believe that men and women behave like this. 'Is it provincial? Sententious? Sentimental? Unreal?'[8] Its portrait of a sophisticated Dublin surgeon, named after one of O'Faolain's school companions at Pres., making a pilgrimage with his mistress, enabled O'Faolain to focus on the issue of the individual conscience caught between the conflicting demands of sexual desire and moral principle. He had good reason to be worried about it. In this story he got away from naturalistic depiction of Irish peasant life, but he wrote of an experience that was something of a curiosity to non-Irish, non-Catholic readers. At the end of the story when the lovers go to separate rooms even though both would clearly prefer to go to bed together, they adhere to the morality of the pilgrimage for one more night. It was a choice that readers in the late fifties and sixties found hard to believe. O'Faolain did not change the ending. His lovers behaved as he and Honor Tracy had done. In matters of sexual morality O'Faolain remained conservative, but his worry about the story was justified: no editor wanted it.

He had troubles of his own: difficulty in paying his income tax, Eileen's preoccupation with dieting – she seemed to be addicted now to white wine in addition to whatever she ate – and mixed feelings about his children. Julia was 'a pretty ticket', but Stephen was 'a total fool'.[9] When Julia got a Travelling Studentship, he envied her. 'O God, to be young, to be young!'[10] It was as though she was having the youth he would have wished for himself. She was a mirror image of the self he might have had and to a large extent she was his creation. They exuded mutual admiration and the enjoyment of each other's personalities. Stephen, on the other hand, was the dullard Sean had never been. He had to study three hours every day to make up for time lost at Glenstal through illness. Sean once again was dissatisfied with Ireland, with the damp, the Church, the State and wanted to get away. Ireland was heaven if one could find *any* excuse for getting out of it three times a year. At the same time he admitted that the country was not doing so badly and had become more tolerable since Independence. He regretted that instead of abusing the politicians, he had not mixed with them and tried to influence them, although he knew that that went against his temperament. He was torn between a wish to see the country become more intelligent and hard like Switzerland or America and his liking for this 'ragtagsloppyexas-perating-laughablewarm Irish-Italian way?' He was not sure which he preferred.[11]

He told Kelleher about a recurrent, wonderful dream:

Last night I was in Cork: the climate was Italian; I lay on the steps of the square in Patrick Street, a great big piazza, with the pagoda of the 1000 Steps dimly lit to the left across a tangential square, and Pigott's front was just two immense doors from roof to pavement in black and gold lacquer, and Egan's the jeweller's had a hallway of great size surrounded by walls covered by lifesize brass repousse goddesses and gods and warriors designed by Harry Clarke. There I lay strewn in the warm night, with a suggestion of flower-sellers. It was dark but the traffic (taxis and whatnot) poured past me leftwards the way it does out of the Corso into the P. Vittorio Emmanuele. Suddenly Jack Hendrick and Kitty O'Leary appeared. Jack wore a lieutenant's uniform, Irish army. He paused, sidled, hesitated, recognised me, and I let him come on, and then, *lo*, and how exquisitely beautiful it was, he flung himself down beside me, threw down the army cap, and Kitty curled up too, and I mocked him

[194]

about the army, and he laughed, and his face was damp with pleasant perspiration, and my God how he laughed and how Kitty laughed, and we were all young again and full of joy and to-hell-with-the-world feelings, and life was our oyster, and Ireland was the world the way it used to be. What woke me up was crying because in my heart I knew it was only a dream I was dreaming. So I put on the light and scrawled down the *immense* wisdom for fear I'd forget it when I really woke up, and this morning there it is on a bit of paper: Youth should go thru the world like a knife thru butter once you begin to calculate its all *up*'.

He wished he could write a play that would similarly capture the memory of past ideals within the present absence of ideals. He felt he was wasting his life. Sometimes he thought that one bottle of Montrachet '25 was worth all Henry James.[12]

Princeton, where Sean arrived on 17 February 1953, provided a social world that he greatly enjoyed. The small university town has a beautiful, rural setting, particularly in the Spring, when its lush, fertile vegetation, trees and flowering shrubs are at their best. Winding roads bordered by fine houses and estates stretch out from the town. The town itself is small and the campus has generous open spaces, trees, shrubs, and lawns. The people Sean met were intelligent, sophisticated, worldly, tolerant and welcoming. There was an active social life of cocktail-parties and dinner parties that he enjoyed. Faculty life, he reported, was either drunken or dull, but the people were 'always sweet and kind and eager to be helpful and most friendly'.[13]

The graduate college in which he lived, complete with fake Gothic quad, trees and Magdalene towers, had a golf course at its door. He could lie there in the sun, shirt off, with Princeton Inn like something out of an advertisement in the *New Yorker*, only a few minutes away across the links. There he could sit on the terrace or in the lounges, drink long drinks or have tea. He found everybody 'overwhelmingly hospitable and kind' and he had no sense of time passing.

The Gauss seminars took place on Thursday evenings at eight o'clock in the Firestone Library. It was a gathering place for all those who were interested, but it was mainly a small group, assembled around Richard Blackmuir, who found each other's company and intelligences congenial, that formed. Šean would speak for an hour, then, after a break, there would be wide-ranging discussion. There were no rules except for the general understanding that it was not the place for old-line academics, details, or the recitation of scholarship. Those taking part included selected members from various departments, some graduate students, some people from the Institute for Advanced Study, and guests. The average size of each group was about twenty-five. The aim of the discussions was to express ideas and tease out implications and they were enlivened by the fact that participants came from several different disciplines, not only literature but music, philosophy, politics and, occasionally, the sciences. Blackmuir had the gift of asking a good question even after a poor talk.[14] It was just the sort of intellectual exchange that O'Faolain liked.

People at Princeton found him immensely attractive. Blackmuir admired him as a man of letters and talked of him as an old friend. Blackmuir's secretary, Jane Jacobi, a warm, friendly, blonde girl, liked him. Unlike some other visiting writers, he would stop by her office for a chat. He discussed his views of writers, told her of his dislike of Virginia Woolf and Marcel Proust, and made no secret of his dislike of academics. He was a good conversationalist on many subjects. Women found him attractive. He dressed well, had elegant taste in shoes, discussed the best places in New York in which to buy clothes. While he was convivial in a hard-drinking group, he was reasonably abstemious, quite unlike the stereotype of the Irish writer. Friends noticed that he set time aside every day for writing. There were occasional excesses. Writing to John Kelleher 'with a reeling head and a sick stomach after a party', he pronounced Princeton 'a soak of a place'.[15]

When he had finished the six lectures Princeton University Press asked to publish them. He was 'flattered'. But giving the lectures had been more of a strain than he had realized. He felt light-headed when he was finished, but found that the subject of the anti-hero 'touched a personal nerve of supreme importance' to him (VM, 349). The loner, the supreme egoist, the ultimate symbol of every American's two main ideals – 'self-reliance and independence' – was independent, aggressive, and self-reliant. He fitted in well with O'Faolain's own style. He, too, liked to work alone and was something of a misfit in Irish society. He, too, had experienced the breakdown of religious belief and still struggled with the conflict between personal independence and church teaching. In a determined effort to liberate himself from the emotional and moral burdens that home, religion and education had imposed, he became 'a loner, a recusant, detached, an *étranger*, an observer, an alien, a spy, a writer' (VM, 51). All his adult life he tried to keep a balance between his instinctive, passionate nature and his strongly rational mind. Increasingly after the war he developed a persona that was civilized, engaging, sophisticated, and detached, one quite different from the man who trudged around West Cork with a horsedrawn caravan.

In *The Vanishing Hero, Studies in Novelists of the Twenties* (1956) Sean argued that the traditional hero was on the side of the law, the church, the headmaster and the head of the family, but had lost his representative status when traditional values lost their appeal. In his place emerged the anti-hero who was puzzled, crass, mocking, frustrated and isolated, as he manfully or blunderingly sought to establish his own personal, supra-social codes. He could not see any pattern in life and rarely its destination. In many respects he resembles O'Faolain who felt *déraciné*, wrote of misfit characters, and battled against a society, and a church, that he felt unable to accept. It was the lack of discernible pattern, the uncertainty of there being a destination, that drove him in historical biographies to examine the past to find some exemplary modes of behaviour.

At the end of February Sean gave the lectures that Dick Ellmann had arranged. He went to Virginia from 8–10 March, to Columbia on the thirteenth, to Minnesota on 4 April for about a week, to Boston on the thirteenth, where Kelleher introduced him to Archibald MacLeish and Harry Levin, and to Dartmouth on 4 May. He was a good speaker, well able to hold the attention of his audiences, and was himself buoyed up by the excitement of the podium. At Northwestern he spoke on 'Six Modern Novelists in Search of a Hero'. Ellmann told him that 'faculty and students alike were charmed, fascinated, impressed; two of my senior colleagues who have been listening to talks here for twenty years said it was the best they had ever heard. The younger ones disagreed, some of them, with your views on Joyce and Faulkner in particular, but this just added to the general excitement. It was an excellent job, and by the way, Zabel also told me he was very pleased with your performance there'.[16]

But it was also hard going and he felt worn out by the end. The conference at Charlottesville was a 'jamboree'. Elizabeth Bowen wanted to renew their relationship, but he declined. He gave a 'highpressure' twenty-five minute talk on Joyce and then Padraic Colum blew it all sky high simply by saying how kind and gentle and indeed princely a man Joyce was.[17] He had the 'fleeting illusion of being a person of some importance'. He went to Minnesota where he lectured at the Newman Centre and raked in '500 bucks'. The earlier mid-West trip had brought in $400.

Not long after his arrival at Princeton Sean got in touch with Alene Erlanger. A wealthy woman with a spacious apartment at 117 East 64th Street in New York, she became the most stimulating woman in O'Faolain's life for the next fifteen years. While still in her teens she had married Milton Erlanger, a wealthy manufacturer of men's underwear, known from coast to coast as BVDs. The marriage was a disaster. He was an opinionated, unreceptive man, and an athlete, who had a good public image but dominated his wife and children.

Five feet and one inch tall, Alene, known as Kick to Sean and to her friends, had taste and style, was very expensively, selectively, spartan about choosing jewellery and always wore the same identical type of shoe. She was very vain, preened before her mirrors, had her clothes designed by Balenciaga. She had a passion for life, had many diverse interests – in books, theatre, music, ballet, horses, poodles. Her library included a full first edition of Jane Austen, the first edition of Joyce's *Exiles*, and some manuscripts. She liked to host soirées and musical evenings. The one thing that could upset her was boredom. Her response, he wrote, was 'spirited, forcible, gutsy', although she never appeared that way as she strolled along Park Avenue or Lexington near her home, with her gloves carried in her hands.

In the spring of 1954 she and Sean saw each other regularly. Sometimes one of his Princeton friends, Lucius Wilmerding, drove him to the Erlanger estate at Oakhurst, New Jersey, a large house with racing stables. Sometimes he borrowed her car. They went to the races at Monmouth Park where the Erlangers had a box. His letter to John Kelleher does not anticipate the consequences of his renewal of contact with Alene. He went to the races, he said, 'with a Jewess I used to adore 25 years ago and who is now about as old as God'.[18]

That Easter weekend was eventful. One afternoon at a Princeton tea-party he discussed the recurrence of evil as a denial of the will. On the advice of his friend, Fr. Demanash, an Egyptian Jew who was attached to the Aquinas Foundation, he went to see the priest-philosopher, Ivan Ilyich, on Easter Saturday in the rectory of the Church of the Incarnation on 175th

Street. The mental torments that drove him there had a varied origin: the hardships of his mother's life; his horror followed by his rage at his first helpless sexual initiation; disillusionment with all revolutions, revolutionaries and reformers; later and above all by his reading of Dostoyevsky's outraged cry in the chapter in *The Brothers Karamazov* called 'The Grand Inquisitor'. These culminated in the thought that, if God is as all-powerful as he is all-loving, why does he allow men and women to do so many hideous things, to suffer so many agonies; why let them occur and go on occurring at every moment of every day and night all over the globe?

He had 'an intense conversation' with Father Ilyich. Ilyich talked about a First Cause, or Divine Will, that created life. It was the cause of everything that happened. It could accept what happened 'once it had happened'. It was, for O'Faolain, a 'dazzlingly simple solution: Heaven is powerless to intervene in any human decision until the act decided on has occurred.' 'The sacred freedom of the will of every human soul takes precedence in time over the will of God. Once the act is done Heaven may judge but not before. Even then, judgement still may be suspended. There is always the road to Damascus. The chains fell from my will. I left that rectory bursting with joy. The predestinatory weight had been lifted'. If God willingly accepted whatever happened, why should he not accept it? For the last time in his life he knelt to confess his sins and receive absolution in a condition bordering on despair. For a man who had had a chip on his shoulder about the injustice of the world and the church, this was a great releasing experience. That day, he recorded in *Vive Moi!* (1964), he accepted himself, loved himself and thereby could love everyone, so that had he met a beautiful woman outside the church 'I doubt if I could have predicted the consequences' (VM, 231).

In fact a beautiful woman was waiting for him, 'a smallish, very attractive woman' in an open, shining Cadillac, who said 'You look absolutely radiant'. 'Alene', he answered, 'I have never felt so happy in my life!' She, a sceptic, a non-believer, a loner, said 'Tell me all about yourself'. As they drove out of Harlem, through Central Park, and down into Fifth Avenue, he told her about his former sense of slavery and his newfound independence. In this uncharacteristic unburdening we may date the beginning of his love-affair with Alene Erlanger.

For obvious reasons they kept their love-affair secret. She only told her daughters about it on her deathbed. Long before then both girls had come to love Sean, because he was so warm and amusing. The son, Michael, found the situation less easy to accept. Years after she met Sean again Alene converted to Catholicism. Michael thought she wanted to be closer to Sean, her daughters said she hated being slighted as a Jew, Sean thought it was a question of conscience.

Meeting her expanded his life. Since she had interests in Ireland, in the world of horse-breeding and theatre, she was a frequent visitor. She was also in the habit of buying her clothes in Paris. Through her he moved in a wider social circle centred round the Shelbourne Hotel and stables in the country, made up of 'an irregular, sexy crowd' that had 'curiosity and colour' and suited him. Alene was 'very beautiful, dynamic, full of life, and a complete extrovert' and Sean had the ability to talk with someone as though that person was the most important person in the world. Eileen, on the other hand, was quiet; she seemed lacklustre besides Alene's brilliance.[19] As he began to move about between America, Italy, London and Dublin, the life that he now began to experience with Alene continued elsewhere as well. He found her attractively comic in her enthusiasms and enjoyed her sexual intensity. Frank and outspoken about her feelings and sexual needs, Alene was very different from any Irish woman he had known. The sexual attraction between them was very strong.

Another result of this stay in America was that through his agent, Emelie Jacobson, he secured a commission from *Holiday* to write articles on Italy. Instead of returning directly to Ireland, he sailed to France on the 'Isle de France', went on to Paris, where he was joined by Eileen, and then travelled to Rome, Naples, Sicily, Florence, Paris, London and back to Dublin.

When he got home Dublin was 'cold and green and pensive' and he was doubly nostalgic for Italy and for New York. He sorted his notes and settled down to writing his *Holiday* article. He recast the last chapter of *Alien with a Passport* but had a recurrence of low blood-pressure blues. He rested, ate steaks and drank red wine. He was nostalgic for New England, it rained all the time, Gus's wife was visiting and she was an 'eedjut'. Gus himself arrived in October, as did F. N. Robinson. Sean's dissatisfaction continued, increased by memories of Italy and by absence from Alene. He lunched with her friend, Ria Mooney, but lacked congenial company. He decided that if he was to tell the whole truth about Ireland he must do so from a protected position, i.e. from exile which he had avoided all his life. He would have to go away to either London, Rome, Paris, or the USA, to Harvard, Princeton, Yale or the environs of New York, or perhaps San Francisco. 'I am too racinated . . . I do not wish to uproot myself in anger or in bitterness, but in regret, indeed in affection – nothing becoming me or Ireland better than my leaving her. I shall be very lonely. However, I will take time – a year, I expect, at least'. As he dramatized 'A Born Genius' for Radio Eireann, that early story about artist-lovers trapped in Cork, he looked around and asked himself, 'Does nobody rebel?' Could these characters not fly away together, or shoot somebody, as in Ibsen, make *some* gesture of revolt? 'Then I suddenly began to look around me with open eyes for the first time, and the hypothesis which I have not fully posited before, that they *do* rebel, however feebly, in secret and I have been astounded by the number of lives I have always known or should have known in which recompenses are surely being sought and found – the men with mistresses, the cars that prowl about Fitzwilliam or Merrion Square at night to pick up the whores . . . the silent men who, one knows somehow, are full of contempt for the blahblah of priests and politicians. It must be all there but they have no Ibsen to put themselves before them on the stage . . . But one cannot write that here. Friendship is too expensive, and so are libel actions, and one has children, and one cannot write in peace and calm, and truth, if half one's mind is looking behind one's back for these things'.[20]

At the age of fifty-four he had realized something that another man might have realized at least twenty years earlier. For all his intellectual analysis and scepticism he had missed something fairly common in human nature. He had also failed to apply experiences he had had: Edward Garnett lived a double life, Liam O'Flaherty had run away with another man's wife, O'Connor had a number of relationships, as he had had himself. One reason for his blindness was the secretive nature of Irish society and his view of its sexual Puritanism. Scandals in Irish public life were rare and were kept out of the newspapers. Nevertheless, his blindness was extreme and damaging for him as a novelist.

He wavered now again, deciding that he would not go into exile; he was reconciled to 'this withering grove: with forays outward'.[21] That was the position he held for the rest of his life. Ireland was tolerable if he could get out regularly and that meant going to Italy about twice a year, with occasional visits to America as well. It was his solution and in time he would find ways of absorbing it into his fiction. He went back to Italy on 1 September, took Stevie with him to London to see plays – *The Cherry*

Orchard, *Tea House of the August Moon*, *Guys and Dolls* – then he travelled on to Venice and was away until 24 September.

When he finished *Alien with a Passport* he sent the ms. to William Plomer, asking him to cast a friendly but very cool eye over it, simply to say that it worked or didn't. Only two people had seen it: Stanley Rhinehart who was prepared to publish it and Eileen who said it was good when it was serious and awful when it tried to be comic. He worried about the possibility of libel and thought of releasing it only in America.[22] He saw the work as a romantic satire, a new genre, something to free Irish fiction from the cliché realism and cliché naturalism and pseudo-satire. The main problem was to learn how to take life calmly and to write in a totally detached manner, to play with the material. 'Just a subject. Stand back, gentlemen! Let a fellow write about this crap, can't you!'[23]

Plomer found the novel 'loose, expansive, various, touching, absurd, muddled', very Irish and deeply and essentially Catholic. A critical reader, however, might be disconcerted by the way it flew along erratically on wings that didn't match, propelled by two impulses, one farcical, the other serious. His comment on the main characters was devastating: 'I don't believe in Stanislaus, I don't find Loopy funny, I lose sight of F.X. and of Miss Smith'.[24] O'Faolain saw what Plomer was saying: his experiment did not come off – it had given the impression of indiscipline instead of planned disorder, inconsequenciality where he had wanted it to seem (but only to seem) irresponsible, and of triviality. He was sick of Irish peasant stuff and had wanted to be detached, sardonically amused, wanted to say 'This is the joke – and behind all your silliness this is the tragedy; i.e. life-refusal, dodging, touch-and-very-much-*go* attitude to love and life'.[25] Three blue-covered copies of the novel, cleanly retyped on instructions from Rhinehart now sat on his desk. He had spent over four years on the work, had put considerable thought into it, and, once again, tried to produce a different kind of novel. Cape wanted to publish, but by then he was too uncertain as to its quality and thought it 'dangerously near libellous'.[26]

[15]

A Wasted Life?

THE new year 1955 brought stresses: Julia, home from Paris for Christmas, was in bed with a suspected ulcer, Stevie had been knocked down by a car and was in hospital, Sean was 'dying of lack of pressure'.[1] It snowed and was bitterly cold in their underheated house. After another trip to Italy in March to lecture in Turin, Milan, Rome, and Genoa, and to visit Sicily, he asked John Kelleher to be '*ice coldly objective*' about *Alien with a Passport*. He had written it 'in an effort to find a way to speak through a hundred emotional and psychological gags'.

He did not care, he added, if he never saw Italy again, apart from Rome. If he could settle down in Ireland it would be good for him. But that was hard. 'I was sailing home on the ould Aer Lingus plane after two enchanting days with Julia in Paris (not to mention four in Rome where I outNeroed Nero) and there on the paper I sees Bishop Lucy of Cork thundering about the rights of the Church over the state in all and every department of life with knobs on: not to speak of other lunacies dotted all over the paper. Well, first I boiled and then I roared with laughter . . . and as we sailed down in the twilight on to this sweet, pleasant, empty, green, sparkling, sunny, misty, little island I felt honestly as one who has come from the world to the Land of the Eternally Infantile'. A Dail deputy wrote to the *Irish Times* expressing his 'horror' at Lucy, saying he'd rather sacrifice his political career than obey, and then signed himself 'Quo Vadis', explaining that he did not want to end his political career before it had begun. What can one do, O'Faolain asked, in such a comedy, but either get sick or burst a bloodvessel in anger or amusement? And he was expected to write 'about this farcical country and its farcical people, calmly, or wittily, or passionately'. Was it any wonder he'd been taking flying jumps out of it for Italy? But the trips did not provide escape, because he could not jump off his own shadow. 'I must either stop here and learn to take it; or stop here and shut up; or get out of it and take it (if it is easier to do so at a distance); or get out of it and shut up.' If Kelleher read his novel and considered how few stories he'd been writing, he would see that he had stopped 'here', 'and not taken it and shut up, or been shut up. My state of soul is a calm lake if Stromboli is a dead volcano. I'm in chassis'. He would have left long ago were it not for physical bonds, Eileen and Steve: 'pray for us lost souls. We are in Purgatory'.[2]

Kelleher wrote two letters: a long, constructive response which was enthusiastic about the quality of the writing in *Alien with a Passport* but critical of the characterization. It was, he thought, the first Irish book written in a major key since God knows when, but the Irish section, which should be the strongest, was the weakest, weaker than the Italian and French sections.[3] In those backgrounds O'Faolain observes objectively, and with respect, the continuum of ordinary life. The Irish scene is observed subjectively through two characters, is sentimental and unsympathetic, and there is no continuum.[4]

The novel, O'Faolain admitted, encouraged by Kelleher's response, meant a lot to him. If he had '*utterly*' failed he did not think he would have the guts to try again, in another way. He was still frightened of possible libel action, chiefly by Opus Dei who might recognize themselves in the novel's Vae Victis. The novel, he admitted, 'does really mean a lot to me, and I put more into it than I pretended'.[5] He began work on his sixth novel, declaring, 'If this is another flop, I surrender. Somebody else must solve the problem of how to write an Irish novel which isn't just an "Irish" novel though being set in Ireland'.[6]

In July 1953 he sent a dramatization of 'The Lonely Woman' to Micheál Ó hAodha, Production Director, Radio Eireann. As it was based on his mother and one of her friends, he wanted the voices to have recognizably Cork accents. It was, he said, his first effort at dramatization for radio and he was only too willing to learn from the experts.[7] Ó hAodha thought it would play well and that the members of the radio repertory company, from Cork and Kerry, would have the right accents. He encouraged O'Faolain to send more scripts.[8] O'Faolain then did 'The Murderer' which Ó hAodha also liked. The fee in each case was £30 with £15 for a repeat. All went well until

'The Lonely Woman' was performed. O'Faolain was infuriated. 'I take my hat off to all concerned', he wrote. 'What was intended as a slight comedy was produced and presented most effectively as a dismal dirge . . . For Christ's sake will you, free, gratis and for nothing . . . do the thing once more – for the sake of radio drama, my vanity, or reputation . . . And *please* let me attend the rehearsal this time'. As for 'The Murderer', he must be allowed to attend rehearsals or he would 'withdraw it'.[9] Ó hAodha soothed him, admitted the pace had been too slow, assured him of a repeat and that he could attend rehearsals. 'The Murderer' also required Cork accents. Knocked out with smallpox as a result of being vaccinated in order to get a visa to go to America, O'Faolain could not attend the final rehearsals, but he thanked the producer for the 'excellent production'. He then dramatized 'The End of the Record' and 'The Fur Coat'. 'A Born Genius' became a full-length play that Ó hAodha found very moving. Somewhat loftily O'Faolain informed Aloys Fleischmann, who thought the play captured the atmosphere of Cork, that it was not really about Cork but about a theme![10]

Sam Lawrence reported favourably on *Alien* to Little Brown but other reports were more negative and the novel was turned down. Sean asked Emelie Jacobson to return the ms. so that he could show it to Cape. *Alien* was turned down by four publishers. He was disappointed and shaken. He was almost fifty-six and the chances of prolonged leisure to do only what he should be doing were remote. 'I fear I lacked courage earlier on. I should have been more poor, more egotistical, never given hostages to fortune'. 'To tell you the truth I feel very depressed these last two months. The practical failure of that novel has been a blow. I have written no story that satisfies me. I sell none. Just for the feck of it read the enclosed. It has been refused by the *New Yorker*, *Atlantic*, *Harper's Bazaar*, *Vogue*, *Mademoiselle*, *Virginia Quarterly*, *Partisan*, *Yale* and *New World Writing*. I can't sell "Lovers of the Lake" either. I have got so I think I can't write stories at all'.[11] At least Little Brown wanted to publish a collection of his stories. He intended to add ten or twelve 'new equally good ones', but warned that Devin Garrity who held the rights on *The Man Who Invented Sin* would be 'tough'. He sent Alan Collins a list of the stories from *The Man Who Invented Sin* (10), *Midsummer Night Madness* (4) and *Purse of Coppers* (6) that he wanted in the proposed collection.

Being commissioned by *Holiday* to do articles on Italy and on American cities increased his earnings, but put increased pressure on his time and energy. He visited Italy in August 1956, flew to New York at the end of September, worked on assignment in Las Vegas, San Francisco and Philadelphia, and prepared a piece on St. Patrick's Day in New York. In January 1957 he went to Los Angeles, Texas and Chicago. In February he was in Boston. While he worked on new articles to meet deadlines, he revised articles already sent in. He wanted to achieve a realistic sense of place, but *Holiday* also had definite ideas as to what they wanted and frequently asked for revisions. He was philosophical about this and his professionalism steadied him: 'one is asked to do a job competently and the rest is a cheque'. He met deadlines scrupulously, revised when requested, worked hard to make his articles informative, alive and factually accurate. He had the true journalist's capacity to become excited by fresh material. When he got back to Ireland early in March he set about writing the articles. Keyed-up about his piece on L.A. he was relieved when Harry Sions at *Holiday* liked it. Sions then wanted the article on Texas and something more on downtown L.A., to cover the Mexicans and Japanese. Sean supplied three additional pages on the Mexicans in L.A., but observed that once he went under the surface too much in these pieces he came upon subsoil of a less appealing nature. In the piece on Texas he skipped the issue of the Mexicans, the Black problem, the finances and politics of oil, on the assumption that *Holiday* was not a sociological periodical. 'One seems better advised to concentrate on the general impression of L.A. as a unique city-type, and on general aspects of Texas, e.g. its variety and its changing nature'.[12] He could only do these assignments at all by working up a fictitious excitement about them, and if he delayed too long they went dead. He analysed his disposition. 'Am I a nervous type? I'd be inclined to think my nerves boss me terribly. To slow down is a painful discipline'.[13]

Sean's mood of sober self-assessment persisted. While he was occupied with assignments, adding a section on Huxley to *The Vanishing Hero* and pottering away at a new novel, called *No Country for Old Men*, he spent the rest of his time either as Eileen's 'felaheen' in the garden or bewailing his wasted life. 'Now 56, and what have I to show for it? About twelve fairish to good stories and that is all. I looked at a couple of my other volumes, e.g. *An Irish Journey*, the other night, and I thanked Hitler and Stalin and Franco and Mussolini and the economic situation that it and most of my other ballsy books are out of print. I have written all my wasted life too fast too much. O to recall the years. (I'd do the same again.) My niche in literature is about the same as a minor metaphysical poet: to appear in anthologies. What a labour to achieve so little! . . . What is this desire for immortality?'[14]

Before Stephen was due to return from Cork, where he had been staying with the Lucys, Sean and Eileen took a trip to Lake Garda. On their way they visited Julia in London where Eileen had to go to hospital because of a recurrence of stomach trouble, but the treatment was so successful that she got her appetite back. After ten years of 'weak tummy' she was now eating steaks, putting on weight, and letting out her frocks.[15] It was, Sean said, a joy to see her eating well in Italy after ten years of struggling along on tea and toast. They spent seventeen days at Lake Garda. When she got back to Ireland Eileen ate and drank as never before since 1945.[16] According to O'Connor she was now known as 'two steak Eily'. In September Stephen went to Wireless College in Wales to become a radio officer, Gus's wife Eileen visited, and Julia was home. With the maid that meant four women in the house and Sean was 'driven mad by them'. He was at the age when the children were less dear to him than they used to be 'chiefly because they made it clear that they were independent entities' and that he and Eileen were expected not to behave like parents anymore – except when specifically invited. He thought this was tough on Eileen in particular.[17]

Despite the enthusiasm at Atlantic Monthly Press about O'Faolain's stories, publication was delayed, partly because they had to search, with Kelleher's assistance, through periodicals for permissions to republish, but mainly because of Devin-Adair's reluctance to release the stories from *The Man Who Invented Sin*. 'The very simple truth', Alan Collins informed Lawrence, is that Garrity, the publisher, Devin-Adair, 'is mad and wants to slap Sean down'. He laid down severe, indeed, 'outrageous' conditions.[18] Garrity's behaviour was determined to some degree by Sean's failure to honour an arrangement to give *Newman's Way* to Devin-Adair, even though he had received an advance of $2000. At the time of the proposed publication of *Finest Stories*, he still owed Garrity $300. The immediate escape from Garrity's claws was to reduce the number of stories from *Man Who Invented Sin*, but O'Faolain insisted that 'Up the Bare Stairs' and 'The Trout' must be included. He wanted the book to be good 'and to hell with money considerations'. He told Collins that there was no use wasting words on Garrity. 'Why should I waste my spirit on him? I'm afraid this is a weakness in me'.[19] But he protested at the terms of his contract. He complained that Cape were getting £50 and that Devin-Adair whom he thought were getting 30% of his advance of $1000 were getting 30% of all the royalties. It was, he said, 'unprecedented' that Garrity should get a share in all royalties, including stories he did not publish.[20] The agreement between Little Brown and Devin-Adair also specified that the permission was granted for this one 'anthology' only; the rights then reverted to Devin-Adair.

But he felt very good about the forthcoming collection and about the approaching (November) publication of his Princeton essays. The rejection of *Alien with a Passport* had been bad for his morale. He felt 'terribly has-been-ish'. The rejection was all the harder to take, because he knew the novel had some good material in it. And while he had begun to write another, his way of life kept intruding. And, as he admitted to John Kelleher, his lifestyle drove him on the treadmill of travel and journalism. Long ago he had opted for a comfortable existence. Why, he asked vainly, could he not be poor and ascetic? At one time he used to say: '£200 and a cottage. I ask no more!'[21] The fact was, however, that when it came to a choice between perfection of the work and perfection of the life, he opted for life and burdened himself to afford it.

He went to Florence in July 1956, was back in Dublin for late July and all of August, was in Italy for the first ten days of September, then back in Dublin for the last two weeks of September. His letters reveal a harried existence. He and Eileen were 'flooded' with visitors from Princeton, Virginia, the Midwest and 'God knows where else'. Julia came home on holidays on 31 July, he expected proofs of the *Vanishing Hero* on 1 August, he hoped Little Brown would bring out the stories, and he hoped Steve knew the facts of life.[22] Eyre and Spottiswoode wanted him to do another travel book. He could, he thought, do one on America, if *Holiday* commissioned three more articles. In the end he was persuaded not to pursue this idea on the grounds that the publication would not add to his stature as a writer.

Meanwhile the enthusiasm continued to grow at Atlantic Monthly Press. Kelleher suggested he should do a 'Books and Men' essay on O'Faolain for the *Atlantic Monthly*. He had in mind a critical and biographical piece to coincide with the publication of the stories. 'I am', Kelleher wrote, 'very interested in seeing that his book gets as good a reception as possible because Sean is, and has been for nearly twenty years, the chief hope of Irish literature'.[23] O'Faolain had wanted to dedicate the book to Kelleher, who had virtually selected the contents and insisted that he include stories from *Midsummer Night Madness* and *Purse of Coppers*, but Kelleher refused on the grounds that he might be asked to do a review. When *Finest Stories* appeared in May 1957, Sean was very pleased. 'It looks damn good and do I need to tell you how exciting it is to see it and handle it. I'd ambitioned it for years.'[24]

Sean had to have a hernia operation in November 1956. Unaccustomed to hospitals, he suffered the indignities of enemas and bedpans, felt most put upon, but gradually enjoyed being helpless and removed from all responsibility. From the Adelaide he wrote to Emmy to thank her for placing a story of Julia's in the *New Yorker*: 'Oh, I am glad and so grateful'.[25] When he got home, he had to rest, but he worried about his position. He knew he should feel that he belonged to his time, but how could he belong if he lived in isolation, in Dublin? But, he reflected, he might as well accept the challenge. 'Here one is dropped. Here is one's fated field'. One thing he felt to be true: it was folly to go on applying the humanist criteria to Ireland, and once he stopped doing so life became much more bearable. The greatest hope for Ireland now was that there was no hope for her. 'She has no progressive future. She really does live on her past'.[26]

He received an unexpected boost to his morale when the Irish Government appointed him Director of the Arts Council. At a meeting at Government Buildings the Taoiseach, John A. Costello, asked O'Faolain if he would accept the position. O'Faolain was flattered. It was, he said, the first honour his country had ever given him and he accepted gladly. But the Archbishop of Dublin appealed to Costello 'to prevent that man being appointed'. Costello asked Thomas Bodkin if he would accept instead. Shocked and embarrassed, Bodkin refused. After all, he pointed out, he had been present when O'Faolain had been offered the job.[27]

The Archbishop's opposition was understandable. Not only was O'Faolain a banned writer and an outspoken anticlerical, but as President of the Irish Association of Civil Liberty (1953–1957) he had drawn particular attention to censorship. During this period the Archbishop, backed by the hierarchy, had spearheaded what the Government recognized as an orchestrated attack on 'immoral' literature. Many Catholic lay organizations engaged in a campaign of letter-writing to the Taoiseach.[28] When the Association held a public meeting in the Mansion House, the right-wing society, Maria Duce, handed out leaflets describing the Association as Communist. Sean defended the Association against that charge in a letter to the papers. At the meeting O'Faolain said that as a writer he objected to the fact that he was denied the right given to an embezzler, a burglar, or an abortionist: prosecution in a court of law. The Association sent the Taoiseach a list of banned books and a petition, signed by 834 people, that he re-examine the workings of the Censorship Act. At another meeting Sean spoke against Government control of broadcasting. In his final year of office he argued against the boycotting of Protestants by Catholics in Fethard-on-Sea on the grounds that no group of citizens had the right to enforce their views on others by physical force. The issue, he said, concerned the civil liberty of every citizen. Work at the Association had its lighter moments. Once, when a Canadian newspaper published a syndicated article referring to Owen Sheehy-Skeffington as a neo-Communist and to the other members of Council as fellow travellers, Council sued for libel and had a good dinner at the United Services Club on the proceeds.

Sean flew to New York on 7 January 1957, despite Eileen's anxiety about his health. She felt he was not sufficiently recovered from his operation. He had a demanding schedule: New York (9–12 January), Los Angeles (16–25), Texas (28–5 February), New York (7–11), Boston (12–15), Chicago (16–25), New York (27–4 March).

Eileen's anxieties were well founded. The L.A. and Texas trips were too much for him. He returned to the Erlangers to rest. He had a bad foot, an ingrown toenail, an abscess on a tooth and had got into 'a rather sleepless rundown condition'. He was not fit enough for another intensive bout of exploration and he had to cancel his visit to Chicago. He warned Ellmann not to tell Eileen.[29]

At first he regarded his part-time job at the Arts Council as the most interesting job in Ireland. The salary of £1000 a year was welcome, but he had only one secretary and no desk. At his suggestion the civil servant and novelist, Mervyn Wall, was appointed Secretary to the Arts Council in 1959, and this eased the burden of O'Faolain's work. Wall was a competent official with a satirical, anecdotal nature. O'Faolain enjoyed working with him, but his own job was frustrating because there was so little money available. What there was he had to dispense as wisely as he could, in response to requests from various parts of the country — local drama groups, music societies, in addition to the more established bodies. What, he asked Denis Johnston, can one do for drama apart from wasting £4000 to get Edwards and MacLiammoir out of bankruptcy, giving Longford £2000 to help rebuild the Gate, Waterford £500 to repair the Royal, and odds and ends of grants to swarms of rural societies?[30] He gave the Cork Ballet Co. a grant and when the Cork Symphony went to Limerick, he attended. He and Eileen opened a Festival in Scarriff, Co. Clare.

He enjoyed watching Council members, Thomas McGreevy, Niall Montgomery, Hayes McCoy, Lord Rosse, Sir Basil Goulding, Muriel Gahan, John Mahar, and Father Donal O'Sullivan displaying their personal oddities and trying to steer them to some agreement on something. By early May all he had done was to get *Irish Writing* an annual grant of £250. He made some attempts to bring about change. In July 1957 he had a meeting with the Minister of Education in which he suggested, as a recommendation of the Council, that the National Gallery and the National Museum should be provided with sales counters where they could provide publications and reproductions about their holdings. He also recommended that the Director of the National Gallery be given professional assistance to produce a catalogue. Lest McGreevy be offended, he stressed that he understood the difficulties of not having sufficient staff and that there was no criticism of the Gallery, its Director, or management.[31]

He organized an international exhibition of printing equipment and books and invited the distinguished English scholar, Stanley Morrison, to give a lecture. Against the advice of the teachers at Bolton Street Technical School where the exhibition was held, he insisted that the Aula Maxima at University College, Dublin, would be a more suitable venue for the Morrison lecture. That turned out to be a disastrous decision. Only seven people turned up. Even though the teachers had strongly advised him not to use the university, he blamed them bitterly for the poor attendance. He had more success in making all the oil and petrol companies agree to cut out rural advertising and got a furious letter from the legal adviser to David Allen, the billboard tycoon, telling him to lay off. One of his wilder schemes was to provide grants to preserve all the thatched cottages in the country. He resigned from the Arts Council in 1959 for the simple reason, he explained later, that the work was futile, since there was so little money.

He went to Italy on 15 May, but decided it was too risky to write about

[211]

the Vatican. He wandered down the coast south of Rimini, visited Florence and Urbino and looked in vain for Italy's famous sun; his was, he thought, 'a restless life, unsuitable to any form of work'. He returned to Dublin on 18 June. He was amused to hear that *Finest Stories* would be the August selection of the Catholic Book Club. That meant a payment of $1520 on publication. He had already signed with Bantam Books for a paperback edition. He was experiencing success as a writer. At the same time he received further recognition when Trinity College Dublin awarded him an honorary D.Litt. degree on 5 July 1957. He prepared an article on Ireland for *Holiday*, wrote a couple of long stories, worked on another novel, and had, he declared, no complaints.[32]

But he had worries before the summer ended. Julia had fallen in love with Lauro Martines, a Harvard Ph.D. student whom she met in Florence. Her parents knew nothing about him and were alarmed at the speed with which the relationship developed; they had met in July and planned to marry in November. O'Faolain asked Kelleher to find out if there was anything about Martines that would justify their telling him to go to hell. 'What can a distracted father and mother do?' Martines was a lapsed Catholic, but O'Faolain felt in no position to hold that against him. They worried about his ability to support Julia. They would be content, O'Faolain said, if Julia was really madly in love and if he got employment in New England, but it was unthinkable that she might end up in Indiana or Ohio. 'Curse all the whole and entire American nation for stealing my daughter'.[33]

Further letters from Julia persuaded them that she knew her own mind, but Sean felt 'uncertain about her man'. In the past she had been involved with a Spanish communist. On that occasion her father had persuaded her to come home for a year to see if the relationship lasted. He and Eileen kept her latest involvement 'very secret for fear of gossip and the desire to be sure'. Sean was anxious not to incur the young people's wrath at being spied on, but felt he had to face it in the cause of paternal duty. He knew he was being pompous, as Julia had 'scornfully' told him.[34]

Julia came home 'on the understanding that we want her marriage to be happy and wish to partake of it, in every normal way, the basic presumption being that Martines was the man for her'. She and Eileen shopped happily, getting clothes for the wedding and the future, making plans for their journey to Florence. At their request it was to be a church wedding. Sean insisted. Julia, who was no longer a Catholic, asked 'What difference can it make to you?' 'It will mean a lot to your mother and me'. There were unpleasant scenes. An occasion that should have been filled with happiness was spoiled. 'We are a rather sad household this morning'. In a postscript he asked: 'You won't tell anybody? Especially Stan??!'[35]

Sean's misery persisted. 'This home has been an unhappy one.' Julia went back to Florence and to Lauro, 'torn between some doubt, much misery at the sorrow she had seen in her mother, and mostly belief in L.M.'. Lauro had written, but Sean still wondered whether Julia was going to starve or 'go nuts' in the prairies. 'And that's enough if it is all . . . Forgive everything you can. It's been rather hell'.[36] Under the strain of his conversations with Julia Sean revealed the source of his information about Lauro. But Kelleher had reported to him in the strictest confidence. The betrayal of that confidence was inexcusable. The wedding took place on 20 November at the Church of Santa Lucia dei Magnoli, Florence. Irish newspapers carried the announcement, but the parents of the bride did not attend.

In 1954 Aloys Fleischmann had proposed that O'Faolain should be invited to open a Book Exhibition in Cork, but the Lord Mayor strongly opposed it. Local IRA antagonism was still strong and O'Faolain was regarded as anticlerical. Now in October 1957 he gave a lecture at University College Cork on the various pleasures of fiction and had his picture in the *Cork Examiner* under the caption 'Writer Lectures in Native Town'. He got word that *The Vanishing Hero* had received 'extraordinarily good reviews' and had sold about 1800 copies. *Finest Stories* had now sold 3900 copies. His new novel, *Arms and the Woman*, was read at Atlantic Monthly Press and turned down. Once again he had failed. He was rather frightened to realize that he could have believed for so long in something that turned out to be nothing. He could only conclude that he could not write novels.[37]

Richard Ellmann arranged for Sean to be invited to teach two courses at Northwestern for a fee of $5000. He had been unable to accept for Spring 1957 because of commitments to *Holiday*. Now he was free. He had decided to lecture on 'The Various Pleasures of Fiction' so that he could analyse the precise nature, scope, variety, depth, and so on, of the pleasure offered by a number of novels; talk on trying to classify pleasure; show how the writer managed it, technically.[38] Sending the list to Ellmann he summed up recent events: Julia was married; he regretted 'like hell' that her husband would take her 3000 miles away; he felt like the G.O.M. of Irish letters, since they had made him a D.Litt. and Director of the Arts Council; he had written two novels in the last three years and both had been turned down in the States; Eileen wouldn't go with him to Northwestern; 'Alas she will probably have Julie while I'm away'.[39]

[16]

Acceptance

THE New Year of 1958 began well with the arrival from Atlantic Monthly Press of Sam Lawrence's 'most wonderful gift' of a calf-bound copy of *Finest Stories* and of *Vanishing Hero*. Stephen exclaimed 'Maw! . . . When Dad conks can I have 'em?' Sean was writing long stories in a 'lyrical-romantic style'[1] one of which, 'Love's Young Dream', Emelie Jacobson sold to the *Saturday Evening Post* for $4000, despite his fear that an editor might say 'Too long. Nice, sensitive. But not for us'.[2] This story confused him. He felt enchantment but also a sort of troubling obscurity; he was not sure he understood the differences between the two girls or between what each meant to the boy.[3] *Post* asked him to cut it; he did not object. He did not mind what happened in a magazine: it was the final version that mattered. He pointed to the example of Thomas Hardy. When Mudies objected to a man carrying a girl across a stream in his arms, Hardy had him wheel her across in a wheelbarrow. It was solely a question of what one could do, without making nonsense of the story.[4] People responded well to his lyrical realism. 'A Touch of Autumn in the Air', which Sam Lawrence thought had 'a magic and evocative beauty in it out of all proportion to its length', was accepted by *The Listener* for Christmas 1958.[5] Sean began to see what he could do with this more expansive form as he rediscovered that he was 'a lyrical, dreamy dope who knows O about people. Anyway . . . people bore me to boredom for the most part: and above all the great noble gallant salt of life common people.'[6]

He had intended to go to Corofin for some shooting, but when Stephen developed a temperature of 105° he stayed at home. Having been 'tormented' by Julia, who was 'absurdly and disquietingly happy', he thought boys were easier to rear than girls.[7] When Stephen was gone, he missed him. 'He's a nice lad but O Jesus so immature. And so assertive'.[8]

Before he left for Northwestern he and Eileen took a holiday in London and saw some plays. On the way to Evanston he stayed in New York to see Alene. With Ellmann's help he got an apartment at 1725 Orrington Avenue and settled in. He taught two courses: 'Essential Pleasures of Fiction' and 'Creative Writing'. In his fiction course there were 110 students, but he had an assistant who read and graded the papers. They studied *Manon*, *Middlemarch*, *Scarlet and Black*, *Fathers and Children*, *The Brothers Karamazov*, *Swann's Way*, *Wolf Solent*, *Knot of Vipers*, *The Razor's Edge*, and *Lucky Jim*. He encouraged students to ask why they liked a particular novel. It was at that point, he said, that intelligent criticism began.[9]

He made a good impression. Moody Prior, Dean of the Graduate School, heard no complaints. He regarded him as a man of great charm, somewhat reserved but not aloof, not an aggressive or argumentative conversationalist, and a pleasure to be with and talk to.[10] Jean H. Hagstrum, Professor of English, was impressed with his 'intelligence, charm and graciousness'.[11] Although he was 'doing wonderfully' as a teacher, Ellmann suspected that he still found Julia's marriage 'disquieting'.[12] He was an over-anxious teacher, and spent a lot of time in Deering library. Later he wrote to Ellmann about 'the imbecile sort of life' he had lived in Evanston. He should have gone round in the evenings to chat, instead of working in the library, 'feeling blue' in the Jongle d'Amour, or going into Chicago to do research for an article for *Holiday*. He attended a few meetings of the *Finnegans Wake* club and before he left was presented with the *Finnegans Wake* cup!

When he got home, Julia was waiting to see him. When she left he was desolate. 'Losing her is like death . . . The ribbon, the torn postcard, the forgotten handkerchief become not so much, or not alone memorials as forewarnings. Everything . . . endures a moment or a day'.[13] It rained for three weeks and was 'misty, maddening and melancholic . . . and so boring'. He asked Alan Collins at Curtis Brown to invite his 'charming daughter' to lunch 'for my sake': 'ask her alone, professionally and MAKE her get at her novel, I don't know what she's up to. She needs to be immediately given the feeling that she is a writer first and a wife after! Anyway I am intensely jealous of her bloody husband'. He and Eileen were about to go to Italy. 'If you want to be a pet and drop me a card about Julia I'd love you for it. She is my Benjamina! My heart is broken to have lost her to your beloved country'.[14] He sent $150 to Sukie at Curtis Brown to give to Julia in case she needed it. 'Why do fathers', he asked, 'hang on so pathetically to their daughters?' He felt foolish worrying about her, but she knew hardly anybody in New York.[15] In late November Sean asked Sukie to put another $150 in his account so that he could send Julia a cheque for Christmas. Both Sean and Eileen continued to feel 'very lonely' after she left. Eileen was well in general, but got a series of colds that left her very debilitated. By November, however, she was very much better.

He and Eileen drove in the sunshine around the Italian lakes. It was a relief from Ireland's incessant rain. It was, Sean said, like motoring all around Brigitte Bardot. 'Not a brain within sight but lots of lovely matter'.[16] When he got back his mind was so full of the lakes that he decided to write on them at once. 'The Lakes are so much a matter of impressions and sensations . . . that one wants freshness'. He was keen on doing St. Louis and New Orleans in March, but burked a bit at Miami.[17] He was concerned that Sions had cut his earnings from $2000 to $1500. He had postponed his article on Chicago, because the books he had ordered had not arrived. He reminded Bob Garry at the Great Expectations bookshop to send them. Exasperated by Garry's slowness, he asked Ellmann to intervene. 'Can you for God's sake ring him or call on him and find out? I am in desperate need of Chicago books and of my own'.[18] But a month later, despite Ellmann's intervention, they still had not arrived. O'Faolain was enraged: 'that ineffable indescribable bastard Bob Garry is the *bottom*'. He could not start his article and to keep *Holiday* calm had to go to Italy and do a different article.[19]

Further articles on American cities would require another trip in the Spring. He began to plan ahead: he asked Denis Johnston at Mount Holyoke to keep him in mind for a lecture. He was, he told Ellmann, always willing to pick up 'fare-paying lectures en route'. He was trying to get to St. Paul in the hope of luring Julia, his exiled masterpiece, from Portland, Oregon, but could stop off in Chicago for a night if there were some dollars to pick up. He spent five days in Minneapolis. Julia flew in for a 'very happy weekend during which we just talked and talked'. He negotiated with Dick Blackmuir about doing a creative literature course as well as another Gauss Seminar. He told him that he would like to go to Princeton for a year, and to bring Eileen. For the seminar he would develop further the idea of applying the Pleasure Principle to the novel. He could do the writing course from his experience at Northwestern. He was 'delightfully excited' by this prospect as was Eileen who had not been in America, since they lived at Appian Way. They would need at least three rooms (two bedrooms and a living room) plus the usuals. Julia was due to have a child on 2 September. So he and Eileen were glad that they would be in America at that time. They were looking forward to the birth of their first grandchild. Already Sean felt possessive. Stephen was home for Christmas. A party he gave for his friends was spoiled when ten gate-crashers 'made a shambles of the place'. O'Faolain had to put them out at one o'clock.[20]

June was an eventful month with the premature birth of his grandson, his investiture with the Order First Class of the Star of Italian Solidarity for furthering knowledge of Italy and Italian culture, and because he became increasingly attracted by the idea of writing a book called *My Ireland*. It could, he thought, be a sort of autobiographical book with the stress on the environment and the individual's struggle with it to shape and hold himself intact. He talked over the idea with his agent in London and with Eyre and Spottiswoode. It would, he told Kelleher, have something to do with how a man finally comes to his identity through Ireland (and England and Italy and America), comes at sixty to the point of saying contentedly at last: 'well, so what? If I am nuts I'm nuts. If I am sensual (or a Puritan) or not Balzac, or a congenital romantic, or a congenital liar, or no good dealing with men, or a humanist lost in a medieval (or Barbarian) outlying island of the world – I *am*!' He had a lovely title: *Vive Moi!*. He had seen this on a wall in Paris: 'Vive de Gaulle, Vive Mollet, Vive Mendes France, all scratched out by some splendidly egotistical lunatic who chalked up after them – Vive Moi! (As one might add: Be Jasus!)'. His agent and publisher and wife were not enthusiastic, but he thought he 'could have great fun with it. Maybe as a personal novel (to give me more scope as a congenital liar) like *La Vie de Henri Brulard*. The Life of Larry Looney'.[21]

By the end of July he had a clearer idea of what he would do and was much excited by it. So were Sam Lawrence and Little Brown. The book, he thought, would be 'part autobiography' or at any rate 'personal', 'part peregrinatory, in so far as it would pass from Ireland to America, to England, to Europe for the background and environment of the *moi*, part cogitative, a little like Yeats's *Reveries*. The theme before me is the discovery of self through the strong tensions of environment, i.e. mainly Ireland, with its assumptions about certain idealised modes of life which I gradually found unviable, after long struggles with them. In the end I have found, though I have learned much from these struggles, I have mainly learned, deeply into myself, a love for and trust in myself — wherefore I would like to call the book *Vive Moi!* At sixty I accept not the universe but *me*. Ireland, England, America and Italy have not "made" me. They and I between us have thrown up on the shore of age a self, an identity, that I can recognise and accept. It has been a sort of journey of innocence — the guiltlessness of being what one finally is. I do not guarantee that the book will be autobiography. Stendhal's *La Vie de Henri Brulard* . . . was not, yet was. I cannot be more clear at this stage. I do not even guarantee that what may result will not be (like Henri Brulard) ostensibly a novel in the first person'.[22]

But he had 'an underlying fear of acceptance'. He knew that he was a sensuous and sensual man, with a regard for the intelligence. It followed that if he accepted that Ireland was still medieval, he would be accepting that he was out of it, that it would be foolish for him to try to do anything in, with, or for it, and he would just retire, 'instead of being cross with it as I now so often am and for years and years have been'. By looking at his material objectively he might have dissociated himself from it imaginatively and thereby produced 'a loss of sympathy, interest, involvement?' His despondency was, he thought, probably the result of age and selfishness. He was tired of the children, tired of John Charles McQuaid, Pigott (Chairman of the Censorship Board), Dublin Corporation and other things in Ireland that he disliked. How could he find a way of accepting all that while not accepting it, 'a way of being Irish and not-Irish simultaneously'? His last two novels in manuscript had been self-portraits of the 3 a.m. self-as-worthless. 'I'm rightly balled-up now! . . . My God, it is hard to take Life any time, but to take Life in Ireland on Irish terms . . .'. He suffered badly because of his stomach.[23] What he really suffered from was a benign ulcer, brought on, he declared, from frustration and bile at not being in America for so long. There was also the emotional strain brought about by his love for Alene and his loyalty to Eileen. His letter to J. F. Powers about Alan Tate's state, when he was trying to get a divorce, is strikingly empathetic. 'When you think of the agonies of longing, of love (it doesn't matter whether it's "real" or not), of a broken life, of age, etc. etc. et-and infinity-cetera that poor Alan and Caroline are going through.'[24]

* * *

[219]

Sean was emotional on leaving Ireland for two years, and perhaps longer. He wrote to Kelleher on his 'last night', adding his signature '(Jack Whelan of 5 Half Moon St. Cork. Slightly drunk and sentimental)'. They had let Knockaderry, sold the car, emptied the drawers and cupboards. They set out with six suitcases, a packing case, five hand-parcels, and a packet of traveller's cheques. Stephen went into digs while awaiting a ship. On 14 August they sailed from Southampton on the Liberté,[25] stayed with the Erlangers and then moved to 20 North Stanworth Drive, a duplex apartment in a complex of about one hundred and fifty garden apartments, which they rented for $140 a month.

For his Creative Writing course Sean met students individually in fifty minute sessions. He had learned at Northwestern that meeting an entire class was not satisfactory: there was no close-up battle, word for word, through a text. In Princeton he held a couple of general preparatory conferences, then met students once a fortnight, three or four on each of two days each week. Physically it was very exhausting.[26] But he was content. He had nineteen students, worked ten hours a week and earned $8000. But since he had nothing lined up for the second year, he also had to write and lecture on the side to end the year with $2000 or $3000, so that he could pay for the summer ahead, his fares and the empty year.

Because he was still preparing his Gauss seminars, he and Eileen declined an invitation from the Kellehers for Thanksgiving on the grounds that he was too nervous and too worked up about his seminars. At that stage he had only two and half written and would have been far too 'uneasy and rattled to be able to enjoy the good company'. He listed the seminars – Dec. 3 'The Pleasure of Moral Shock: *Chéri* (Colette)'; Dec. 10, 'The Pleasure of Having it Both Ways: *Manon Lescaut* (Prévost)'; Dec. 17, 'The Pleasure of Dismayed Recognition: *Lord Jim* and *Lucky Jim* (Conrad and Amis)'; Jan. 7, 'The Pleasure of Getting Away from it All: *Little Women* (Louisa Alcott)'; Jan. 14, 'The Pleasure of Tension and Extension: *Fathers and Sons* (Turgenev)' and Jan. 21, 'The Pleasure of Imaginative Order: *Le Rouge et le Noir* (Stendhal)'. When the invitations to attend were being sent out on 19 November, he asked that Alene Erlanger be one of the special guests. Normally the seminars were only attended by men, but when Sean spoke on women novelists, he suggested that women should be invited with the result that Eileen Simpson was then included. The format was as before: one hour's lecture followed by an hour's discussion. They got a Christmas card from the Kellehers but had not sent one. 'Blame all', Sean said, 'on the bloody Christian Gauss Seminars which have to date lost me 9 lbs avoirdupois and worn my nerves and Eileen's ragged'. He had not realized how long it takes to do such things properly. At the end, as usual, he felt suddenly tired. The second series of seminars, more in the nature of discussions of novels that he liked, sometimes for odd reasons, were not as interesting as the first.[27]

When the seminars were over he could relax. Princeton had invited him to stay for another year, raised his salary to $12,000, and asked him to teach only Creative Writing, which would have nine students. That was easy, since it required little preparation. It was also unusual. He owed that invitation to his success in the classroom and his friendship with Blackmuir who ran the Creative Writing Programme. On 7 February he gave a public lecture in McCosh Hall on 'The Various Pleasures of Fiction' and was introduced by R. P. Blackmuir. Later that month he went to Boston to give lectures at Brandeis and Boston College, and to see Sam Lawrence, Jack Sweeney, and Kelleher. He received an invitation from Phi Beta Kappa to be one of their peripatetic scholars for about six weeks in 1961–62. The fee would be $6000. His new lecture agent had raised his fee to $500 and $700 plus expenses which he thought 'phenomenal'.

Their lives, O'Faolain wrote, were uneventful apart from toil, an occasional party (what Eileen called 'First Folio-Second Quarto sort of conversation'), a drive in the Western New Jersey country, a rare movie – that was about all! They were also lonely for Julia and delighted when she joined them at Christmas. They had not seen their grandson, but Julia told them he was 'sweet, pretty, smiles' and would soon talk. Sean envied John Kelleher his home and family. They spent much of the Christmas vacation in New York near the Erlangers.

University life, Sean told Norah McGuinness, was rather dull, but New York was truly beautiful at all hours, in all weathers. He and Eileen went there to see Dick Ellmann receive a National Book Award for his life of Joyce. They had dinner with Sean's publisher at the Harvard Club, stayed at the Gotham at the publisher's expense, had lunch at Ellmann's expense at a good French restaurant, saw the Soviet film 'The Cranes Are Flying', bought a few French cheeses and returned to Princeton by bus. Stephen, he added, was last heard of off French Equatorial Africa on a French tanker on his way to southern Italy! 'Full of beans'.[28]

Apart from having people round for drinks, Eileen and Sean did not entertain much, but they gave a small dinner party on St. Patrick's Day to celebrate Sean's sixtieth birthday. The O'Faolains had some close friends, including the Moynahans, McAndrews, Simpsons and Jacobis. Eileen, however, was homesick. She thought Princeton was inward looking and complacent; the people seemed cold, impersonal and boring. She missed her garden, complained about the smallness of her kitchen and made it clear that she preferred to live in Ireland. One night at dinner she sang an Irish song and spoke nostalgically of their visits to the Irish speaking west. On another occasion on hearing a recording of Irish songs, she and Sean were so overcome that they had to leave the room. When the Moynahans told her they had been to Clonmacnoise, she said 'But you haven't seen the hidden Ireland, Gougane Barra'. When the young book editor, Alan Williams, played a recording of Siobhán McKenna reading the Molly Bloom soliloquy, Eileen became uncomfortable as the language became 'smutty'. She was very sensitive and took offence easily. Once when the Moynahans gave a party for the O'Faolains, they included a number of Dublin people. Instead of being pleased, Eileen clutched Julian by the arm, exclaiming 'Julian, I don't know how you do it!' 'Do what?' he asked. 'You have brought all my enemies together'.

Princeton friends had mixed views on the relationship between Sean and Eileen. Eileen Simpson thought they were good comrades who slept in separate beds. While Eileen was reserved and not as sensual as Sean, he was devoted to her. Adultery, Blackmuir told Julian Moynahan, was O'Faolain's favourite mortal sin. That characterization did not prepare him for the 'gentlemanly, genial, mostly sedate and kindly man who turned up'. But there was some truth in it, as Jane Jacobi discovered when Sean drove her home from the hospital where she had been visiting Bill. She did not realize what he had in mind until he made sexual advances.

The O'Faolains went back to Ireland at the end of June and rented Norah McGuinness's cottage in Wicklow. Sean tried to find Stephen. He telephoned his ship to see if he had left London on it, discovered he had not and tracked him down to the home of an English woman, Patricia McDaniel, with whom he was living. Her husband, an American, had been killed the previous year. Sean disapproved, persuaded Stephen to leave, set him up in a flat and got him a job doing electrical work.[29]

Sean and Eileen worried about Stephen, but Sean took refuge in working on the anthology of stories: *Short Stories: A Study for Pleasure* and the autobiography. He enjoyed Ireland mainly by ignoring it. When September came he returned to Princeton, where he told a long, funny story about searching for Stephen and ejecting him from the woman's home. He did not seem to mind being on his own again. 'I come in the door', he said, 'and there's my typewriter smiling at me'. He went to the races at Monmouth, Camden and other places with Alene. They saw Shelagh Delaney's *A Taste of Honey* and took in a couple of foreign films. As usual work was a great solace. In the world of the imagination he could close the door on the intrusions of the real world. He had been disappointed when Stephen took up with someone whom he considered socially inferior: pointing to his typewriter he asked 'Did I do all this in vain?'[30] He wrote rather airily to John Kelleher about an eventful summer 'crowned by the madcap and seemingly happy marriage of my son Steve to an English girl aged 31, mother of three children'.[31]

Eileen remained behind. She went as far as Shannon to see him off. He had a dreadful cold and flew out into a hurricane. She rented Paul Henry's house in Bray, tried to put 'anxiety' out of her head, but continued to worry about her 'problem child'. 'I do not see much prospects of it ending happily in marriage, as he, the poor boy thinks. He seems under a dreadful strain'.[32] The wedding took place on 26 October in the Church of St. Michael, Rathdown. Eileen left for America on 4 November and had a 'barbarous journey'. She told Ria Mooney she avoided the wedding. Later that month she and Sean stayed for a weekend with the Erlangers at their country estate in Elberon, New Jersey, where everyone was 'so happy and so kind'. They also spent Thanksgiving with them.[33] That winter Stephen came to Princeton and was very ill at ease with his parents, particularly his father. Patricia was expecting their baby. Sean was anxious that it should not be called Sean.

The O'Faolains returned to Knockaderry in July. 'It is', Sean wrote 'heaven to be back in our home'. He could enjoy being back in the knowledge that he would be going away again in October. 'No life, no place is now perfect for me if I feel I'm stuck there. So long as I know I'm not there permanently all is well'. When their daughter-in-law called they drove to Hunter's Hotel for lunch and a walk on the beach. He did a bit of gardening, building a low wall to shelter a flower-bed. But they employed a gardener and a painter to do the more strenuous tasks, bringing the house and garden back into shape after being rented for two years.

Sean corrected proofs of *I Remember! I Remember!*, 'quite a nice collection', he thought, 'a bit Celtic and dreamy, a very long way from the Tough School. Not an eye gouged out. Not a single dirty word. Not a bulging muscle'.[34] It sold well but was, he thought, a '*very* pensive book'. The 'superb' title story describes two sisters, one confined to a wheelchair who remembers facts, the other who has left Ireland imagines more. One is a paralysed Irish symbol of truth in contrast with the wandering Diana of her American sister. Diana has been imagining a lot about reality (i.e. herself). There is no other way to see truth (i.e. self) but to imagine (i.e. create) it. We create ourselves. 'The essential thing is to imagine sanely. The paralysed sister didn't imagine at all. She just remembered the data and buried them like a squirrel'.[35]

It was a key story, as important in the directions now taken in his work as 'A Broken World' had been in *Purse of Coppers*. From now on he would imagine more, record less. From now in his struggle against naturalism he would use facts to give the impression of accuracy of location but would be more detached from social issues pertaining to a particular society. He would be the wandering Diana, seeing truth by imagining it, creating himself, or versions of himself, in a multiplicity of rôles and in a variety of places. Remembered data were grist to this imaginative transmutation. Autobiographical writing, even letters, would also veer towards the transforming Diana and away from the recording angel in the wheelchair. He considered honesty in autobiography as 'a most promising area for ambivalence, suggestibility, comedy, complexity, an area (literally) for playing about with'.[36]

Sean was happy about *Vive Moi!*, a fine piece of impressionistic writing, as selective and evasive as Yeats's *Memoirs*, deceptive in its loops in time, and stopping short of his engagement with Irish life in the thirties and forties. Even what he left out prior to that period, such as his adolescent struggle with religion, his first involuntary sexual experience, his vulnerability in the presence of strong women, his failure to earn Stockley's approval, his aggressive and arrogant manner, his suspicion of others, also contributed significantly to the shaping of his imagination and left their mark on his early writings.

I Remember! I Remember! came from the mood of self-assessment and recollection that Sean experienced in the fifties. 'Love's Young Dream', that poignant recreation of adolescent uncertainties and strange intuitions, focusses on the boy's miseries and exaltations in a manner that is more emotional than the cold analysis in 'Lovers of the Lake'. But when the boy's romantic view of life is crudely shattered, how will he cope? 'Like everybody else I would pretend for the rest of my life. I would compound. I would invent – poetry, religion, common sense, kindness, good cheer, the sigh, the laugh, the shrug, everything that saves us from having to admit that beauty and goodness exist here only for as long as we create and nourish them by the force of our dreams, that there is nothing outside ourselves apart from our imaginings' (CS, 177). That has the ring of truth and it fits well with O'Faolain's way of dealing with a world that never fully satisfied him. He had been let down time and time again, by Ireland, the Church, leaders, the new society, children, his inability to accept; his idealism drove him into the walls of experience like young Joyce bashing into Knockaderry's wall. He would recover and cope, he could make a life by imagining, could come to understand himself better, could create friends, in particular women-friends, in accordance with the image of them that satisfied him. He could be two-faced about this: charming and courteous to people when they were present, lacerating them when they had gone; he could write flirtatious letters to women he disliked, flattering letters to people he wished to influence. He knew the power of his charm. But his fictions go deeper, taking us to the man for whom fiction was the supreme and perhaps the only true happiness.

'We are not one person', he concludes in 'Dividends'. 'We pass through several lives of faith, ambition, sometimes love, often friendship. We change, die and live again' (CS, 307). In story after story, in 'The Human Thing', in 'Billy Billee', 'Two of Kind', 'The Bosom of the Country', this sense of humanity enables him to look into people's twists and turns, changes of mood and of mind. But we are free within what we are. There is the striking discovery in 'A Shadow, Silent as a Cloud', about a selfishly ambitious architect who accepts the searing insight that 'there is no such thing as saving your life or squandering your life because nobody knows what life is until he has lived out so much of it that it is too late then to do anything but go on the way you have gone on, or been driven on, from the beginning. We are free to be, to act, to live, to create, to imagine, call it whatever you like, only inside our own destiny, or else to spit in the face of destiny and be destroyed by it' (CS, 136). Outside this discovery is the unintelligible universe. Inside it is the grain of wisdom from 'Lovers of the Lake' – one cannot give up everything for love – and the bitter truth of 'Up the Bare Stairs'. In opting for a softer portrayal, *Vive Moi!* lacks the cold objective analysis of some of these stories. *King of the Beggars* and *The Great O'Neill* also had more steel.

O'Faolain liked to play with the figure of the successful man and the quest for happiness. 'One Night in Turin' is about the unattainable: a woman seen once, a snow-maiden on stage in a moment so full of revelation and rapture that the Irishman packs his bags, returns to Cork and never declares his love. He is middle-aged, diffident, pursues her after her husband dies, tries in a thousand ways to bring her into the nets of his desire, and fails.

With this Walter Hunter type O'Faolain created the perfect vehicle for his detached, sophisticated, Jamesian approach. At home in Ireland, Italy, or France, lightly connected with a place, or a profession, free when it suits him to travel, to be available for amorous pursuits, to indulge his passion for fine food, wine, good tailoring, Italian opera, unconnected with social or political concerns, a man who enjoys good conversation, he was the ideal personality through which O'Faolain explored human nature. Man, he liked to say, is not a roll of wallpaper. He is infinitely variable, unendingly interesting, apart altogether from social or political issues. If we see in these wandering men, these self-creating sophisticates, the outline of Sean O'Faolain from Halfmoon Street, Cork, who was inclined to display his knowledge of wine, or food, or opera, who as a highly successful travel writer could create the solidity of place in Italy, America or Dublin, that is only to recognize that in imagining so well he was to a degree imagining himself. Those who lost track of him after 'Lovers of the Lake', or with *I Remember! I Remember!* often failed to connect the later life with the later work and could not see how the chameleon self profoundly explored and discovered its own multiple selves, in these apparently disconnected narratives, often set in distant places and often dealing with characters without much obvious connection with the O'Faolain most people knew, or thought they knew. Art reveals personality, but it also conceals. It may give a partial reflection of the life, it may be an adaptation of the life. In O'Faolain's case we are dealing with someone who concealed more than he revealed, who destroyed letters and manuscripts, played a rôle even with close friends, and considered writing as a transcending reality. He lived at a considerable distance from his work. His life, in so far as we may ever really know it, may help us to see why he wrote about certain subjects, why he expressed certain concerns or strategies for dealing with them.

He made an extensive American tour from 1 October to 13 December, as a Phi Beta Kappa lecturer at about sixteen colleges or universities. His topics included 'Trial by Pleasure', 'How a Writer Writes', 'The Angry Young Men', 'So You Want to Write a Short Story?', 'Art and Science: The Single Culture', and 'An Irishman Looks at the World'. In the following year he added 'Education for Everybody: A Modern Will-o'the Wisp?' He made a similar tour in the Autumn of 1962 and a shorter one in 1967. At each institution he was expected to give one public lecture to the entire academic community, take part in classroom discussions and meet informally with students. In practice a visit could entail much more – lunch or dinner with faculty, interviews for local newspapers, a radio station or the student paper. But he was a seasoned lecturer. All the reports on file at the Phi Beta Kappa office in Washington are favourable and the fact that he did three tours indicates his success. In mid-October 1961 he made a quick visit to Princeton to the McAndrews and other friends. He also met Katharine Anne Porter, 'still as attractive as a girl'. Ten years off both their lives, he assured Sam Lawrence, and they would have made a chapter in each other's. He had 'an amiable evening at the Harvard Club with Lawrence and visited a 'dirty sex shop'".[37]

Sean and Eileen had a quiet Christmas, broken by rows between Stephen and Patricia. Stephen's marriage was unhappy. Patricia was alcoholic and may have been taking drugs. He claimed that she was drunk on their wedding day and wanted to know if that could be used as grounds for annulment. He had just returned from a ten-and-a-half-month round-the-world voyage. His emotional instability had become more pronounced. Eileen was frightened of him. One night she and Sean were called to his home on the Vico Road where he was shouting and threatening violence.

Sean was sadly conscious of age. 'So many words and so much struggle!' 'Being left behind isn't so much fun'. He was incensed when Edward Weeks at *Atlantic Monthly* turned down excerpts from the early section of *Vive Moi!*. 'He really is the most stuffed-shirtest editor in the U.S.A.'[38] In May he accepted an assignment to revisit the South of Italy to see how the American reclamation scheme had progressed. He would stay in Rome for ten days in July, and spend most of August in Florence with Eileen, Julia, Lauro and Lucien. While the grandparents looked after Lucien with the aid of an Italian maid, Alene Erlanger took Julia and Lauro to the music festival in Salzburg. Then they went back to the 'dark hobgoblin island' and remembered sunny Tuscany.[39] After three years in which he had paid no tax, he had to pay the arrears, including tax on his Princeton earnings.

On 20 September Sean left for his second Phi Beta Kappa tour and was away for two months. In Boston he stayed at St. Botolph's Club, and met Sam Lawrence, the Kellehers and Dan Binchy. He was distressed to hear that Jean McAndrew had had a mastectomy just two weeks after John died. He stayed with Alene for Thanksgiving, visited Jean and took her to an Italian restaurant. When he got home on 30 November he had sciatica so badly that he had to go into a nursing home. He was there from 3 December to January 1963, then had to stay in bed at home. Even as late as April the pain was fading 'inch by inch'. From his sick bed he wrote to various friends – Jean McAndrew, Julian Moynahan, Alan Collins. Eight weeks to the day since the sciatica hit him he was downstairs, limping about on crutches. The winter was 'arctic', the hardest on record. Fortunately they had got in oil-fired central heating when they returned from Princeton and that made the house comfortable.[40]

He got back to his Underwood early in February and was well for his birthday. He planned to visit Italy twice – in May to do the piece on southern Italy, and again in July after a trip to Lourdes. This fitted in with their desire to be in Florence with Lauro and Julia. They stayed at the pensione in Fiesole run by the Blue Nuns, a lovely villa in quiet grounds which they enjoyed.

Eileen also enjoyed her grandson – 'the sweetest child that ever lived' – and felt well after their month abroad. They hated Dublin when they got back. She had, she told Jean McAndrew, made the mistake of allowing her family to keep her in the kitchen and found that it was 'bad for her, bad for them and bad for Sean'.[41] He was tired of his three professions of teaching, journalism, and lecturing. Despite his irritation with Ed Weeks, he sent him another fragment of *Vive Moi!* It was, he said, the most difficult task he had undertaken. Nothing that he did before had prepared him for 'this discipline of controlling or subjecting the artist's subjective desire to give shape and form to actuality, which is both natural and dominant in him, to the insistent demands of actuality *not* to be reshaped. It is a fascinating task and an exhausting struggle'. The rewriting was to get things 'moderately, objectively true'.[42] In fiction, he could play about with material, but in autobiography he felt in conscience bound by actuality. It was subjectively true and objectively true, he felt. When Weeks cabled a warm response, he was pleased. A writer, he explained, toils alone, but there comes the point 'when he (O so unwillingly!) relinquishes his manuscript (I feel quite lonely here without it! Is it warm, well-fed, exercised daily on the Common?) and then he must for all his earlier boasted indifference to what the world thinks of his child, be in a tremble lest nobody else loves it as he has loved it'.[43] He had, he explained, planned the book as an integral whole, playing off chapters against chapters. Atlantic Monthly Press issued his contract at the end of October: an advance of $5000, 10% royalty to first 7,500 copies, 12 and a half to 10,000, 15% thereafter. In October the manuscript stopped short at an awkward period of his life, aged twenty-six, at Harvard, which he did not quite know how to handle. By mid-November he was almost at the end of this chapter, but was not finished until 13 December; only London and Home remained. He worked through Christmas on the final chapter. Eileen's sister, Alice, visited for Christmas. They enjoyed the 'euphoria and optimism' of the Moynahans who were in Ireland for the year. Eileen Simpson visited from Paris. Julia was happy in Florence, Stephen was on the high seas off Australia – 'clever youth, to get rid of a wife and four kids at the age of twenty-five'.[44] Sean took a quick, surreptitious break in London by arranging for Sam Lawrence to cable him to go there. The letter was headed 'Pussonal. Between Men and All That'. 'Nobody must know . . . be an angel and do it now. Time presses and the ageing heart beats in the hardening arteries'. In a box he wrote: 'Tear this up in small pieces, masticate slowly and swallow with a small brandy'. He stayed at the Hyde Park Hotel, Knightsbridge and from there wrote again to Lawrence: 'I had a luvvely time and silently praised you, mon ami'.[45]

[17]

A Writer in Residence

'I AM tired and sad – almost like a man after a long night of love'.[1] He had sent the last of *Vive Moi!* to be typed. It had been a labour of love, the manuscript frequently rewritten and revised, carried about and worked over while he went on his journalistic assignments to various American cities, set aside in Knockaderry while he wrote articles on Italy and America and Ireland, set aside while he dashed off to Italy for research and recreation, at his side while he went about his duties as visiting professor, writer-in-residence, or Phi Beta Kappa scholar. The pattern of his life was now well established. He was making a good living through the three parts of his career. He did not complain now about not having enough time to write, because he made enough as a journalist and professor to keep him going for long stretches of time. In fact, instead of prolonging these periods he sought opportunities for travel, often suggested ideas to *Holiday*, sought visiting appointments in America, loved to go to Italy, was writing and working at an intensity unmatched since the years of *The Bell*. He enjoyed what he was doing, was writing well, producing more stories per year than he had for years. He felt involved and fulfilled, knew he was valued by editors and university people. Influential figures in the literary market-place wanted to meet him. In May 1966 Emelie Jacobson arranged a cocktail party at her home so that he could meet some of his admirers. These included Mrs. Neal Stuart, *Redbook's* fiction editor, Robert Stein, editor *McCall's*, David Mopress from *Life*, and people from Curtis Brown. In 1968 a similar group of editors wanted to meet him to talk about possible contributions: Arnold Ehrlich from *Holiday*, William Wright from *Ventura*. He made good money from the glossies: he was paid between $2000 and $2500 for each of about twenty articles for *Holiday* between 1955 and 1964; *Post* paid $2500 to $3500 per story; *McCall's* $3500; *Playboy* paid $3000 to $3500 for a story, gave an occasional bonus, and ran annual fiction awards. He had friends in America, such as Richard Ellmann, John Kelleher, Peter Davison, Sam Lawrence, Robie Macauley, who made no secret of their admiration and friendship. Emelie Jacobson said he was 'one of the most brilliant people she had ever known as well as one of the most delightful'.[2] He had a reputation as a moral leader. Robert Penn Warren admired the way in which Yeats had played that rôle in Ireland and, thinking that Yeats should have made the position respectable, wondered why O'Faolain met with such hostility. Warren, Alan Tate, and others were interested in him as a controversialist and intellectual *provocateur*. In Knockaderry he lived with style and entertained a wide variety of interesting people. He admired Yeats's *sprezzatura* which he defined as 'seeming nonchalance, *disinvoltura*'. Whereas the decade leading up to and including *The Bell* years was productive and important to him as a writer, he himself saw these later years as the good years.

The winter of 1963–64 was mild; he and Eileen went swimming on Christmas Day. From September on they had a 'spate' of elderly relatives staying with them, Jean McAndrew made a rushed visit, and they enjoyed having the Moynahans as neighbours in Dunlaoghaire. Julia was in Florence. Eileen was finishing a book of translations of Irish Folk Tales and Sean prepared for his visit to Boston College. *Vive Moi!* was still not quite finished. After a few days of enjoyable idleness, he broke the last chapter into two – 'I don't want to see the blasted thing for a long time . . . has me worn down'.[3]

O'Faolain was Writer-in-Residence at Boston College from 10 February to 5 April 1964. He stayed at the St. Botolph Club again on Commonwealth Avenue. Even in 1964 the campus retained some of its original rural atmosphere with its avenue of lindens, its cherry trees, apple trees, Japanese Maple, and small forest of firs. There were many birds – orioles, blue jays, woodpeckers and oven birds. Swifts flew about the spires and towers. St. Mary's Hall, Gasson Tower and the Bapst library were all gothic in style. Bapst, which had a medieval staircase and a reading room with lofty arches, housed a good Irish collection, with first editions, manuscripts, and work

[231]

by contemporary Irish artists. When O'Faolain arrived the trees, lawns and buildings were snow-covered.

On Thursdays he lectured on the pleasures of fiction. His texts were the old reliables already worked over at Northwestern. Every Tuesday and Wednesday he held conferences with students in his writing class. He spent about twenty to thirty minutes discussing their work individually. His comments often began with 'Couldn't you . . . ?' or 'Why don't you try . . . ?' He was, John Vernon recalled, 'like a kindly driving instructor who can't help but feel some disquiet in a vehicle driven by a novice; and I was like the driving student who barges straight ahead despite what the instructor says'. Even when a piece of writing tried his patience he had a way of both showing and not showing that impatience. He did the best he could, taught by his presence and example, was gentle and understanding, and avoided false or misleading enthusiasm.[4] When Frank Bergon arrived for his appointment in O'Faolain's cinderblock office in Carney Hall, he saw him sitting at the far end of the room, wearing glasses, a blue suit and a solid coloured tie, and holding a copy of the student magazine containing one of Bergon's stories. With an impish grin he said, 'Well, it's obvious you're a writer. But God only knows what kind'. With faint pencilmarks in the margin he had broken up the story into numerous scenes and anecdotes, 'chapters' he called them. Bergon, he said, had enough material for any number of stories. That criticism was one all the students heard. In the extravagance of youth, he told them, they squandered material. 'One of these days', he predicted, 'you'll be knocking your head against the wall trying to think of something to write about and here you are throwing away all these potential stories'. He urged Bergon to strive for focus and referred to Chekhov's economical methods as the great example. The best kind of story, one that narrowed into something similar to an immediate, vivid, scenic, dramatic one-act play, was what he should aim at, if he aspired to the artistry of Chekhov or Hemingway.

He was both encouraging and straightforward, praised moments of vividness and turns of phrase. He instilled the need for discipline – 'You can be wildly excited about an idea for a story, but when you come to write it down you have to be like ice' – and downplayed the students' desire to get published. 'I can't even get my own things published', he once said. This was truer than his students realized. In 1961 four periodicals turned down 'Two of a Kind' and the following year five turned down 'The Younger

Generation'. His work was becoming more sensual and this occasionally raised eyebrows in editorial offices. *Post* asked him to substitute shoulder-kissing for breast-kissing in 'A Sweet Colleen', to eliminate a reference to syphilis and the 'bra-business' in the last scene. It was another case of Hardy's wheelbarrow.

O'Faolain returned to Boston College in the Spring term of 1965 and was there again in October 1966. His salary was $5000 the first year and $6000 the next, but in the second year when he and Eileen rented a house in Cambridge, they spent most of his salary. Bergon, a senior in 1965, still showed him stories. O'Faolain was still perceptive, still encouraging. 'That's a fine character. I wanted more of that old man'. Two or three years later, he sent O'Faolain some stories and got back a three-page, somewhat formal, Jamesian letter. 'I do want to say how much your mss. interested and intrigued me, as your mss. have always done, and if they did not give me the rounded, concentrated pleasures of a brew matured in the cask, a single potion that condenses the essence of you, or of your natural way of seeing reality – of defining reality – they all did and do, in parts, point to a future total success that even yet (I know how impatient one is at your advanced age) you have not managed to achieve, but I feel sure, will. Let me bore you by pausing on this essential word "reality" . . .' He had a more playful, sometimes contradictory way of talking about art and reality. Once at a cocktail party he was holding forth about the elusive beauty of Hemingway's story 'A Clean Well-Lighted Place'. 'That story opens just like a star', he said and swept a smooth arc through the air with one hand, gradually spreading apart his thumb and forefinger to indicate the gathering brightness of a bursting star. Bergon mentioned one of Joyce's stories in comparison. O'Faolain disagreed. 'Most of those stories in *Dubliners* aren't very good'. Before Bergon could protest, he straightened his back, widened his eyes, and said, 'But, of course, I have high standards. I'm an artist'. 'And what am I?' Bergon asked. 'You?' he snapped, arching an impish brow. 'You, I suspect, are a novelist'.[5]

Peter Davison gave a welcoming party for him. Among those he met was the Keats biographer Aileen Ward. He asked her what she intended to write about next – 'Another five-letter poet'? He had guessed correctly: her next subject was Blake. Davison had several parties at his home during O'Faolain's visits to Boston College. He invited Ernie Simmons, knowing he was an old friend. Simmons was rather ponderous in contrast with

O'Faolain's light, witty and charming personality. Like others in the Boston area associated with the Press, Davison found O'Faolain a well-balanced and stable personality. Peggy Yntema was his editor. While Sam Lawrence, and later Peter Davison, handled O'Faolain's contract arrangements, generally set policy and were fond of O'Faolain, he liked having a woman editor to confide in and pretend to flirt with. For her part she liked working with him because he was 'a pro'. He was eminently free of the neuroses that often affect writers. He never minded working stories over again, in response to her corrections or suggestions. While money was a worry, he was never stingy. While she did not probe, he was always direct in answering questions. He admitted that Stephen was a problem. He praised his son-in-law whose car he could borrow when he went to Florence. As part of his flirtation he told Peggy that the woman in 'A Faithless Wife' was based on her. But she could see no resemblance. To her, 'Sean was no womaniser'. He told her he had had only three affairs. She knew Elizabeth Bowen and could see why they were attracted to each other – both attractive looking, both literary, and even the different social backgrounds would have been part of the attraction. He liked to pretend that all women were intriguers and dissemblers and that their manoeuvres and affectations delighted him. He prided himself on his appearance, spent money on good clothes, had good taste, except for an old raincoat and hat that he liked. Eileen, by contrast, had less style, did not have good dress sense. While she seemed to like America, she complained of the cold and did not like the shops. Peggy found her dreary and irritable. She would get cross about things and complain.

When he went to Boston he usually asked Peggy to lunch at the Vendome which had an air of faded Victorian elegance. They always had a chicken sandwich and a split of good champagne, and he made a gleeful parade about ordering it and fascinating the waiter. 'He loved style and good living. He had a fine, straight, long-legged figure, wore very good suits, and strutted a bit'. She remembered him at her spacious, elegantly furnished home on Brattle Street, tasting new Bermuda potatoes for the first time and becoming quite pink and misty-eyed with pleasure. 'But they-re so tender, they-re like grapes!'. Seeing a woman outlined against a window, he quoted Yeats's Lissadell. He loved to hear stories about what went on during the Dublin Horse Show Week – the wild antics of the men, the pile of drunken debutantes in the Land-rover.[6]

* * *

His appointment during April–May 1965 at the Centre for Advanced Studies at Wesleyan University in Connecticut, where he was paid $4500 plus airfare and had free accommodation, was less demanding. It gave him the opportunity to proceed with his own work, with the understanding that he might be available to students and faculty for informal meetings.

He alternated his academic work with work for *Holiday*. He valued this connection, appreciated their $2000 cheques ($1800 after agent's fees had been deducted), but wondered if they realized that costs had gone up since he began his 'happy Holiday-ing' some ten years earlier.[7] Sending Emelie Jacobson an itemised list of his expenses, and always scrupulously honest in such matters, he told her he had had to make two trips to Lourdes, but did not feel *Holiday* should have to pay for both, since that would add another $100 on to his expenses. As usual he had ideas for future articles: would definitely do Florence, would definitely not do Italian industrialists, would like to do Torino and, later, Sardinia. He spent six 'strenuous and exciting' weeks in Florence in early summer 1964, but found the heat, the noise and the crowds very wearing. He had a heavy cold. Fortunately he had the use of Lauro's white Giuletta and he and Eileen could go out of the city into the hills and the Val d'Arno. He explained his method: 'Normally I tear around a place with all antennae out at full-sensitivity nonstop like Hawkeye and S. Holmes rolled into one'. The usual minimum expense in the past had been about $500, but Sardinia would be more expensive, since he proposed to sail around the island with Christo Gore-Grimes and bring a Suzuki or a Honda strapped on board for exploring the interior of the island. Could Emelie clarify Harry Sions's attitude to more expenses?[8]

When he got back he corrected the page proofs of *Vive Moi!*. He worried about the possibility of libel in his account of the priest at the retreat in University College Cork. London lawyers held the remarks to be defamatory. Christo Gore-Grimes read the passage for him and told him that the line 'He had the right to betray me' was defamatory, as was the use of the word betrayal earlier in the same paragraph. Sean changed the latter to 'memory', meaning the pain of memory, and the former to 'But did he really speak? I felt surrounded by malice and suspicion'. He was also warned about the references to O'Rahilly; he would need his permission to use the letter he had quoted. O'Rahilly gave his permission.

When *Vive Moi!* appeared he went to America to promote it. He found being interviewed and talking on radio and tv 'most interesting, and equally exhausting'; so he preferred to do it all in an intense eight or nine days. Then he could visit Alene and see friends in Princeton and elsewhere.

When he went back to Boston College in 1965 Eileen stayed at home. 'Somehow he does not seem to be so involved as I am'.[9] She went to London to be with her sister, Alice, who was dying, sat by her bedside for four days, then got sick herself and was taken by stretcher to St. Vincent's Nursing Home the day after she got home, on 2 March. She had to keep quiet, since it would take a long time for the infection and inflammation to clear. She left the nursing home on 25 March but would be a semi-invalid for some time. Sean, she knew, was blithely making plans for a May holiday in Italy. They did not tell him at any stage how serious her condition was, but he postponed his trip.[10]

They were able to go to Florence at the end of August. Julia joined them. From there Sean could visit Torino, work on material for the spas, and have a holiday. He went to America in October to give the keynote lecture on Yeats at Princeton for the Yeats Centennial and stayed for eight days. He was introduced by Robert Goheen, president of the university and gave a 'superb lecture'. He 'revelled in every blessed moment' of his American visit, saw foreign and native films, including Garbo in *Grand Hotel* and Wallace Beery in *Dinner at Eight*, ate good lobster, dined with Francis Brown of the *New York Times* and 'enchanted him as I always do with anybody from whom I know I'll get away within an hour or two.' He spent a couple of happy hours in the Frick Museum and a weekend with Alene in New Jersey.

In December, annoyed that they never initiated anything he changed his London agents from Curtis Brown to A. P. Watt. Hilary Rubinstein at once set about getting him released from his obligations to Jonathan Cape. O'Faolain then urged Curtis Brown in New York to see to it that his rights to his US publications reverted to him. A year later he was still pressing them to find out exactly how many copies Devin-Adair had left of each of his books; he would buy them back. He had no intention of doing so but wanted by this means to find out just how many unsold copies there were. When Emelie asked for a reversion of rights, Devin-Adair sent royalty statements and a cheque for $96.81, thereby claiming the books were in print. In 1974 she was still trying to get copyright, especially for *The Man Who Invented Sin* and *Summer in Italy*. O'Faolain was irritated. Garrity, he complained, made no sales yet the books were supposed to be in print. 'He just gets my goat'.[11] In England by contrast Hilary Rubinstein continued to recover titles with the result that paperback rights could be sold. In June 1975 Devin-Adair refused to revert the rights in five of O'Faolain's books. In December 1965 Sean got flu. Then Eileen caught it and had a temperature for three days from a bronchial infection. They abandoned their plan to go to Corofin for Christmas. Instead Sean cooked a pheasant, with Lyonnaise potatoes and string beans and selected a bottle of Volnay.[12]

Although he began to feel that his filibustering days were over, he spent two days in London in early January 1966, where he met V. S. Pritchett for a meal at the Garrick and saw an Italian film. He had enjoyed Pritchett's company when he was in Dublin. He was, he thought, 'very solid English . . . writes good English stories, beef and plenty of horse-radish sauce . . . a very splendid writer of the art, not least because I'm so dopey and off-the-ground myself, or want to be'. The two men got on well together. They went occasionally for walks in the Dublin mountains. Eileen 'gardens, or sews, or cooks, or reads'.[13] He gave a talk to the Royal Dublin Society and one to the Kilkenny Literary Society, but missed meeting younger writers. He was at Wesleyan University in April–May and in Florence and Turin in June. In July Julia and Lauro were preparing to leave Florence. He asked Sukie to send her $1000. He decided to return to Turin on 2 September for further research and spent three weeks in Florence with Julia. His visits abroad now were affected by his concern for Eileen's health: he did not want to leave her on her own for long periods.

When they spent five days in London, Eileen, who had had a crippling attack of arthritis since March, had to rely on pain killers. She blamed her arthritis on everything – the awful weather, gardening, saccharine in her tea, but mainly on having brought back a piece of white basalt from the top of the mound at New Grange. She got relief from cortisone, but wanted Sean to take the stone back. During March and April he 'had a hard domestic round',[14] but they got away to Florence in July and he began gathering material for an article on the Vatican.

[237]

In the Autumn, from 24 September to 9 November, he was Phi Beta Kappa speaker in eight American colleges, but he found it unprofitable. The lecture agent took half the fee, paid the circuit fare inside the U.S. and therefore arranged as many talks as he could. 'The result is pure hell'.[15] In New York his briefcase, containing several talks and notes, was stolen.

In December Eileen had polymyalgia, an arthritic type of bone-cementation, and had to spend over three weeks in a Nursing Home. He went to see her every day. She was home just before Christmas. Getting some relief from physiotherapy, traction and exercises, made her 'more hopeful for the future',[16] but they did not have their usual Christmas party and went to none. Even though they had invited friends to call in at any time for a drink, they saw very few. Since neither enjoyed cocktail parties, they were content to be quiet. Sean's ulcer troubled him again in February.

Even by March Eileen could barely take a quarter of a mile 'toddle' on fine days. Sean went to Frankfurt and Bonn in mid-April to participate in an Irish week arranged by the Irish Embassy in Godesburg and by the English Department (seminar) at the University of Frankfurt. His books were displayed in an exhibition of work by Irish writers in German translation. From Bonn he went to France on 22 May to investigate Normandy but had to leave quickly before the supply of petrol stopped. He drove 350 kilometres to Brussels, phoned twenty-two hotels to find a bed, and waited days for a plane to London.

His social life was greatly inhibited by Eileen's immobility. Through sheer inertia, hatred of mobs, and no family in Europe they had no holiday there this year. His life was in the sear and yellow, 'and a very fine leaf it is to be in. All passion (nearly) spent . . . All I do is garden for Eileen, sit and write stories . . . a dull, easy old age'. Being made a Trustee of the National Library by the Minister for Education, he boasted untruthfully that he went to one meeting, found them all about eighty, decided there was nothing to be hoped for, and never went back.[17] At least the Irish summer was lovely, 70 degrees for days.

There were changes elsewhere. *Holiday* wanted lighter pieces and paid less. When they asked him to do Corsica at a reduced fee, he refused, regretting what appeared to be the end of his 'long and happy association' with the magazine.[18] He was, therefore, interested when *Ventura* proposed that he do some work for them. He was, he said, considering an article on the Irish cop. Emelie promptly got in touch with *Ventura*, then discovered

[238]

that Sean had been flying a kite, with his 'natural conspiratorial Irish mind', in the hope that they would suggest a second American subject and thereby make it worth his while to travel to the USA.[19] Instead they suggested the British Museum which did not appeal to him. He agreed to do Taranto, subsequently divided into two, one on Taranto, the other on the Ionian Shore. He hoped that writing for them would not stop *Holiday* from using him. Harry Sions reassured him of their 'continuing admiration' and 'gratitude'.[20]

He was back in the States in late September and spent several days in New York, but wanted more. He had 'a belly-craving for America'.[21] He got flu and bronchitis in January and was confined to the house from 3 January to the eighteenth. Even then his bronchial tubes were not clear, his nose was moist and he lacked energy. Eileen also caught flu. He found her hypochondria both pathetic and amusing. She was, he told Alene, 'health-absorbed to a degree that was sometimes funny: as when she said that it was not so dangerous (bug-wise) to go to church because the roof is high, but it had got much more dangerous since they introduced the spoken Mass with everybody gasping and puffing out Confiteors and microbes. This she said quite seriously'.[22]

Still angling for a trip to the States he wondered if Rutgers or Princeton had a summer school where he could earn his fare at a lecture a week or something. He floated the idea of an article on the Stock Exchange. In late September he and Eileen flew to Los Angeles where they stayed with Julia, while Sean did some lecturing. Eileen needed sun for her arthritis. So did he, but he got his 'annual bout of bronchial semipneumonia'. On his return Ireland was 'pure and clear and empty and good for the lungs and the spirit, very soothing for sex, too. All the women *d'une chasteté formidable*' and the men with baffled looks.[23] Before Christmas he heard of Mary Ellmann's aneurysm and the failure of the first operation; he wrote a sympathetic letter to Dick.

Nevertheless, he was remarkably active and productive. In Sam Lawrence he had an editor who liked his work and encouraged him to publish collections: *I Remember! I Remember!* (1961), *The Heat of the Sun* (1966) and *The Talking Trees* (1971). His reputation as a writer was high: *Finest Stories* sold well; the Bantam paperback had sold 26,000 copies by June 1965; *Vive Moi!* was acclaimed as an important autobiography. The London edition sold 2000 copies in the first month. *The Vanishing Hero* was a critical success. His travel articles brought him a wide audience. He regularly appeared in the American glossies: *Saturday Evening Post*, *Holiday*, *McCall's*, *Ladies' Home Journal*, *Playboy*. Each short story collection added to his reputation and he had the satisfaction of knowing that he was writing well. He always had a store of half-finished stories to be rewritten.

Julia's emergence as a writer meant that he could try out his stories on her before sending them to Emelie. She was good at giving practical advice: she provided useful historical information about Italian partisans for 'A Sweet Colleen', and proposed an alternative ending, which he accepted, for 'How to Write a Short Story', later known as 'Hymeneal'. He accepted advice from Julia, Emelie, Peggy Yntema and Robie Macauley; when necessary he consulted others with specific knowledge: Michael Lester at the Oratory, London, Peter Connolly at Maynooth. In 'The Talking Trees', he felt squeamish about the scene in which the girl strips for the boys. 'I didn't know if I could do it without embarrassment or anticlimax'.[24] But Robie Macauley liked the story and Sam Lawrence liked 'In the Bosom of the Country', in which the Major's expressions were based on John Lucy. Sean could accept revisions from *Holiday*, but had a 'big row' with Ed Weeks who shortened a story by ten lines without telling him. He swore he would never again allow anything of his to appear in the *Atlantic Monthly* while Weeks was editor. '*Never send him anything by me*'.[25]

In 1968, with Eileen incapacitated, he spent his time gardening and writing stories. He wrote four 'good stories' in 1967, seven in 1968, felt 'madly excited privately almost all day long'.[26] The short story, 'one of the most cunning of all the arts invented by man' continued to fascinate him. There was 'an enormous amount of craft concealed inside all successful short stories'.[27] 'The good ones outlast the writer – who will never know'.[28] He liked the element of 'discovering what he had to say in the process of writing and rewriting'; he was never sure how a story would end and found it difficult to know when a story succeeded and when it did not.[29]

He enjoyed writing for *Playboy* and liked working with Robie Macauley. Occasionally they gave a bonus fee; his first was for $200. He was indignant when Emelie took her agent's commission: 'A bonus is a bonus, Emmy, outside all stipulated pay. It is a gift. Do you take cuts on gifts??? How could

Sukie do this to anyone, least of all to me?'[30] But his big money market was contracting. The *Post* folded and *Holiday* paid less.

During these years many American friends came to visit, but there were more frequent signs of mortality. 'All our friends and contemporaries are dying'.[31] One evening, while Peter Davison was at dinner in Knockaderry, O'Faolain answered the phone. Next morning as they walked by the sea he told him that Edwin O'Connor had died: he and Eileen had saved their guest from the bad news.

Frank O'Connor's death was a hammer-blow. Sean went to the morning funeral, but Eileen was too distressed to attend. He was surprised at the Catholic service. 'Who's responsible for this imposture?' he asked. Since O'Connor had been anticlerical for most of his life, the funeral seemed to be a betrayal of the man and what he stood for. When Ernest Blythe also expressed surprise, Hector Legge joked 'Did you not hear? O'Connor returned to the Church. He's been a Mass-goer and daily-communicant'. Blythe passed on, shaking his head. O'Faolain said 'That's the best short story I ever heard!' Nevertheless Sean received the Eucharist. At the graveside he wore a large artist's hat and was clearly distressed. He did not know that he had been rejected as grave-side orator by Harriet O'Connor and Maurice Sheehy, because he and Michael had quarrelled.

His feelings found expression in letters to John Kelleher:

Well, that is theoretically all over. A sudden death blesses those who receive it and blasts those who bury them. If you have been feeling the same sense of blackness, blankness and emptiness I have, I have just about enough feeling left in me to be sorry for you with the kind of miserable sorrow relatives of the dead dully feel for one another – no more. And I think you like me feel more – regrets, the 'too-late' guilt, remorse, and an unappeasable anger with the certain among the living, more among the dead, and last of all and most of all with whoever made us and kills us.

It is not his genius I miss. That's in his books. It is not even the man – we had both lost him before now. I hate the simple fact of his not being alive; not solely but mainly because while he lived he was so abundantly alive . . . so vitally, combustively, explosively alive. This fellow was the incarnation of livingness.

His genius depended on it. It was a flame. No alloy. No coldness of the intelligence to make it a blend with some other form of apprehension. Pure undiluted intuition. A rare marvel. Of course, death always telescopes and simplifies a man. We think of him only as his essence. You and I know his many hours and days of near-lunacy from depression, boredom, fury, frustration, and we know too how his essential sensitivity and sensibility would leak away into their opposites — even into cruelty and brutality and blind insensitivity. It had to be that way. He just had to be what he was — a receptacle for every emotional storm, as for every least gentle and tender whisper of the softest wind of feeling, of the mystery and the poetry of life.

. . . He had to have emotion. Those who slapped back outburst for outburst were those he loved . . . Such men make their deaths our death. They fill life with life and death. It is all about me these days — this sense of waste, whence my obscure rage — so futile, so frustrating, so unmanning.

It is rounded off. The turbulent life, the mellowing — that did not decline into apathy, capable of fine indignation to the last — the big public success abroad, the return to Ireland, the happy years with Harriet, not declining into mere dull domestic habit, the grand old man admired still (and intensely) by the young, his gifts intact, and then the hammer-blow. Leaving us all to sorrow for the loss of a completed man. The tree was in full leaf when it crashed. My deep sympathy with you, dear John, in this total loss.[32]

Others remembered the 'quarrel' of which there were many versions: jealousy because they had both loved Eileen as young men; anger at the 'betrayal' because while O'Faolain looked after Joan O'Donovan and her baby O'Connor took up with Harriet Rich in America and never told Sean; O'Faolain's punning on Harriet's name; his anger that O'Connor let Ita O'Leary down; O'Connor's envy of O'Faolain's education and mental discipline; O'Faolain's jibe, in connection with O'Connor's association with the *New Yorker*, that he liked to write his stories himself and not have them written by editors. There were many elements in the relationship between the two men, there were many disagreements, many rows and explosions, great competition and stimulation, lots of shared youthful ambitions. But at the end O'Faolain, his mind 'still deeply troubled by memories of Michael', explained that their estrangement was not a quarrel —

no one incident blew them apart – O'Faolain 'just grew exhausted by his wild emotionalism'.[33]

While he and Eileen had been confined to the house with flu in January 1969, Sean longed to get to the post office where he knew there would be a letter from Alene Erlanger. There was. This was his reply:

Your glorious letter as they say 'to hand'; that is to heart, to soul, to body, deep in me as if an x-ray were after tatooing my insides with I Love You. I don't know why but as I drove home with it, to read over and over at my leisure, savouring every letter, every thin penstroke from the hand I adore, seeing my love sitting up in bed at night . . .

I just had to get that letter or die. And there it was . . . and I raced home with it, and E is in bed with her cold and catarrh . . . so I could sit and read and reread and kiss the page and feel about seventeen with your love turning the universe into a lot of glowing stars swooping into my heart. I thought the other night, If I was young she'd have ruined me for life. Ruined in the frivolous sense that no other woman could ever mean anything to me ever after . . . Other women no doubt have soft hands, no doubt, and desirable limbs. They might as well be manufactured by General Motors for all the touch of them could mean to me who knows and feels the pulsing power of love that flows from the tip of your little finger, one smile, one word. I just want you, and nothing and nobody else in all creation since Alpha time. . . . After all, my darling darling in February I will enter my 70th year. I think I won't give you up until I'm 75. Can you believe it: we became one when I was a young fellow of 54. Last night I had a great desire. I want to buy two wedding rings, one very small and one bigger, and I want to take you in my arms in the dark, and I want to ask you if you'd ever think of marrying me, and you'll say it is a bit sudden but I will plead and plead and at last you will let me put your little ring on your finger, and you will put mine on mine. And then, my darling, that will be the start of our honeymoon. Why didn't we do this ceremoniously like that long ago? Mrs Johnny? . . . The follies and fantasies and joys and longings of all true lovers! . . . for the last five minutes I have been gazing out of the window. At you.

[243]

... O, my darling ... Do you get bored ever with my telling you that you are my love, and that I love you so much I feel like a Zeppelin, blown out with it, and that I thank God and you that I have you to think of and of so much joy, gaiety, happiness and living and loving that we have created between us and that nothing can destroy. There's me, yes, and a you, yes, but really there's only a meyou and youme, so that all I do is done by us and felt and thought, and the same must be true of you, my own and only. *Omd, je t'embrasse, partout.*

What a wonderful life you have given to me! Without you I would not have known at all what life is and what love is . . .[34]

In *Vive Moi!* (1993), he celebrated Alene's personality: her need for self-assertion, her love of horses, of flying old airplanes, of the company of actors, actresses, musicians, writers, gifted people who dominated the arena like gladiators. He admired her combustible, life-seeking, life-enhancing spirit. He admired the way she prepared for her own death and had a Mozart concerto played over her ashes. On his last visit she was sick with cancer, but he recorded an incident from his previous visit: when he suddenly smacked her bare bottom, she whirled, they struggled, he said, 'Go on, hit me again'. She said 'Don't be so submissive'. Knowing how vulnerable he had been to strong women, her remark was a dagger-thrust that stayed in his mind. Her death in June 1969 was also a hammer-blow. 'I am very downcast today . . . So vital a spark, so life-loving a woman. It puts a big hole in New York for me'.[35] One month later Milton also died. 'We've had a sad time'.[36]

[18]

The Wonderful Seventies

HE had a 'fine' seventieth birthday: *Playboy* had accepted 'Of Sanctity and Whiskey' (he sent Robie Macauley a bottle of Paddy); 'A Sense of Ireland' had been published in the *TLS* (15 February); he sent an article to the *New York Times*; Cape were going to publish *The Talking Trees*; Hilary Rubinstein had sold four stories to Granada T.V.; two paperback editions were being prepared; and he got 'lots of letters, telegrams and a case of champagne, so I wish I were 70 every month. It feels wonderful, completely absolved of responsibility on all sides, and living posthumously.'[1] During the next ten years he wrote more stories and the novel, *And Again?*, travelled to Italy, France, London, and America, continued his journalism, gave occasional lectures, and made a number of programmes for Irish television.

Because he had written *The Irish* Niall McCarthy turned to him when he had the idea of doing a series of TV programmes on 'We. The Irish'. He had been warned that O'Faolain was crusty and aloof, but when he telephoned to explain what he had in mind, O'Faolain said 'Come out here, young man, and talk to me'. The series examined Irish life in the period between the commemoration of the fiftieth anniversary of the Easter Rising and Ireland's entry into the European Economic Community. The old order had not disappeared: De Valera was still in power, John Charles McQuaid was still Archbishop of Dublin, but there were signs of change: an increase in industrial production brought about by a Government programme that encouraged foreign investment, a rising tide of relative prosperity, a diminishment in censorship, greater freedom of expression, a closer connection with Europe, and social and cultural changes. It was, McCarthy judged, a good time for reassessment, for the kind of revisionist approach that O'Faolain had pioneered in *The Irish*.

O'Faolain wrote and presented three programmes: 'Saints and Soldiers' (6 June 1971), with locations in Clonmacnoise, St. Gallen, Bobbio and Rome; 'The Money Men' (3 November 1971), which examined the new type of wealthy businessman in Irish society; and 'The Exiles', which looked at the Irish in Boston. In 'Prospect' (1 December 1971), Conor Cruise O'Brien, Owen Dudley Edwards and O'Faolain speculated on the possibility of Ireland's retaining individuality at a time of increasing internationalism. 'The Politicians' (17 November 1971), written and presented by O'Faolain, took the form of a public lecture by Conor Cruise O'Brien, followed by a discussion with leading politicians.[2]

While they had been filming for 'We. The Irish', O'Faolain urged McCarthy to do places outside Ireland. A series called 'Neighbours' began with the Italians and was filmed in Rome, Naples and rural areas of Sicily (22 November 1972). For 'The English' (27 December 1972) O'Faolain chose Sheffield, which had a Labour Council, to see what the English genius had produced, apart from the aristocracy. In 1974 they did a programme on the Vatican (12 June).

Although he was initially distant, O'Faolain quickly adjusted to the camaraderie of the camera crew. The hours were long; full of enthusiasm, he worked hard, often in poor conditions, studied his script and could speak for several minutes without referring to it. He had a stamina unusual for a man of his years although the young crew often made him feel like ninety. Sometimes his age came against him. When they filmed in Antrim he had to work in a strong wind and went down with bronchial trouble when he got home.[3]

Because of his interest in film he understood camera work, patiently endured the retakes and liked to be present in the cutting-room. He also understood the structure of a film and the need for a precise use of voice-over. Of all the writers with whom the camera man, Godfrey Graham, worked, and they included Robert Graves and John Betjeman, O'Faolain had the best grasp of the technology. His interest in film went back to his days with *Ireland Today* when he had become a member of the Irish Film Society. The young people who worked with him admired his personal discipline and lack of pretensions. He did not object when McCarthy made changes in his script, knowing that it had to be adjusted to meet the needs of the medium. The two men got on well together. McCarthy admired O'Faolain's ability to live a civilized life, to be professional by day, then to relax in the late afternoon. His day ended at five o'clock. Then it was time for a drink and relaxation. McCarthy found that Catholicism fascinated O'Faolain for whom the very fact of its survival suggested worthwhile qualities. He was interested that McCarthy did not harbour any resentment towards Catholicism. He told him that he was attracted by the possibility of a divine source, beyond the Church's ethical scheme.

What Graham most admired was Sean's youthfulness of spirit and his intelligent, shrewd observations on human nature. When, for example, they went to meet him at the airport in Rome, he strode out of the Arrivals area dressed in an immaculate grey suit, wearing a smart panama and carrying an old brief-case. 'Great to see you, boys,' he said, 'I know just the place where we'll dine to-night', as though they were starting on a holiday. This was his city. He took them to favourite nooks and crannies, to his favourite restaurants, including one in which nuns served at table and advised on the choice of wine. He reminded them of human frailty: even the Pope was only a man of flesh and blood like them; he might aspire to greatness, but he and the Church, for all its solemnity of manner and apparent certainties, were highly frail. They should never forget that.

O'Faolain was attracted by beautiful, intelligent women. One evening a young woman arrived. O'Faolain left with her for dinner and did not return until the following morning. He spoke about the need 'to make arrangements', maintained that since time began men and women have been attracted to other partners. Therefore arrangements had to be made and made with discretion. While he had wished a hundred times that he was not married, it had taken him forty-five years to realize that there was 'no substitute for the restfulness of a relationship you can take for granted'.⁴ When they went to Harvard Square they discovered a demonstration in progress: young women marching through the area, bra-less and with lots of cleavage on show. McCarthy asked O'Faolain if he was still bothered by sexual desire. O'Faolain replied that the fever in the head did not diminish; one might admire beauty, long to possess it, but be unable to do so. But in affairs of the heart, he also had the ability to be detached. When a woman teased him by saying she was seeing another admirer of the same age and asked if that made him jealous, he realized that he had never felt sexual jealousy. 'Envy, yes; regret of loss, yes'. He wondered if introverts have a way of intellectualizing away disasters where men of action would go berserk.[5] He reflected that if he were to live all over again, he would marry a woman who would be 'mature, wilful, life-loving, intelligent, entertaining and above all — his opposite — realistic'.[6]

His sexual needs could cause him to behave badly, as Eilis Dillon discovered when she returned to Dublin with her husband, Cormac, who was dying. O'Faolain's attentions took the form of interest in her writing. He was, he said, afraid that Cormac's death might stop her from writing. He would telephone her to see how she was doing with her novel, *Across the Bitter Sea*. He took the manuscript with him on holiday and wrote her at length about it, but he also pursued her, turned up at St. Vincent's Nursing Home, accompanied her to the Shelbourne for tea or a drink, visited her at home, and seemed not to understand how distressed she was, in the first place by her husband's condition, and in the second by his advances, fearing, as she did, that she had unwittingly encouraged him.

He considered sexual desire to be a primary imperative, was proud that his sexual energy remained strong and regretted that Eileen had always insisted on separate rooms. When Eilis Dillon married Vivian Mercier, he approved on the grounds that she was a full-blooded woman who needed a sexual partner. Subsequently, in 'A Faithless Wife' he made comic use of the situation in which he had placed Eilis. When Cormac died the O'Faolains often invited her to their Sunday afternoon gatherings in order to help her to recover. Then, they dropped her.

His literary advice was not merely a disguise for romantic pursuit, although he wrote to her about her novel almost every day from Florence. He was 'filled with interest and anticipation'. He rhapsodized on the possibilities of the novel's plot: a young peasant girl taken out of her normal situation by a rich, powerful, handsome, presumably normally passionate man, sent off to a remote island to be educated as a 'lady', married as a lady, loved, adorned, given power. 'Eilis! It is a tremendous and most fascinating and most complicated (humanely speaking) problem'. Add to this that another man of her own class and traditions wants her and loves her. Add further that she feels that she really loves him. 'My God! What a drama! What depths, storms, fears, wonders of the heart must be hers on that island'. He wanted more detail, more passion, less telling, more seeing. Back in Knockaderry his enthusiasm cooled. He illustrated different kinds of style sometimes bluntly: 'A modern writer *inside* Morgan would not write "If he had forced her then", but "if he had fucked her then".' He and Eilis, both nineteenth century writers, would say 'If he had thrown her on her back then'. 'You are', he tells her, 'too bloody genteel with these people of simple, strong, primitive passions'.[7]

Robie and Anne Macauley had first met Sean when he was teaching at Northwestern. They admired his stories and regarded him as a 'witty, warm and delightful man'. As fiction editor of *Playboy*, between 1966 and 1974, Robie selected and published most of O'Faolain's later stories. O'Faolain developed a great respect for him as an editor and frequently sought Macauley's advice. Sending 'How to Write a Short Story', he asked him to read it as a fellow-writer, and say as a fellow-writer, how the usual three questions struck him: what is he trying to do? How far does he succeed in doing it? And was it worth doing? In the midst of his bronchial attack early in 1971, it did him good to hear that Macauley accepted 'Murder at Cobbler's Hulk'. He needed the 'fillip just then, feeling . . . discouraged for various reasons mostly subjective and irrational'. He got a $500 bonus. When he read the proofs he was astonished at how good the story was and at how very well the writer had done it. He had a dream that *Playboy* was offering a reward of $5000 for the best short story of the year in English, or say $10,000, and offered his services as one of five judges.[8]

From September to June he worked at 'Falling Rocks, Narrowing Road, Cul-de-Sac, Stop,' with the result that when he sent it off he had come to the conclusion that he 'was washed-up and impotent'. When Robie liked it, he was 're-energized' and '*so* happy'.[9] When he sent 'The Inside Outside Complex' to Emelie, he wanted Robie to see it. 'I *do* want a perfectly professional word about it from a colleague. It is me, but that to hell, is it successfully me as a *work of art*'.[10] Robie was 'quite bowled over by it' — 'may well be the best literary story we've ever published' — and had really only one comment, or question, 'how does a writer manage to get better and better and better as time goes by?' He liked the idea in the story that 'we are in love with our own longings, that in completion is life and consummation is depressingly final'. It was, he thought, beautifully carried out.[11] The story, or 'parable' meant a lot to O'Faolain. 'I felt it was in orbit, I felt I knew what it was about, i.e. what my psyche was in his usual fumbling way, eedjut that he is, trying to say, in fact that I knew rather better than he did, having lived for twenty years "forever panting and forever young" . . . in pursuit of the Perfect that is most a dream when most or over-possessed'.[12] When Macauley accepted 'Venus or the Virgin', subsequently called 'Something, Everything, Anything, Nothing', he felt that his belief in him was justified. Robie was the only one he could sound out a story on. Julia, he felt, had become kind to the old boy and flattered him.

He was excited by the prospect of attending a lunch of contributors to *Playboy*. Since Eileen would be unable to travel, he arranged for Julia to take her place. He enjoyed himself and delighted his audience with his reading of part of 'Murder at Cobbler's Hulk' at the dinner. The Macauleys were 'sweet' to them. He was appalled when Anne Macauley had to go into hospital for a serious operation. 'Times are', he wrote, 'when I wish I were an Italian, rending the hair and screaming to heaven – letting the whole steaming misery out. If I were more Irish and less Anglo I'd do it all the time. You Americans are even more stoical!' He was, he said, still living on memories of those five days in Chicago, 'giving little grunts of amusement and bewilderment at it all and pleasurable nods of the head'.[13]

He was to get another cheque and medallion from *Playboy* in 1972, this time in New York. He contacted Julia about joining him and felt 'excited as a boy going to his first pantomime at the idea of seeing New York again before Christmas', but he got another bronchial attack and could not go. '*Damn!* . . . I lie here and cough and cuss'.[14] He felt forgotten. Ellmann assured him that he had not joined the forgotten generation, but the classic one. 'That is hard but there are worse fates'.[15] He felt out of favour with the young. He knew his own worth, he said: he was a talented minor writer, not one of the great writers, like Shaw, Yeats, Joyce, O'Casey, Synge. 'The rest of us are minor writers, talented perhaps, but not men of genius'. Men of talent often write better than men of genius, but not with the same fire.[16] He was lonely – 'I have so very few friends' – but enjoyed life. 'Happy Birthday to me! Survival feelings and a conviction about Life that with all its faults I love it still'.[17] He found growing old hard. The future had vanished. The past was part of the present. 'I see nobody' he commented, resigned. 'I am only moderately discontented'. One of the irritants of age, he discovered, was that the older he got, the younger he felt; 'the only complaint I have about life is that there isn't more of it'.[18] 'I sometimes feel the world is a looneybin. The only cure for it is to write a story about it'.[19] He had no illusions about his own achievements, he dismissed his three novels. Any merit he had as a writer depended on two points of view: a) as an *homme de lettres*, intelligent, like a lesser Gide contributing his mite to the general intelligence of his developing country, and b) as a writer of short stories. That, he claimed, had been his ambition, but he had all his life been distracted by having to earn a living. He might have written six to ten stories that would last.[20] When he sent 'Durling', later called 'The Faithless Wife' to Emelie he asked if it was any good at all, or whether he should quit. That recurrent doubt changed to delight when Robie liked it.

He frequently thought of James Joyce as an example: 'the man we should all of my generation have harkened to . . . because he was "cold", would not yield an inch, no palaver, no Godhelpus stuff, the whole stinking mess of life coldly observed, one cannot say accepted, but may say "acknowledged", and by being presented clearly and coldly . . . once more coldly condemned. Bertrand Russell was right. "Life is Horrible! Horrible! Horrible!" Once you accept this you can begin to enjoy it. Joyce did. He would hug his suffering.' But the coldness, O'Faolain remarked, the necessary coldness, the admirable, thin-lipped coldness would be a natural counterpart to the introverted loneliness which he cultivated. Life whipped him . . . and his revenge was to unmask 'horrible' life.[21] Much as he might admire that, he knew it was not his way. He was a softie, O'Connor a toughie. ('HOW he mistreated, maltreated his women for example'.)[22] Of the stories he was writing he preferred those which were 'gauzey, more suggestive, imperfect, hazardous, not clear even to me'.[23] But he was persistent. Writing was like trench warfare. 'Constant, relentless, no truce . . . push on a hundred yards (words), retreat fifty, or five hundred, start again, ding dong, borne only because one's soul knows that over Hill 365 or so there is a Promised Land. Gold, pardner! Gold! Nuggets of it . . . I know at seventy-four (all but a month) that when I tire of word-pushing I will have tired of living.'[24] 'Should an old gent of 74-ish be prolific? My Muse is screaming for a chastity belt'.[25]

Peter Davison mentioned the possibility of doing a *Collected Stories*, but meantime Sean had *Foreign Affairs*, a new collection that he dedicated to Robie Macauley. Five of the eight stories had been published in *Playboy*. He thought highly of this collection, in which he had tried to get away from the 'peasant' Irish scene.[26] What he was doing now required concentration, since he wanted to expand stories, to write tales, to retain unity inside movement. A short story he compared to a child's kite, a small wonder, a brief, bright moment. But he found that difficult now, because the tale enabled him to go further, to cover more ground, to have more suggestibility. Like Chinese globes that rotate one inside the other, the tale had one meaning inside another. A short story accreted, a tale was constructed. He also acknowledged his preference for women characters. His men were all 'cads' – pitiful, amusing, entertaining, cunning; the women were strong, heroic, and tiresome in their heroism.[27] He wanted his *Selected Stories* to represent what was most likely to endure. He left out virtually all he had written prior to 1957, selecting only 'Passion' and 'The Silence of the Valley' from *Teresa* (1947) and 'Lovers of the Lake' from *Stories* (known, in America, as *Finest Stories* 1957). All the rest were from the later collections: fourteen in all.

Of the stories in *Foreign Affairs* (1976) 'An Inside Outside Complex' is the perfect late O'Faolain story. It is almost a summary of his lifelong search for the unattainable, his difficulty in being satisfied with reality, his need for an alternative. It tells of a man who, from the outside, sees a woman within her room, finds the scene hauntingly attractive, cleverly gains admission, woos her, wins her and takes possession of what he had desired only to be disappointed, and to imagine the scene outside the room to be more attractive. He leaves her, is drawn back, sees her again inside the attractive room, knocks, enters, is welcomed, and together, looking out, they see themselves reflected in a mirror which he has brought to enhance her room only to find that it will not fit in through the door. Like many of these later stories, the story is a parable and floats free of its realistic tetherings. While its theme of never-ending idealistic pursuit runs throughout O'Faolain's work, it is present in many of these later stories, such as 'Marmalade', 'The Bosom of the Country', 'Liberty', 'Brainsy', or 'How to Write a Short Story'.

To a degree these stories illustrate how O'Faolain survived in a world he often found unsatisfactory and sometimes almost unbearable. Many involve the figure of the man who creates a rôle in which he can flourish, Bertie Bolger in 'An Inside Outside Complex', Walter Hunter in 'One Night in Turin', the Major in 'The Bosom of the Country', Georgie Atkinson in 'Foreign Affairs'. Because he has to be constantly created he is vulnerable to experiences that threaten his portrait of himself as gay dog, cosmopolitan, professional, or sophisticate. But these connoisseurs lack security. They fumble and fail in their pursuit of love, romanticize it, are tentative in pursuit, damagingly self-questioning.

Every man, Hanafan cries in *Purse of Coppers*, lives out his imagination of himself and every imagination needs its background and it is this strength and security that these figures lack. Ireland, tangentially present, is incomplete. O'Faolain gives rein to the foolish illusions of his romantics, but is coldly analytical in exposing their weaknesses. His style is versatile, often knowingly so, and histrionic. He walks the tight-rope of his divided nature showing off like a skilled acrobat. In art, as in life, he liked to preen and flap his wings. Behind the performance and the *sprezzatura* lay hurt, disappointment, pride, compassion and understanding.

O'Faolain needed the caparison of cosmopolitanism. He was as shrewd as ever in his analysis of Irish affairs, and occasionally driven to anger or anguish by them, but, as he told John Kelleher in 1970, he was no longer interested in Ireland. The price paid for his portrait of the artist as cosmopolitan was that his work had little connection with Irish conditions. He was less an Irish writer in the old sense. He wrestled less with Irish conditions.

He had little choice. Half of his world had been taken away. The Ireland of his boyhood had been swept away by revolution and social change. The touchstone of life in the West was no longer a force. The struggle with the Church was removed with the Church's own loss of power. Like a man who had wrestled with a strong opponent, the struggle lost its challenge when that opponent went limp in his arms. The young had little interest in old-fashioned Fenian anticlericalism. His later stories acknowledge the pleasures of the good life, but show little awareness of the other side of Irish life: shady standards in high places, greed, or social deprivation. He was out of touch with them and in any case had never been much of a socialist. But the loss that one detects in the later stories goes deeper. It is not merely that Aunt Nan's half-door is gone. There is a psychological gap, an intellectual absence, an entire cultural failure. Against that background he could construct ironic, paradoxical parables, and fabricated social backgrounds of clubs in Stephen's Green, a legal career vaguely pursued, a little mansion somewhere in Cork or Limerick, and visits to Italian cities or Sicily. He created types and amalgams and was free of realism.

He could in these detached, distanced stories find forms for his frustrations and pleasures, his divided loyalties, his need for flair and style, the attractions of Irish life. 'A Dead Cert' is an ironic portrayal of this inside-outside complex also in its account of the woman from Cork who dallies for a day in Dublin with another man, lures him again, teases him, entertains the notion that if her husband died for a week she might have a fling, then drives through the night back to her home in Cork. She leaves the man in Dublin with the notion that maybe, next time, he might take up the implications of her wish that her husband might die for a week. What fools these mortals be!

In real life O'Faolain knew when to cut the painter. In Alene Erlanger he had a woman who liked the world she had in New York and all that went with it, loved him because he was bright, sensual, enjoyed many of the things she liked, travel, books, theatre, music, added lustre to her table, and was as able as he was to lead a double life. Women who wanted more learned quickly that he was not available.

He made a good living by spinning threads of fantasy out of his own innards. He loved to be with Alene or other friends in New York, Boston, or continental Europe, to be with Julia, to conform to the cosmopolitan, knowing that he could fly back to his green, medieval, hobgoblin island, there to recuperate, and to spin again his fantasies of flight and adventure. His own estimation of his ability was accurate: he was not a genius. His words did not boil onto the page in uneven brilliance. He was a man of great talent who might, if lucky, create something that would endure.

O'Faolain attended the Irish Week in Frankfurt in May 1970, but what he most wanted was to visit Italy. RTE's decision to do a programme on the Italians suited him. He and Eileen did Dublin-Lourdes-Rome-Bari 'all in one run'. Julia met them in Rome. Taranto offered a swimming pool, hotel and mediocre food, some interest 'of an oldtime picturesque type, lots and lots of scalding sun and of course noise'. It was 'the blessed, empty silence' along the coast that he liked best. They returned north via Brindisi to Rome, where he spent two days filming. He went to Naples, rejoined Eileen and Julia in Orvieto and drove to Florence where 'we simply lie in deck chairs among the olives, in the sun and shade, hearing only the chirruping of birds and the muted sounds of cars in Fiesole, looking down at the rosered city below'. He found Florence impossible – 'noise, traffic, heat, crowds, noise, heat, crowds, da capo' but recommended their pensione for its silence, the view of the city below, its old olive trees and fair food'.[28] Eileen, he noted, went on eating, drinking, sleeping without worry of any kind. Physically, he felt the holiday would do her very little good but morally it was 'a great victory'.[29]

They stayed on. He gave up trying to read Henry James, abandoned Muriel Spark 'in contempt', could not bear Edna O'Brien, but was saved by Unamuno's *L'Agonie du Christianisme* which was full of ideas. He was deeply impressed with Silone's *Bread and Wine*. With the cooler weather and Julia gone, he began to read Eilis Dillon's novel although Italy's hot climate, he told her, was not for work, and, subtly, 'hardly even a climate for love-making'.[30] He wished she were a lizard lying beside him in the sun.

He wanted to return to America, but his proposed lecture tour did not work out, because of cut-backs in the Californian universities. Then, unexpectedly, he went to Boston, filming. Boston now meant lobster, cheese, bookshops, food, music and, above all, friends.[31] Eileen's arthritis was so bad in 1971 that they went to London instead of Italy. When they returned they found that their house had been burgled. Fear about what might happen in their absence now troubled all future holiday plans. They became increasingly housebound. In addition to arthritis, Eileen had occasional asthma and a floating temperature. He did the shopping, daily tidying and some light cooking. He had developed claustrophobia. 'Why go out? Here is warmth, coffee, drinks, music, books, a wife, one's slippers and an occasional dropper-in'. But he knew it was 'madly bad for the spirits'. He went to London for five days, to stay with Julia, meet friends, see a couple of movies and a play or two, smell petrol and see 'crrrroowwdds' all around him.[32] His annual bout of bronchitis and the inevitable fits of coughing made Eilis Dillon say 'For God's sake, Sean, will you give up the pipe'. He had tried before, turned to cigarettes, using a holder, but reverted to the pipe. Now he sent his pipes to J. F. Powers: two meerschaums in a leather case with the maker's name – D. P. Ehrlick and Co., Boston, but Powers, awed by the gift, only smoked them about a dozen times.

When he moved to A. P. Watt he came into contact with Carol Smith, an outgoing, vibrant and independent young woman, whose job it was to handle short stories. Soon after they started corresponding on a business level, he wrote to say he was going to London and would like to take her to

[255]

dinner. She went to the restaurant in Knightsbridge, nervously expecting to meet someone terrifying, like George Bernard Shaw or James Joyce. Instead, she found a handsome, urbane, silver-haired sophisticate, smoking a cigarette and drinking a dry martini. Their friendship started at once. He took her home in a taxi and insisted on kissing her. 'Well', he said, 'I was expecting to meet an old lady'. 'Well', she said, with more justification, 'I was expecting to meet an old man'. He wrote to her at home so that his letters would not go into the agency's files and their friendship accelerated. He would go to her flat for a drink, then take her out to a local restaurant. Sometimes they met at Julia's house. He was very romantic and fairly amorous, asked her to sleep with him, but she found the age difference embarrassing, although it was difficult to refuse an older man whom she liked and admired.

He was, she discovered, an extraordinarily good listener who had the knack of drawing one out and finding out all one's secrets. He was interested in every single incident in even the most insignificant life. Her life, to him, seemed crowded, happy and glamorous. He was openly jealous of her relationship with another man. He talked about himself, his love-affair with Elizabeth Bowen, the woman he had loved most, but refused to talk about Stephen. In her flat he met a number of interesting people, most of whom were connected with writing and publishing: Susan Blackburn, a wealthy Texan socialite; Arianna Stassinopoulos, who wrote biographies of Callas and Picasso; Caro Hobhouse, a publisher who used to be an editor at Macmillan, to whom he was particularly attracted. She was a good-looking, intelligent, blond woman, who sat at his feet after dinner. He clearly enjoyed the company of these lively, sophisticated people and fitted in well. Eileen, by contrast, the few times she was present, was quiet and unworldly and did not fit in.

In a humorous letter to Carol Smith in which he pretended to write a seventeen-year-old's passionate love letter, he said he longed to see her, was sure that she saw that he had 'a finely inhibited set of feelings' and that he was comporting himself very well. He loathed age.[33] His inherent romantic nature was forever breaking out. He made a brief visit to Muriel Spark in Rome, but his letters to her were romantic and playful. He could not remember, he claimed, how they parted in body 'but the meeting and you are unforgettable. I hope I behaved myself and said or did nothing unforgiveable'.[34]

* * *

The burning of the British Embassy in Dublin in reaction to Derry's Bloody Sunday stunned and confused him. He organized a petition to be signed by English intellectuals and artists and published in the London *Times*. The letter pleaded for a phasing-out of internment as a way of inducing the elected political representatives of the minority to come to the negotiating table without loss of pride. They had, he believed, most foolishly, said they would not do so until the last man was released.

He sent out a personal handwritten letter to sixty-three people, seventy-five according to Eileen, and wined and dined a number of them in London. They got over thirty replies saying 'yes', thirty-three by his reckoning, twenty-five 'nos' and the rest did not answer. Those who signed were those he either knew personally or who knew enough of him to trust him (Lord Annan, Lord Snow, Sir Kenneth Clark, Cecil Day Lewis, A. J. P. Taylor, V. S. Pritchett, Sir Freddy Ayer, Pamela Hansford Johnson, Henry Moore, Graham Greene, Iris Murdoch, Muriel Spark and others). The response gave a rough indication of his standing in England, and he was rather proud of it. But it had been arduous. Tired after the strain, he longed to see Carol, if only for a drink and a quiet chat. He enjoyed the visit, saw *The Decameron*, *Claire's Knee*, and the opera *Seraglio*, and 'had lots of lunches, dinings and drinkings'.[35]

Eileen had another bad flare-up of her arthritis, this time in her hands, knees and feet. She was very despondent about the future. He had just finished 'The Inside Outside Complex' and was writing well even though he was also housekeeper, laundry-boy, shopper and what not. They got into such a flap about Eileen's health and his age, and the size of the garden, and the impossibility of getting domestic help that he went out one morning and bought a small, four-roomed house with a garden in a quiet cul-de-sac, called Rosmeen Park. He got men in: 'contractors, painters, electricians, kitchen experts, plumbers, central-heating wallahs, gardener'. He redesigned the house and kitchen, organized the drainage in the garden, selected materials for the garden, and went in his little green car to collect old bricks from a building site. He hoped Eileen would like it. Although they hated to leave Knockaderry after thirty-three years, they just could not cope. They would sell at a profit 'and after that if once she utters any more fears of being sent off to some Saint Biddy's Nursing Home if I get sick, leave her for a Burmese Jewess with a hump, or depart for the immortals, I will . . . I will . . . I will just not hear her!'[36]

Knockaderry was on the market for four weeks. They had to endure prospective buyers 'tramping about'. He felt isolated. Julia had gone back to UCLA for six months, so he had no excuse for a trip to London. He had another attack of 'bronchitic flu' after he had been to Manchester filming in the rain. That meant about ten days of coughing, followed by a week in which he would be limp and housebound. He was just recovered in time to move, but the moving went slowly: the heat went off, the telephone went dead.

They moved to Rosmeen Park on 28 November to a semi-detached house with 'a bit of grass in front and a bigger lawn in the back, a "study" of $7'6'' \times 7'6''$ instead of one $13' \times 30''$. It was 'marvellous', he declared with typical gusto, 'to change the pattern of one's life at seventy-two'; 'Sing no sad songs for me'.[37] He had just sold his last book of stories to the Bancroft Library for £1500, so had good reason to feel buoyant. He was pleased with his 'pet of a wee house, so quiet, so warm, so easily run, so near service that we have a part-time maid, a shop that delivers daily'. He also liked the location – five hundred yards from the sea, one thousand from Joyce's tower, a straight run out to the country, and a commuter railway line only two hundred yards away to take him to Dublin. A delegation of local residents came to the door: they understood he was a writer; this was a quiet district; they hoped he would not be holding any late night parties. He was delighted.

He had wearied of Italy. 'One would have to be *very* much in love with a place or person to arrive at the ultra-romantic decision (which has only once been my happiness to make) that "the beloved can do no wrong"'.[38] He, Eileen and Julia went to Provence on 20 June for almost a month. They stayed in Mouries, Bouches du Rhone. He had hoped to write about Daudet's Provence but discovered and wrote about the Massey instead. When they returned he was aware of the 'depressing life' in their cul-de-sac where the neighbours trimmed their hedges over and over. In July 1973 he joined the University Club on St. Stephen's Green, where Patrick Lynch, Christo Gore-Grimes and other friends had membership. He was able to entertain friends there, such as V. S. Pritchett and James T. Farrell.

Eileen was 'arthritic, asthmatic, sees badly' and he had to drive her once a week to her eye specialist. They were, he declared despondently and inaccurately, back to their days in Appian Way when they used to grovel for ten cigarettes and light holy candles to their American friends who sent an occasional packet of tea. He bought a butane gas incandescent lamp. He hoped to be in London for Christmas or New Year to see Julia and Lauro, and to gaze at Carol's 'dear puss and elegant form again, and take your cardiac-erotic temperature and talk to you like an Irish uncle'.[39] They had recurrent difficulty in getting help, partly because Eileen had old-fashioned expectations as to the relationship that should prevail between servant and mistress. Once, when she interviewed a potential housekeeper that Helen Fahy had already vetted and thought would be suitable she found her 'totally unacceptable'. 'Do you know what she did?' she asked Helen. 'She shook hands with us!'

In January 1974, when he had just sold a long story to *Playboy* and had just finished another, he wrote to Carol Smith ('Charlie Smiff'), telling her that he was a worrier by nature. During the years when he had travelled a lot, he had constant bad dreams about missing trains, planes and other forms of transport. He was anxious not to spoil this relationship. He wrote two letters to her in March but tore them up as just possibly striking the wrong note. He was surprised to discover that the 'child' he worried about was in fact thirty-five years old. He felt concerned: was it not 'a very great heart searching decision for any married man to make about whether or not he is preventing an unmarried girl from getting married by becoming her lover and an equal decision for her'? He sadly acknowledged that the age difference made anything more than friendship with Carol impossible. 'I talk nonsense to you only because . . . if I didn't talk nonsense I might make the mistake of . . . Ah, well! *you* know! Cheers! I *do* like you lots, dear Carole. When you are fifty my passionate ghost will visit you'.[40]

He and Eileen went to Venice for ten days. Julia spent a week with them and that 'enlivened' Venice for them. He wanted 'blazing sun' but it rained. They hired a car and drove to Brenta and Padua, then south to Vicenza, Ferrara, Bologna, but the rain sent them back up to Trieste. He read Ellmann's account of the city and had Stendhal, Svevo, Ibsen, Rilke and others in mind. He read Svevo's *Senilità* with the real city before him, very 'Dubliny' in geography, sea, port, hills, foreign domination, swank and poverty. He lunched with Signora Svevo but she was too old for his purposes. So was Pesante. He needed to meet a hard-nosed industrialist and a few students. What charmed him was how much of the old time was left: nineteenth century façades, patriotic memories, industrialists. But he doubted if he could write a travel piece about it.[41]

He got food poisoning which awakened his ulcer and then the 'blow' struck: Gus had a stroke. Sean flew back quickly, watched Gus linger but thought he had not recognized him. He returned to Ireland, knowing that Eileen needed him, and feeling that Gus would be 'happier when he does go – it is his wish, he is already half asleep. And he haunts me.'[42] He rang the hospital every day. His nephew, Dennis Michael, promised to ring him when the crisis came. When Gus died in late July Sean felt so 'wretched' that he asked Julia to deputize for him at the funeral. His food poisoning lingered on but he had a check-up and got a clean bill of health. Now he was dieting his way back to health. He does not seem to have realized that his brother, Pat, had already died in April.[43]

With the death of his two brothers he felt even more alone. He wrote long letters to Carol Smith, to Ellmann, to Robie Macauley: 'O dear Robie come, please, and show me how the hell you make a martini. Or I'll meet you in London'.[44] He worked at stories. In old age he wrote more meticulously and more slowly than ever. On 31 October he flew to Los Angeles, where he stayed with Julia. From there he went to Berkeley to open an exhibition of his manuscripts at the Bancroft Library. He gave the Beckman Lecture on 'The Creative Reader'. Jim and Ruth Hart took him to dinner at Trader Vic's. Hart also took him to lunch at the old Bohemian Club. He thanked Jim Hart for his warm welcome and hospitality. 'I grew a whole inch!' but the ten days were 'too tiring to be enjoyable'. It 'nearly killed' him. He was too old to fly 5000 miles. Of course, he told Carol Smith, he was 'marvellous' but the only reason he went was to see Julia 'who is genuinely a marvel'.[45] She was, he told Emelie, 'the apple of my eye, my masterpiece'.[46] He did not like her novel, *Godded and Codded*, withdrawn because of a threatened libel action, but called *Women in the Wall* (1975) his masterpiece, as though his literary gifts had been passed on to Julia and improved.

In February 1975, in a ceremony at the Gresham Hotel, he was awarded the Allied Irish Banks Literary Award: a cheque for £500 and in addition an especially bound copy of Yeats's *The Shadowy Waters*, a first edition originally owned by St. John Gogarty. It had a Gogarty book plate and Yeats's signature. Michael MacLiammoir spoke of O'Faolain as a sophisticated European writer. At the head table, evoking memories of more embattled days, sat O'Faolain and Peadar O'Donnell; in the room were many younger writers, many of whom had benefited from his advice or example or from the way he had helped to clear the air of suspicion. O'Faolain spoke of his early struggles when he had written for sums which could be counted in pennies. He praised the new approach by which commercial institutions, like the banks, honoured writers. The *Irish Times* ran an editorial entitled 'Sean O'Faolain'. 'I was so delighted at being made much of and gave a good speech'.[47] The following year he was elected as a Foreign Honorary Member of the American Academy of Arts and Sciences.

He received recognition in various ways. Maurice Harmon did a special issue of *The Irish University Review* on him with articles by Robie Macauley, Eilis Dillon, Vivian Mercier, Dermot Foley, Julian Moynahan, Hubert Butler and others. In preparing a biographical note with the editor Sean omitted all reference to the birth of his second child. David Marcus appointed him resident reviewer for the *Irish Press* for 1976. Richard Ellmann nominated him for the Nobel Prize. The National University of Ireland conferred an Honorary Doctor of Literature on him. In 1978, when Gerald Goldberg was Lord Mayor of Cork and Joe McHugh was City Manager, they invited him to accept the Freedom of the city of Cork, but he declined. Undeterred, they presented him with a scroll of honour. Explaining his refusal to write an Introduction to a book of photographs of Cork that McHugh was preparing, he concluded by giving him permission to use anything in his writings that he might find useful.

He painted the railings round the little front garden. Dublin was 'still comparatively quiet, uncrowded, lazy, personal and inefficient, inquisitive, unlearned, but at 75 we ask less . . . We are too old, too select, won't be shoved and pushed . . . so we have done with European holidays'.[48] Since Trieste he had to watch his diet; this meant cutting out wine and reducing the number of martinis. By Autumn he was a 'bit in the rats [i.e. depressed] by that tiresome woman Annie Dominie, but by dint of saying Corraggio! every morning am brisk again'. He ran over to Julia for succour.[49] In November Eileen had a cataract removed from one eye and a plastic lens installed; it worked almost perfectly. The following March she went back to hospital to have a cataract removed from the other eye.

He had flu in March, was full of antibiotics and whiskey but what he really needed was a south of France 'pick-me-up holiday', if he could find the £500 required. Eileen was in hospital, but he had become quite adept at roasting chicken, lamb and beef, could make excellent Greek soup, Scotch broth, Italian tripe (out of a tin), could cook any vegetable. Constable's jacket for *Foreign Affairs* did 'wonders' for his self-image. After five weeks as Editor's Choice in the *New York Times* Peter Davison ordered a second printing. David Marcus printed 'Liberty' to coincide with the London imprint.

Christmas was quiet: there were no friends to be visited. He was 'thrown back' on his 'senile novel', *And Again?*; he 'got into a frazzle' about 'the whole damn blessed thing'. But he had reread the 330 pages and liked it.[50]

When Carol Smith moved from A. P. Watt in 1975, their relationship abruptly ceased. He began corresponding with Elfreda Powell in 1975, writing flirtatious letters to her even before they met and when she, in turn, left Constable in 1984, their friendship also ended, as though it depended solely on her usefulness to him. It was a pattern that repeated itself. When John Kelleher became absorbed in the old Irish annals, O'Faolain stopped visiting him in Boston and wrote to him infrequently. For no reason that Robie Macauley ever knew, O'Faolain suddenly stopped writing to him. When they moved to Rosmeen Park, they no longer asked Norah McGuinness to visit. People came to the conclusion that he was 'cold'. There were additional reasons. He was self-absorbed much of the time, and had much to do looking after Eileen. Letter writing was to some extent self-indulgent, another version of fiction, in which he spun his fine mesh of friendship, played his part as a romantic, indulged in a dream of amorous pursuit. The chase in itself was a delight, a veil spun between him and the harsher realities of age, decreasing sexual power and the requirements of everyday life. He still felt 'the urgent urge' but at seventy-nine knew it was only a dream.[51]

He was romantic with Elfreda Powell but made no sexual advances. After his prostate operation in 1977, he told her, that was no longer possible. But they became good friends. He confided in her, as he had confided in Carol, in Peggy Yntema, in Eileen Simpson, and Alene Erlanger. He was, as he freely admitted, a woman's man. Women were more sensitive and understanding. He regarded himself as bisexual. At the same time he was inclined to undervalue them, or at least take them for granted, as he had for years with Eileen, and when Carol and Elfreda were no longer involved with his work, he simply abandoned them, without considering their feelings.

He talked freely with Elfreda. They discussed children and parents at length, how fathers idolize daughters, mothers sons, the rows and tensions occurring in families and the tensions individual members ended up feeling. He told her that he never intended to communicate with Stephen again. She noticed that he assigned rôles to people: Stephen was a disappointment, Julia was warm and loving, he imposed his view of her on Elfreda and played a part himself. He never revealed his background, presented himself as sophisticated, as one who had lived in Italy, had an affair with Honor Tracy, had a homosexual experience.

At their first meeting, over lunch, he told her about Honor Tracy, but much later about Elizabeth Bowen, during the writing of *And Again?* when old memories were revived. He was, he told her, deeply ashamed of having belonged to the I.R.A. and was very reluctant to allow Constable to reprint stories from *Midsummer Night Madness*. He liked Englishness, liked being published by Constable which he regarded as a very British kind of publishing house with an old Etonian at the helm.

The frankness of his conversations with Elfreda contrasted with the secrecy of his meetings with Victoria Glendinning. When she was preparing her life of Elizabeth Bowen, she wrote to him saying she would like to see him. She was out when he telephoned saying 'Will you tell Mrs. Glendinning I have nothing to say to her'. Two weeks later he wrote saying he would meet her. Eileen, he explained, had objected to him talking with her. Such caution was characteristic; he wanted to protect his reputation. He asked Victoria Glendinning not to mention that he and Elizabeth had stayed in the same hotel in Salzburg. He even asked her to omit the name of the people who owned Alta Villa which he had mentioned in a letter to Elizabeth. In the past he had been over cautious. Once when he and Elizabeth were having lunch in Dublin, he kept looking around in case anyone might see them together. Elizabeth thought such nervousness was ridiculous: two well-known writers ought to be able to lunch together without feeling anxious about being seen.

In July 1977 it was his turn to go to St. Vincent's Nursing Home. He had endured an enlarged prostate for five years, but now it was time to have it dealt with. He wrote jokingly to Robie Macauley: 'Age! It's bad enough doing without the lovely things of life . . . — but to have to relinquish one's one and only prostate!!!'[52] The cure was a drilling up the penis to pound the

[263]

gland away. He would, he said, not visit the U.S. again. 'I am a retired unretiring man'.[53]

He kept up his spirits in wacky, Joycean letters to Elfreda, as when 'slightly tiddly', he responded to her reassurances about copyright. 'Copyright means the sole right to publish, produce, perform, reproduce etc anyfink, and of course the creator of the anyfink owns this right until he sells it to some other guy who thereupon exercises his right which the first guy totally had up to then and may have again if the second guy give his right to copy back to the first guy . . . I rejoyce in having discovered that under your calm coll but inwardly seething dark abyssimus Cornish pussynality you are a bluddy pedant lawyer theologian theorist with your bland talk about of course the author owns . . .'[54]

He needed such outlets, conscious as he was of the death of friends — Susan Blackburn, his 'best pal' Christo Gore-Grimes, Doctor Jerry Slattery, Owen Sheehy-Skeffington and others. When Skeffington died, Sean delivered the graveside oration, describing him as one of the noblest and most complete men the country had ever produced, the inspiration and very often the conscience of those who knew him. 'We will always remember Skeff with joy and gratitude, taking from his memory in love and admiration, as we so often took from his laughing, living presence, a renewal of belief in all that was best in man'. He spoke of the man's untiring devotion to his liberal, humanist principles in the face of enough harassment, discouragement, even personal obloquy from the damned compact majority to have silenced anyone less tenacious, patient and persistent. 'Let us salute then a man who, in a country and time not rich in moral courage, was a giant of honesty, who never swerved or changed, and who kept his youthful spirit to the very end . . . It is all too common for a man to hold high ideals in his youth and let them fade in his old age . . . It is no occasion for eloquence or grief. It is enough to say only "Goodbye Owen. You won." '[55] The words could as easily have been applied to O'Faolain himself.

The winter was hard; heating bills soared, but with the arrival of daffodils, he and Eileen began to think of an Italian holiday. He was holding out for Venice, but Eileen would not risk it, because it rained every day when they were there in 1976. In the end they went to Siena in June where they spent seventeen days, sent postcards to a few friends, and celebrated fifty years of marriage.

[19]

Rosmeen Park

And Again? took over two years to complete, but he 'got a continuous pleasure out of the writing'[1] and whenever he read the manuscript, it stood up to his scrutiny. It was, he knew, the work of a romantic who believed that one is born as a certain kind of person and nothing changes that. Man is like the sea, the ever-renewing sea. He repeats his loves precisely. We have not got free will. Only wilfulness.[2] By taking his characters on the level of sex and passion he had escaped from the constrictions of society and thereby freed himself from the preoccupations with place and character that had impeded his imagination in his published novels. He had always admired Yeats's ability to burn away character, the social carapace, and get to personality, the human essence.

Elfreda Powell's response set his nerves 'a-tingle with happiness'. Of all literary activities cutting, he declared, was his favourite: was it not Chekhov who said one can always cut the beginning, and also perhaps the end, and it does not do a story a damned bit of harm to cut the middle too. 'The trouble is to decide how little to leave!' Elfreda said he was too modest. 'I am modest', he replied, 'because I tend to have the arrogance to match myself with those I admire beyond our common test – words – and rarely, only now and again, feel (arrogantly) "Pretty good!" when my Muse nudges me at the right way.' (26 September 1978). Later he told her she was the inspiration for the novel which was throughout 'a lament for lost youth'. Henceforth her name was not Powell but Perkins, namely Maxwell P., that most patient editor. She was 'a marvellous blend of the judicious, the sensitive (or responsive) and the totally efficient' (24 Oct. 1978).

When Emelie Jacobson found the novel 'marvellously original, rich, beautiful, erudite, funny, bittersweet, passionate and generally superb', he read it again and found the author's life-view 'rather appealing' (29 October 1978). Elfreda suggested cuts, mentioned 'longueurs' and persuaded him to remove a long discussion on Jansenism. She was, he acknowledged, 'dead right'. He did not want to be a 'tiresome . . . incompetent, author argufying with an editor' (24 October 1978). He accepted suggestions for emendations and corrections, sweated blood to get around her objection to the 'artificial contrivance' of a letter, that he could not eliminate, since his hero, a man without a memory, had to have some documentary proof that certain events did actually occur, but he reduced the ten pages to five or six and the actual letter to about three, and broke the whole sequence up by transferring the content of most of the letter to conversational form. He then reworked 196 pages she had sent back with suggestions. Sending them back he longed to see what she had found to 'growl at' in the next lot. He urged her to watch for inconsistencies; he pointed to several and gave the corrections.

Elfreda and O'Faolain had a good working relationship. She found him fun to work with, spirited, witty, shrewd, responsive to suggestions, willing to cut. He was able to stand back from what he had written and look at it objectively. He had unusual mental energy for a man who was close to eighty, even though he was 'emotionally exhausted' in December by her persistent questioning. She had, he said, become his 'collaborator' rather than his editor. He did not have a final title for the novel and thought of *Younger*, and *Return Ticket*, but left the decision to her.

He was taken aback when Peter Davison rejected the novel. At the heart of his many objections was, O'Faolain judged, the troubling attitude of a man complaining that a fantasy-imaginative novel was not being realistic. Davison's objections were so fundamental that O'Faolain told Emelie not to send the ms. to other American publishers until he and Constable, that is, Elfreda, had decided on the final version. He was disappointed that no American publisher could be found.

A prolonged postal strike in the Spring of 1979 cut him off from the outside. He and Eileen had begun gardening again, watching the sky for fear it might rain. He helped with the cooking, bearing a special grudge against marble-sized new potatoes which he found impossible to clean. As an antidote to amateurishly prepared meals he got a case of wine they had discovered in Siena – Brolio 1973. Eileen was the practical one. She insisted on the lawns being mown in an especial pattern, a spiral at the front, stripes at the back. She was tough with gardeners and other workers; she knew what she wanted, could not easily accept deterioration in the garden – weeds growing, neglected plants dying. Sean was vaguer about how things should be done. For him shopping was irksome. Because he could be forgetful, Eileen had to give him a list of items. But she often added to this list, hammering with her stick on the floor just as he was about to leave, hallooing after him, so that he had to go upstairs again and again. Once he cried out 'My God, will she ever stop?' He sacrificed himself to her and she was demanding. But usually he was patient, as he had been for years, lamenting the 'dung and diamonds' nature of life that allowed him rude health while she was in terrible pain. Sometimes they mentioned Stephen far away in New Zealand, his cancer and his alcoholism.

Sean continued to write, sold 'Marmalade' to *Playboy* for $3500, sent another to Emelie Jacobson, and was finishing a third, a reduction of Henry James's *Wings of the Dove*. He had seven unpublished stories, the latest 'A Girl in a Grave'. Writing, as always, was a hedge against the discomforts of life. 'I am', he told Julian Moynahan, 'suffering all the maniacal despair that comes with old age, and the death of dear friends, and loneliness, and desire for life and living foiled either by flat feet, shortage of breath, oncoming impotence, claustrophilia, the trickling away of the elan vital'.[3] He liked to write about people who try to do new things but do not succeed. The main thing was that they tried. He reread *And Again?* with the 'warmest' feelings and found therein a 'remarkably endearing personality' by which he meant that his hero was 'a total shit and loved by all and sundry'.

He had discussed the theme so often with Eileen that she was bored by it. When he asked her if she would like to live her life over again, she answered 'Count me out'. Elisabeth Schnack liked the idea but thought that living life backwards was crazy. 'But', Sean said, 'that's the whole point. Without any memory. He doesn't recognise his old flame when he runs into her, and that gives rise to the most wonderful complications'.[4] As in a detective story the working out of the complications is part of the fascination the novel holds. Given the opportunity to live his life over again, Robert Younger's search for a self sends him on false trails and brings him to half-truths; he is frequently baffled. It also involves disguises, secrecy and evasions as he grows visibly more youthful or is faced with questions about himself, his family, or his past that he cannot answer. O'Faolain regretted that readers missed the comedy of all this. In his love affairs, first with Ana, his old flame, then with her daughter, then with her granddaughter, he repeats himself; in essence each is the same woman. That has its comic side, but the novel takes it seriously. In the end, Younger has to dwindle in America while his daughter grows up, and has one more love affair there. But the affairs are accompanied by psychological analysis of each of the women and Younger's characterization is not as lightly done as comparable figures in the short stories. O'Faolain realized, after publication, that the novel is too long. It is, as he said, a lament for lost youth, but it is also self-indulgent.

He managed to get to London in December. He and Julia saw 'La Marinella', a weepy play by Eduardo da Filippo. Holding hands, they wept copious tears. He took Elfreda to the Café Royal where he used to take 'dear Lizzie Bowen'. Once a fashionable place for writers and artists, it had been redecorated in loud red plush, and was patronized by tourists. They spent most of their time laughing at the incongruity of the setting. He was in a romantic, nostalgic mood and looked very dapper with his silver-headed cane and impeccable manners. He looked more like a bank manager than a writer and his conversation, being anarchic, flirtatious and very frank, was often at odds with the appearance.

Their conversation was always lively. They had much in common: both loved Italy, she had edited translations of Cesare Pavese whom O'Faolain also liked and they both liked *Le Grand Meaulnes*. They discussed religiosity, living according to a framework, Joyce, Stendhal, O'Faolain's prostate operation, and his dismissal of Stephen out of his life. A great tease, he used Elfreda as a sounding-board for ideas. He had his particular view of her: 'hearty, thoroughly well-balanced, life-loving, not too-complicated, active Cornish extrovert'. He was her 'opposite in every way (and snobbishly proud of it.' (20 July 1981) She was extremely fond of him: even at eighty he was still attractive to women.

He read voraciously from his own shelves, all of Maupassant, all Chekhov, Scott Fitzgerald, Robert Fitzgerald's *Odyssey*, Ronald Firbank, Muriel Spark, Henry James, Pritchett on Turgenev, his own work, books sent by the British Library, such as Harold Acton's *Naples under the Bourbons* and *The Last of the Bourbons*, John Richard Green's *History of the English*, Scott's *Staying On*, Santayana's *History of Reason*, the latest Updike, Mary Gordon, Peter Taylor, Nabokov, Fowles, Joan Didion,

Mollie Keane, Tanysaki, Robert Browning, Toni Morrison, John Hawkes, Ruth Prawer Jhabvaśla *Esmond in India*, and Jacques Lacarrieres's *The Gnostics*, a 'frightening book' that 'nevertheless makes one proud of mankind to have created so many lovely things, people, hours out of a diabolical mess, in short it makes one a Humanist' (1 July 1980). Noting that even the stature of the great short story writers had 'dwindled', he was willing to allow Constable to issue a *Collected Stories*. He knew he too had 'committed' many 'undistinguished stories', but seeing how so many of those by Maupassant and Chekhov were poor and thin, decided to let Constable go ahead. It had been a shock to discover such imperfections in the old masters. What particularly interested him was that the whole art of writing stories had been deeply affected by the tempo of his age. 'Time, speed, greater knowledge of psychology, tougher approach all tend to *force* us to use infinitely more technical skill. Naturalism and Realism also complicate matters in so far as the public are coarser in their appetites, are impatient with subtlety, want to arrive at the fullest visual close-up: the influence of the camera and TV are patent here'.[5]

He reflected on himself. 'The fact is I possibly never became fully mature, but I only began to get as mature as I now am very late'. One of the pleasures of age was that he could feel 'blissfully irresponsible . . . Guiltless of my country's blood. Inculpable. A blameless delinquent lamb' (13 February 1980). He was 'old and given to listening to music, reading endlessly, thinking and thinking, and feeling content, lazy, irresponsible, lethargic and claustrophilic'. When Pat Egan, Chairman of the Cork Adult Educational Council, asked him to name his six desert island books, he chose: *Charterhouse of Parma*, *Le Grand Meaulnes*, *A Nest of Simple Folk*, *The Ambassadors*, *Dead Souls*, *Mansfield Park*, *Jude*, any Colette, *A Room with a View* or *Where Angels Fear to Tread*, *The White Hotel*, or possibly *Manon Lescaut* and *Princess of Cleves*. Technique, he had decided, did not matter where the heart is warm.

For many years he had struggled to draw a line between faith, probably as good a religion as the world had invented, and the Church which had 'bitched it up century after century'. While admitting that the Church had produced good architecture, painting, music, sculpture, he pushed it far aside and thought about it as little as possible (22 July 1981). He took Eileen to Mass in St. Joseph's Church, Glasthule where they got to know the parish priest, Father Lorcan Foley who visited Eileen in Rosmeen. He was not always welcomed. Sometimes Sean would not allow him in and when he wanted to say Mass in the house Eileen would not allow it. In an interview in 1979 Sean said 'I'm not a Catholic. I'm not anything in fact. I have no religion'. He did not believe in the afterlife.[6] Newman, he said, had never been truly free. He left the confines of one Church to find himself confined by another. Sean himself put an extreme value on independence; as he said in *Vive Moi!* 'I simply want to owe nothing to anyone' (355). 'When I die I'm going to be eaten by worms'.

He celebrated his eightieth birthday very quietly. Julia published 'Sean at Eighty' in the *London Magazine*. Two German friends, Ambassador Von Boehmer and his wife, took him to a small private luncheon at the Shelbourne. He received flowers and telegrams from a few friends in Ireland, England, the USA and South America. His heart reacted, giving 'extra-systolic jumps', common and harmless, according to his doctors, but it was an uncomfortable experience. He was convinced it must mean *something*. It decided him against going to London for the launch of Volume One of *Collected Stories*.

He got a cold in late June and almost lost his voice for two months. He was still coughing in September. Losing his voice affected his confidence and he was in low spirits. He avoided people. Then it was discovered that he had a cyst on his larynx that had to be removed. The cyst was cancerous and for several months he had to have radiation therapy. He was in poor spirits and had little energy. He pottered at his writing. 'One writes fiction . . . to make life seem real' (15 September 1980). Responding to a letter from Muriel Spark in his usual, gallant, flirtatious fashion he wished he could fly to see her, but he hadn't the energy to fly to London to see his 'lovely and clever daughter'. 'So there you and I are: you to be dreamed of, outrageously idealized, admired – and unobtainable. It is the very nicest and most unsatisfactory way possible to love anyone'.[7]

He and Eileen switched to Vin Blanc Cassis. He had discovered that it required much less expenditure of energy to pour a few glasses for visitors than to make tea. On Sunday afternoons they would invite one or two friends at a time: Patrick Lynch – 'a most courteous man, and loyal friend, as well as a charming man' – Dan Binchy, Richard Murphy, Ita Daly and David Marcus, Maurice and Maura Harmon, an occasional visitor from abroad. Telephoning the invitation Sean would explain, with a half-laugh, that they kept nursing home hours: Eileen would stay in bed until early afternoon and then come down to the living room for two hours of 'high revels' with the visitors. He was, he claimed, a shy, retiring, pseudo-intellectual bloke with a hazy heart of imagination that he let out to bark and gambol for a few hours. Like most Irish writers he considered that human beings are alive for about an hour a day when they escape from the grinding machinery of living into their own selves, their own secret spy-world of the imagination. 'We believe that the imagination creates its own private world which acts as a dissolvent of the public world. I do not think we Irish are ever very happy or satisfied with the public world: we are inclined to distrust it, mock it, laugh at it, satirise it, make a raree-show [a peep show] of it, so that although we are as keen as anybody else on success . . . we do not measure real happiness that way . . . If you look at some of my . . . most characteristic stories, you will find this theme of Ever-Elusive-Happiness dramatised . . . What is at issue, ultimately, in this Irish dualism, is our search for the true Self . . . Every Irishman is all the time living out dramatically an inner search for the unattainable'.[8] He had what he jokingly called 'nominal amnesia', or Name Block. 'I'm reading a book called NB by NB published by NB, reviewed in the NB by NB. Dearest NB do forgive your own true NB' (29 July 1982). It was not as bad as that, but it was annoying.

The first volume of *Collected Stories* lay ostentatiously on the dining room table in October 1980: 'I will say, "Oh, that?" and explain that there are publishers *and* publishers'.[9] The second volume followed the next year, the third a year later and then Penguin issued all three. The reviews were excellent. They admired the social range, the energy of expression and variety of invention. He was pleased with the extra cash 'in these desperate times'. He owed money to the Revenue Commissioners and had to pay Capital Gains Tax on the sale of Knockaderry, and did not want to have to sell off his stock which had been bought at 71 and was due to mature at par in 1983. A. P. Watt sent him £1,876 in June 1982 and that helped. His correspondence with Hilary Rubinstein at this period shows him to be precise and professional about financial matters and still quoting what Eric Linklater had said: if he once accepted an inferior fee he would be rated that way forever. From her hospital bed Eileen questioned about payments due on volumes of the *Collected Stories*. He and Eileen, 'his accountant', worried about finances, but when he got a pension of £6000 from Aosdana their worries were eased. Sean wrote a gracious letter to Colm O'Briain at the

Arts Council, quoting what Yeats had nobly said when Patrick McCartan had secured a pension for him: he accepted with gratitude 'that something more which is precious to an old man'.[10]

Even as he wrote amusingly to Elfreda about his inability to remember names, Eileen was in hospital again, rushed there by ambulance on 23 August. She was brought back for three weeks, then taken off again, and brought home just before Christmas. Cortisone and other pain-killing drugs had weakened her stomach; she was threatened with peritonitis. Reluctant to use surgery, the doctors fed her exclusively by drip on glucose and liquid, and gave her blood transfusions so that the stomach could heal itself, but in November she had to have surgery to remove an abscess in her stomach and to cover it with a skin graft. 'It was all a near thing – if it really is over'.[11] Without the support of friends, he would have gone 'quite off his chump'. At Christmas she was still very weak, but improving. Thin and frail, weighing only seven stone, she kept as quiet as possible and got up about three o'clock. Sean also got up late, about 10 a.m., and retired early. They had their evening meal at about six o'clock, watched television, used a video to record what they would miss by going to bed early. In this struggle with death, he felt he had lost touch with life, and neglected friends. They were 'like two apples waiting to fall off the tree from over-ripeness'. They made their will: the trustees held all royalties from his books, radio and TV broadcasts for Julia, and were to purchase a holding of £75,000 in long-dated Government stock and pay the income to Stephen over his lifetime. On his death the holding would become Julia's property. The trustees were also instructed to sell and convert the residue of his estate and out of the proceeds to pay £30,000 to Lucien and the residue to Julia. The estate came to £301,915.

He got a cold in February and had to go to bed. On the eve of his eighty-third birthday he asked Emelie Jacobson to send Stephen $1000. He had been simultaneously hit by the recession in New Zealand and by an accident. He intended to help him occasionally. Stephen had been sending tapes, since he was not good at letter writing, but his father would have preferred a letter. He admitted, however, that when Stephen had written, he had commented on the grammar and syntax.

In 1986 O'Faolain received the American Irish Foundation Literary Award and was presented with a cheque for $7500 at a luncheon in the Ambassador's residence. He was elected to the honorary position of *saoi* in

Aosdana. The President of Ireland, Dr. Hillery, came to Rosmeen Park to present him with a gold torc and stayed for forty-five minutes. Colm O'Briain and Patrick Lynch were there as well.

Eileen had become so incapacitated that she could not walk downstairs. His architect friend, Nial Montgomery, helped to instal a small lift in the hallway behind the front door. It worked on a system of counter weights, like an old sash window: her seven stone against seven stone of lead, occasionally aided by his walking stick when she reascended. A wheelchair took her from the hallway into the living room. She was still lively and alert in conversation, although inclined to tell visitors in detail about her illness. On Sunday afternoons, when they entertained, the conversation was often of the latest books. They both read what was current, were interested in younger writers, but were 'rather lonely and cut off'. Elfreda had gone from Constable. Sean had not been to London for a long time. He had 'shot his bolt as a writer'. Eileen was immobilized and that meant he had virtually shot his bolt on the front door, since she could not be left alone. Their 'mutual occasional bites at one another' were always 'preliminaries to exquisite renewals of love (whatever that word means)'.[12] He wrote a warmly enthusiastic letter to Bryan MacMahon who had sent him a copy of *Sound of Hooves*, praising his 'daring spontaneity' and commenting on individual stories.[13]

In May 1987 they had a visit from John and Helen Kelleher. In the summer Munira Mutran and her husband visited. *And Again?* was translated into Russian and Dutch. If visitors asked what he was writing, O'Faolain replied 'nothing', or 'just rewriting', which usually caused Eileen to ask, 'Well, why are you spending so much time in your study?' He would shrug or smile, enigmatically. In fact he was not only rewriting stories, but working on a shortened version of *And Again?*, revising *Vive Moi!*, and writing its sequel.

Things began to go seriously wrong for them in November 1987. Sean, who had been confused, went into hospital for examination. He had to have a bladder operation. Julia came to see him. He returned home by the twenty-first, but then Eileen had a haemorrhage and was taken to hospital by ambulance on 29 November. Patrick Lynch spent the afternoon with Sean.

In March he wrote a warm letter of commiseration to Dermot Foley who had suffered a stroke and was in a nursing home. I brought him news about

Dermot and other friends. He was not well enough to get to Cork to receive the Freedom of the city. He wrote a cordial letter to the Lord Mayor, Tom Brosnan. Julia went in his place. The ceremony took place in the Council Chamber of the City Hall. The Lord Mayor presented Julia with the scroll of Freedom: it bore the arms of Cork city, the familiar picture of the two pillars, the ship and the motto 'Statio Bene Fida Carinis'. He praised O'Faolain as 'one of the great men of letters of our time', among the greatest short story writers the world has known, renowned as novelist, biographer, literary critic, playwright and travel writer. He recalled his leadership and courage as editor of *The Bell* and stressed his persistence in helping Ireland to overcome her isolation and thereby making her more ready to take her place within 'the enlarged European Community and in a wider world'. Among those present were Aloys Fleischmann, Nancy McCarthy, Gerald Goldberg, Tadgh Ó Ciardha, President of University College Cork, Mairead Murphy, Sile and Eilis MacCurtain, and Isabel Healy whose father had accompanied O'Faolain to the SS. München in 1926.

Some kind of reconciliation had been achieved in O'Faolain's acceptance, the Lord Mayor's speech, and Julia's reply. The *Cork Examiner's* headline said 'Cork Comes of Age in Honouring O'Faolain'. Isabel Healy's account was critical: it should have been a major civic occasion; instead there was a 'lacklustre drab little affair' – the handing over of the exquisitely wrought and locally made silver Freedom Box, followed by salad sandwiches, wine or mineral water. But it was, at least, a symbolic gesture – Cork's disenchanted son had made his peace with the place where he was got. He had other things on his mind.

Eileen died on the morning of 21 September 1988. She had had a recurrence of internal bleeding and was taken to St. Vincent's Hospital. Late the previous night the hospital phoned Patrick Lynch to tell him she was weak and might not survive until the morning. He phoned Mary Moloney, who through him knew the O'Faolains and whose parents became friends of Sean in his last years. He asked her to drive him to the hospital and to collect Sean on the way. Eileen was without pain up to five minutes before she died, from a stroke. A sister suggested that Sean have a cup of tea. While he was having it, Eileen died. They took Sean back to Rosmeen, very distressed. Patrick Lynch offered to stay with him, but Sean would not have that. He phoned the housekeeper who arrived about five o'clock. Julia arrived from London that evening.

There was no funeral. Eileen's body had been bequeathed to Trinity College for medical research. Her ashes were subsequently scattered in Gougane Barra. Requiem Mass was celebrated in the College Chapel on the twenty-seventh. There was a small attendance, which included Julia and Lauro, Maura Harmon, Harriet Sheehy, and Patrick Lynch. President Hillery sent his aide-de-camp, a tribute that Sean appreciated. Mass was said by Father Foley. When it was over Sean sat still, feeling the emptiness of the service. Stephen wrote to his father and sent a photograph of himself. Sean sent him a card occasionally, sometimes written by Mary Moloney and signed by him. Although Stephen threatened to come home, he did not: it had been arranged years before that he would stay away in return for a regular allowance. After the Chapel service Sean took Julia, Lauro and Patrick Lynch to lunch at the Montrose Hotel.

Back at Rosmeen Sean found it difficult to realize that Eileen was gone. He would go into her room to tell her something and then remember she was no longer there. He suffered remorse over her death and regretted that he had not paid more attention to her. Neighbours and friends worried about him being on his own, but he seemed to be managing. He was free now to come and go as he wished. Helen Fahy, who had been a good friend and neighbour to both of the O'Faolains, since they moved to Rosmeen, now became indispensable. He visited her almost every day, often had his meals in her home and enjoyed being with her family. He did the shopping, wrote to friends, talked on the phone with Dan Binchy. 'A truly terrific thing has happened to me with Dan Binchy. I quite literally have ceased to remember him – he is become the Irish mirror of my son (in is it New Zealand or America?)'. He had, he joked, found 'a quite interesting author . . . More than interesting. A discovery. Name – O'Faolain. You see? I am a good former writer'.[14] For the first time he could talk freely about his additions to *Vive Moi!* and in particular about the women figures. He told me that he wanted that story told: the women had been important to his development. He had not been able to write freely about them, because Alene Erlanger lived on to 1969, Honor Tracy was still alive (she died in June 1989) and had always opposed the idea of being included in his autobiography, and because of Eileen.

In February he signed a contract with Constable for a reprint of *A Nest of Simple Folk* and got an advance of £500. In May Constable decided to extend Penguin's licence on *And Again?* and *Midsummer Night Madness* for another five years and arranged for an advance of £2000. In a feature that earned her a literary award Mary Moloney interviewed him for the *Evening Press* on his birthday. What, she asked him, was the worst part of becoming old? 'Being alone', he answered. 'And silence . . . you spend a lot of time keeping your spirit up. Writing is a heavenly relief. It takes you out of yourself and out of the present'. Did he believe in the afterlife? 'I don't believe in it, which doesn't mean I deny its existence. I should think the body probably disappears and the spirit is as it was in the beginning, so it is in the end'. He recalled the banning of *Bird Alone*. 'I felt like dirt, that I needed a wash . . . Somebody had thrown me out of an accepted club without my knowing what I'd done'. He could not say exactly when he left the Church. He had to leave because ultimately it interfered with his freedom as a writer. Of Eileen he said that he appreciated her capacity for friendship. 'I respected her enormously. Her capacity for endurance was one of her greatest gifts and it made me feel I've got to bear up'. He wished he had read more of her work while she was alive. 'I'm a woman's man', he admitted. 'I like the company of women more than the company of men. They're more sensitive'.

In March 1989 he was taken to hospital suffering from loss of memory and confusion. He had also experienced paranoia and was threatening people. Helen Fahy and the housekeeper watched over him. He seemed to be sleeping, but he crept downstairs, dressed only in a pullover and long underpants, and could not be restrained. He rushed screaming and shouting into the roadway and burst into a neighbour's house. It took five or six people, Hugh Fahy, his two sons, Helen and the housekeeper to bring him back. That evening he was committed to St. John of God's mental hospital in Stillorgan.

He was put in a room with two men, then with six. His mental condition improved. He hated the constant locking, the noise of keys turning. He broke out one afternoon and made his way to Patrick Lynch's home. Patrick rang Helen Fahy to help him to bring him back. It took hours to persuade him. When they arrived attendants had to force him back in. He was suffering from a deficiency in folic acid. His doctor thought there was no need for him to remain any longer in St. John of God's but that he should be in a nursing home.

He was made a ward of court. Under the terms of this order he was given

£40 a week spending money, his royalties were paid directly into his account, but he was unable to deal with his bank and was deprived of his cheque book. The solicitor dealt with his affairs. These restrictions on his independence and self-esteem troubled him greatly.

The house at Rosmeen Park, which had been broken into while he was away, was put up for sale. Thieves stole a fine bookcase with first editions and a hunting table. Julia and Helen Fahy searched for a suitable nursing home and found Aclare House in Dunlaoghaire. O'Faolain moved there in July 1989. He had a double room on the second floor, with a single bed, a comfortable armchair, a small table at the window overlooking the garden, a desk for his typewriter, and a small bookcase for his Chekhovs, Turgenevs, his six copies of *A Nest of Simple Folk* and other books. He had a beaten copper Celtic cross on the dressing table and an abstract painting, acquired when he was Director of the Arts Council, over his bed. Although the front door was locked, he was free to come and go as he wished. He adapted to these circumstances surprisingly well, mingled easily with the other residents, had his meals with them, entertained friends in his room, enjoyed his freedom of movement. He frequently phoned people inviting them to visit, or go out with him; he dined in restaurants in Dunlaoghaire, had a couple of favourite pubs, and was generally in good form. He deliberately rejected self-pity, sometimes joked about himself, about his failing memory, his occasional confusion, and refused to speak of Aclare House as a nursing home. But, inevitably, he was more cut off than ever. Editors and friends from abroad who used to phone him at Rosmeen now either did not know where he was or were unsure about his state of health.

A small circle of friends continued to visit. Helen Fahy came to see him frequently and he often walked to Rosmeen Park to visit her, sometimes as much as three times a day. Mary Moloney took him for drives into Wicklow, including one to Killough House; Patrick Lynch took him to lunch at least once a week. Sean frequently called him on the phone and Patrick, knowing he was bored, lonely and restless, always went to see him. James Plunkett took him to his home in Wicklow where they were joined by Val Mulkerns. He was sometimes absent-minded, sometimes pretended not to remember names, could be careless with his money. Once when Ita Daly took him to lunch, he clearly had no idea who she was. When they got to Realt na Mara he immediately became gallant, ushered her in, was attentive and flirtatious, circuitously established who she was. She drove him back with Sean holding her hand. He kissed her, said he had had a lovely time, that they must do it again. Next time, he said, they must also arrange not to have David present. I drove him to the Dalkey Island Hotel every week. We would sit looking out over the sea and chat for about two hours.

He looked well. He had a nice grey suit that he wore going out; another outfit was a sports jacket with grey slacks, blue shirt and lightly coloured tie and brown shoes, and a particularly elegant paisley waistcoat. He discovered my *Sean O'Faolain: a critical introduction* (1985) on his bookshelf and was fascinated with the evidence of his life as a writer. He often took it with him when we went to Coliemore harbour. Sometimes he joked about having been 'bonkers'. He was puzzled by the financial arrangement and hated the indignity of going to Mrs. Jones, the proprietor of the Aclare, for money. He complained that the Irish Government was depriving Irish writers of royalties.

He reached his ninetieth birthday. Aclare House put on a birthday party: Julia phoned from California, friends went to see him, James Plunkett paid tribute to him on television, the *Irish Times* carried articles by Thomas Kilroy, Mervyn Wall, Fintan O'Toole and me. The Arts Show, on radio, had a discussion of his work. Jack Nagle sent him a birthday card: 'to a nonagenarian from an octogenarian'. He was, instinctively, courteous and gallant to the staff at Aclare or when he went visiting, to the Moloneys' one Christmas, to the Harmons for another.

He was unable to carry on a coherent conversation, nor could he express himself clearly. Sometimes he was quite lucid. One of the great losses in his life, he said, had been loss of belief in the afterlife. He regretted the placidity of modern life, the lack of a rebellious spirit. He was envious of Julia's ability to create a world for herself in the United States, England, Italy. But he felt her marriage inhibited her. If someone says 'I'm going to get married', the answer should be 'don't'. He sometimes felt he had lost contact with Julia. He could no longer have a conversation with her: she visited, took him out, but he felt she had no real interest in him or in what he thought. He spoke of his parents: his father had understanding even if he was not articulate; his mother had elemental fears. Neither had spoken of his relationship with Eileen. They were much more worried about his relationship with Kathleen Ni Houlihan, but Eileen represented what he had discovered. His parents need not have worried on moral grounds. Both he and Eileen overcame sexual passion. She was 'a very good girl'. Once, in November 1990, as he looked out to sea O'Faolain sighed 'Oh, my!' and explained, with tears in his eyes 'My wife died'. Stephen had rung him up and talked 'balls'. He had had to hang up on him.

Sean's occasional mental sharpness was evident in his response to the newspapers. He read the *Irish Times* every day. During the presidential elections when the paper carried an interview with one of the candidates, Brian Lenihan, O'Faolain cut it out and underlined it heavily, wanted to know if anyone was going to challenge some of the statements. He had felt his gorge rising, he said.

In December the New Zealand sculptor, Anthony Stones, spent two afternoons working on a head. Sean spoke of Stephen abandoning his roots, something that had never seemed to bother him. He regretted that Julia would not visit him for Christmas. When the head was finished he said 'It has life'. He noted that it looked different from each side. Rubbing his hand over his chest he said 'I feel part of me has been taken away'.

In February 1991 he was alarmed by a letter in which Julia described the American preoccupation with the war in the Gulf. He worried that she might be in danger. He hoped to see her 'for the last time'. He had a number of slight heart attacks, but on 17 February he had a bad attack. The doctor advised that Julia should be notified, since the next few hours would be crucial. Helen Fahy telephoned Patrick Lynch and me. Patrick went to see him and found him very weak. But he had a good night, was out of bed next morning at eight o'clock, did not remember anything from the previous day's alarms. I went to see him in the afternoon, intending to stay with him in his room. To my surprise he was fully dressed, with Gus's black homburg on, his umbrella over his arm, and determined to 'sneak out'. We looked for the last time together on the view across Dublin bay that had been part of Sean's life for over fifty years. He had a chest infection that did not respond to antibiotics. He became restless at night, was violent, would not stay in bed, required an attendant at all times. He developed pneumonia and was not well enough to attend a small birthday party arranged by the Harmons.

In March he was much weaker. Helen Fahy phoned Julia who told her she would arrive in two weeks.[15] 'Why didn't she come two weeks ago?' Sean asked and got back into bed, curled up, his head deep in the pillow. Next day

[279]

he talked about age and death: he had lived long enough; he thought there was just so much time allotted to each person. He had no belief in the afterlife. It was just baloney. Old Nobodaddy amused by foolish humans with their expectations. 'I have never accepted "shalt not"'.

He could be violent and abusive. Because of the changes in mood the nurses now called him Jekyll and Hyde. When angry and frustrated he could be very aggressive, using violent language. Then on good days he was his usual witty, gentlemanly self. Mrs. Jones feared her staff, including the male nurse, would not be able to handle him. In the daytime he had to be sedated. Julia was expected on Saturday, 9 March. When we visited him that afternoon, he thanked Maura for the flowers which were in his room. He was much brighter, roguish and flirtatious. He was looking forward to seeing Julia who arrived that night. She began visiting him every day.

She talked with Patrick Lynch about funeral arrangements. His remains would go to Trinity College, as he had wanted, and there would be a memorial Mass at Trinity. She prepared the death notice. Next day, 16 March, Aclare House phoned me to say Sean was dying. I phoned Julia at Helen Fahy's. In a vague response to a priest's invitation O'Faolain had received Extreme Unction some months previously in a general absolution of all the Aclare residents.

On 22 March, much to his astonishment, Dr Donal McCafferty had a fluent and coherent conversation with O'Faolain in Irish lasting twenty minutes. It included a discussion of the grammatical differences between Donegal and Munster Irish. Patrick Lynch visited the same day, then Julia. I arrived just as she was leaving, but got little response from him. Julia went to London, feeling that there was not much more she could do. He did not communicate much now. On Good Friday I read to him, including Frank O'Connor's translation of 'Kilcash', and sang the original. Then, with Sean smiling in recognition, I read a passage from 'The Silence of the Valley'. We had an intense communication.

'I am very miserable. It is horrible. The pain'.

'Are you in pain?'

'Yes. It is terrible. Not being able to speak'.

'You can think?'

'Yes'.

'You have ideas?'

'Yes. It is horrible. Where can I get sympathy? Pity?'

'You have my sympathy'.
'Yes'.
'Have you hope?'
'No'.
'But you have courage'.
'Yes.'
'You have dignity'.
'Dignity and courage'.
And then our familiar exchange on parting.
'Always nice to see you, Sean.'
'Always nice to see you'.
'I'll see you again'.
This time O'Faolain added 'Please do, please do. God bless you. God bless', his head against my hands, pressing in agony.

Karl Hayes, the solicitor in the Gore-Grimes firm, instructed Mrs. Jones to move O'Faolain downstairs to shared accommodation and to discontinue the special nurse because of the expense: the twenty-four-hour care was costing £1700 per week and Sean's doctor could not predict how long it might be required. Thinking that O'Faolain might die within a couple of days, since he was weak and declining, Mrs. Jones waited until after the weekend to move him. When I visited in the afternoon I found him downstairs in a smaller bare room with one window, that looked upwards at the garden, and a silent old man. In the downstairs room he was closer to the nurses' room and could be observed more easily. The alternative, which Julia and Helen Fahy wanted to avoid, was to send him back to St. John of God's. O'Faolain was aggressive and angry, his speech clear and sharp. 'What do you want?' Mrs. Jones asked. 'I want to die'. He ground the words out strongly. Later Patrick Lynch was refused admission.

Sean O'Faolain died at 4.00 p.m. on 20 April 1991. That afternoon about 3 o'clock I found him weak, his breathing short. Just after 4 o'clock the nursing home rang to give me the news. I phoned Patrick Lynch who phoned Julia. The body was removed to Trinity at 7 o'clock. The Sunday papers carried the news. There were tributes from James Plunkett, Cyril Cusack, President Mary Robinson, Francis Stuart, Benedict Kiely and my long appreciation in the *Sunday Independent*. There was a memorial Mass on 4 May in St. Joseph's Church, Glasthule. The celebrants were Father Lorcan Foley, F. X. Martin, O.S.A., Father Roland Burke-Savage, S. J. and

Mark Tierney, O.S.A. Present were Julia, Lauro and Lucien, James Plunkett, Conor and Maire Cruise O'Brien, Ita Daly and David Marcus, Eilis Dillon, Helen Fahy, Bryan MacMahon, Jack Nagle, Maura Harmon, Mary Moloney, some of the Dublin cousins, some of Julia's friends — Maureen Charlton, Nuala and John Mulcahy, and various friends, neighbours and writers.[16] Both the President and the Taoiseach were represented by an aide-de-camp, but the Government failed to honour him. In fact there was not a single politician present. In his Memorial Address Conor Cruise O'Brien spoke of Owen Sheehy Skeffington, the Irish agnostic, Hubert Butler, the Irish Protestant, and Sean O'Faolain, the Irish Catholic, all liberal, courageous intellectuals who had served their country well. Afterwards Julia took the mourners to lunch at the National Yacht Club, a setting that reminded some of them that Sean had used the Dun Laoghaire yacht clubs as settings for his ironic romantic portraits of Irishmen in pursuit of an Ever-Elusive-Happiness.

Notes

Chapter 1. Cork

Autobiographical material is based on a number of sources: *Vive Moi!* (1993), another version in manuscript, *Vive Moi!* (1964), *An Irish Journey* (1940), several radio scripts, and interviews. For this chapter interviews were held with John O'Flaherty.

1. Articles by John O'Flaherty in the *Evening Echo* 14 and 22 October, 1974.
2. SOF interview with John Quinn, Radio Eireann 1980.
3. Even at no. 16 the Whelans had one lodger, a travelling salesman. They had a seventeen-year-old domestic servant at no. 5, called Annie McCarthy.
4. Letter to SOF April 1965.
5. SOF letter to Andrew O'Shaughnessy, n.d.
6. Letter 1938. He referred to Robinson's play in a letter to the *Irish Times* (2 March 1938) in which he praised its 'faithfulness and reality', and its 'intricate and earnest searchings of the national consciousness'.
7. 'A Writer Growing Up', Westdeutscher Rundfunk, 6 June 1969. He also wrote about this in *Puck's Fare* (1941).

Chapter 2. Education

Interviews with Nancy McCarthy, Brother Reen, Bridie Markham, Neddy Kennedy, Brother Matthew, Bill Twomey, T. J. McElligott, Frank Johnson, P. J. O'Connor, Dan Frawley, Peter Brennan, Kitty Madden, Isabel Healy.

1. Letter to SOF, April 1965.
2. 'An Irish Schooling', *Life and Letters*, 10, 5 (April 1934), 30.

3. SOF letter to Andrew O'Shaughnessy, n.d.
4. P. J. O'Connor, *Exploring Limerick's Past*. Newcastle West (1987), 138, 158.
5. Letter to SOF, April 1965.
6. Presentation Brothers College. *Extension Souvenir (1887–1954)*, 57.

Chapter 3. Revolution

Interviews were held with Margaret Phelan, Aloys Fleischmann, Sophia Mallin.

1. SOF interview with Justine McCarthy, *Irish Independent*, 24 March 1990.
2. SOF interview with Andy O'Mahony, Radio Eireann, 1970.

Chapter 4. Civil War

Peter Lucey, Dan Kelleher, T. P. O'Neill, Maire McCarthy, Lily Twomey, and Ruth Moller provided some of the information for this chapter.

1. Document No. 129, Military Archives.
2. Manuscript in Cork City Museum.
3. *Guests of the Nation*, 124.
4. Mary MacSwiney letter to Patrick Ruttledge, 3 October 1923.
5. BBC Northern Ireland, 17 March 1978.
6. SOF letter to Horace Reynolds, 3 May 1937.
7. Tim Pat Coogan, *The IRA*, 6.
8. *The Bell*, 10, 3 (June 1943), 200.
9. *Cork Examiner*, 5 April 1924.
10. *Sinn Fein*, 11 October 1924. He quoted Whitman's observation that there is nothing more terrible than the sight of a people being led by leaders who do not believe in men.

Chapter 5. Corkery's Glugger

Interviews with Aloys Fleischmann, Gerald Goldberg, Declan MacSwiney and Patrick Maume.

1. Sean O Tuama, 'Daniel Corkery, Literary Critic: a Memoir', 119.
2. 'Daniel Corkery', *Dublin Magazine*, 1936.
3. *Irish Times*, 26 May 1977.
4. *The Day* gives the flavour of the Club's activities. It contains short articles by T. C. Murray and Con O'Leary, reviews of local dramatic performances, and an attack on 'dirty' books and films that regrets that the Vigilance

Committee is inactive. There are summaries of lectures and occasionally a chronicle of Club meetings. The list of topics indicates the intellectual level of the meetings: 'Extracts from a Treatise on English as Spoken in Cork' by J. Leahy, MA; 'The Short Story' by Daniel Corkery; '. . . A Symposium. Irish History' by Dennis Breen; and so on. The 'chronicle' recorded in March 1918 has a similar list, with many of the same speakers. There is no record of O'Faolain's talk on Tolstoy because *The Day* ceased publication in December 1918.

Aloys Fleischmann remembered how devastatingly effective O'Faolain was at a meeting of the Twenty Club when Father Patrick McSwiney gave a talk on 'Chopin and the Historical Background', but devoted most of the time to the background. Sean stood up and protested at this imbalance. He 'wiped the floor with him'. On another occasion during a concert at which some students were unruly, Sean suddenly gathered other students together, and threw the unruly ones out. Kitty Madden remembered how Sean walking out of a meeting of the Literary and Historical Society at which he was giving a talk, when some students heckled him.

5. Letter to John V. Kelleher, 8 September 1948.
6. Letter to Horace Reynolds, 22 January 1937.
7. Letter to Horace Reynolds, 16 December 1936.
8. SOF letter to *An Phoblacht*, 14 May 1932.
9. Letter to John V. Kelleher, 8 September 1948.
10. *Irish Statesman*, 5 September 1925.
11. *Irish Tribune*, July 1926. Since Corkery was Literary Editor the attack had a personal sting.
12. *Irish Tribune*, 23 July 1926, 23.

Chapter 6. Harvard

1. SOF letter to Edward Garnett, August 1926.
2. Mrs. F. W. Bateson letter to MH, 3 May 1990.
3. 'Liam O'Flaherty: A Tribute', Radio Eireann, 11 September 1984.
4. 'The Philological Syndicate in Harvard', *Harvard Alumni Bulletin*, 23 October 1964.
5. Report by Max Ferrand to the Commonwealth Fellowship.
6. n.d. Sean, of course, could not be a scoundrel, but he could be quick-witted in an emergency as when he drove across the traffic in Boston and was whistled to a stop by an enormous cop. 'What's your name?' the cop asked. 'Sean O'Faolain,' Sean answered, adding to his accent a top-dressing that Eric Linklater had never heard before. 'What's that you said?' asked the cop. 'Sean O'Faolain'. 'Where do you come from?' 'Cork', said Sean, but he pronounced it so that it sounded like 'Caorrk', and as he spoke he smiled

with a sort of shy complicity. 'Is it Caorrk, do you say?' asked the cop. 'It is', said Sean. 'Then get to hell out of here before anyone sees what you've done to the traffic'. (Eric Linklater, *Fanfare for a Tin Hat*, 129.)

7. *Harvard Union Catalogue, 1928–29*, 636.
8. SOF letter to Edward Bliss Reed, 28 December 1927.
9. Father Harry O'Connor letter to MH, October 1988.
10. George Russell letter to SOF, 20 May 1927.
11. Eileen Simpson, *Poets in their Youth* (New York 1982), 11.
12. SOF to Edward Garnett, n.d.

Chapter 7. London

Some of the material on St. Mary's was obtained from staff and former students, including Father John Hurley, Father Kevin Cronin, Father Desmond O'Beirne, Father Michael Prior, Michael Fitzpatrick, John McHugh.

Sean O'Faolain wrote frequently to Edward Garnett during these London years. When dates are available they are given in the text.

1. SOF letter to Frank O'Connor, June 1946.
2. Frank Naughton letter to Father Michael Prior, 4 September 1988.
3. *Simmerian Newsletter*, Winter 1977.
4. Eric Linklater, *Fanfare for a Tin Hat*, 30.
5. H. E. Bates, *Edward Garnett*, 47–48.
6. The Abbey already had a Parnell play. According to Frank O'Connor, Lennox Robinson did not like O'Faolain's because it 'twisted' dates and facts. (Letter to Nancy McCarthy, 18 September 1930.) Ten years later he and O'Faolain also worked on a Parnell play.
7. SOF interview *Windmill* 1962.
8. *Bookman*, LXXXII (April–September 1932).
9. *New York Times*, 27 March 1932.
10. SOF letter to Edward Bliss Reed, 31 March 1931.
11. Frank O'Connor letter to Sean Hendrick, 13 April 1929.
12. SOF letter to Edward Bliss Reed, 3 November 1929.
13. SOF letter to Lincoln Kirstein, 20 April 1931.
14. Aloys Fleischmann letter to MH, 29 April 1991. Confirmed by Mrs. Sophia Mallin, daughter of W. F. P. Stockley.
15. Materials concerning the applications are in the archives at University College, Cork. At the same time Sean applied for a Lectureship at Queens University in Belfast.
16. Aloys Fleischmann letter to MH, 7 October 1991. One other candidate received minimal support. There was considerable student resentment at the failure to appoint O'Faolain.

17. SOF letter to Lincoln Kirstein, 2 October 1931.
18. SOF letter to Cape, 30 May 1933.
19. SOF letter to Benjamin Huebsch, January–February 1932.
20. SOF letter to Eric Linklater, 24 February 1932.
21. George Russell letter to SOF, 18 February 1932.
22. Frank O'Connor letter to SOF, n.d.
23. James Mathews, *Frank O'Connor*, 397.
24. File H 315/114 National Archives.
25. SOF interview with Andy O'Mahony, Radio Eireann, 26 July 1971.
26. Eileen O'Faolain letter to Edward Garnett, n.d. Objecting to the attacks on *Midsummer Night Madness*, including the banning, Sean defended the individual's right to freedom of expression. Much of modern Irish nationalism, he said, was a cloak for bigotry and intolerant jingoism. The absence of intellectual freedom, he declared, kept Ireland in a worse state of slavery than it was before Independence. He regretted the growth of religious, racial and cultural intolerance. (*An Phoblacht*, 14 May, 4 June, 9 July 1932.)
27. SOF letter to Lincoln Kirstein, 19 May 1931.
28. Jonathan Cape letter to SOF, 12 June 1933.
29. Frank O'Connor letter to Nancy McCarthy, 11 April 1933.
30. George Russell letter to SOF, 5 April 1933.

Chapter 8. Killough House

Interviews with Victoria Glendinning, Micheál O hAodha, Cyril Cusack, Patricia Boylan, Terence de Vere White, Aloys Fleischmann.

1. In an Irish issue of *The Bookman* (August 1934) he was seen as the leading figure: Lennox Robinson praised him as one of the new realists; Stephen Gwynn noted how writers on the Civil War, including O'Faolain, describe its bitterness and violence; Norreys Jephson quotes his advice to a writer to read no newspapers, take no periodicals, hear nothing of politics, meddle with controversy no more than a writer need for pride and literature, allow beauty to rise to him of her own desire, ignorant and wanton as the dawn; in two articles he is even mentioned as likely to write poetry which judging by his few published poems was most unlikely. O'Faolain himself contributed 'Criticism by Forgetting' in which he states a personal preference for a literary criticism based on an instinctive response to particular moments or scenes.

   It was significant of his emergence as the leading literary figure of his generation that he was invited to give a lecture under the auspices of the Irish Academy of Letters in 1934. He was excited by the opportunity to

present his ideas on the rôle of the Catholic novelist. He noted that the three priests who were members, including Father Aubrey Gwynn, stayed away.
2. SOF letters to F. W. Bateson, 1933.
3. Michael O'Donovan letters to Nancy McCarthy, 10, 16 and 13 August 1933.
4. Diary, 22 August 1933. Other entries given in the text.
5. Christopher Gore-Grimes letter to MH, 18 September 1975.
6. SOF letter to Francis Hackett, 1933.
7. Signe Toksvig letter to Florence Hackett, 1 December 1933.
8. Signe Toksvig letter to Francis Hackett, February 1934.
9. Signe Toksvig letter to Francis Hackett, 24 February 1934.
10. SOF letter to Scott James, 28 September 1934. When he returned to Ireland he tried for a teaching position at St. Patrick's Training College, Dublin, but was turned down because of his former IRA association.
11. SOF letter to F. W. Bateson, 7 May 1934.
12. 'The Dangers of Censorship', *Ireland To-Day*, 1, 1 (November 1936), 57–63.
13. *Ireland To-Day*, 1, 2 (July 1936), 32. O'Faolain's fundamental belief that Irish democracy began with O'Connell came from a lecture given by Frank O'Connor for the Irish Academy of Letters (3 March 1935). After the defeat at Kinsale, O'Connor said, the literary classes were lost to any sense of reality. After the Siege of Limerick the aristocratic leaders had left. Those who remained, the ordinary Irish people, were the components of the new democracy. In 'The Lament for Patrick Sarsfield', Ireland, for the first time, had the voice of a whole people. O'Faolain's *King of the Beggars* develops these ideas. He often acknowledged his debt to O'Connor.
14. During this period O'Faolain wrote several important articles about Irish society and the difficulties facing the writer, e.g. 'Provincialism and Literature', *Motley*, 1, 3 (August 1932), 3–4; 'New Directions in Irish Literature', *Bookman*, LXXV, (5 September 1937), 447; 'Letter from a Novelist to an Idealist', *Motley*, 11, 7 (November 1933), 3–5. 'Celts and Irishmen', *New Statesman & Nation*, IV, 74 (23 July 1932), 93–4; 'De Valera – Rebel or Reformer', *New Statesman & Nation*, IV, 77 (13 August 1932), 173–174. 'Emancipation of Irish Writers', *Yale Review*, 23 (Spring 1934), 501; 'Re-orientation of Irish Letters', *Irish Times*, 21 September 1935, 12.
15. SOF letter to Eric Linklater, March 193[5].
16. 'Principles and Propaganda', *The Bell*, 10, 3 (June 1945), 197–200.
17. O'Faolain constantly examined De Valera's character, policies, philosophy and influence: in 'Irish Year', *New Statesman and Nation*, 6 (9 December 1933), 44; a letter to Eric Linklater, March 193 [5]; in *Commonweal*, 15, 10 (6 January 1932), 273; 22, 18 (3 August 1933); and the *Yale Review*, Winter 1936, 325–327. In the 1939 *De Valera* he presents the statistical and factual evidence for the consolidation of this middle-class. He particularly disliked De Valera's attempt to justify his decision to take the Oath of Allegiance to

the British Crown so that he could enter the Dail. He did not blame him for changing his mind. He did blame him for pretending that no change was involved. It was another example of the labyrinthine Irish mind at work.

He preferred the humanity of Theobald Wolfe Tone, a man of charming personality and with civilized ideas about life. He was attracted by his 'merry, insuppressible, eager, all too human nature, so sceptical, so serious, so gay, so indiscreet, so utterly removed from all posing and false dignity' (IR, 120). He was, O'Faolain claimed, the only sensible definition of what Irishmen meant when they talked of being Republicans. He was certain that Tone would not have liked the mode of living that De Valera had allowed to develop, would have resisted 'sectarianism, puritanism, middle-class vulgarity, canting pietism, narrow orthodoxies whether of Church or State'. (*Autobiography of Wolfe Tone*, ed. SOF, 123).

18. Francis Hackett letter to SOF, 10 November 1934.
19. Francis Hackett letter to SOF, June 1935.
20. He was attracted to her as a 'warm, passionate, active woman'. He admired a woman who told her governess she was 'a bigoted bloody Sassenach' and washed her car 'in the middle of Rathmines Road in her red knickers' (SOF letter to Edward Garnett). Initially Derek Verschoyle, then R. N. D. Wilson were to have shared the work with him; they would do the Ascendancy background. In the end he wrote the book on his own, much of it from interviews. He welcomed later, more scholarly biographies.
21. SOF letter to Horace Reynolds, 18 September, n.d. Garnett wanted him to remember Balzac. That idea attracted him. Ireland, he thought, resembled France under Louis Philippe when a nascent democracy was trying to establish itself. Ireland needed a Balzac to express the drama of their post-revolutionary period. Literature should become public and stop being subjective and private and keep the continuity of the literary movement alive. (SOF letter to Joseph Walsh, 27 June 1938.) He admired what Balzac had done, but he loathed naturalism.
22. 'An Irish Letter', *Hound and Horn*, 7, 2 (January–March 1934), 271–273.
23. 'Plea for a New Type of Novel', *Virginia Quarterly Review*, 10 (April 1934), 197. 'A.E. and W.B.', *Virginia Quarterly Review*, 15, 1 (January 1939), 55. These examinations of the novel are part of a wider scheme in which O'Faolain studied writers who had influenced him and other Irish writers, not only AE and Yeats, but Moore, Pater, Flaubert, Chekhov. He said he would call the proposed book of essays 'Always Kill Your Da'. (SOF letter to F. W. Bateson, 1936.)
24. SOF letter to John V. Kelleher, 8 September 1948.
25. n.d. These undated letters were written in 1937. He often mentioned the importance of the novelist being able to make use of many levels of society, as Hardy and the Russians did. Neither he, nor O'Connor, nor O'Flaherty knew the Big House. 'It is', he wrote, 'that the *consciousness* of the existence

of many modes of life, and some intimacy with them, heightens the treatment of any one mode of life, gives the sense of echo, reverberations wider than the scene displayed, as well as more colour and more variety in a writer's work taken as a whole'. 'Gamut of Irish Fiction', *Saturday Review of Literature*, XIV (1 August 1936), 19–20.

26. Quoted by Patricia Craig in *Elizabeth Bowen*, 92.

27. SOF letter to Francis Hackett, 27 June, n.d..

28. SOF letter to Francis Hackett, n.d. Parnell, he said, was big enough to embrace divergencies. He had 'an extraordinary power of acceptance', but being Anglo–Irish he did not incarnate Irish life and character. (SOF review of Leon O'Broin's biography of Parnell, *Irish Press*, 20 May 1937.)

29. SOF letter to Patrick McCartan, 17 October 1937; Hugh Hunt, *Irish Independent*, 3 September 1967.

30. SOF letter to Patrick McCartan, 17 October 1937.

31. SOF letter to Evelyn Bowen, 1937.

32. Evelyn Bowen letter to MH, 20 October 1988.

33. *The Bell*, 6, 4 (July 1943).

34. SOF letter to Frank O'Connor, 1938.

35. SOF letter to Eric Linklater, July 1938.

Chapter 9. Knockaderry

Many people have memories of being at Knockaderry. They include Leon O'Broin, Rita Quinn, Nial McCarthy, Eilis Dillon, Val Mulkerns.

1. SOF letter to Frank O'Connor, Easter 1939. He wrote many letters to O'Connor in this period. Many are undated but were written between 1939 and 1940. When available dates are given in the text.

2. He had conducted a public campaign against the deteriorating standards. In reply to a Yeats interview he denied that there was a decrease in playwriting by Irish dramatists; there was no need for the Abbey to fall back on old plays. The policy of producing continental plays, he said, discouraged young dramatists. (*Irish Independent*, 26 January 1935.) In an Open Letter to Yeats he recalled his experience of seeing Lennox Robinson's *Patriots* and urged the Abbey to remember the enchantment such realistic plays gave (*Irish Independent*, 2 March 1935). At the same time he praised the 'timely' production of *The Silver Tassie* (*Irish Independent*, 3 September 1935). He thought their *Coriolanus* had vigour and zest (*Irish Independent*, 15 January 1936). In response to the Abbey Theatre Festival (1938) he praised some of the 'electrifying performances', but criticized the lectures because they had no common ground of agreement. The Directors were

neither able to formulate a revolt against the Abbey's old tradition nor to adapt it to modern conditions. (*Irish Times*, 20 and 21 September 1938.)

3. Frank O'Connor letter to Dermot Foley, 4 June 1940.

4. The publisher's apology was a slap in the face for O'Faolain. Written as a letter to the editor it said: 'The Solicitors of the Most Reverend Doctor Michael Browne, Lord Bishop of Galway, have drawn our attention to certain passages appearing in *An Irish Journey* by Sean O'Faolain, the Irish Edition of which has been issued through our firm, and have pointed out that the passages referred to defame His Lordship and his Diocese.

'We acknowledge that the statements referred to are offensive and untrue, and we very sincerely regret that such statements should have appeared in a Book published by us and we desire to apologize and to express our deepest regrets to His Lordship.

'Immediately our attention was drawn to the matter we withdrew the book from circulation and have undertaken not to reissue it with the passages in question.

'We desire to add that we were associated only as Publishers and these passages were unfortunately overlooked in our office.' (*Irish Press*, 15 August 1940.)

5. In 1935 he was almost ready. He thought of a weekly newspaper, drew up a list of names to be involved – George O'Brien, A. E. Malone, Francis Hackett; they would raise £550 once they could offer attractive editorial control and guaranteed contributions; he had ideas on the religio-educational policy; Catholicism must be Europeanized by printing liberal continental Catholic writers; he was against attacking the Irish; they should be able to get out a live paper if they stuck together as people did during the revolution. He was determined to start a magazine 'or burst': 'something faintly astringent', named *Order*, or *The Lance*, or *Now*. These plans were forestalled by the appearance of *Ireland To-Day* (1936–38), owned by J. J. O'Leary and printed by Cahills. O'Faolain became Literary Editor but was not happy with the paper's apparent lack of editorial consistency and direction.

Chapter 10. The Bell

Interviews with Vivian Mercier, Patrick Lynch, George Hetherington, James Plunkett, Bryan MacMahon, Eilis Dillon, Val Mulkerns, Michael O'Beirne, Mary Lavin, Mrs. Lochlinn McGlynn, Dermot Foley.

1. Her memoirs were published under the title 'Orphans'.

2. The Russian magazine, *Kolokol,* was anti-Government, anti-Censorship and anti-isolationism. When O'Faolain decided on *The Bell* as title, he said 'I will be the hammer'.

3. SOF letter to L. A. G. Strong, 6 October 1940.
4. SOF to Frank O'Connor, 1940. O'Faolain wrote frequently to O'Connor. References, when dated, are given in the text.
5. O'Connor expressed his reservations about *The Bell* to Dermot Foley. The second issue, he said, was deplorable: at least 4 dud articles, 2 dud reviews, not a single outstanding contribution, and a sketch 'by the fellow who employs him to edit the *English Digest*' (1940). He was less scathing about the January 1941 issue, praising poems by Cecil Day Lewis, his own story, and a sketch called 'Poachers', but Robinson's 'playlet' he found 'incredibly awful' and, he added in disgust, 'Jack Yeats! Peadar O'Donnell!!!'. He had told them, he said, that a paper without a policy would be meaningless; everything he said would happen had happened; the loss had jumped from £20 a month to £45. He told O'Faolain that *The Bell* had an 'alien breath'. O'Faolain found that '*devastating*'. Fortunately, he said, he had 'earplugs' to all criticism or he'd go daft. (1940.)
6. The Belfry featured the work of new poets.
7. Letter, n.d.
8. 'O'Faolain. The Encourager', *Cork Review* (1991), 55–56.
9. 'In the Beginning. James Plunkett and *The Bell*', *Cork Review* (1991), 45.
10. 'Monotonously Rings the Little Bell', *Irish University Review*, 6, 1 (Spring 1976), 54–62.
11. SOF letters to Lochlinn MacGlynn, 12 August 1942; n.d.; 5 April 1944.
12. SOF letter to Lochlinn MacGlynn, 8 October 1943. He also got a job on the *Irish Digest* for Michael O'Beirne, another of the writers he encouraged, after O'Beirne wrote saying he needed a job badly. He advised O'Beirne to put himself forward, not to be like an animal who lays eggs in a dark tunnel. He should come out into the light. O'Beirne enjoyed O'Faolain's vivacity. Once when they went into a restaurant in which the waitresses were dressed like bunnies, O'Faolain attracted one with long black stockings, rubbing his fingers softly together and whispering 'puss, puss, puss'. He made light of his fame, saying 'yesterday I was famous' (Michael O'Beirne interview with MH, April 1993).
13. SOF to Edward Sheehy, 26 May 1941. He tended to overpraise what he liked. As they said in Dublin 'all his mice were elephants'. But he had a good nose. When David Marcus sent him a short story, he turned it down, but said 'your name or pen-name suggests you are a Jew. I'll give you 8 gns. for an article on Jews in Cork'.
14. 'Sean O'Faolain and the Younger Writer', *Irish University Review*, 6, 1 (Spring 1976), 37–44.
15. The first 'Republican' Irish parliament, or Dail, he liked to recall, met in Dublin in 1919. It should have produced or at least discussed and decided on a social programme to define the kind of society that would develop under an Irish Republic. It did produce a Democratic Programme. It

contained the vaguest generalization. 'It was read aloud and discussed for precisely 20 minutes and 50 seconds, and was then buried *for ever*'. 'O the earning of the green', review of Dorothy Macardle's *The Irish Republic*, *New York Herald Tribune*, 10 March 1965, 3.

16. Diary, 1942.
17. He wrote in gloomy terms to James Hogan. Ireland, he said, was 'beyond all hope now', there was 'utter apathy'. (13 December 1945.)
18. Evelyn Bowen letter to Dermot Foley, November 1941.
19. SOF letter to Denis Johnston, 1941.
20. SOF letter to James M. Cain, 21 January 1941.
21. Sean McEntee letter to SOF, 17 October 1942.
22. Diary 1945. Shortly before he resigned he set up an Advisory Council consisting of Owen Sheehy Skeffington, Vivian Mercier, Thomas Woods, Conor Cruise O'Brien, Hubert Butler, Valentin Iremonger and Patrick Lynch. It was an ideas-body, but never did much work. At the meeting at which Sean handed over to Peadar O'Donnell, O'Donnell made a short speech. 'I'm proud to follow in the footsteps of Sean O'Faolain, but my emphasis will be different. I want to open the windows to look at a distant horizon'. 'For God's sake, Peadar', Sean interrupted, 'speak English'.
23. SOF letter to Hubert Butler, n.d.
24. Julia O'Faolain, 'Sean at 80', in *Fathers. Reflections by Daughters*, 120–131.
25. 'I'm being steeped in the Modernist thing. It's terrifying'. (SOF letter to Frank O'Connor, 19 September 1942.)
26. SOF interview with Brian P. Kennedy, 7 February 1987, *Cork Review* (1991), 4–6.

Chapter 11. The Bell *Years*

Interviews with Mervyn Wall, Leon O'Broin, Nancy McCarthy, Ann Hughes and John V. Kelleher.

1. *Irish Times*, 6 March 1943.
2. *Irish Times*, 26 April 1941.
3. WAAMA was founded to promote the solidarity of, and to secure better working conditions for, the four Guilds of which it was composed: the Writers', Actors', Artists' and Musicians' Guilds. The Association wanted to get a decent minimum wage for all its members. O'Faolain was the President which meant that he had to attend meetings of each of the Guilds and to preside over the organization of a WAAMA week from 17–22 May 1941. That began with a sponsored radio programme, saw the launch of *Puck's Fare*, held three flag days for the Association's Benevolent Fund, ran a Symphony Concert in the Mansion House, and concluded with a

Grand Arts Ball in the Metropole. *Puck's Fare* contained a 'Meet Sean O'Faolain' by The Bellman.

The following year O'Faolain was Vice-Chairman of the Committee organising a Book Fair for the Thomas Davis Centenary. It was opened at the Mansion House (24–27 March) by Sean MacEntee; O'Faolain also spoke. A month later he and Eileen spent two days cycling in Co. Cavan with Frank O'Connor.

4. R. O Faracháin letter to SOF, 23 April 1941.
5. SOF letter to R. O Faracháin, 25 June 1941.
6. SOF letter to Frank O'Connor, 1941. Where dated these letters are noted in the text.
7. SOF letter to Dermot Foley, 1942.
8. *Horizon*, V, 25 (January 1942), 55–63.
9. Frank O'Connor letter to Dermot Foley, 15 October 1942.
10. Frank Duff letter to Frank O'Connor, 29 December 1942.
11. Frank O'Connor letter to SOF, n.d.
12. Leon O'Broin . . . *Just Like Yesterday*, 152–155. Father John Heuston, a Dominican theologian vetted questions submitted in advance for a Questions and Answers session. This was O'Faolain's idea.
13. SOF letter to Hilton Brown, 18 December 1942.
14. SOF letter to Frank Hugh O'Donnell, 3 March 1943.
15. Some of the family's happiest holidays were spent at the Brandondale Guest House near Graiguenamanagh. O'Faolain wrote about the town in 'A Tale of a Town', *The Bell*, May 1945. See also Hubert Butler, *Escape from the Anthill*, 90. Brandondale had a dark, laurelled walk in which there was a well with steps leading down to it. Hearing the story about there being a trout in the well, Sean wrote 'The Trout'. Many years later he commented about this story. Art, he said is 'a mosaic of teeny bits and pieces of memory, come from all over one's life and wanderings'; when they 'magnetically come together they are impelled to take the shape they do partly by design but also – and this is the lovely mystery of personality – by some indefinable force of longing in me that seized on the tiny hint, or spur, or attraction, or revelation in the image of there possibly being a trout in a tiny well in the dark walk'. (SOF letter to Ann Hughes, 24 January 1983.)
16. SOF letter to John V. Kelleher, July 1943.

In his diary he noted that what Flaubert did for novel-writing is perfectly expressed in Flaubert's own words. It differentiates the novel as a work of art from the novel as popular entertainment: 'Whatever may be the thing one wants to express, there is only one word to express it, only one verb to animate it, only one adjective to qualify it. One must look for them until one finds them, that word, that adjective, that verb, and never be satisfied with an approximation'.
17. In 'The Silence of the Valley' Denis appeared under his own name and was

bluntly described. He said the story was 'all bloody lies' (Interview with MH, 1960).

18. SOF letter to Nancy McCarthy, 31 July 1943.
19. SOF letter to Irving Erdman, 16 October 1944.
20. SOF letter to Nancy McCarthy, n.d.
21. Nancy McCarthy letter to MH, 29 July 1988.
22. Eileen O'Faolain letters to Nancy McCarthy, 18 July and 4 December 1944.
23. SOF letters to Nancy McCarthy, 7 and 15 December 1944.
24. Eileen O'Faolain letter to Nancy McCarthy, 1 January 1945.
25. Frank O'Connor letter to Sean Hendrick, n.d.
26. Frank O'Connor letter to SOF, 23 January 1945.
27. Frank O'Connor letter to SOF, 31 January 1945.

Chapter 12. *Italy and* Newman's Way

1. Page references to *Summer in Italy, South to Sicily* and *Newman's Way* are given within the text.
2. 'The Irish and the Latins', *The Bell*, 19, 1 (December 1953), 145–150.
3. Enriqueta Frankfurt interview with MH, 25 March 1990.
4. SOF letter to Richard Ellmann, 2 June 1948.
5. SOF letter to BBC, January 1949.
6. SOF letter to BBC, 1 April 1949. One Sunday Sean, Honor Tracy and Christo Gore-Grimes went to Mass in the Basilica of S. Maria Maggiore. They knelt close to a confessional which had an open side for the penitent. Mass had already started, but Gore-Grimes, who was closest, noticed a young and beautiful girl with bare legs and sandals making her confession just a few feet away from where they were kneeling. As she told her sins her toes relaxed and touched the tiled floor softly, but as soon as she stopped whispering and listened to the words of her confessor, the toes tied themselves into knots. Trying to concentrate for a moment on the Mass, Gore-Grimes turned towards the altar and caught the eyes of Sean and Honor gazing past him and focussed on the toes. When Mass ended the interpretations began. Sean was certain that the twitching was due to questioning by the priest as to how she could lose – outside wedlock – the greatest treasure a young girl has; Honor was certain that she was being rebuked for having joined the Communist Party. The argument ended when laughter took over (Christo Gore–Grimes letter to MH, 10 September 1975).
7. Harriet Sheehy interview with MH, 4 August 1989. Frank O'Connor noted that she was 'besotted' with O'Faolain.
8. SOF letter to John V. Kelleher, 30 October 1951.
9. 'Autoantiamericanism', *The Bell*, 16, 6 (March 1951), 7–18.

10. 'Sicily', *Holiday*, 19 (May 1956), 48.
11. 'Southern Italy', *Holiday*, 36 (September 1964), 38–46.
12. SOF letter to John V. Kelleher, 8 September 1948.
13. SOF letter to Richard Ellmann, 25 September 1954.
14. SOF letter to John V. Kelleher, 30 October 1951.
15. SOF letter to John V. Kelleher, 30 October 1951.
16. SOF letter to Elisabeth Schnack, 13 December 1951.
17. SOF letter to Elisabeth Schnack, 26 March 1952.

Chapter 13. Ireland

Interviews with Eilis Dillon, Hector Legge, Father Mark Tierney and Sr. Philibin.

1. SOF letter to A. S. B. Glover, 6 March 1946.
2. SOF letter to Allen Lane, 9 September 1947.
3. SOF letter to John V. Kelleher, 14 May 1948.
4. SOF letter to P. S. O'Hegarty, 4 June 1946; SOF to Frank O'Connor, June 1946.
5. His column in the *Sunday Independent* ran from January 1946 to July 1948.
6. SOF letter to Curtis Brown, September 1946. The article was turned down by the *Atlantic Monthly* but appeared in *Life*.
7. Sr. Philibin interview with MH, 3 February 1990.
8. SOF letter to Curtis Brown, December 1946.
9. SOF letter to John V. Kelleher, 12 April 1947.
10. Eileen O'Faolain letter to John V. Kelleher, 21 May 1947.
11. SOF letter to Arthur O'Shaughnessy, 28 November 1946.
12. SOF letter to John V. Kelleher, 14 March 1948.
13. 'The Dilemma of Irish Letters', *The Month*, 2, 6 (December 1949), 375.
14. SOF letter to John V. Kelleher, 13 March 1947.
15. SOF letter to John V. Kelleher, 1947. He had been bored with peasant subject matter for several years and regarded 'Lovers of the Lake' as a break with it.
16. SOF letter to Ronald Boswell, 3 March 1947.
17. SOF letter to John V. Kelleher, 12 April 1947. In his Introduction to *Finest Stories*, he commented on the difficulty of writing about people who combine 'beautiful, palpitating, tea-rose souls with hard, coolly calculating heads'.
18. SOF letter to John V. Kelleher, 31 August 1948.
19. SOF letter to John V. Kelleher, 30 October 1951.
20. SOF letter to Richard Ellmann, 29 July 1948. His claim to be half in love with Margaret was part fantasy. Although he visited her, did some programmes for her and stayed with her in Paris, he never made any advances. She saw him as a Maurice Chevalier figure — dapper, suave, international — but without Chevalier's panache.

21. SOF letter to Louis MacNeice, 21 September 1948.
22. SOF letter to Aloys Fleischmann, 25 October 1948.
23. SOF letter to Raynor Heppenstall, November 1948.
24. SOF letter to Theodora Fitzgibbon, 19 December 1951. The meeting was not organized by Skeffington as some people thought.
25. SOF letter to Sylvia Beach, 16 May 1948.
26. SOF letter to Eric Linklater, 1950.
27. SOF letter to Father Columba, 12 November 1949.
28. SOF letter to Father Columba, 17 April 1950.
29. SOF letter to Father Columba, 16 January 1951. Sean wrote frequently to Glenstal, usually to Father Columba, sometimes to Father Matthew Dillon. Where available the dates are given in the text.

Chapter 14. Princeton

Interviews with Liz and Julian Moynahan, Ed Cone, Eileen Simpson, Lucius Wilmerding, John and Jane Jacobi.

1. E. B. O. Borgerhoff letter to SOF, 18 April 1953.
2. SOF letter to E. B. O. Borgerhoff, 23 February 1953.
3. Richard Ellmann letter to SOF, 22 December, 1953. Sean was interested in intellectual Catholicism and had agreed to edit a Catholic weekly. But nothing came of this scheme. He lectured John Kelleher on the need for an intellectual Catholicism in America and told John Deedy of *Commonweal* that Catholic journals should be inherently Catholic and not feel obliged to stress it. His first travel articles on Italy had been sent to *Commonweal* for which he had written reviews and articles since December 1927, but they paid badly. Even in August 1953 their fee for 'A Visit to Padre Pio' was $50.
4. SOF letter to E. B. O. Borgerhoff, 1 December 1953.
5. E. B. O. Borgerhoff letter to SOF, 8 December 1953.
6. SOF letter to Richard Ellmann, 29 December 1953. O'Connor had stayed with the O'Faolains in February 1952 and they attended a dinner to celebrate his fiftieth birthday in 1953, but the row over O'Connor's abandonment of Joan O'Donovan and the secrecy with which he acted caused a major disruption in the friendship. When O'Faolain was in America in 1955, he did not visit O'Connor even though he knew O'Connor had had a serious heart attack. When the O'Faolains met him at a reception in Dublin, Eileen refused to speak to him and Sean was merely polite. In April 1957 Sean did not even recognize him when he saw him in the street.
7. SOF letter to John V. Kelleher, 12 January 1954.
8. SOF letter to John V. Kelleher, 1 December 1953.

9. SOF letter to Eric Linklater, 3 September 1953.
10. SOF letter to John V. Kelleher, 6 October 1953.
11. SOF letter to John V. Kelleher, 22 (?) 1953.
12. SOF letter to John V. Kelleher, 7 December 1953.
13. SOF letter to John V. Kelleher, 1 April 1954.
14. Hans Aarloff letter to MH, 2 January 1989.
15. SOF letter to John V. Kelleher, 17 April 1954.
16. Richard Ellmann letter to SOF, 13 March 1954. Sean also arranged other lectures through Kelleher, Ellmann, William York Tyndall, and others. He insisted on a fee of $100 per lecture, not $50 as some universities were offering. Ellmann arranged for him to lecture at Northwestern University, the University of Chicago, and the University of Illinois. He advised him against undertaking the long trip to Minnesota to see J. F. Powers (letter to SOF, 18 January 1954).
17. SOF letter to John V. Kelleher, 11 March 1954.
18. SOF letter to John V. Kelleher, 1 April 1954.
19. Valerie Cooper interview with MH, 30 May 1991.
20. SOF letter to John V. Kelleher, 18 August 1954.
21. SOF letter to John V. Kelleher, 20 October 1954.
22. SOF letter to William Plomer, 11 October 1954.
23. SOF letter to John V. Kelleher, 20 October 1954.
24. William Plomer letter to SOF, 5 November 1954.
25. SOF letter to William Plomer, 11 November 1954.
26. SOF letter to Marc Longman, 22 November 1954.

Chapter 15. A Wasted Life?

1. SOF letter to John V. Kelleher, 21 January 1955.
2. SOF letter to John V. Kelleher, 16 April 1955. .
3. John V. Kelleher letter to SOF, 29 April 1955.
4. John V. Kelleher letter to SOF, 18 May 1955.
5. SOF letter to John V. Kelleher, 4 May 1955.
6. SOF letter to John V. Kelleher, 4 September 1957.
7. SOF letter to Micheál O hAodha, July 1953.
8. Micheál O hAodha letter to SOF, 15 July 1953.
9. SOF letter to Micheál O hAodha, 20 October, 1953.
10. SOF letter to Aloys Fleischmann, 18 August 1953.
11. SOF letter to John V. Kelleher, 29 January 1956.
12. SOF letter to Emelie Jacobson, 8 May 1957.
13. SOF letter to John V. Kelleher, 28 October 1956.
14. SOF letter to John V. Kelleher, 24 June 1956.
15. SOF letter to Elisabeth Schnack, 1956.

16. SOF letter to John V. Kelleher, 9 July 1956.
17. SOF letter to John V. Kelleher, 28 October 1956.
18. Alan Collins letter to Seymour Lawrence, 20 June 1956.
19. SOF letter to John V. Kelleher, 9 July 1956.
20. SOF letter to Alan Collins, January 1957.
21. SOF letter to John V. Kelleher, 9 July 1956.
22. SOF letter to John V. Kelleher, 27 July 1956.
23. John V. Kelleher letter to Edward A. Weeks, 15 August 1956.
24. SOF letter to Nancy Reynolds, 9 April 1957.
25. SOF letter to Emelie Jacobson, 25 November 1956.
26. SOF letter to John V. Kelleher, 13 December 1957.
27. Mervyn Wall interview with MH, 22 September 1989.
28. National Archives S 2321–25.
29. SOF letter to Richard Ellmann, 21 February 1957. *Holiday* required an itemized list of expenses and this was always something of a worry for Sean.
30. SOF letter to Denis Johnston, 25 November 1957.
31. SOF letter to Thomas McGreevy, July 1957.
32. SOF letter to Nancy Reynolds, 27 May 1957.
33. SOF letter to John V. Kelleher, 24 August 1957.
34. SOF letter to John V. Kelleher, 1957.
35. SOF letter to John V. Kelleher, 26 September 1957.
36. SOF letter to John V. Kelleher, 5 October 1957.
37. SOF letter to Seymour Lawrence, 1957.
38. SF letter to John V. Kelleher, 4 September 1957.
39. SOF letter to Richard Ellmann, November 1957.

Chapter 16. Acceptance

People interviewed for this chapter included Eileen Simpson, Jane Jacobi, Liz and Julian Moynahan, Ed Cone and Harriet Sheehy.

1. SOF letter to Seymour Lawrence, 7 January 1958; letter to John V. Kelleher, 8 January 1958.
2. SOF letter to Emelie Jacobson, February 1958.
3. SOF letter to Curtis Brown, 20 February 1958.
4. SOF letter to Emelie Jacobson, 12 March 1958.
5. Seymour Lawrence letter to Emelie Jacobson, 16 January 1959.
6. SOF letter to J. F. Powers, 20 May 1959.
7. SOF letter to John V. Kelleher, 8 January 1958.
8. SOF letter to John V. Kelleher, 15 January 1958.
9. *Northwestern University Alumni News*, 37, 4 (July 1958), 3–11.
10. Moody Prior letter to MH, 20 February 1988.
11. Jean Hagstrum letter to MH, 25 September 1988.

12. Richard Ellmann letter to John V. Kelleher, 17 April 1958.
13. SOF letter to Richard Ellmann, 10 July 1958.
14. SOF letter to Alan Collins, 26 July 1958.
15. SOF letter to Sukie, 26 July 1958.
16. SOF letter to Seymour Lawrence, 1 September 1958.
17. SOF letter to Harry Sions, 3 September 1958.
18. SOF letter to Richard Ellmann, 4 October 1958.
19. SOF letter to Richard Ellmann, 6 November 1958.
20. SOF letter to Denis Johnston, 1 January 1959; Stan Stewart told Dermot Foley that Eileen had an 'unhappy time with teenagers at Christmas', 19 January 1959.
21. SOF letter to John V. Kelleher, 26 July 1959.
22. SOF letter to Curtis Brown, 28 July 1959.
23. SOF letter to John V. Kelleher, 15 January 1958.
24. SOF letter to J. F. Powers, August 1959.
25. SOF letter to J. F. Powers, August 1959.
26. SOF letter to Father Sweeney, 21 March 1963.
27. Ed Cone letter to MH, 20 January 1959.
28. SOF letter to Norah McGuinness, 25 March 1960.
29. Jean McAndrew letter to MH, 30 June 1989.
30. Elisabeth Schnack letter to MH, May 1991.
31. SOF letter to John V. Kelleher, 24 November 1960.
32. Eileen O'Faolain letter to Mabel Henry, 4 October 1960.
33. Eileen O'Faolain letter to Ria Mooney, 19 November 1960.
34. SOF letter to Seymour Lawrence, 11 August 1961.
35. SOF letter to John V. Kelleher, 1 September 1962.
36. SOF letter to Michael O'Beirne, 20 November 1980.
37. SOF letter to John V. Kelleher, 3 June 1961.
38. SOF letter to Seymour Lawrence, 18 November 1961.
39. SOF letter to Emelie Jacobson, 24 March 1962.
40. SOF letter to John V. Kelleher, 1 September 1962.
41. Eileen O'Faolain letter to Jean McAndrew, 7 July 1963.
42. Sean O'Faolain radio interview with John Boyd, The Arts in Ulster, 12 December 1963.
43. SOF letter to Edward Weeks, 23 October 1963.
44. SOF letter to Jean McAndrew, 23 December 1963.
45. SOF letter to Seymour Lawrence, 26 November 1963.

Chapter 17. A Writer in Residence

Interviews with Sally Bierer, Alene Bricken, Hector Legge, Peter Davison, Robie Macauley, Thomas Kilroy, Peggy Yntema, Julia O'Faolain, Terence de Vere White and Father Francis Sweeney.

1. SOF letter to Seymour Lawrence, 21 January 1964.
2. Emelie Jacobson letter to A. P. Watt, 24 February 1966.
3. SOF letter to Seymour Lawrence, 29 January 1964.
4. John Vernon letter to MH, 28 January 1990.
5. Frank Bergon letter to MH, 25 September 1990. O'Faolain was similarly mischievous when he and William S. Rukeyser were having a drink in the Nassau Tavern in Princeton. Thinking to impress O'Faolain Rukeyser, then an undergraduate, coolly ordered Bushmills on the rocks. 'He'll have Jamesons', O'Faolain said. 'No', said Rukeyser. 'You'll have Jamesons', O'Faolain said again. 'No', Rukeyser insisted amiably. 'I drink this stuff all the time, and it's definitely Bushmills I want'. 'What do you want with that filthy stuff?' O'Faolain asked, and Rukeyser noticed for the first time that this was more than just social chitchat. '*It's made in the North*'. Like many other students Rukeyser was impressed with O'Faolain's presence, his white mane, great dignity, talkativeness and the glamour that attached to his personal history as a revolutionary at a time in America when most students did not know anybody in that line of work. (William S. Rukeyser letter to MH, 19 May 1993.)
6. E. S. Yntema letter to MH, 1 December 1989; interview with MH, 13 May 1991.
7. SOF letter to Emelie Jacobson, 14 September 1964.
8. SOF letter to Emelie Jacobson, 14 September 1964.
9. Eileen O'Faolain letter to Jean McAndrew, 2 January 1965.
10. Eileen O'Faolain letters to Jean McAndrew, 22 & 25 March 1965.
11. SOF letter to Emelie Jacobson, 17 April 1974.
12. SOF letter to Emelie Jacobson, 24 December 1965 and to Father Francis Sweeney, 26 December 1965.
13. SOF letter to J. F. Powers, 16 November 1965.
14. Eileen O'Faolain letter to John and Helen Kelleher, 31 May 1967.
15. SOF letter to Margaret Phelan, 14 December 1967.
16. SOF letter to Elisabeth Schnack, 14 December 1967.
17. SOF letter to Richard Ellmann, 19 July 1968. Appointed in May 1968, initially he attended meetings quite frequently and was supportive of the Director. He resigned in 1975.
18. SOF letter to Emelie Jacobson, 7 November 1968.
19. SOF letter to Emelie Jacobson, 18 November 1968.
20. Harry Sions letter to SOF, 28 February 1969.
21. SOF letter to Julian Moynahan, 18 January 1969.
22. SOF letter to Alene Erlanger, 18 January 1968.
23. SOF letter to Emelie Jacobson, 22 November 1969.
24. SOF letter to Emelie Jacobson, 21 March 1968.
25. SOF letter to Emelie Jacobson, 11 October 1965.
26. SOF letters to Julian Moynahan, 11 January & 17 December 1968.

27. SOF Radio Eireann, 'Focus', 11 February 1969.
28. SOF letter to Robie Macauley, 25 September 1968.
29. SOF and J. F. Powers, 'Towards a Tradition', BBC, 12 August 1968.
30. SOF letter to Emelie Jacobson, 13 December 1968.
31. Eileen O'Faolain letter to Elisabeth Schnack, 4 January 1967.
32. SOF letter to John V. Kelleher, 14 March 1966.
33. SOF letter to John V. Kelleher, 18 March 1966.
34. SOF letter to Alene Erlanger, 18 January 1969.
35. SOF letter to Emelie Jacobson, 28 June 1969.
36. SOF letter to Emelie Jacobson, 6 August 1969.

Chapter 18. The Wonderful Seventies

Some of the material in this chapter is based on interviews with Niall McCarthy, Godfrey Graham, Eilis Dillon, Robie Macauley, Peter Davison, Gerald Goldberg, Joseph McHugh, Helen Fahy and Victoria Glendinning.

1. SOF letter to Emelie Jacobson, 6 March 1970.
2. O'Faolain took part in a number of other television programmes: one on the burning of *The Tailor and Ansty* (31 October 1978), another on *The Bell* (21 December 1978), one about ageing, three about events that shaped Ireland in the twentieth century (23 February 1976, 15 March 1976, 12 April 1976), and various book review programmes.

   In the programme on *The Tailor and Ansty* he was asked to what he attributed the fervour of censorship in the thirties and forties. Drawing upon his reading of Marina Warner's *Alone of all Her Sex* (1976), a book he admired, he invoked the hypocritical sexual puritanism of the English Victorians which had been transmitted to the equally hypocritical, colonized, urban Irish males. Since the Tailor and his wife lived in Gougane Barra, a remote Gaeltacht, they represented an older, racier tradition which had escaped the Victorian influence. He also mentioned the emphasis on virginity in the churches and in the Irish educational system of his boyhood which had an exaggerated cult of the Virgin Mary. He also suggested that there was a double, or treble, standard among the Victorian males, both in England and Ireland: the Virgin on the one hand, the Magdalen, or whore, on the other, and in between the wife who was supposed to have a totally different sexuality from the male, i.e. to have none at all other than the trivially minimum amount necessary for procreation. In his letter to Colum Kenny, in which he outlined these remarks, he also recommended Edward J. Bristow's *Vice and Vigilance* (1978) for those interested in the subject of state-controlled chastity.

3. SOF letters to Julian Moynahan, 3 February 1971 and to Robie Macauley, 1 March 1971.
4. SOF letter to Robie Macauley, February 1975.
5. SOF letter to Robie Macauley, 16 October 1973.
6. SOF letter to Robie Macauley, 1 January 1975.
7. SOF letters to Eilis Dillon, July 1970.
8. SOF letters to Robie Macauley, 4 October & 1 November 1970.
9. SOF letter to Robie Macauley, 7 July 1971.
10. SOF letter to Emelie Jacobson, 14 March 1972.
11. Robie Macauley letter to SOF, 23 March 1972.
12. SOF letter to Robie Macauley, 29 March 1972.
13. SOF to Robie Macauley, 3 November 1971.
14. SOF letter to Emelie Jacobson, 21 November 1972.
15. Richard Ellmann letter to SOF, 20 November 1971.
16. SOF letter to Munira Mutran, 6 May 1973.
17. SOF letter to Richard Ellmann, 22 February 1973.
18. SOF letter to James Hart, 8 December 1973.
19. SOF letter to Carol Smith, 30 November 1973.
20. SOF letter to Munira Mutran, 17 February 1973.
21. SOF letter to Richard Ellmann, 26 December 1974.
22. SOF letter to Richard Ellmann, 29 May 1974.
23. SOF letter to James Hart, 8 December 1973.
24. SOF letter to Richard Ellmann, 1974.
25. SOF letter to Emelie Jacobson, 22 January 1974.
26. SOF letter to Munira Mutran, 26 July 1974.
27. SOF interview BBC, 13 April 1976.
28. SOF letter to Robie Macauley, July 1970.
29. SOF letter to Eilis Dillon, June 1970.
30. SOF letter to Eilis Dillon, 1 July 1970.
31. SOF letter to Robie Macauley, 9 June 1971.
32. SOF letter to Robie Macauley, 3 December 1971.
33. SOF letter to Carol Smith, 15 April 1973.
34. SOF letter to Muriel Spark, 20 September, n.d.
35. SOF letter to Robie Macauley, 14 March 1972.
36. SOF letter to Robie Macauley, 5 June 1972.
37. SOF letter to Carol Smith, 7 November 1972.
38. SOF letter to Munira Mutran, 24 September 1973.
39. SOF letter to Carol Smith, 18 November 1973.
40. SOF letters to Carol Smith, 25 March 1974 & January 1975.
41. SOF letter to Richard Ellmann, 2 August 1974.
42. SOF letter to Richard Ellmann, 26 July 1974.
43. Monsignor Patrick Whelan died 1 April 1974. Sean remembered him as a pompous and righteous man who used to lecture his younger brothers.

From 1919–1923 he was a curate at Dulwich Hall, then an assistant priest at a number of parishes, before being appointed parish priest at Lithgow in 1937. This was a mountainous, mining area where he was greatly liked. In 1964 he was transferred as parish priest to Stanmore in Sydney. There he celebrated his golden jubilee on 5 May 1968 and was created a chaplain to His Holiness with the title Very Reverend Monsignor.

44. SOF letter to Robie Macauley, 10 May 1974.
45. SOF letter to Carol Smith, January 1975.
46. SOF letter to Emelie Jacobson, 27 January 1970.
47. SOF letter to Robie Macauley, 3 March 1975. His appointment to the Cork Radio Advisory Committee in 1974 was another sign of recognition; he was clear and trenchant about their vague terms of reference and eventually stopped going to meetings. In 1973 he served as a juror in connection with an Architectural Award Scheme. Other jurors appreciated his perceptive comments. The Award went to the US Embassy building in Dublin.
48. SOF letter to Richard Ellmann, 10 June 1975.
49. SOF letter to Robie Macauley, 15 October 1975.
50. SOF letter to Elfreda Powell, 1 January 1977.
51. SOF letter to Robie Macauley, 8 November 1978.
52. SOF letter to Robie Macauley, 1 July 1977.
53. SOF letter to James M. Cain, July 1977.
54. SOF letter to Elfreda Powell, 26 November 1977.
55. *Irish Times*, 10 June 1970.

Chapter 19. Rosmeen Park

For this chapter interviews were held with Eithne Jones, Helen Fahy, Mary Moloney, Patrick Lynch, Elfreda Powell, Ita Daly, David Marcus, Hugh Powers and Bryan MacMahon.

1. SOF letter to Elfreda Powell, 26 September 1978. The dates of other letters are included in the text.
2. SOF letter to Muriel Spark, 29 August 1980.
3. SOF letter to Julian Moynahan, 21 August 1979.
4. Elisabeth Schnack, *Spiegelungen. Autobiographisches*, 1984, 111–113.
5. SOF letter to Elisabeth Schnack, 20 March 1980.
6. SOF interview with Brian Kennedy, 7 February 1987.
7. SOF letter to Muriel Spark, 29 August 1980.
8. SOF letter to Father Daniel Griffin, 17 June 1982.
9. SOF letter to Ben Glazebrook, 29 October 1980.
10. SOF letter to Colm O'Briain, 30 June 1982.

11. SOF letter to Hilary Rubinstein, 18 November 1982.
12. SOF letter to Richard Ellmann, 13 August 1986.
13. SOF letter to Bryan MacMahon, 27 June 1985.
14. SOF letter to David Marcus and Ita Daly, December 1988.
15. She had already booked her flight and since her father tended to recover from these set-backs, she could never be certain how critical the latest one was and in fact he did rally again.
16. Maurice Harmon was in America.

Bibliography

BOOKS

Lyrics and Satires from Tom Moore. Cuala Press, Dublin, 1929.

Midsummer Night Madness and other stories. With an Introduction by Edward Garnett. Jonathan Cape, London, 1932.

The Life Story of Eamon De Valera. Talbot Press, Dublin, 1932.

A Nest of Simple Folk. Jonathan Cape, London, 1934.

Constance Markievicz, or The Average Revolutionary. Jonathan Cape, London, 1934.

Bird Alone. Jonathan Cape, London, 1936.

A Purse of Coppers. Jonathan Cape, London, 1937.

She Had to Do Something: A Comedy in Three Acts. Jonathan Cape, London, 1938.

The Silver Branch: A Collection of the Best Old Irish Lyrics, Variously Translated, Chosen by Sean O'Faolain. Jonathan Cape, London, 1938.

King of the Beggars, A Life of Daniel O'Connell, the Irish Liberator. A Study of the Rise of the Modern Irish Democracy (1775–1847). Thomas Nelson & Sons, London, 1938.

De Valera. Penguin, London, 1939.

Come Back to Erin. Jonathan Cape, London, 1940.

An Irish Journey. Longmans, Green & Co, London, 1940.

The Great O'Neill, A Biography of Hugh O'Neill, Earl of Tyrone, 1550–1616. Longmans, Green & Co, London, 1942.

Teresa and other stories. Jonathan Cape, London, 1947.

The Irish. Penguin, London, 1947.

The Short Story. William Collins Sons & Co, London, 1948.

The Man Who Invented Sin and other stories. Devin-Adair, New York, 1949.

A Summer in Italy. Eyre & Spottiswoode Ltd, London, 1949.

Newman's Way, the Odyssey of John Henry Newman. Longmans, Green & Co, London, 1952.

South to Sicily. William Collins Sons & Co, London, 1953.
The Vanishing Hero, Studies in Novelists of the Twenties. Eyre & Spottiswoode Ltd, London, 1956.
The Finest Stories of Sean O'Faolain. Little, Brown & Co, Boston, 1957.
The Stories of Sean O'Faolain. Rupert Hart-Davies, London, 1958.
Short Stories, A Study in Pleasure, edited by Sean O'Faolain. Little, Brown & Co, Boston, 1961.
Selected Stories. Constable, London, 1978.
Collected Stories. Constable, London, 1980–1982.

ARTICLES AND STORIES

'A Parisian Duel', *Irish Outlook*, 26 April 1913.
'False and True', *Irish Outlook*, 17 May 1913.
'Teach', *An Grianan. Paipear cinn bliadhna do Ghaedhealaibh Chorcoighe*. Craobh Naomh Fionn-Bharra i gCorcoig. n.d.
'An Malairt', *An Grianan*. n.d.
'Prendergast', *Earna* (11, 5), 12–16, Meitheamh, 1924.
'Deich mBliana d'Fhas i mBeatha Fhile', a study of Daibhidh Ua Bruadair's development between the ages of forty and fifty. *Earna* (11, 7), 26–33, Feile Padraig, 1925; (8), 14–17, Nodlaig, 1925.
'The Best Irish Literature', *Irish Statesman* (4, 26), 816, 5 September 1925.
'A Plea for a New Type of Scholarship', *Irish Statesman* (5, 10), 296–97, 14 November 1925.
'An Irish Dominican Poet (Padraigin Haicead, 1600–1654)', *Irish Rosary* (XXX, 1), 52–59, January 1926.
'In Lilliput', *Irish Statesman* (5, 22), 680–81, 6 February 1926.
'The Gaoltach Tradition', *Irish Statesman* (6, 7), 175–76, 24 April 1926.
'The Language Problem', *Irish Tribune*, (1, 18), 20–21, 9 July; (5, 19), 6–8, 16 July; (1, 20), 9–10, 23 July; (1, 21), 13–15, 30 July 1926.
'Under the Roof', *Dial* (81, 3), 220–23, September 1926.
'The Bomb Shop', *Dial* (82, 3), 197–209, March 1927.
'Fugue', *Hound and Horn* (2, 1), 7–28, September 1928.
'Style and the Limitations of Speech', *Criterion* (8) 67–97, September 1928.
'Cruelty and Beauty of Words', *Virginia Quarterly Review* (4), 208–25, April 1928.
'Almost Music', *Hound and Horn* (2, 2), 178–180, January–March 1929.
'Young Man', *Living Age* (336), 195, May 1929.
'The Spurious Fenian Tale', *Folk-Lore, Transactions of the Folk-lore Society* (41), 154–68, June 1930.
'William Butler Yeats: *Selected Poems, Lyrical and Narrative*', *Criterion* (9, XXXVI), 523–28, April 1930.
'New Irish Revolutionaries', *Commonweal* (15), 39–41, 11 November 1931; letter, 273, 6 January 1932.

'A.E: *Enchantment and Other Poems*', *Criterion* (10, XLII), 748–50, July 1931.

'Synge and Anglo-Irish Literature', *Criterion* (11, XLII), 140–42, October 1931.

'Meeting an Irishman on His Own Ground', *The Listener* (VII, 176), 764–765, 25 May 1932.

'The American University', *The Simmarian*, 5–6, May 1932.

'A.E: *Song and its Fountains*', *Criterion* (11, XLV), 725–27, July 1932.

'Celts and Irishmen', *New Statesman and Nation* (4, 74), 93–94, 23 July 1932.

'De Valera, Rebel or Reformer?', *New Statesman and Nation* (4, 77), 173–74, 13 August 1932.

'Provincialism and Literature', *Motley* (1, 3), 3–4, August 1932.

'New Directions in Irish Literature', *Bookman* (75), 446–48, September 1932.

'Irish Year', *New Statesman and Nation* (6), 733–34, 9 December 1933.

'Literary Provincialism', *Commonweal* (17, 8), 214–15, 21 December 1932.

'The Suburban Novel?', *The Listener* (VIII, 206), 895, 21 December 1932.

'Confessional', *New Statesman and Nation* (6), 104–05, 22 July 1933.

'Letter from a Novelist to an Idealist', *Motley*, (11, 7), 3–5, November 1933.

'Jubilee in the North Abbey', *Lovat Dickson's Magazine*, 60–74, December 1933.

'An Irish Letter', *Hound and Horn* (7, 2), 271–73, January–March 1934; *New Statesman and Nation*, 9 December 1933.

'Autobiographical Sketch', *Wilson Bulletin* (8, 6), 380, March 1934.

'Emancipation of Irish Writers', *Yale Review* (23), 485–503, Spring 1934.

'An Irish Schooling', *Life and Letters* (10, 52), 27–32, April 1934.

'Plea for a New Type of Novel', *Virginia Quarterly Review* (10), 189–99, April 1934.

'A Born Genius', *Lovat Dickson's Magazine*, 468–98, April 1934.

'The Governess', *Listener* (XII, 300), 623–624, 10 October 1934.

'Sullivan's Trousers', *London Mercury* (31), 42–52, November 1934.

'Novelists See Too Much', *Spectator* (154), 385–386, 8 March 1935.

'W.B. Yeats', *English Review* (9) 686–88, June 1935; *Irish Times*, 13 June 1935.

'The Modern Novel: A Catholic Point of View', *Virginia Quarterly Review* (11), 339–51, July 1935.

'A.E.', *London Mercury* (32, 190), 361–64, August 1935.

'Meeting', *Living Age* (349), 66–69, September 1935; *Story* (7, 40), 5–53, November 1935.

'Irish Letters: To-day and To-morrow', *Fortnightly Review* (138), 369–71, September 1935.

'Re-Orientation of Irish Letters', *Irish Times*, 21 September 1935.

'It No Longer Matters, or the Death of the English Novel', *Criterion* (15, LVIII), 49–56, October 1935.

'New Ireland', *Yale Review* (25), 321–29, December 1935.

'Pigeon-Holing the Modern Novel', *London Mercury* (33), 159–64, December 1935.

'The Coorter', *Harper's Bazaar* (XIII, 5), 16–17, February 1936.

'Connemara', *Harper's Bazaar* (XIV, 3), 56–57, 102–104, June 1936.

'Daniel Corkery', *Dublin Magazine* (11, 2), 49–61, April–June 1936; *Commonweal* (22), 35–37, 6 November 1936.

'In Defence of "Oh Yeah"', *Spectator* (157), 53–54, 10 July 1936.

'The Gamut of Irish Fiction', *Saturday Review of Literature* (XIV), 19–20, 1 August 1936.

'Pater and Moore', *London Mercury*, (XXXIV), 330–38, August 1936.

'Lonely Lives', *Story* (9, 51), 93–101, October 1936.

'The Dangers of Censorship', *Ireland To-day* (1), 27–36, November 1936.

'Exiles', *Harper's Bazaar* (XV, 2), 38–39, 91–95, November 1936.

'Chronos Ate His Children', *London Mercury* (XXXV), 108–109, December 1936.

'A Broken World', *London Mercury* (XXXV), 123–32, December 1936.

'My Son Austin', *Harper's Bazaar* (XV, 3), 26–27, 96–100, December 1936.

'The New Ireland. A Letter from any Irishman to any Englishman', *Yale Review* (25), 320–29, Winter 1936.

'The Squinty Tinker and the Black Powlraddy', *Harper's Bazaar* (XV, 5), 65, 80–84, February 1937.

'Proletarian Novel', *London Mercury* (XXXV), 583–589, April 1937.

'Kitty the Wren', *Story* (10, 57), 81–94, April 1937.

'The Priests and the People', *Ireland Today* (11), 31–38, July 1937.

'Discord', *London Mercury* (XXXVI), 239–45, July 1937.

'The Old Master', *Story* (11, 61), 38–47, August 1937.

'On a Story by Tchekov', *Life and Letters* (17, 9), 60–69, August 1937.

'Don Quixote O'Flaherty', *London Mercury and Bookman* (XXXVII) 170–175, December 1937.

'Abbey Festival', *New Statesman and Nation* (XVI), 281–282, 20 August 1938; *Irish Times*, 20 and 21 September 1938.

'The Three Clever Sisters', *The Listener* (XX, 505), 564–65, 15 September 1938.

'A.E. and W.B.Y.', *Virginia Quarterly Review* (XV, 1), 41–57, January 1939.

'William Butler Yeats', *Spectator* (CLXII), 183, 3 February 1939.

'Two Kids', *Harper's Bazaar* (XX, 1), 48–49, 88–90, April 1939.

'Murderer', *Virginia Quarterly Review* (XV, 3), 371–78, July 1939.

'The Warder', *Listener* (XXVI, 656), 203–4, 5 August 1941; *Virginia Quarterly Review* (XVI, 4), 513–22, Autumn 1940.

'Ah, Wisha! The Irish Novel', *Virginia Quarterly Review* (XVII), 265–74, Spring 1941.

'The Lonely Woman', *Yale Review* (31, 20), 269–78, December 1941.

'What Little Town?', *Puck's Fare*, 29–33, 1941.

'Yeats and the Younger Generation', *Horizon* (V), 43–54, January 1942.

'Two Kinds of Novel', *Bell* (IV, 1), 64–70, April 1942.

'The Spoken Word', *Listener* (XXVII, 700), 764, 11 June 1942.

'The Barbaric Note', *Listener* (XXVII, 701), 783–787, 18 June 1942.

'Lady Lucifer', *Bell* (5, 1), 55–62, October 1942.

'Drama in Wexford', *Bell* (V, 5), 390–96, February 1943.

'Antonio Fogazzaro', *Bell* (V, 6), 475–481, March 1943.

'The Strange Case of Sean O'Casey', *Bell* (VI, 2), 112–21, May 1943.

'Case of the Young Irish Writer', *Commonweal* (38), 392–3, 8 August 1943.

'Personal Anthologies 1', *Bell* (VI, 6), 496–502, September 1943.

'Sense and Nonsense in Poetry', *Bell* (VII, 2), 156–69, November 1943.

'Teresa', *Virginia Quarterly Review* (20, 2), April 1944.

'The Craft of the Short Story', *Bell* (VII, 4), 337–44, January 1944; (VII, 5), 403–10, February 1944; (VII, 6), 529–36, March 1944; (VIII, 1), 46–54, April 1944; (VIII, 4), 306–14, July 1944.

'The Man Who Invented Sin', *Bell* (IX, 8), 219–232, December 1944.

'Thoughts of a Juryman', *Bell* (IX, 5), 369–79, February 1945.

'Passion', *Virginia Quarterly Review* (21, 2), 250–55, April 1945.

'A Tale of a Town', *Bell* (X, 2), 106–121, May 1945.

'The Trout', *Colliers* (XV), 23, 12 May 1945; *Bell* (X, 6), 489–92, September 1945.

'Shaw's Prefaces', *Bell* (XII, 5), 425–32, August 1946.

'Vive La France', *Irish Writing* (I, 1), 9–18, 1946.

'Rebel by Vocation', *Bell* (13, 2), 98, November 1946.

'Innocence', *Yale Review* (n.s. XXXVI, 2), 257–61, December 1946.

'The Silence of the Valley', *Virginia Quarterly Review* (XXIII, 2), 209–30, April 1947; *Bell* (XII, 6), 466–89, September 1946.

'The Sugawn Chair', *Bell* (XV, 3), 22–25, December 1947.

'Getting at Which Public?', *Virginia Quarterly Review* (24, 1), 90–95, January 1948.

'The Younger Generation', *Listener* (XXXIX, 1008), 829–32, 20 May 1948; 'Eden', *Bell* (XVII, 9), 18–26, December 1951.

'The Evening Star', *Irish Writing* (5), 9–20, July 1948.

'On Translating from the Irish', *Poetry Ireland* (4), 24–17, January 1949.

'Romance and the Devil', *New English Review* (1, 3), 193–96, November 1948.

'The Art of the Short Story', *Listener*, (XLII, 1070), 145–46, 28 July 1949.

'End of the Record', *New Statesman and Nation* (38), 381–82, 8 October 1949.

'Persecution Mania', *Kenyon Review* (XI, 4), 588–94, Autumn 1949.

'The Song of Salesman MacGinty', *Envoy* (I, 1), 20–26, December 1949.

'The Dilemma of Irish Letters', *Month* (2, 6), 366–79, December 1949.

'The First Kiss', *Blarney Annual* (V, 2), 42–46, 1949–50.

'The U.S. and Europe: The Emigrant Looks Back', *Listener* (XLII, 1091), 1085–6, 22 December 1949.

'The City of Rome', *Commonweal* (11), 575–76, 10 March 1950.

'The Sighing Age', *Irish Writing* (XII), 5–18, September 1950.

'The Ould Jug', *Bell* (XVI, 2), 52–56, November 1950.

'Religious Art', *Bell* (XVI, 4), 39–42 January 1951.

'The Liberal Ethic', *Bell* (XVI, 5), 5–11, February 1951.

'Autoantiamericanism', *Bell* (XVI, 6), 7–18, March 1951; (XVII, 2), 8–28, May 1951; (XVII, 3), June 1951.

'Changing Calabria', *The Listener* (XLV, 1153), 535–6, 5 April 1951.

'The Death of Nationalism', *Bell* (XVII, 2), 44–53, May 1951.

'From Italy', *Commonweal* (LIV), 139–41, 18 May 1951.

'The Dail and the Bishops', *Bell* (XVII, 3), 5–13, June 1951.

'The Shaken Tapestry of Sicily', *Listener* (XLVI, 1170), 165–6, 2 August 1951.

'From Sicily', *Commonweal* (54), 546–7, 14 September 1951.

'The Bishop of Galway and the *Bell*', *Bell* (XVII, 6), 15–17, September 1951.

'The Divided Generation', *Bell* (XVII, 11), 5–11, February 1952.

'The New Criticism', *Bell* (XVIII, 3), 133–142, June 1952.

'The Lonely Woman', *Bell* (XVIII, 4), 205–212, July 1952.

'Gamblers', *Virginia Quarterly Review* (28, 3), 417–34, July 1952.

'Imaginary Conversation', *Bell* (XVIII, 5), 261–73, October 1952.

'Persecution Mania', *Bell* (XVIII, 6), 325–30, November 1952.

'Ireland After Yeats', *Books Abroad* (XXVI), 325–33, Autumn 1952.

'Enduring Friendship', *Commonweal* (57), 355–7, 9 January 1953.

'On a Recent Incident at the International Affairs Association', *Bell* (XVIII, 9), 517–27, February 1953.

'Golden Hill Towns of Italy', *Commonweal* (57), 571–3, 13 March 1953.

'Love Among the Irish', *Life* (34), 140–27, 16 March 1953.

'Landscape Without Figures', *Listener* (XLIX, 1264), 836–7, 21 May 1953.

'On Being an Irish Writer', *Spectator* (191), 25–6, 3 July 1953; *Commonweal* (58), 339–41, 10 July 1953.

'Visit to Padre Pio', *Commonweal* (58), 507–9, 28 August 1953.

'The Irish and the Latins', *Bell* (XIX, 1), 145–50, December 1953.

'Miracles Don't Happen Twice', *Irish Writing* (3, 28), 18–21, September 1954.

'Childybawn', *Bell* (XIX, 10), 11–20, November 1954.

'Italy: Her Wonderful People', *Holiday* (17), 36–43, April 1955.

'Venice', *Holiday* (18), 42–7, October 1955.

'Sei romanzieri in cerca di un eroe', *Quaderni ACI*, 39–65, 1955.

'Doomed Daredevil's of the I.R.A. Warm Up their Forty Year's War', *Life* (39), 139, 7 November 1955.

'St Patrick's Day: Thoughts about Ireland', *New York Times Magazine*, 17, 11 March 1956.

'Angels and Ministers of Grace', *Irish Writing* (4, 34), 8–19, Spring 1956.

'Sicily', *Holiday* (19), 46–51, May 1956.

'Las Vegas', *Holiday* (20), 56–61, September 1956.

'Naples', *Holiday* (20), 96–104, October 1956.

'Looking Back at Writing', *Atlantic Monthly* (198), 75–6, December 1956.

'End of the Record', *Atlantic Monthly* (198), 53–5, December 1956.

'Philadelphia Tradition', *Holiday* (21), 50–67, May 1957.

'World of Los Angeles', *Holiday* (22), 50–63, October 1957.

'Are You Writing a Short Story?', *The Listener* (LIX, 1507), 282–3, 13 February 1958.

'Ireland', *Holiday* (23), 54, June 1958.

'A Touch of Autumn in the Air', *Listener* (LXI, 1553), 19–21, 1 January 1959.

'Texas', *Holiday* (24), 34–49, October 1958.

'Flavour of Boston', *Holiday* (24), 92–101, December 1958.

'Lovely Lakes of Italy', *Holiday* (25), 90–7, March 1959.

'Love's Young Dream', *Saturday Evening Post* (232), 40–1, 3 October 1959.

'Touch of Autumn in the Air', *Atlantic Monthly* (204), 76–9, November 1959.

'Pontifical Splendour', *Holiday* (27), 82–91, April 1960.

'New Spirit of St. Louis', *Holiday* (27), 80–5, May 1960.

'Three Chicagos', *Holiday* (28), 74–87, December 1960.

'Entre deux silences', *Mademoiselle* (52), 130–1, March 1961.

'I Remember! I Remember!', *Mademoiselle* (53), 93, July 1961.

'Sugawn Chair', *Atlantic Monthly* (208), 59–60, August 1961.

'New Orleans', *Holiday* (30), 50–63, November 1961.

'Beyond the Riviera', *Holiday* (31), 80–7, January 1962.

'Writer at Work', *St. Stephen's*, 25–36, Michaelmas 1962.

'Irish Families', *Nation* (196), 269–71, 30 March 1963.

'Fair Dublin', *Holiday* (33), 72, April 1963.

'One Man, One Boat, One Girl', *Saturday Evening Post* (236), 48–49, 19 October 1963.

'Too Beautiful, Too Good', *Ladies Home Journal* (80), 84–7, October 1963.

'Southern Italy', *Holiday* (36), 38–46, September 1964.

'The Philological Syndicate in Harvard. Reflections of a Commonwealth Fellow', *Harvard Alumni Bulletin*, 24 October 1964.

'Miracle at Lourdes', *Holiday* (36), 66–7, November 1964.

'Don Juan in Dublin', *Saturday Evening Post*' (238), 48–51, 19 January 1965.

'Three Shapes of Love', *Atlantic Monthly* (215), 124–28, March 1965.

'In Search of Sardinia', *Holiday* (39), 52–3, January 1966.

'The Heart of Sardinia', *Listener* (LXXXV, 1935), 607–09, 28 April 1966.

'To: Some Old Republican Somewhere', *1916–1966. What has Happened?*, 7–8, 1966.

'The Art of Autobiography', *Listener* (LXXXV, 1938), 720–21, 19 May 1966.

'Operation Rosebud', *Redbook* (127), 58–60, August 1966.

'Jungle of Love', *Saturday Evening Post* (239), 54–63, 13 August 1966.

'Dividends', *McCalls* (93), 114–15, September 1966.

'Heat of the Sun', *Atlantic Monthly* (218), 70–5, September 1966.

'Smithsonian: Biographer to the World', *Holiday* (42), 44–9, August 1967.

'Turin', *Holiday* (43), 58–65, February 1968.

'Fool of a Man', *Saturday Evening Post* (241), 60–5, September 1968.

'This is Your Life: Louisa May Alcott', *Holiday* (44), 18, November 1968.

'What a Stunning Night!', *Saturday Evening Post* (242), 46–7, 28 December 1968.
'Vatican City: Where the Decisions are Made', *Holiday* (44), 68–71, December 1968.
'Kitchen', *Atlantic Monthly* (223), 42–5, June 1969.
'Planets of the Years', *Ladies Home Journal* (86), 102–3, September 1969.
'Florentine Hill Towns: Suburbs Tuscan Style', *Holiday* (46), 42–3, September 1969.
'Portrait of the Artist as an Old Man', *Listener* (87), 605–8, 11 May 1972.
'Dürling, or the Faithless Wife', *Playboy* (21, 1), 175, January 1974.
'Venus, or the Virgin?', *Playboy* (21, 8), 66, August 1974.
'Good Night, Sweet Sherlock', *Playboy* (22, 1), 109, January 1975.
'Liberty', *Atlantic Monthly* (235), 73–7, April 1975.
'Frank O'Connor', *Irish Press*, 26 May 1977.
'Valedictory', *Irish Press*, 6 January 1977.
'How Not to Write an Irish Short Story', *Irish Press*, 29 April 1978.
'A Present from Clonmacnoise', *Irish Press*, 10 May 1980.
'May I Have some Marmalade, Please?', *Playboy* (27), 168, December 1980.
'What It Feels Like to be a Writer', *Boston Irish News* (6, 1), 4, January 1981.
'Hate, Greed, Lust and Doom', *London Review of Books*, May 1981.
'From Huesca with Love and Kisses', *Irish Press*, 4 November 1982.
'Nora Barnacle: Pictor Ignotus', *London Review of Books* (6, 1), 23–24, 2 August 1984.

BACKGROUND

Bates, H.E., *Edward Garnett*. Max Parrish, London, 1950.
Butler, Hubert, *Escape from the Anthill*. Lilliput, Dublin, 1985.
Craig, Patricia, *Elizabeth Bowen*. Penguin, London, 1986.
Glendinning, Victoria, *Elizabeth Bowen. Portrait of a Writer*. Weidenfeld & Nicolson, London, 1977.
Mathews, James, *Voices. A Life of Frank O'Connor*. Atheneum, New York, 1983.
O'Broin, Leon, *. . . Just Like Yesterday*. Gill & Macmillan, Dublin, 1986.
Connor, P.J., *Exploring Limerick's Past*. Oirlacht na Mumhan Books, Newcastle West, 1987.
Owen, Ursula (ed.), *Fathers. Reflections by Daughters*. Virago, London, 1983.
Simpson, Eileen, *Poets in their Youth*. Random House, New York, 1982.
Schnack, Elisabeth, *Spiegelungen. Begegnungen mit angelsächsichen Austoren*. Pendo-Verlag, Zurich, 1984.
Cork Review, Sean O'Faolain Special Issue, 1991.
Irish University Review (6, 1), Sean O'Faolain Special Issue, Spring 1976.

A more complete bibliography is available in Maurice Harmon, *Sean O'Faolain: a critical introduction*, Dublin, 1967, 1984.

Index

Abbey Theatre, Dublin, 88, 116, 117,
119, 122, 124, 128, 144, 145, 146,
287n, 291n; Board, 120, 144
'AE' (George William Russell), 67, 69,
70, 79, 80, 82, 90, 97, 99, 117, 119,
127, 132
All Hallows College, Dublin, 23
Allan, Maud, 24
Allen, David, 211
An Dun, Queen St, Cork, 63, 64, 65
An Grianan (literary annual), 63
An Long (periodical), 65
An Poblacht (Southern Edition), 56
An Phoblacht 59–60, 67
Annan, Lord, 257
Anouilh, Jean, 191
Arnold, Matthew, 46, 49; *Literature and
Science*, 75
Arts Council, 272; Sean appointed
Director of the, 209, 210–11, 214,
277
Ayer, Sir Freddy, 257
Aymé, Marcel, 191, 192

Babbitt, Irving, 75, 78; *New Humanism*,
76
Ballingeary, 43, 44, 56, 57; Irish college,
44
Ballymakeera, 57
Barea, Arturo, 191
Barrington, Margaret, 133

Barry, Tom, 50, 52
Barry, Vin, 122
Bates, H.E., 87, 97
Bateson, F.W., 74, 87, 99
Bateson, Jan, 102
BBC, 98, 122, 123, 154, 156, 167, 174,
181
Beach, Sylvia, 183
Behan, Brendan, 188
The Bell, 152, 153, 170, 177, 182, 183,
188, 230, 231, 303n; Sean's editorship
of (1940–45), 126, 127–50, 155, 156,
157–9, 163, 164, 176, 188, 274, 292
Benson, Frank, 24
Benson, Theodora, 191
Bergon, Frank, 232, 233, 301n
Berlin, Isaiah, 114
Bernanos, Georges, 192; *Sous le Soleil de
Satan*, 192
Berryman, John, 81
Betjeman, John, 188, 246
Binchy, Dan, 228, 270, 275
Blackburn, Susan, 256, 264
Blackmuir, Richard, 82, 191, 195–6, 217,
221, 222
Blythe, Ernest, 133, 241
Bodkin, Thomas, 209
The *Bookman*, 88, 98, 288n
Borgerhoff, E.B.O., 192
Boston College, 221; Sean teaches Anglo-
Irish literature at, 78, 82, 83; and

Writer-in-Residence at (1964/65/66), 231–4, 236

Bowen, Elizabeth, 127, 133, 136, 158, 159, 160, 191, 268; Sean's relationship with, 113–15, 116, 121, 234, 256, 263; *Another September*, 113, 121; *Friends and Relations*, 113; *House in Paris*, 115

Bowen, Evelyn, 116, 117, 119, 120, 144, 147, 148, 156, 169, 189, 192, 193

Boydell, Brian, 188

Boyhan, Kate (née Whelan: aunt), 34, 35

Boyhan, Lena (cousin), 34, 35

Boyhan, May (cousin), 34, 35

Boyhan, Owen (uncle), 34

Boyhan, Tom (cousin), 34–5, 40

Breen, Dennis, 68, 285n

Brennan, Robert, 59

Brosnan, Tom, 274

Brown, Francis, 236

Browne, Michael, Bishop of Galway, 121–2, 123, 291n

Browne, Dr Noel, 182

Buchanan-Riddell, Sir Walter, 70, 90, 92

Buckley, Ansty, 160

Buckley, Jack, 177

Buckley, Tim ('The Tailor'), 139, 160

Burke, Michael, 132

Burke-Savage, Father Roland, 281

Butler, Hubert, 133, 183, 261, 282

Cahills, 43, Parkgate St, Dublin, 128, 129, 137, 145, 149, 158, 292n

Calabria, Sean in, 170–1

Campbell, Mrs Patrick, 24

Campbell, Georgie, 24

Camus, Albert, 191

The Cancan't Club, 176

Cape, Jonathan, publisher, 71, 97, 98, 99, 100, 101, 106, 202, 205, 207, 236, 245

Carl Rosa Opera Company, 25

Casey, Lazy, 24

Chamberlain, John, 88

Chambers, Frank, 74

Chambéry, 181, 183

Charlton, Maureen, 282

Chekhov, Anton, 47, 109, 160, 164, 232, 265, 268, 269, 277

Chelmsford, Viscount, 70

Chesterton, G.K., 106

Childers, Erskine, 44, 56, 60; execution of, 61

Childers, Mrs Erskine ('Molly'), 59–60

Christian Brothers School, Ennis, Sean appointed Head Class Teacher in (1924), 68–9

Civil War (1922–23), 50, 54, 55–62, 63, 66, 108, 166, 179

Clark, Sir Kenneth (James), 257

Clarke, Austin, 139

Clarke, Thomas J., 52

Cohalan, Bishop, 52, 92

Collingwood, R.G., 175

Collins, Alan, 205, 207, 216, 228

Collins, José, 24

Collins, Michael, 54, 62, 67, 104

Collis, Bob, 120

Colum, Padraic, 197–8

Columba, Father, 184, 185, 186–7

Common Ground Society, 157, 158

Commonweal, 170, 298n

Connolly, Cyril, 114

Connolly, Brother E.I., 38–9, 42

Connolly, Jim, 143

Connolly, Peter, 240

Connolly, Violet, 161

Conrad, Joseph, 87, 220

Constable, publishers, 262, 263, 269, 273, 275–6

Coppard, A.E., 97

Corcoran, Rev. T., 93–4

Corelli, Marie, 25

Cork Butter Exchange Band, 24, 181

Cork Examiner, 15, 40, 55–6, 57, 213, 274

Cork Park races, 22, 36

Cork Radio Advisory Committee, 304n

Corkery, Daniel, 44, 55, 59, 63–4, 65–8, 69, 97, 104, 110, 143, 156, 285n; *Rebel Songs*, 55; *Poblacht na h'Eireann*, 55; 'King and Hermit', 64; 'Israel's Revenge', 64; 'Clan Falvey', 64; *The Threshold of Quiet*, 66, 94; *The Hounds of Banba*, 67, 94; *The Hidden Ireland*, 67, 94, 95; *Synge and Anglo-Irish Literature*, 89, 94; *A Munster*

Twilight, 94; *La Pléiade*, 94; *The Labour Leader*, 94; *The Yellow Bittern and other plays*, 94; *The Stormy Hills*, 94; appointed Professor of English Language and Literature at UCC (1931), 90, 94–5; *Fohnam the Sculptor*, 122
Corrigan, Margaret, 133
Cosgrave, Aunt Nan, 31, 32, 33, 161, 253
Cosgrave, Uncle Tom, 32, 33
Costello, John A., 209
The Criterion, 82, 98, 126, 143
Craig, Harry L., 149
Cronin, Dinny, 160
Cross, Eric, *The Tailor and Ansty*, 139, 177, 302n
Curragh, Kildare, 34, 35
Curran, Con, 188
Curran, Elizabeth, 133, 175, 188
Curtayne, Alice, 145
Curtis Brown, literary agents, 216, 217, 230, 236–7
Cusack, Cyril, 188, 281

D'Alton, Louis, 146; *The Money Doesn't Matter*, 139, 144
Daly, Ita, 270, 277–8, 282
Davison, Peter, 231, 233–4, 241, 251, 262, 266
De Valera, Eamon, 44, 54, 55, 59, 60, 64, 104–5, 108, 111, 119, 122, 126, 141, 142, 144, 148, 164, 172, 175, 179, 245, 289n; Sean's biography of, 104, 119, 123, 142, 175, 289n
De Vere, Aubrey, 40
Declan, Brother, 30
Deedy, John, 298n
Delaney, Shelagh, *A Taste of Honey*, 223
Demanash, Fr, 198
Devlin, Denis, 106
Dillon, Cormac, 248
Dillon, Eilis, 138, 188, 248–9, 255, 261, 281, 282; *Across the Bitter Sea*, 248, 255
Donnchadha, Eamon O., 63
Donne, John, 68, 86
Dooley, Jim, 24

Dopré, A.J., 86–7
Doran, Charles, 24
Douglas, Norman, 170
Dostoyevsky, Fedor, 47, 53
Dowling, P.J., 86
Doyle, Dr James, 86
Doyle, Lynn, 132
Dublin Drama League, 124, 146–7
The Dublin Magazine, 97
Duff, Frank, 156, 157, 158, 188
Dunsany, Lord, 105
Duxbury (USA), Kennedy's cottage at, 76, 77, 78

Earna (magazine), 47
Easter Rising (1916), 39, 40, 44, 62, 107, 245
Educational Company of Ireland, 79; Sean works as travelling salesman with, 53–4
Edwards, Owen Dudley, 246
Egan, Pat, 269
Ehrlich, Arnold, 230
Eliot, T.S., 73, 82, 83, 87, 102
Ellmann, Mary, 239
Ellmann, Richard, 172, 176, 188, 191, 192, 197, 210, 213–14, 216, 217, 221, 231, 239, 250, 259, 260, 261, 298n
English Digest, 128, 129, 137, 158, 292n
Ennis, Christian Brothers School, 68–9
Envoy, 189
Erlanger, Alene ('Kick'), 72, 73, 210, 220, 221, 223, 228, 236, 239; Sean's relationship with, 198, 199–200, 216, 219, 223, 228, 236, 243–4, 254, 262, 275; death of (1969), 244
Erlanger, Michael, 199–200
Erlanger, Milton, 198, 210, 220, 221, 223, 244
Evangelis, Brother, 36
Eyre and Spottiswoode, publishers, 165, 208, 218

Fahy, Edward, 132, 133
Fahy, Helen, 259, 275, 276, 277, 279, 280, 282

Fahy, Hugh, 276
Farrell, James T., 258
Farrell, Michael, 101, 120, 127, 132, 158
Faulkner, William, 191, 197
Fenians, 26, 43
Filippo, Eduardo da, 'La Marinella', 268
Finbarr, St, 45
Fitzgerald, Barry, 128
Fitzgerald, Desmond and Mabel, 102
Fitzgerald, Molly, 58–9, 68, 69
Fitzgerald, Theodora, 183
Fitzpatrick, Michael, 87
Flaubert, Gustave, 138, 295n
Fleischmann, Aloys, 116–17, 161, 181, 182, 205, 213, 274, 285n
Fleischmann, Tilly, 48
Flower, Robin, 92
Flynn, Christopher, 38
Foley, Dermot, 116, 135–6, 155, 261, 273–4, 292n
Foley, Father Lorcan, 269–70, 275, 281
Ford, J.M.D., 73
Fortnightly Review, 126
Friends of the Academy, 124, 125, 145

Gaelic League, 40, 51, 63–4, 65, 68, 94, 95, 138–9
Gaelic Revivalists, 68, 103
Gaeltacht, 45
Gahan, Muriel, 211
Gallagher, Frank, 39, 56; articles on the 'Volunteer Spirit', 62
Gardiner's Hill (Cork), Corkery's home, 65
Garnett, Edward, 70, 71–2, 74, 75, 80, 82, 83, 87–90, 96, 100, 102, 103, 201, 286n
Garrity, Devin-Adair, 205, 297–8, 236–7
Garry, Bob, 217
Gibbings, Robert, 98
Gibbon, Monk, 133
Giltinan, D.J., 157
Gissing, George, 170
Glendinning, Victoria, 263
Glenstal Abbey, Co. Limerick, 184, 185–6, 187–8, 194

Gogarty, St John, 260
Gogol, Nikolay, *Dead Souls*, 54
Goheen, Robert, 236
Goldberg, Gerald, 261, 274
Golden Cockerel Press, 98
Goldsmith, Oliver, 48
Good, Herman, solicitor, 146
Gore-Grimes, Christo, 102, 176, 188, 235, 258, 264, 276, 296n
Gougane Barra, 44, 45, 56, 96, 139, 159, 160, 176–7, 222, 275, 303n; Cronin's Hotel, 160, 176
Gould family, 42–3
Gould, Alice (sister-in-law), 229, 236
Gould, Eileen *see* O'Faolain
Gould, Gerald, 97
Gould, Jo (father-in-law), 43, 59, 108
Goulding, Sir Basil, 211
Graham, Cunninghame, 97
Graham, Godfrey, 246, 247
Graham, J.K., 155
Grauer, Sally, 114
Greacen, Robert, 133
Green, Julien, 191, 192; *Moira*, 192
Greene, Graham, 165, 191, 257
Gregory, Lady, 155
Griffith, Arthur, 39, 62, 104
Guiney, Denis, 133
Gwynn, Father Aubrey, 49, 92, 145, 288n
Gwynn, Denis, 102
Gwynn, Duffys, 145
Gwynn, Stephen, 93–4, 288n

Hackett, Francis, 102, 103, 104, 196, 115–16, 129, 291n
Hagstrum, Jean H., 216
Halfmoon Street (Cork), O'Faolain's home at no.15, 20; and at no.5: 20–1, 58, 122, 220
Hampshire, Susan, 114
Hardy, Thomas, 47, 122–3, 181, 215, 290n
Harmon, Maura, 270, 275, 279, 280, 282
Harmon, Maurice, *Sean O'Faolain: a critical introduction*, 270, 278
Harmsworth Award (IAL), 105, 115
Harris, Enriqueta (later Frankfurt), 166

Hart, Jim and Ruth, 260
Harvard University, Sean at (1926–9),
   73–84, 92, 172, 229; Widener Library,
   73–4, 78, 83; Appointments Office,
   81–2
Hastings, Father William, 86
Hawthorne, Nathaniel, 179, 180
Hayes, Karl, 281
Hayes, Richard, 116, 120, 133
Healy, Isabel, 274
Healy, Joe, 72
Healy, Maurice, 16
Healy, Tim, 16
Hemingway, Ernest, 191, 232; For Whom
   the Bell Tolls, 191; 'A Clean Well-
   Lighted Place', 233
Hendrick, Jack (Sean), 55, 56, 58, 64, 75,
   160, 163, 194–5
Henry, Paul, 121, 189, 223
Hewitt, John, 133
Higgins, F.R., 139, 148, 188
Hillery, Dr, President of Ireland, 273,
   275
Hindman (Kentucky), Sean's stay at, 76
Hobhouse, Caro, 256
Hoctor, Brother, 79
Hogan, James, 134
Hough family, 33, 34
The Hound and Horn (journal), 82, 98,
   126
Huebsch, Alfhild, 103
Hulme, T.E., 191
Huxley, Aldous, 206
Hyde, Douglas, 63, 106
Hunt, Hugh, 116

Ilyich, Ivan, 198–9
Inishfail, 99
IRA, 50–1, 52, 63, 64, 67, 98, 114, 213,
   262; Civil War, 55–62
Ireland Today, 246, 292n
Irish Academy of Letters, 99, 100, 105–6,
   115–16, 124–5, 129, 139, 145, 158,
   288n
Irish Association of Civil Liberty, 176,
   209–10
Irish Bulletin, 56

Irish Digest, 128, 137, 149–50, 293n
Irish Film Society, 246
Irish Literary Revival, 64, 67
Irish Outlook, 26–7
Irish Poems Today, 163
Irish Press, 105, 261
Irish Short Stories Today, 163
Irish Society (An Chuallach Gaedhlach),
   46
Irish Statesman, 69, 82
Irish Times, 109, 125, 139, 144, 154, 158,
   163, 189, 203, 261, 278, 279
The Irish University Review, 261
Irish Volunteers, 39, 40, 42, 50–1, 52
Irish Writing, 189, 211

Jacobi, Jane, 196, 222
Jacobson, Emelie, 200, 205, 215, 230,
   231, 235, 237, 240, 249, 251, 260, 266,
   267, 272
James, Henry, 179–80, 195, 255, 267,
   268
Jephson, Norreys, 288n
Johnson, Pamela Hansford, 257
Johnston, Denis, 124, 133, 146, 211, 217
Johnston, Fred, 117
Jones, Mrs, proprietor of Aclare House,
   278, 280, 281
Josephus, Brother, 30
Joyce, James, 68, 83, 87, 118, 147, 148,
   191, 192, 197–8, 225, 250, 251, 256,
   268; A Portrait of the Artist as a
   Young Man 47; Ulysses, 66, 82; Exiles,
   76, 198; Dubliners, 88, 233

Kauffman, Anna Maria, 72–3, 76, 77, 126
Kavanagh, Patrick, 132, 188
Keane, Sir John, 139
Kelleher, Dan, 57
Kelleher, Helen, 273
Kelleher, John V., 81, 159, 176, 177, 188,
   193, 194, 196, 198, 203, 204, 207, 208–
   9, 212, 213, 218, 220, 221, 223, 228,
   231, 241, 253, 262, 273, 298n
Kenafick, T., murder of, 56
Kennedy, Albert and Edith, 76, 77
Kennedy, Ray, 50–1, 55, 56

Keynes, Lord, *Two Memoirs (My Early Belief)*, 192
Kiely, Benedict, 281
Kiernan, Dr Thomas, 155
Killiney *see* Knockaderry
Kilmichael, 52
Kilroy, Thomas, 278
Kirstein, Lincoln, 82, 98
Knockaderry (Killiney), Sean's home at, 34, 117–18, 121, 122, 150, 157, 159, 178, 181, 184, 189–90, 220, 223–4, 231, 241, 248, 257–8, 271; 'At Homes', 188
Koszul, Professor André, 73

Labour Monthly, 69
Lampedusa, Giuseppe, *The Leopard*, 170
Lancasterian School, Cork ('Lancs'), Sean's education at, 28–31, 35, 185
Langford, Bob (Robert), 57, 147
Laverty, Maura, 133, 134
Lavery, Sir John, 148
Lavin, Mary, 134
Lawrence, T.E., 154
Leahy, D.J., 91
Lee, River, 44, 45, 46
Legge, Hector, 241
Legree, Simon, 24–5
Lenihan, Brian, 279
Leonard, Father Joseph ('Bunt'), 86, 88–9, 176
Lester, Michael, 240
Levi, Carlo, *Christ Stopped at Eboli*, 170
Levin, Harry, 75, 197
Lewis, Cecil Day, 133, 257, 292n
Lindsay, Mrs, 98; shooting of, 52
Lindsay, Tom, 161
Linklater, Eric, 87, 97, 101, 118, 184, 271, 286n
The Listener, 98, 177, 215
Little, P.J., 156
Little Brown, publishers, 205, 208, 218
London, 122, 154, 158, 160–1; Sean in, 85–99 *passim*, 101, 180, 182, 201, 216, 229, 255–6, 268, 270
London Magazine, 270

Longford, Christine, 133
Longford, Lord, 120, 124
Lough Doohyle, 33
Lowes, John Livingstone, 73, 75, 76, 79, 90, 92, 93; *The Road to Xanadu*, 75
Lowry, Dan, 24
Lucey, Christy, 56, 80
Lucey, Mary, 58, 59
Lucey, Peter, 57
Lucy, Bishop of Cork, 203
Lucy, John, 240
Lynch, Patrick, 176, 188, 258, 270, 273, 274, 275, 276, 277, 279, 280, 281, 293n
Lynd, Robert, 102
Lyon, W.C., 79

MacAndrew, Jean, 222, 227, 228, 231
MacAndrew, John, 222, 227, 228
MacArdle, Mary, 62
Macaulay, Anne, 249, 250
Macauley, Robie, 231, 240, 245, 249–50, 251, 260, 261, 262, 263, 304n
Macaulay, Rose, 161
McBride, Maude Gonne, 116
McCafferty, Dr Donal, 280
McCalls, 230, 231, 240
McCartan, Patrick, 116, 272
McCarthy, Desmond, 88–9
McCarthy, Hannah, 177
McCarthy, Nancy, 44, 107, 116, 118, 161, 162, 176, 274
McCarthy, Niall, 245–7
McCarthy, Father Vincent, 86, 92
McCormack, John, 24
McCoy, Hayes, 211
MacCurtain, Mary, 52
MacCurtain, Sile and Eilis, 274
MacCurtain, Tomas, murder of, 51, 64
McDaniel, Patricia (Mrs Stephen O'Faolain), 222, 223, 227
MacDonagh, Donagh, 133
MacDonagh, John, 132
McEntee, Sean, 148, 294n
MacGlynn, Lochlinn, 'The Dam', 136–7
McGrath, Joseph, 128
McGreevy, Thomas, 211

MacGrian, Michael, 'Myself and Some Ducks', 134
McGuinness, Nora, 127, 188, 221, 222, 262; 'Make Your Windows Gay', 132
McHugh, Joe, 261
McHugh, John, 87
McHugh, Pat and Roger, 176
McKenna, Siobhán, 222
Mackenzie, Compton, 97
McKenzie, Scottie, 44, 56
MacLeish, Archibald, 197
MacLiammoir, Michael, 133, 155, 211, 260–1
MacMahon, Bryan, 131, 134–5, 180–1, 282; 'The Breadmaker', 135; *The Lion-Tamer*, 180; *Sound of Hooves*, 273
MacManus, Francis, 132, 157
MacManus, M.J., 132, 141–2, 143–4
MacNeill, Eoin, 63
MacNeill, Josephine, 133
McQuaid, John Charles, Archbishop of Dublin, 157, 209, 219, 245
MacSweeney, Myles, 181
MacSwiney, Mary, 59
McSwiney, Father Patrick, 285n
MacSwiney, Terence, 44, 51–2, 63, 64; *Principles of Freedom*, 52, 62
Magennis, Professor, 139
Magny, C.E., 192
Mahar, John, 211
Manchester Guardian, 189–90
Manhood, H.A., 87
Mansergh, Nicholas, 161
Marcel, Gabriel, 191
Marcus, David, 189, 261, 262, 270, 282, 293n
Markham, Bridie, 33
Marsh, Alexander, 24
Martin, Eamon, 128, 147
Martin, F.X., 281
Martines, Julia *see* O'Faolain
Martin, Lauro, 228, 234, 235, 237, 259, 275, 282; marriage to Julia (1957), 212–13
Martines, Lucien (grandson), 218, 221, 228, 272, 282
Mathews, Denis, cobbler, 20

Matthew, Father, 187
Mathew, Father Gervase, 191
Maupassant, Guy de, 47, 268, 269
Mauriac, François, 191, 192
May, Freddy, 120
May, Sheila, 134
Mercier, Vivian, 248, 261, 293n
Meredith, George, 'Love in the Valley', 47
Merriman, P.J., President of UCC, 79, 92
Mespil House, Dublin, Sarah Purser's teas at, 102
Meyer, Kuno, 47, 67
Micheál Óg Ó Longáin Prize, awarded to Sean (1922), 47
Moloney, Mary, 274, 275, 276, 277, 278, 282
Montgomery, Niall, 188, 211, 273
Moody, T.W., 175
Moody Manners Opera Company, 16, 24
Mooney, Ria, 128, 200, 223
Moore, G.E., *Principia Ethica*, 191, 192
Moore, George, 83, 139
Moore, Henry, 257
Moore, T.C. Kingsmill, 134
Moorhead, Gillman, 134
Mopress, David, 230
Moravia, Alberto, *L'Amore Coniugale*, 192
Morrell, Lady Ottoline, 103, 115
Morrison, Stanley, 211
Morrow, H.L., 133, 158
Mortimer, Raymond, 191
Moynihan, Julian and Mrs, 222, 228, 229, 231, 261, 267
Mulcahy, Nuala and John, 282
Mulkerns, Val, 134, 277
Mulvany, Tommy, 24
Murdoch, Iris, 257
Murphy, C., 133
Murphy, grandmother, 33
Murphy, Mairead, 274
Murphy, Michael, 132
Murphy, Richard, 270
Murphy, Russell, 190
Murray, T.C., 64, 65, 285n
Mutran, Munira, 273

Nagle, Jack, 278, 282
The Nation, 129
National Foresters, 16
Naughton, Frank, 86
New Statesman and Nation, 98, 101
New York Herald Tribune, 107
New York Times, 88, 107, 236, 245, 262
New Yorker, 205, 209, 242
Newman, Cardinal John Henry, 167, 170,
   172–3, 174, 184, 270
Nicholson, Harold, 89
Noon, Mrs Theodore, 81
Nunn, Sir T. Percy, 70, 92

O'Beirne, Michael, 189, 293n
O'Briain, Colm, 271–273
O'Brien, Conor Cruise, 189, 246, 282,
   293n
O'Brien, Edna, 255
O'Brien, Kate, *Land of Spices*, 139
O'Brien, Marie Cruise, 282
O'Brien, Molly, 114
O'Brien, William, 16
Ó Broin, Leon, 157, 158
O'Bruadair, Dáibhí, 47
O'Casey, Sean, 128, 139, 250; *The Plough
   and the Stars*, 117
Ó Caoimh, Pádraic, 39
Ó Ciardha, Tadhg, 274
O'Connell, Daniel, 32, 86, 100, 104, 105,
   110–13, 126, 143, 152, 153, 172
O'Connor, Frank, 43, 44, 52, 55, 56, 63,
   65, 66, 68, 69, 72, 99, 101–2, 107, 109,
   116, 118, 119–21, 124, 125, 135, 139,
   144–7, 148, 153, 160, 172, 176, 180,
   188, 189, 192–3, 201, 207, 241, 242–3,
   251, 280, 288–9n, 291n, 298n
O'Connor, Father Harry, 79
O'Connor, Nicky, publican, 15, 26
O'Connor, Rory, 67–8
O'Dea, Denis, 144
O'Dea, Jimmy, 133
Ó Dómhnaill, Pádraig, 38, 39, 40–1, 42,
   43
Ó Donnchadha, Eamonn, 48–9, 63
Ó Donnchadha, Tadhg (pen-name
   Torna), 48–9, 63, 74, 80

O'Donnell, Hugh, 153
O'Donnell, Peadar, 106, 128, 130, 131,
   132, 134, 145, 148–9, 157, 158, 188,
   261, 293n
O'Donovan, Joan, 169, 192, 193, 242,
   298n
O'Dwyer, William, 145, 161
O'Faolain, Eileen (*née* Gould: wife), 51,
   58, 72, 119, 120, 123, 149, 150, 155,
   159, 160, 164, 169, 172, 174, 176, 177,
   189, 194, 204, 208, 216, 217, 231, 266–
   7, 269–71, 276; Sean's relationship
   with, 42–33, 44, 45, 46, 60, 68, 69, 75,
   76–7, 178–9, 189–90, 219, 278–9;
   arrested and jailed (1923), 58–9; trips
   to Paris, 71, 116, 174, 200; Sean sends
   engagement ring to, 76; trips to USA,
   76, 77–84 *passim*, 217, 218, 220, 221–
   2, 223, 233, 234, 239; marriage to Sean
   (1928), 79–80, 81; in London (1929–
   33), 85–99 *passim*; birth of daughter
   Julia (1932), 98; at Killough House,
   100–3, 107, 114; move to Knockaderry
   (Killiney), 117–18; birth of son
   Stephen (1938), 118; ill health (and
   hypochondria) of, 121, 158, 162, 178,
   181, 187, 236, 237, 238, 239, 240, 243,
   255, 257, 258, 261, 262, 272, 273;
   enters Portobello Nursing Home, 162;
   trips to Italy, 167–8, 207, 216, 217,
   228, 235, 254–5, 259, 264; worries
   about Stephen, 183, 184–8, 222–3;
   marriage of Julia, 212–13; translation
   of Irish Folk Tales by, 231; and death
   of Frank O'Connor, 241, 242; death of
   (1988), 274–5
O'Faolain, Julia (Mrs Lauro Martines:
   daughter), 101, 107, 117, 121, 159,
   160, 162, 174, 176, 194, 207, 208, 215,
   221, 228, 229, 231, 236, 237, 239, 250,
   254, 255, 256, 259, 260, 263, 268, 272,
   273; birth of (1932), 98; education,
   177, 183, 184, 188, 194; awarded
   Travelling Studentship, 194; illness,
   107, 157, 158, 203; story published in
   New Yorker by, 209; marriage to
   Lauro Martines (1957), 212–13, 216–17;

birth of son Lucien (1958), 218, 221; Sean accepts her literary advice, 240; Provencal holiday with parents, 258; 'Sean at Eighty' by, 270; death of mother, 274, 275; death of her father (1991), 279, 280, 281, 282

O'Faolain, Stephen (son), 121, 159, 160, 162, 164, 172, 178, 201, 204, 208, 215–16, 218, 220, 221, 229, 256, 267, 268, 279; birth (1938), 118; illnesses, 158, 174, 176, 185, 187, 194, 203, 215; education, 177, 181, 183, 184, 185–8, 194, 207; marriage to Patricia, 222–3, 227; parents' worry over, 183–8, 222–3, 234, 263, 272; Sean sends money to, 272; death of mother, 275

Ó Faracháin, Roibéard, 154–5, 156, 157

O'Flaherty, Liam, 71, 75, 82, 87, 97, 139, 201

O'Gorman, Eric, 191

O'Growney Award (IAL), 105

Ó hAodha, Micheál, 204–5

O'Hegarty, P.S., 176

O'Higgins, Brian, 39

O'Leary, Con, 285n

O'Leary, Ita, 242

O'Leary, J.J., 128–9, 130–1, 145, 147, 150, 158, 292n

O'Leary, John, 143

O'Leary, Kitty, 194–5

O'Leary, William, 129

O'Malley, Ernie, 50, 116

O'Neill, Joseph, 133

O'Neill, Margaret, 181, 297n

O'Rahilly, Dr Alfred, 63, 73, 75, 90, 91, 92, 95, 161–2, 183, 236

O'Reilly, Francis, 98

O'Shea, Katherine, 85

Ó Súilleabháin, Tomás Rua, 41, 43

O'Sullivan, Father Dick, 23

O'Sullivan, Father Donal, 211

O'Sullivan, Brother Loyola ('Lolly'), 36

O'Sullivan, P.R., 134

O'Sullivan, Sean, 157, 175

O'Toole, Fintan, 278

Ó Tuama family, Tuirin Dubh, 43, 44, 57

Parnell, Charles Stewart, 43, 85, 87–8, 90, 107–8, 116, 142, 143, 287n, 290n

Pater, Walter, 83; Marius the Epicurean, 68, 160

Pavese, Cesare, 268

Pearse, Padraic, 52, 63

Peel Memorial Prize, awarded to Sean (1921), 47

PEN, 100, 103, 106, 154; Edinburgh conference, 101

Penguin Books, 123, 175, 177, 271, 276

Percy, Esmé, 24

Phi Beta Kappa lecture tours in USA, 221, 227, 228, 230, 238

Philip, Brother, 30

Playboy magazine, 231, 240, 245, 249, 250, 251, 259, 267

Plomer, William, 202

Plunkett, Horace, 67

Plunkett, James, 135, 188, 277, 278, 281, 282

Poems from Ireland, 163

Porter, Horace, 59

Porter, Katharine Anne, 227

Pound, Ezra, 102

Powell, Elfreda, 262–3, 264, 265–6, 268, 272, 273

Power, Arthur, 188

Powers, J.F., 219, 255

Presentation Brothers College ('Pres'), 56; Sean's education at (1912–18), 35–6, 37–41, 42, 185

Princeton University (USA), 200, 217, 227, 228, 239, 301n; Sean's seminars at (1954/58), 191–2, 195–7, 198–9, 217–18, 220–3; Yeats lecture (1965), 236

Prior, Moody, 216

Pritchett, V.S., 188, 237, 257, 258, 268

Proust, Marcel, 140, 196

Purser, Sarah, 102

Radio Eireann, 122–3, 137–8, 154–5, 156, 157, 174, 181, 201, 204–5

Rathkeale, Co. Limerick, 31–4, 35, 40, 80, 96

Read, Herbert, 87

Redmond, John, 16

Reed, Edward Bliss, 70, 90, 92–3
Rhinehart, Stanley, 202
Rich, Harriet (Mrs O'Connor), 192, 193, 141, 142
Richards, Shelah, 117
Ritchie, Charles, 115
Robinson, Dave, 56–7
Robinson, Professor F.N., 73, 74, 75, 76, 78–9, 92, 93, 200
Robinson, Lennox, 65, 69, 70, 79, 102, 132, 144, 146, 287n, 288n; *Patriots*, 26, 27, 291n; 'The Round Table', 65
Robinson, Mary, President of Ireland, 281
Roche, Gussy, 16
Rodgers, W.R., 133
Rogers, Brother Sebastian ('Battling Billy'), 29
Rooney, Paddy, accountant, 149
Rosmeen Park, Sean's home at, 257, 258, 261, 262, 269–70, 273, 274, 275, 277, 281
Rosse, Lord, 211
Royal Dublin Society, 237
Royal Irish Constabulary (RIC), 16, 50, 51, 53
Rubinstein, Hilary, 236, 237, 245, 271
Rukeyser, William S., 301n
Rush, Marie, 162
Russell, Bertrand, 251
Russell, Circle, 175–6
Ruttledge, Patrick, 59
Ryan, John, 189

Sacred Heart School, Monkstown, 177, 183
St John of God's mental hospital, Stillorgan, Sean committed to (1989), 276
St Mary's Training College, Strawberry Hill, 85, 86, 92, 286n
St Vincent's Nursing Home, 236, 263, 274
Salzburg festival, 114, 228
Saroyan, William, 180
Sartre, Jean-Paul, 191, 192; *Les Chemins de la Liberté*, 192; *La Nausée*, 192

Saturday Evening Post, 215, 240, 241
Schnack, Elisabeth, 174, 267
Seignobus, Charles, 175
Sexton, Dean, 117
Shakespeare, William, 47, 48
Shaw, George Bernard, 89, 102, 250, 256
Sheehan, 'Doggy', 38
Sheehy, Anna, 133
Sheehy, Edward, 137
Sheehy, Harriet, 275
Sheehy, Maurice, 241
Sheehy-Skeffington, Hanna, 134
Sheehy-Skeffington, Owen, 176, 183, 188, 210, 264, 282, 293n
Shelley, Percy Bysshe, 47, 53, 73
Sheridan, Margaret Burke, 133
Sheridan, Niall, 132
Sheridan, Richard Brinsley, 48
Shúilleabháin, Bean Ui, 45
Silone, Ignazio, *Bread and Wine*, 25
Simmons, Ernie, 74, 80, 233–4
Simpson, Eileen, 220, 229, 262
Sims, George, *The Lights o'London*, 26
Sinn Fein, 51, 68, 104, 107; Sean appointed Assistant Director of Publicity for, 59–60
Sinn Fein (newspaper: *Eire*), 59, 62, 67, 68
Sions, Harry, 206, 217, 235, 239
Sitwell family, 83
Slattery, Dr Jerry, 264
'Sloppy Dan', headmaster of Lancasterian School, 29
Smith, Carol, 255–6, 257, 259, 260, 262
Snow, Lord, 257
South End House, Union Park, Cambridge (Mass., USA), 76, 77, 79
Spark, Muriel, 255, 256, 257, 268, 270
Speaight, Robert, 117, 156
The Spectator, 69, 98, 101, 163
Stassinopoulos, Arianna, 256
Stein, Robert, 230
Stendhal (Henri Beyle), 47, 110, 220, 259, 268; *La Vie de Henri Brulard*, 218, 219
Stepinac, Cardinal, 183

Stewart, Stan, 121–2
Stockley, Germaine, 48, 63, 117
Stockley, Professor W.F.P., 48, 59, 63, 73, 74, 90, 92, 93
Stones, Anthony, 279
Strong, L.A.G., 136
Stuart, Francis, 139, 281
Stuart, Mrs Neal, 230
The Studio, 66
Sunday Chronicle, 98, 101
Sunday Independent, 177, 281, 296n
Sutherland, Halliday, *The Laws of Life*, 139
Svevo, Italo, *Senilita*, 259
Sweeney, Jack, 221
Synge, J.M., 155, 177, 250

The Tablet, 101
Tate, Alan, 219, 231
Tatlock, J.S.P., 73
Taylor, A.J.P., 257
Taylor, Geoffrey, 129
Terry, Fred, 24
Tierney, Mark, 282
Tierney, S.J., 282
Times Literary Supplement, 66, 69, 245
Toksvig, Signe (Mrs Francis Hackett), 102–3, 116
Tone, Theobald Wolfe, 105, 143, 289n; *Autobiography*, 52
Torna *see* O Donnchadha, Tadhg
Tracy, Honor, 149, 150, 178, 181, 188, 263, 296n; Sean's relationship with, 150–1, 162, 166, 167, 168–9, 172, 176–7, 193, 275; *Mind You, I've Said Nothing!*, 188
Traynor, Father Tim, 44, 160, 176, 177
The Treaty, Anglo-Irish (1921), 53, 54, 55, 60
Trinity College, Dublin, 150, 275, 280, 281; Sean awarded Hon. D. Litt. by (1957), 212
Tuama, Bean Ui ('Nan Nan'), 44, 45
Tuirin Dubh, 43–5, 56, 80
Turgenev, Ivan, 47, 64, 83, 220, 268, 277; *Torrents of Spring*, 65, 96, 160
Twenty Club, 63, 64–5, 66, 91, 285n

Twomey, Maurice, 188
Twomey, Willie, 80

Unamuno, Miguel, *L'Agonie du Christianisme*, 255
University Club, St Stephen's Green, 258
University College, Cork (UCC), 40, 43, 46, 73, 87, 90, 162, 213, 235, 274; Sean's studies at, 39, 42, 45, 46–50, 52–3, 55, 63, 69, 79, 92; Republican Branch, 51–2; Philosophical Society, 46; Students' Representative Council, 46; Corkery appointed Professor of English Language and Literature at (1931), 90–5
University College, Dublin, 184, 188, 211
Ussher, Arland, 132

Vann, Father Gerald, *On Being Human*, 113
Vendler, Helen, 81
Ventura, magazine, 230, 238–9
Vernon, John, 232
Viking Press, 98, 101
Virginia Quarterly Review, 82

WAAMA (Writers Artists Actors Musicians Association), 154, 156, 158, 163, 294n
Wall, Mervyn, 157, 158, 210, 278
Wallace, Sheila, 64
Walpole, Horace, 86
Walsh, Maurice, 128, 133, 157
Walsh, Roisin, 128, 145
Ward, Aileen, 233
Warner, Marina, *Alone of All Her Sex*, 303n
Warren, Robert Penn, 231
Watergrasshill, Siege of (1904), 18–19
Watt, A.P., literary agents, 236, 255, 262, 271
Waugh, Evelyn, 191; *Vile Bodies*, 191
Webster, Eileen, 134
Weeks, Edward, 227, 228, 229, 240
Wells, E.M., 132

Wells, H.G., 106, 140
West, Rebecca, 97
Whelan, Bridget (née Murphy: mother),
    15–16, 17, 19–20, 21–2, 32, 33, 36, 37,
    43, 50, 58, 72, 113, 278–9; ill in North
    Infirmary, Cork, 122, 161; death of
    (1944), 161
Whelan, Denis (father), 15, 16–20, 25,
    32, 36, 37, 38, 43, 50, 58, 72, 278–9;
    death of (1928), 82
Whelan, Eileen (wife of Gus), 23, 207
Whelan, Gus (Augustine: brother), 17,
    21, 22–3, 28, 38, 39, 82, 161, 174, 200,
    279; death of, 260
Whelan, Patrick (brother), 17, 21, 22–3,
    28, 39, 161, 260, 304n
Whitaker, Malachi, 87
White, H.O., 175
Williams, Alan, 222

Willow Park preparatory school, 177,
    184
Wilmerding, Lucius, 198
Woods, Thomas, 293n
Woolf, Virginia, 115, 191, 196; *Diary*,
    192
Wright, William, 230

Yeats, Jack, 132, 133, 175
Yeats, Michael, 176
Yeats, W.B., 47, 65, 68, 76, 81, 82, 83,
    94, 97, 102, 106, 110, 115, 116, 117,
    119, 124, 139, 144, 145, 155, 231, 234,
    250, 265, 272, 291n; *Countess Cathleen*,
    26; 'September 1913', 47; 'Easter 1916',
    47; *Reveries*, 218; *Memoirs*, 224; *The
    Shadowy Waters*, 260
Yntema, Peggy, 234, 240, 262
Young Irelanders, 105